The Study of
Medieval Records

KATHLEEN MAJOR

The Study of Medieval Records

Essays in honour of
KATHLEEN MAJOR

Edited by
D. A. BULLOUGH
and
R. L. STOREY

OXFORD
AT THE CLARENDON PRESS
1971

Oxford University Press, Ely House, London W. 1

GLASGOW NEW YORK TORONTO MELBOURNE WELLINGTON
CAPE TOWN SALISBURY IBADAN NAIROBI DAR ES SALAAM LUSAKA ADDIS ABABA
BOMBAY CALCUTTA MADRAS KARACHI LAHORE DACCA
KUALA LUMPUR SINGAPORE HONG KONG TOKYO

PRINTED IN GREAT BRITAIN
AT THE UNIVERSITY PRESS, OXFORD
BY VIVIAN RIDLER
PRINTER TO THE UNIVERSITY

AN APPRECIATION

OXFORD, in the winter of 1945, was a cold place. Michaelmas Term started sunny, with St. Luke's little summer, but soon a damp chill settled upon Bodley and its associated reading rooms, a chill so penetrating that even intellectually-starved ex-servicemen, used to discomfort, were only half-heartedly resentful when Sir Thomas's bell tolled for their 5 o'clock ejection into a world still short of everything: clothes to hold off the frost, food to warm the body, sherry to cheer the soul. Even the poor scholar, prepared to endure hunger and cold, soon felt the pinch of wartime conditions, for paper upon which to make his notes was difficult to find and of atrocious quality—yellow, rough, friable. But however cold the weather and hard the life, academic activities were beginning to expand again after years of forced curtailment. Service cadets were gradually replaced by ex-servicemen and women, the younger of whom became elderly undergraduates, while those lucky enough to have completed their first degree before the war tried to settle down to research, some of them wondering if they had been wise to leave the shelter of the army or the civil service as they wrestled with the mysteries of the Bodleian catalogue or tried to recall the details of academic controversies. It was not altogether easy to adapt to scholarly disciplines after years of living according to very different standards, and those who did so most easily were those fortunate enough to find friends, and particularly teachers, who could give them the confidence and stimulus they so badly needed. It was into such an academic world that Kathleen Major came in 1945, when she returned to her old university as Lecturer (and soon Reader) in Diplomatic. She has been a guide and friend to many research students, but I doubt if she was ever more helpful than to those who comprised her first class, held in draughty discomfort in a room on the ground floor of the Bodleian, in that bleak winter of 1945–6.

The working out of academic genealogies is an ancient game and a very illuminating one. Although Lord Annan has taught us to look to heredity to explain why certain men and women become dons, it is well recognized that others, both fortunate in experiencing and quick in assimilating a favourable intellectual environment, are made into scholars even if they spring from entirely unacademic families. In the case of Kathleen Major, the trail leads us back, first of all, to St. Hilda's College, where under a remarkable tutor, Agnes Leys, a succession of keen medievalists was bred up, several of whom went on to work for research degrees and to make valuable contributions to historical knowledge. If, in her time, the atmosphere inside the college was favourable to medieval studies, it was equally propitious in the university as a whole. In 1928, when she had just taken Schools, Sir Maurice Powicke was appointed to the Regius Professorship of Modern History; in the same year the man who was to succeed him in the same chair, Vivian Galbraith, returned to Oxford as Reader in Diplomatic, after some years in the Public Record Office. To the stimulus of Mrs. Leys as tutor was now added the intellectual influences of two great historians who, in many ways, were the perfect complement to each other. Kathleen Major was quick to respond to their teaching and to appreciate what she could learn from each of them.

Special Subjects in the Oxford History School have done much to shape the pattern of research in English Medieval History. Kathleen Major's choice, Medieval Boroughs, was no exception; the sources set for detailed study took undergraduates straight into the world of medieval records and faced them uncompromisingly with the problem of their interpretation. When the time came for her to choose a subject for her B.Litt., her mind turned naturally to some extension of her work in medieval municipal history. Mrs. Leys was anxious, however, that if possible she should work under Professor Powicke who, she rightly thought, would guide the promising young historian into a subject best suited to her talents. Fortunately he agreed to become her supervisor, suggesting that she should collect the *Acta* of Stephen Langton, the assembly and editing of which he had already singled out as a desideratum in an appendix to his Ford Lectures of 1927. Subject and scholar were excellently matched. Her strong interest in constitutional, legal, and administrative history was given full rein; she had the easy command of Latin required, and she soon acquired the palaeographic skill to enable her to read and date documents. At the same time, and with a past master of the art, she began the study of Diplomatic with Vivian Galbraith. Before she started a systematic tour of cathedral libraries and archives to trace Langton's *Acta*, she was as well equipped as any young scholar could have been for her task.

Even after the war access to ecclesiastical records was not always easy to obtain, nor were working conditions ideal. When Kathleen Major began her search, things were even more difficult; to the somewhat shy girl, the difficulties standing between her and the records she needed to examine must often have seemed almost insuperable. Working hours were generally very short; the light in search rooms was often poor; on occasion it proved virtually impossible to persuade a reluctant custodian to allow a thorough search of the archives. The fees charged could be high. But there were compensations. As she has herself recorded in the preface to the *Acta Stephani Langton* (published by the Canterbury and York Society in 1950), from many people she met with extraordinary help and kindness. She derived as much pleasure and profit from meeting eccentric canons and curmudgeonly clerks as she did from reading in medieval cathedral libraries; as a historian she was quick to realize that it was in such surroundings, and to men not unlike those with whom she now had to work, that the records she was looking for had been sent; and it was such men who handled them. No one who has been her pupil could fail to realize what valuable experience she gained in those years of travelling and searching; not only did she compile an invaluable collection of documents, but she also saw, in the office of the bishop's registrar or the chapter clerk, where she often had to work among the clatter and bustle of the daily routine administration of the diocese or the cathedral, how a largely unaltered ecclesiastical legal system actually worked. Documents were issued; documents were received; both had to be registered; some had to be sealed or came with seals. Common forms remained close to medieval precedents; medieval bishops' registers were still working records. To the future Reader in Diplomatic such an apprenticeship, superimposed upon a thorough knowledge of the great national libraries, was invaluable.

Few cathedrals and dioceses had, in the early 1930s, learned archivists with professional standards. Lincoln was among the exceptions. Here Canon C. W. Foster had made himself master of the marvellous collection of material which, stage by stage, he was arranging, calendaring, and publishing in the excellent volumes appearing under his editorship in the Lincoln Record Society series. Kathleen Major first met this remarkable scholar when she went to Lincoln to look for Langton's *Acta*; shortly after submitting her thesis she was asked to become co-editor with him of the *Registrum Antiquissimum of the Cathedral Church of Lincoln*, the publication of which, in ten superbly edited volumes, six undertaken by her alone, will soon be completed. About the same time, Canon Foster's pioneer work on the Lincoln archives so much impressed the Pilgrim Trust that they agreed to make a grant to establish a Diocesan Record Office, with Kathleen Major as the first full-time archivist, an appointment particularly suitable in view of her family connections with the county. She therefore settled in Lincoln, which is still her home and where as an active and public-spirited citizen, she has made many friends. Throughout the years her name has become known throughout Lincolnshire and indeed, much more widely, as the General Editor of the Lincoln Record Society publications.

To the list of those who make up Kathleen Major's academic genealogy one name must be added: that of Sir Frank Stenton. He was one of the examiners of her thesis; he became, with his wife, one of her closest friends. Like the other historians who have done so much to further her career, he was a man of broad interests, a medievalist with an extensive knowledge of other periods and an appreciation of problems well outside his own field. During those years at Lincoln, when the Lincoln Record Office in the cramped quarters in the Exchequer Gate became a model for what such places ought to be, Kathleen Major was not only its very efficient archivist, but also a rapidly developing scholar. No one could have been better fitted to profit from the wealth of archives stored there; no one could have realized more profoundly, from her daily handling of them, how English administrative history and its records are part of a continuing process of evolution, no section of which can be properly understood without a knowledge of the past, indeed of every period of the past, out of which they grew. Those who studied Diplomatic with her must all have realized, as soon as they began to attend her classes, that she would give them a thorough grounding in it from the Dark Ages to the twentieth century. Few can have failed to profit from the broadness of her vision of a subject which can easily become narrow and sterile.

Such was Kathleen Major's academic genealogy when she was elected to the Lecturership in Diplomatic at Oxford in 1945; within three years she had been promoted Reader. For the next ten years in Oxford, many graduate students beginning their research learnt from her not only that administrative history is absorbingly interesting, but also a great deal about the practical side of scholarship. Even when she relinquished the post to become Principal of St. Hilda's during a period when the college was rapidly expanding (1955–65), she always found time to supervise some medievalists. More recently, it has been at Nottingham University, where she has been a part-time Professor of History, that students have profited from her learning and her kindness. She has advised all who have come under her care as well about the great national collections of archives as about the most obscure ecclesiastical and private caches of papers; she has given them sound recommendations about places to stay in distant towns and generously written them letters of introduction to make their visits to strange parts of the country less lonely. She is always approachable, always helpful; she seems to have endless time in which to sort out problems or to entertain her pupils. And all the time she has carried on with her own research, so that year by year the work on 'Antiquissimum', as it is affectionately called by her friends, has gone on in spite of all the distractions of life in the university, and of the many calls upon her to sit on committees and to help with learned projects of all kinds. All who have worked with her, as pupils or colleagues, have learnt to respect the extent and depth of her knowledge, her sound judgement, and her unshakeable scholarly integrity.

Kathleen Major is, her friends are delighted to say, very much alive and still very busy; it is, in fact, absurd to think of the word 'retirement' in connection with her, as so indefatigable a scholar never retires. But from the obligations of regular teaching she now, understandably, seeks release, though it is hard to think that so gifted a teacher will not from time to time find herself entangled in supervision or informal instruction, whatever her good intentions. But none of her old pupils will grudge her more time to get on with 'her own work'; indeed, they hope that she will have as much leisure as possible to publish still more learned editions to instruct them. For she has always been a teacher who has taught as much by practice as by precept—in that surely lies much of her success. In the volume of essays now presented to her she can see for herself how her tuition has brought forth fruit.

ANNE WHITEMAN

PREFACE

A COLLECTION of essays by various hands, on a limited number of aspects of Diplomatic, necessarily falls far short of being that Manual of Diplomatic for English-language readers and for students of the documents of Medieval England the lack of which has long been regretted and which her pupils always hoped that Kathleen Major would one day write. The present volume may none the less serve partially to fill the gap as well as honour the scholar to whom it is offered. It was originally conceived by two of her colleagues at Nottingham in order to show the affection in which she is held by former pupils and colleagues, and how younger historians, active far beyond the limits of the medieval diocese of Lincoln, have profited from her teaching and scholarship.

The requirement of a unifying theme for the volume has involved the exclusion of several who would like to have participated in it: their tribute must therefore be offered in the form of a silent *confraternitas*, the powerful reality of which was none the less evident to at least one medieval bishop of Lincoln. We have been fortunate that the contributors have been ready to accept a sometimes ruthless editorial treatment of their manuscripts to give the volume still greater coherence. We are happy to thank collectively, on behalf of the individual contributors, the staff of the various archive-repositories in the British Isles and abroad, who have willingly made available documents in their custody, provided microfilms, photostats or plates, and answered queries. We are grateful to the Delegates for making it possible for the volume to be published under the imprint of the Clarendon Press. Its staff have displayed their usual acuteness and care in the preparation of the manuscript for press and in the printing. Help with the proofs has been given by Dr. Michael Jones.

D. A. BULLOUGH
R. L. STOREY

ACKNOWLEDGEMENTS

PLATES 1 and 4 and the transcripts of Crown Copyright records in the Public Record Office appear by permission of the Controller of H.M. Stationery Office.

Plate 2 is published with the approval of the Keeper of the Records of Scotland.

CONTENTS

LIST OF ILLUSTRATIONS

ABBREVIATIONS

BIHR *Bulletin of the Institute of Historical Research*

B.M. British Museum

B.R.O. Buckinghamshire Record Office

CCR *Calendar of Close Rolls* (H.M. Stationery Office, 1892–1963). The first volume in the series, for 1227–31, is a full edition of the Latin text

CPL *Calendar of Entries in the Papal Registers relating to Great Britain and Ireland: Papal Letters* (H.M.S.O., 1894–1960)

CPR *Calendar of Patent Rolls* (H.M.S.O., 1891–). The first two volumes, for 1216–25 and 1225–32, are full editions

C.U.L. Cambridge University Library

C.Y.S. Canterbury and York Society

E.D.R. Ely Diocesan Records (in Cambridge U.L.)

EHR *English Historical Review*

JEH *Journal of Ecclesiastical History*

L.A.O. Lincolnshire Archives Office

L.R.S. Lincoln Record Society

P.R.O. Public Record Office. (The office's class-number is cited with its title for a class and this number only is cited for second and later references in the same paper)

P.R.S. Pipe Roll Society

PUE *Papsturkunden in England*, ed. W. Holtzmann, 3 vols. (Abhandlungen der Akademie der Wissenschaften in Göttingen, Phil.-hist. Klasse, Neue Folge, Bd. xxv. 1, and Dritte Folge Nr. 14, 15, 33, Berlin, 1930–5, and Göttingen, 1952)

R.C. Record Commission

RF *Il regesto di Farfa compilato da Gregorio di Catino*, ed. I. Giorgi and U. Balzani, 5 vols. (Rome, 1879 [vol. ii]–1914 [vol. i])

R.S. Rolls Series

TRHS *Transactions of the Royal Historical Society*

VCH *The Victoria History of the Counties of England*

I

The Writing-office of the Dukes of Spoleto in the Eighth Century

EVERY early medieval historian is familiar with periods and regions where even the narrative or political history has to be reconstructed largely or wholly from the evidence of documents. In a small number of cases this reconstruction may depend primarily on quite small but seemingly significant changes in the wording of the protocol and eschatocol of documents: it was from these that the late Sir Frank Stenton was able to build up his picture of the Mercian supremacy in eighth-century England; another example, of which, however, the political context is far from clear, is provided by the striking changes in the diplomas issued in the name of the emperor Louis II in the *regnum Italiae* in the early 860s.[1] The historian of the last years of the independent Lombard kingdom and the early years of Frankish rule in Italy is in a slightly different position.[2] There is no continuous narrative source from the kingdom after Paul the Deacon's *Historia Langobardorum* (written *c.* 790) tactfully breaks off with the death of King Liutprand in 744. The *Liber Pontificalis* provides a partial substitute, but is obviously primarily concerned with events that directly affected Rome and

---

[1] F. M. Stenton, 'The Supremacy of the Mercian Kings', *EHR* xxxiii (1918), 433–52, repr. in Stenton, *Preparatory to Anglo-Saxon England*, ed. Lady Stenton (Oxford, 1970), pp. 48–66; and compare E. John, *Orbis Britanniae* (Leicester, 1966), pp. 1 ff., esp. 17–37, whose views demand serious consideration even if they are not in all respects acceptable; G. v. Pölnitz-Kehr, 'Kaiserin Angelberga. Ein Excurs zur Diplomatik Kaiser Ludwigs II v. Italien', *Historisches Jahrbuch*, lx (1940), 429–40.

[2] The best general accounts are still T. Hodgkin, *Italy and her Invaders*, vii, viii (Oxford, 1899), and L. M. Hartmann, *Gesch. Italiens im Mittelalter*, ii/2 (Gotha, 1903): their place in the historiography of Early Medieval Italy is considered in my Nottingham University Inaugural Lecture, *Italy and her Invaders* (Nottingham, 1968). Certain aspects of the political history of the period to 774 are treated much more fully in O. Bertolini, *Roma di fronte a Bisanzio e ai Longobardi* (Bologna, 1941). F. Manacorda's excellent *Ricerche sugli inizii della dominazione dei Carolingi in Italia* (Ist. Stor. Ital. per il Medio Evo, 1968) is essentially institutional.

its region and the other territories that had previously formed part of the Exarchate, on which its evidence can be substantially supplemented from the papal letters copied in the last years of the century into the remarkable *Codex Carolinus*. Even so, the eighth-century documents from the Lombard duchy of Spoleto preserved by the late eleventh-century 'Farfa Register'—a type of collection corresponding to the English monastic cartulary which is, how-ever, very uncommon south of the Alps in the pre-communal period—are indispensable to the historian trying to give precision to the often deliberately vague or one-sided statements of papal and, subsequently, Frankish writers.[1]

The majority of documents in the Register are concerned with only one part of the duchy, namely the city of Rieti and its terri-tory, which until at least 781 included most of the Sabina—the region on the left (east) bank of the Tiber, extending to within a few miles of Rome, in which the abbey of Farfa lay: and this indicates both their value and their limitations.[2] There are virtu-ally no other early documents from this region, with the apparent exception of a grant of June 772 by duke *Teuduycus* to the bishop of Rieti: known until recently only from Ughelli's copy which was so faulty as to make the document universally suspect, it has been re-edited from a twelfth-century manuscript in the Rieti cathedral archives and its authenticity vigorously defended by Professor Pierre Toubert.[3] Professor Toubert's unique familiarity with the medieval agrarian history and topography of central Italy gives his comments on the dispositive clauses, with their difficult-to-

---

[1] Put together by the monk Gregory of Catino in the years immediately after 1092, with a few subsequent additions, it is now Vatican MS. Lat. 8487: the com-piler's own title was *Liber Gemniagraphus sive Cleronomialis Ecclesiae Farfensis*. Gregory's purpose and methods are interestingly described in his *praefatio* (*RF* ii. 6–7) and again in the preface to his *Liber Largitorius*, ed. G. Zucchetti, i (Rome, 1913), 5: he makes it clear that he has sometimes omitted the purely formal parts of documents although in general he has sought to transcribe them exactly.

[2] Small numbers of documents come from Viterbo (in the *regnum* proper, not in the duchy), Amiterno, Marsi, and a few other places; and there is a unique document of 767 dated by the Emperors in Byzantium (*RF* ii, no. 41) which I believe comes from Civittà Castellana in the *ducatus Romae*: the words printed as *castri Viterbii* by the editors are *castri vr b̄b* in the MS., which was clearly already unintelligible to Gregory.

[3] F. Ughelli, *Italia sacra*, 2nd edn., i (Venice, 1717), 1196; P. Toubert, 'Recherches de diplomatique et d'histoire lombardes', *Journal des savants*, an. ccc, Jan.–Mar. 1965, pp. 171–203, the text at pp. 175–6.

identify place-names, a special authority; and he establishes a link with Lombard royal grants to other beneficees of (confiscated) lands at *Narnate* and elsewhere in the critical and difficult years from 770 to 774.[1] The wording even of these clauses, however, presents difficulties which Professor Toubert has only partially met: the name of the recipient *Idemundus*, however emended, does not seem to be Lombardic and he cannot easily be fitted in to the episcopal succession at Rieti in this period;[2] *mansus*, 'peasant (servile) holding', described by Toubert as a term 'tout à fait exceptionnel en Sabine au Moyen Age', is in fact a word otherwise totally unknown in pre-774 Italy and is one of the many institutional terms apparently introduced by the Franks; the unusually elaborate appurtenance formulas . . . *cum petris et lignamine* . . . *cum montibus et planitiis* etc., have no contemporary parallel in either ducal diplomas or private charters from the Rieti–Spoleto region nor very close parallels elsewhere in the eighth century.[3] There are equally

[1] For the place-names and estate organization, see Toubert, op. cit., pp. 196–202, where 'Sabine' is used for the entire territory of the ancient *Sabini* and not merely for the medieval and modern Sabina. Toubert's location of *Narnate*—which he rightly regards as a zone rather than a place—between Antrodoco and Leonessa is not necessarily wrong but the place-name S. Angelo, a deserted hamlet in this area, is hardly relevant, since the church of S. Angelo at *Narnate* granted to Farfa in 780 (by *RF* ii, no. 129) was merely an appurtenance of the monastery of the Archangel Michael at Rieti (the donor, Bishop Wicbert, was not bishop of Rieti) and clearly not the main church of the district: see further 'The Church of the Archangel Michael at Rieti and the Bishops of Rieti in the Eighth Century' which I have in preparation. For the historical context, see Toubert, op. cit., pp. 192–5. The related diplomas are A. Chroust, *Untersuchungen über die langobardischen u. Herzogs-Urkunden* (Graz, 1888), tab. 1 ('Die Königsurkunden'), no. 39, new edn. *RF* v, no. 1225, with the corrected date 770–4 (thus extending Bresslau's dates '747–67' for the period of activity of the royal notary Gau(s)pert: *Urkundenlehre*, 2nd edn. i. 356); and Chroust, tab. 1, no. 36.

[2] For Lombardic personal names W. Bruckner, *Die Sprache der Langobarden* (Strasbourg, 1895; repr. 1969), pp. 215–326, is still indispensable in spite of its many defects. Compare E. Förstemann, *Altdeutsches Namenbuch*, 2nd edn. i (Bonn, 1901; repr. 1966), who lists Frankish *Hildimunds* but nothing relevant under *Hid-* or *Id-* (cc. 833, 815 ff., 943 ff.). Room has to be found for *Idemund* between Bishop Teuto who was active in the earlier years of Duke Theudicius, and probably still in the duke's later years, and either Bishop Gumpert who took part in a court at Rieti in Mar. 773 (*RF* ii, no. 83) but cannot be shown conclusively to have been bishop of that city, or an Agio (apparently a close relative of Teuto) who was *electus* but not consecrated in the latter part of 775 and the early months of 776: for the details see 'The Church of the Archangel Michael at Rieti' (forthcoming).

[3] *Mansus*: Toubert, op. cit., p. 197; and add to the references in nn. 85 (p. 197), 94 (p. 201)—none of which suggest an early appearance of the word in Italy—the entry *mansus* in Niermeyer, *Mediae Latinitatis Lexikon Minus*, 643–5, and D. Herlihy, 'The Carolingian *mansus*', *Econ. Hist. Rev.*, N.S. xiii (1960–1), pp. 79–89, which confirm its

objections to features of the protocol and eschatocol: apart from those defended—not always convincingly—by Professor Toubert, the *sanctio* in its present form ('. . . a nullo nostro colono vel clientulo seu nostro actore . . . contradicatur') is surely impossible; and the names of the supposed witnesses are highly suspect, if not also impossible, in a document of 772—as indeed is the form of their subscription.[1]

Professor Toubert would see a connection between the admittedly anomalous form of the Rieti charter and the subjection of the dukes of Spoleto to the effective authority of the Lombard kings since 756: 'le glissement formel de l'acte ducal spolétain vers l'acte privé auquel on assiste depuis le duc Gisolf' (*c.* 759–62) and which culminates in the 772 charter, and the corresponding dissolution of the ducal writing-office, 'ne [font] ainsi que traduire la sujétion

absence. Appurtenance clauses (strangely said by Toubert, p. 188, to be lacking in the Rieti charter): those in pre-774 diplomas are normally short (Chroust, op. cit., p. 158) but longer ones are found after that date, as *RF* ii, nos. 105 of 778; more elaborate examples in Rieti private charters 766–77 are *RF* ii, nos. 72, 79, 84, 85, 108, etc.: none of them include the words quoted in the text or anything like them and the nearest comparable forms (which are not in fact very close) are in documents from Lombardy such as L. Schiaparelli (ed.), *Codice diplomatico longobardo*, ii (Rome, 1933), nos. 137, 257. The substantive *pertinentiis* occurs in, for example, the diploma *RF* ii, no. 48 of 761, but never in conjunction with a list of accessories. P. Rasi, *Le pertinenze e le cose accessorie* (Padua, 1955) to which Toubert refers, was not available to me.

[1] The erroneous and anomalous dating by the eighteenth year of Desiderius and Adelchis (*sic*) is explained away by a reference to a private charter of 762 (*RF* ii, no. 50) written by a monk not a notary, although all the surviving diplomas of the 760s and *RF* ii, no. 80 of July 772 have the correct form; *excellentissimus dux*, to which there is no parallel in Spoleto documents, is defended by a reference to a Benevento document (where the parallel is in any case not exact) and to usage in the Exarchate (!) (Toubert, op. cit., pp. 185–7). The standard form of the *sanctio* is . . . *a nullo castaldio vel actore nostro contradicatur*: see *RF* ii, nos. 48 of 761, 80 of 772, 104 of 778, etc. and Chroust, op. cit., pp. 160–1. The first name in the witness-list is obviously corrupt; the other three, *Racter(i)us*, Arderardus, and Crescentius are characteristic of a later period than the eighth century (see *RF* i, pp. lxxxiii, cxxxii, xcv), the first probably, the second almost certainly, being of Frankish origin. *Rogatus* is normally found only in 'autograph' subscriptions, and those introduced by *signum manus* usually end with *testis*. On the other hand I agree with Toubert (op. cit., pp. 189–90) that no formal objection can be raised against the concluding phrase (for the significance of which see below, p. 6) *Sub eodem actionario et Fabiniano conductore*—except for the meaningless *eodem*, which suggests a formulary—although there is no exact parallel to the naming of a *conductor*: the Farfa *conductores*, often of very humble status (*RF* ii, nos. 30 (p. 41), 29; cf. v, p. 271), are bailiffs of a domanial estate, not contractors (compare Toubert, op. cit., p. 189, with e.g. P. J. Jones in *Agricoltura e mondo rurale* = *Settimane di studio del Centro italiano sull'alto Medio Evo, XIII* (Spoleto, 1966), 85.

politique des derniers ducs à Didier et Adelchis'.[1] This point of view does not seem to me to be justified by the available evidence. A re-examination of the Spoletan ducal diplomas and *notitiae* along rather different lines from those followed by Chroust and by Professor Toubert himself and extending into the early Carolingian period, also provides an opportunity for testing the claim of the late Professor Cesare Manaresi, in his fine and indispensable edition of the Italian *placiti* (records of judicial proceedings) of Carolingian date, that the duchy of Spoleto boasted an 'ufficio giudiziario' in this period which worked through 'una speciale cancelleria dei placiti'.[2] The conclusions will, I suggest, be of interest not only for the history of the duchy in the period which saw the change over from Lombard to Frankish rule and of early medieval notarial practice in Italy but may also throw light on the general question of what can and cannot be legitimately inferred from changes in diplomatic forms.

The series of extant Spoletan diplomas begins in May 724 (the year being inferred from the indiction, which is the only dating-evidence supplied) with a grant by Duke Trasmund (II) to the abbey of Farfa of 'the church of St. Gethulius where his body rests' and its dependent property. It was written by a 'Theodaldus notarius, ex iussione domini mei iam dicti ducis et ex dicto Hilderici sculdahis'.[3] The place in which the duke gave his order for the preparation of the document, *datum iussionis*, is not named. Spoleto is obviously not excluded: but Rieti or somewhere in the Sabina, which at this period probably belonged to the gastaldate of Rieti, is more likely. 'The church of St. Gethulius' is seemingly the one from which the *curtis S. Gethulii*—south of the river Farfa and west of the Via Salaria—was named;[4] the see of Bishop

---

[1] Op. cit., p. 190.

[2] C. Manaresi, *I placiti del 'Regnum Italiae'*, vol. i (Fonti per la Storia d'Italia, Rome, 1955), p. xii.

[3] *RF* ii, no. 5.

[4] Cf. *RF* v, no. 1279, iii, nos. 407, etc., with *Passio Getulii et soc., Acta Sanctorum*, Iunii ii. 266 D, where the saint's burial-place is given as *in fundo Capreolis in Salaria ab urbe Roma plus minus millario tricesimo supra fluvium Tyberim*. The Salaria was not, however, near the Tiber at its 30th mile—the supposed site of the martyrdom of S. [H]Iacinthus (*Martyrologium Hieronymianum*, ad Sept. 8) and presumably of the *casa* or *basilica* of that saint (*RF* ii, no. 27 of 747, etc.). Could the *memoria* which E. Stevenson claimed to have discovered at the 25th mile and strangely identified

Audelahis who is to copy the document in *matricula* (presumably to be translated 'register', although of what kind is indeterminable) is not known, but his name—Gothic, if it is not Lombard —may be a slight argument in favour of Rieti: it is, however, not established that the Sabina or a substantial part of it came under the ecclesiastical jurisdiction of that city.[1] The place of origin of the document or of its notary is unfortunately not even established conclusively by the inclusion of the words *sub Scaptolfo gastaldio* in the eschatocol and the evidence of a much later text that he was gastald of Rieti: for this peculiarity of Spoletan diplomas seems intended to indicate the ducal official who has hitherto had jurisdiction over the property which is the subject of the diploma.[2]

A second charter of donation by Trasmund in favour of Farfa, ordered to be written in indiction 8 and prepared by *Arichisius notarius ex dicto Rimonis gastaldii* (in whose jurisdiction the property also lay), was dated by the editors of the Farfa Register to January

as that of Iacinthus (de Rossi, *Bulletino di Archeologia Cristiana*, ser. 3, v (1880), 107) really be that of Gethulius? It is in the right general area to give its name to the *curtis* and not impossibly far from the Tiber.

[1] For the *matricula* see below, p. 8, n. 2. For the name Audelahis see Förstemann, c. 197 (Audelachis). The existence of propertied Goths in the vicinity of Rieti after the destruction of the Ostrogothic kingdom is established by J.-O. Tjäder, *Die nicht-literarischen italienischen Papyri Italiens aus der Zeit 445–700*, i (Lund, 1955), no. 7 of 557. The original three or four sees along the Viae Salaria and Nomentana south of Rieti had been reduced to one, Mentana, by the eighth century, and although it is likely that the diocese of the latter straddled the political frontier (cf. *Deutsches Archiv*, xviii (1962), 230) there is no evidence to show which bishopric was responsible for the northern Sabina. No argument can be based on the right granted to the abbot and community of Farfa by the papal privilege Jaffé-Ewald no. 2144, *RF* ii, no. 2 of 705 to call when they chose on a (? or the) *vicinus episcopus* to perform certain religious functions, for this was a normal feature of early grants of papal protection: compare, for example, Pope Constantine's privilege for Woking and Bermondsey (Jaffé-Ewald no. 2148; W. de Gray Birch, *Cartularium Saxonicum* (London, 1883–93), no. 133), discussed in relation to the Farfa privilege by Stenton, 'Medeshamstede and its Colonies', *Historical Essays in honour of James Tait*, ed. J. G. Edwards *et al.* (Manchester, 1933), pp. 320–3, repr. in Stenton, *Preparatory to Anglo-Saxon England*, pp. 185–8. It is not impossible that the mysterious English-born Bishop Wicbert was brought to the Sabina in the ?760s to help overcome the inadequacies of the diocesan organization in that region: for the details see my 'The Church of the Archangel Michael at Rieti' (forthcoming).

[2] So, correctly, Toubert, op. cit., p. 188 and n. 57, against Chroust, *Untersuchungen*, pp. 150–1 (but an *archiporcarius* is not named only in *RF* ii, no. 48; another figures in *RF* ii, no. 11—after the gastald and before an *actionarius*). For Scaptolf as gastald of Rieti see *RF* ii, no. 103; Manaresi, *Placiti* i, no. 3 of 777: '. . . tempore patris mei Scaptolfi, qui fuit castaldius in Reate'.

740.[1] This dating is, however, virtually excluded by a document copied on to one of the later folios of the manuscript Register which is dated with reference to Duke Hilderic and is certainly to be attributed to December 739: even without this document to help him the Abbé Duchesne argued that the narrative of events recorded at the beginning of the *Vita* of Pope Zacharias must be understood to mean that Trasmund was expelled from Spoleto in favour of the king's nominee Hilderic in the spring of 739 and only re-established himself in the duchy in December 740.[2] The date of Arichis's document is therefore almost certainly January 725. Even if it were not, we would probably be justified in identifying the notary of the diploma with the *Arichis notarius* who wrote a charter of sale to the abbey in 718 and a private charter of donation two years later, the first at a place in the Sabina 'at the order of' Sindolf gastald of Rieti, the second at Rieti itself.[3] The content of the two charters and of the diplomas is too different for a comparison of their formulary to provide decisive support for this identification, but one feature is strongly in its favour: in all three the linking phrase between the context of the document and its final clauses is the unusual *ita sane*, in contrast with Theodald's *quamobrem*, the *ita* or *ita ergo* (744 and subsequently) of documents written by Godipert, and the *quatinus* or *quamobrem* (745 and subsequently) of Dagarius.[4]

The conclusion that in the early years of Duke Trasmund the same notary might write both ducal diplomas and private charters (the earlier of them at the order of a ducal official) is not necessarily in conflict with Professor Toubert's assertion that 'aucun notaire ducal n'est connu pour avoir d'autre part établi des actes privés qui soient parvenus jusqu'à nous'—although the dictum is in fact false.[5] The notaries responsible for the diplomas of 724 and 725

---

[1] *RF* ii, no. 7.

[2] *RF* v, no. 1220; *Lib. Pont.* i. 426, 436; Hartmann, ii/2. 138–9, 154 n. 11, with references to additional sources. [3] *RF* ii, nos. 3, 4.

[4] *RF* ii, nos. 5, 8, 21, 9, 10, 11, etc. The distinctiveness of *ita sane* was noted already by Chroust, op. cit., p. 160 but he did not draw any conclusion about the identity of the notary.

[5] Toubert, op. cit., p. 189 n. 62. An unequivocal example to the contrary is *RF* ii, no. 54 of 763 written by Dagarius (significantly *in curte domnica in Musileo* which was evidently in the Assisi–Foligno area); a probable example is *RF* ii, no. 20 written by

wrote *ex dicto* of (which in this context seems to mean 'the content of the document having been supplied by')[1] a sculdahis and a gastald respectively, that is to say, by officials responsible for ducal domains or other rights; the remarkable and seemingly unique provision in the 724 diploma that 'pro stabilitate nostra virum venerabilem Audelahis sanctissimum aepiscopum in matricula praecipimus scribi' leaves it uncertain what kind of register the bishop was assumed to be maintaining:[2] but it does not suggest a very developed palace organization at Spoleto at this date, even if the building itself belongs to the period of Ostrogothic rule.[3] Clearly we cannot infer the existence of an organized ducal writing-office with two or more permanent notaries or other officials. The implication is rather that a local (lay) notary might be called on to write ducal documents as well as ordinary private charters; and there was as yet no 'court' official who had the particular responsibility of passing on the ducal *iussio* and the content of the dispositive clauses. On the other hand, documents of the two types had already acquired appropriate and different forms. Thus, whether by imitation of the notarial practices of the *regnum* proper or (which seems less likely) because of the use of similar models for both types of document in the two regions, private charters had their main dating-clause at the beginning and in the ablative,

Landemarius at the palace at Spoleto (see below, p. 13). For other possible examples of private charters written by ducal notaries see below, pp. 13, 14.

[1] The significance of *ex dicto* in Lombard documents was convincingly established by L. Schiaparelli, 'Note diplomatiche . . . VI. Dictare, ex dictato, ex dicto, dictator', *Archivio Storico Italiano*, ser. 7, xxi (1934), 21–37. In royal documents *ex dicto* is normally used where ducal diplomas have *ex iussione* and the equivalent of the Spoletan *ex dicto* is *ex dictatu*: but if Schiaparelli is right (op. cit., p. 24), until 762 *ex dicto* occasionally replaces *ex dictatu* in royal documents also—in which case it was unnecessary of Bresslau, *Urkundenlehre*, i. 353 n. 7, to have emended Chroust, op. cit., tab. 1, no. 18; *RF* ii, no. 18.

[2] Neither Bresslau, *Urkundenlehre*, nor A. de Boüard, *Manuel de diplomatique* (i–ii, 1929–48) give any references to *matricula* for the early medieval period. Niermeyer, *Lexikon*, 661 s.v. 1, 2 provides some useful indications but no obvious parallel. If the (?)Rieti *matricula* was not basically a roll of beneficiaries or clergy of the church, could it have been something like the English liturgical books or Gospel books in which charters were entered in the eleventh and twelfth centuries?—for which see F. Wormald, 'The Sherborne "Cartulary" ', *Fritz Saxl: a Volume of Memorial Essays*, ed. D. J. Gordon (London, 1957), pp. 101–19.

[3] For which see my remarks in *Aspetti dell'Umbria dall'inizio del secolo VIII alla fine del secolo XII = Atti del III Convegno di Studi Umbri*, 1965 (Perugia, 1966), p. 214 and n. 13.

diplomas a less elaborate dating-clause introduced by *datum* towards the end of the document; private charters gave ducal years, ducal diplomas did not, while neither type of document indicated the regnal year of the monarch; private charters had witnesses, diplomas did not; diplomas had a simple *apprecatio*, the one word *Feliciter*.[1] Finally, there is the possibility (which seems never previously to have been considered) that diplomas and some other kinds of document issued in the duke's name were sealed, even though there is no reference to this in any eighth-century text.[2] At the same time formulaic phrases that were peculiar to Spoleto notaries for many decades occur in the earliest extant documents whether ducal or private: which suggests an already well-established local notarial tradition.[3]

After the grant of 725 there is an unfortunate gap of twenty years in the series of ducal diplomas. Nothing issued in the name of either Hilderic or Agiprand is now extant: the next examples belong to the first year of Duke Lupus, i.e. ?July 745–?July 746.[4] The one that is probably the earlier of the two, written at Rieti by the notary Andreas, differs significantly from the diplomas of the 720s only in its rearrangement of the final clauses, in a more logical way, and the inclusion in the date, for the first time, of the ducal year (*anno ducatus nostri*): inevitably it also displays those distinctive turns of phrase that are the 'signature' or—as exponents

---

[1] Chroust, *Untersuchungen*, pp. 135–53; Bresslau, *Urkundenlehre*, ii. 450–1. The not infrequent absence of the *apprecatio* from the texts in the Farfa Register is probably an example of Gregory's deliberate omission of unnecessary words.

[2] This is suggested by the very consistent presence in the Register of a medallion-bust of the dukes at the end of diplomas and some other kinds of *notitia* (*RF* ii, no. 95, Manaresi, *Placiti*, i, no. 1) but not at the end of *notitiae iudicati* and the presence of similar medallions at the end of royal and imperial diplomas. For the sealing of ducal diplomas from Benevento see Chroust, op. cit., pp. 134–5; Bresslau, *Urkundenlehre*, ii. 186–7. But Gregory's medallions are in no sense facsimiles of the putative seals, for those of the Lombard kings are identical with those of Frankish kings and emperors and the form of the diadem etc. would hardly have been possible before the mid ninth century at the earliest: see the plate at the end of *RF* ii.

[3] It is unfortunate that the Rieti papyrus of 557 (p. 6 n. 1) is of a type of document which has no parallel in the Lombard period and therefore offers no real basis of comparison with later documents: but it certainly does not suggest that there was an unbroken tradition through the next one and a half centuries. On the other hand, the use of phrases like 'formulario lombardo-toscano' by the late P. S. Leicht and others to describe the basic forms of documents common to many parts of the Lombard kingdom and in many cases to the duchy of Spoleto, also tends to conceal the small but significant local variations.   [4] *RF* ii, nos. 9, 10.

of the modern school of musical analysis, which has much in common with diplomatic analysis, express it—the 'finger-prints' of the individual notary.[1] The new form of final clause is used, with only trivial differences, in Lupus's other diplomas. But the diploma dated December 745 has a novel feature which then recurs in four of the seven diplomas (plus one mandate) issued in the duke's name between October 746 and April 751: the notary who writes the document, Dagarius in 745—thus beginning a recorded career of nearly forty years—and again in 747 (twice), Landemarius in 749/50 (twice), declares that he does so *ex dicto Andreatis referendarii*.[2]

As is well known, the referendary was originally a judicial clerk or messenger of the Emperor. In Francia from at the latest the second half of the sixth century, when it had already fallen out of use in the Empire, the title was given to laymen who played a leading part in the preparation or authentication of royal documents; it subsequently appears in a similar sense in documents from Lombard Italy.[3] The evidence that the *referendarius* was an established and permanent feature of the Lombard royal writing-office for many years before the appearance of a man with the same title in the duchy of Spoleto, is much less satisfactory than is sometimes realized. No referendary figures in the final clauses of the surviving and unquestionably authentic diplomas of Cunincpert, Aripert II, Liutprand, or Hildeprand, covering the years 688 to 744; and since the man who conveyed the royal order to write and the *dictator* of the diploma are both commonly said to be *notarii*, there is no analogy with the evidence of Merovingian diplomas where the title-less authenticating official is known from other texts to have been a referendary. There is no reference to an Italian *referendarius* in the *Historia Langobardorum*, nor in the *Liber Pontificalis* before the last years of the independent Lombard kingdom.[4] On the other hand, it would be hypercritical to reject

[1] Above, p. 7 and n. 4.

[2] *RF* ii, nos. 12, 13, 16, 28.

[3] A. H. M. Jones, *A History of the Later Roman Empire* (Oxford, 1964), i. 575, ii. 1236; Bresslau, *Urkundenlehre*, i. 359–69 with 744; ibid., 352–6; P. Classen, 'Kaiserreskript u. Königsurkunde', *Archiv f. Diplomatik*, i (1955), 74–5, ii (1956), 71–2, 85.

[4] Bresslau, *Urkundenlehre*, i. 352–5 with Chroust, *Untersuchungen*, pp. 35–56 and tab. 1. The referendary Andreas was sent as a legate to the papal court in 773: *Lib.*

the apparent evidence for a *Teodoracus referendarius* in a diploma of Perctarit of the year 673 because the bad twelfth-century copy which is our only source reads *referut*: indeed the most recent edition and commentary, that of Professor Bognetti, suggests that the original reading was *refer.v.c.*, that is to say *referendarii viri clarissimi*, and moreover proposes the reconstruction *Albino ref(e)ren(dario)* for an even more distorted part of the context. It is possible although not very likely that the false diploma of Liutprand for S. Pietro Ciel d'oro at Pavia preserves an authentic reference to an early eighth-century referendary; and the fact that a *referendarius* is named as the *dictator* of nearly every Beneventan ducal diploma from 715 onwards can be and has been used as an argument for supposing that the contemporary royal court had a similarly titled official in charge of the writing-office.[1] The fact remains that after 673 there is no unequivocal evidence for a Lombard royal referendary until March 746.

It is at least arguable, therefore, that the almost simultaneous reappearance (if that is what it was) of the office of *referendarius* at the Pavian court and its first appearance at the court of the dukes of Spoleto were a consequence of the changed political situation following the second expulsion of Duke Trasmund and the deaths of Kings Liutprand and Hildeprand, and of the close links between King Ratchis and Duke Lupus. Lupus's third diploma, of October 746, declares that the salvation of the king was among the objects of the grant and it was said in a later document to have been made to Farfa at the royal command: *publicum*, 'domanial or fiscal land', in the duchy of Spoleto was now, it seems, as much royal as ducal.[2]

Pont. i. 492. H.L. iv. 35 records that early in the seventh century 'misit rex Agilulf Stablicianum notarium suum'.

[1] G. P. Bognetti, 'Il gastaldato longobardo e i giudicati di Adaloaldo, Arioaldo e Pertarido nella lite tra Parma e Piacenza' (pub. 1940–1) in *L'età longobarda*, i (Milan, 1966), 234–9: the existence simultaneously of two referendaries would be in line with the possible evidence for two referendaries in 751 (Bresslau, *Urkundenlehre*, i. 354–5), but the force of Bresslau's arguments has been greatly weakened by Manaresi, *Placiti*, i, no. 106 with the editor's comments on p. 387, although his own explanation of the difficulty created by the wording of *RF* ii, no. 31 of Nov. 751 is not entirely convincing; Chroust, *Untersuchungen*, tab. 1 no. 7, with Bresslau, *Urkundenlehre*, i. 356 n. 5; Chroust, tab. 2, with Bresslau, i. 354.

[2] *RF* ii, no. 11. In spite of various partial attempts there is still no proper study of *publicum* in the Lombard and Carolingian duchy of Spoleto.

The next diploma gave full effect to another grant made at the king's request and completed when the duke was actually at the capital and in the presence of the king—which suggests very strongly that he had his entire writing-office with him and not merely Andreas; while in 747 and again in 749 a royal *missus* visiting the duchy helped to give judgement in disputes involving Farfa.[1] No later texts before 774 bear witness to a comparable degree of acceptance of monarchical superiority by a duke of Spoleto: and clearly there is no significance, other than notarial conservatism, in the continuing omission of regnal (royal) years from documents of all types—even though, only a few decades later, the inclusion or omission of the name of a monarch in a dating-clause is a generally reliable indication of political allegiance.[2]

Lupus's notaries were not only responsible for diplomas of the standard kind. In 749 Dagarius wrote a document of anomalous form which forbade women to use certain paths around the abbey of Farfa: declaring itself to be a *contextum* but perhaps also a *mandatum*, it begins like a *notitia* of judicial proceedings but concludes like a diploma.[3] In 750 the same man recorded judicial proceedings before the duke in a *iudicatum* of the typical current type:[4] the proceedings are of special interest because they involved the rejection of a charter produced in evidence as fraudulent on the grounds that neither a 'true notary' nor witnesses were recorded in it; and it is the first surviving document to use the phrase *domus culta* for a 'centre of agrarian exploitation' or 'centre of a group of estates', although the phrase may have originated on papal estates near Rome—a reminder of the part played by notaries in the invention and spread of institutional terminology.[5] An earlier

---

[1] *RF* ii, nos. 12, 30, 22. Chroust, *Untersuchungen*, p. 152, seems unduly sceptical about the presence of the ducal writing-office with the duke himself at Pavia: that Dagarius normally travelled round with the duke (which at this period one would surely normally expect) is strongly suggested by *RF* ii, nos. 15, 46, and especially 45 and 54.

[2] See, for example, Erchempert's comments on the submission of Grimoald III of Benevento to Charlemagne, *Hist. Lang. Beneventorum* c. 4 (in *Mon. Germ. Hist., Script. rerum Lang.*, p. 236); Grierson in *Revue belge de philologie et d'histoire*, xxx (1952), 829; and the successive changes in the dating-clauses of documents from the 'papal states' in the late eighth and early ninth centuries.

[3] *RF* ii, no. 15.   [4] *RF* ii, no. 25.

[5] In some documents *domus culta* is simply an alternative form for *domus cultilis*,

record of proceedings by a royal *missus* shows that copies of important documents were now being kept at Spoleto, presumably in
the ducal palace.[1] The ducal writing-office was clearly well
organized in the time of Lupus: there was nothing to suggest that
it was of any great size. If the referendary Andreas is identified with
the notary of Lupus's (?) first diploma, then for the better part of
Lupus's dukedom he and Dagarius are its only known personnel;
and if the two Andreases are distinguished and the notary identified
perhaps with the Andreas responsible for a number of later private
charters,[2] there is nothing to connect him with the ducal court
after the date of the diploma. Not until the appearance of Landemarius after September 749, or more correctly perhaps in December
748 when he wrote a private charter at the palace at Spoleto,[3] can
the writing-office be said to have had three writers or officials
simultaneously. The fact that all the documents are concerned
with property in the western party of the duchy and with the abbey
of Farfa is of little importance in this connection: they were written
at Spoleto, Rieti, probably Pavia and two different rural residences.[4]

There is no evidence from other sources to explain why, at some
date between November 749 and November 751, the most active
private notary in the Rieti region, Gudipert, introduced the
regnal years of King Aistulf into his initial dating-clauses. But it is
a safe inference from the documents that, following the death or
expulsion of Lupus between April and July 751, the Lombard
king administered the duchy directly through the local gastalds:[5]

etc. But for *domuscultae* as a distinctive form of papal estate organization in the second
half of the eighth century and the early decades of the ninth see Jones and Bertolini
in *Agricoltura e mondo rurale* (above, p. 4, n. 1 *ex*), pp. 84–9, 237–41 and P. Partner
in *Papers of the Brit. School at Rome*, xxxiv (1966), 68–70.

[1] RF ii, no. 30. Four copies were to be made (*breves consimiles*) of which the first
'nobiscum detulimus ad domni regis vestigia, qui in sacro palatio debeat esse . . . et
tertium appare dedimus Luponi duci quod sit in Spoleto'. This is one of a number of
pre-774 texts in which the phrase *sacrum palatium* is used of the Lombard royal palace
at Pavia, although this has been repeatedly denied by scholars writing on the background of, and preliminaries to, the Imperial coronation of 800.

[2] See p. 14 n. 3, below.

[3] RF ii, no. 20: a grant by Bona *relicta cuiusdam Averolfi gastaldii castri Pantani* to
Farfa *actum Spoleti in palatio.*

[4] *In gualdo nostro in Pontias* (RF ii, no. 11); *in curte nostra ad Varianum* (RF ii, nos.
15, 28).

[5] RF ii, nos. 31 (private charter from Rieti), 34 (*iudicatum* from Rieti); ibid., nos.
32 (*Rimolfus notarius* at Spoleto), 37 (*Mellitus diaconus* in the Sabina).

for having also introduced the regnal years into the final dating-clause of a *iudicatum* and the practice having been adopted also by two other notaries, Gudipert and his fellows drop them again when Alboin was established as duke of Spoleto at the very end of 756 or the beginning of 757. The period of direct royal rule none the less left a permanent mark on Spoletan notarial practice: intermittently in the time of Alboin and consistently thereafter ducal years (*anno ducatus eius N.*) are included in the dating-clauses of private charters as well as diplomas.[1] If then there is any significant break in the organization of the ducal writing-office, as Professor Toubert has suggested, it is surely at Duke Lupus's death and not at the time of Desiderius's accession.[2] Landemarius disappears completely from the records; so does the referendary Andreas, unless (like the editors of the Farfa Register) we identify him with the notary of that name who writes private charters as late as 770 —an identification which gains considerably in plausibility from the presence of *Andreas notarius* as *missus* of the duke in courts of justice in 747 and 749 and in the reference to him in one of his later charters (if it can be trusted in spite of some impossible dating-elements) as *iudex* as well as notary.[3] Dagarius goes into obscurity for a decade. Self-evidently there are no ducal diplomas for the years 752–6; none of those issued by Alboin has survived; and a briefer ducal inter-regnum and period of direct royal rule, from which no documents of any sort are extant, seem to have followed Alboin's dukedom.

In 756/7 Spoletan notaries revived the forms of dating-clause in use in the time of Duke Lupus, with the minor modification already noted. Notarial practice in the early years of Duke Gisulf, whether or not he owed his position to King Desiderius, was the same. Private charters of April 760 (Gisulf's year 1) and of January and March 761 (in year 2), written by three or four different

---

[1] So in *RF* ii, no. 38; v, no. 1224; ii, no. 40; but not in ii, no. 39—all of 757.

[2] Compare Toubert, op. cit., p. 190, with its insistence 'sur l'importance de la coupure que l'avènement de Didier a marquée dans l'histoire et dans la diplomatique des ducs de Spolète'.

[3] *RF* ii, nos. (?)66, 84, 85; and the *iudicata* of 747 and 749, *RF* ii, nos. 30 (*Andreas notarius missus ducis*), 22 (*Andreas notarius domni nostri Luponis ducis*). The use of *iudex* in a fairly general sense (of prominent officials, etc.) is characteristic of eighth-century Italy.

notaries, date by ducal years and the indiction;[1] so do *notitiae iudicati*, recording proceedings under the duke's presidency (at the earlier of which he has the assistance of a royal *missus*), of February and April 761, which mark the reappearance of Dagarius —in the first case as writer, in the second as *dictator*. The fact that Gisulf adds his subscription to the record of the February judgement seems to be of no particular significance, although the practice becomes standard after 774.[2] Gisulf's only surviving diploma, of April 761, written by Dagarius without the participation of a *dictator*, is novel in two respects: for the first time in a ducal document a dating-clause follows immediately after the invocation, although *datum iussionis* with the indiction still figures at the end of the document; and in the initial dating-clause the regnal years of the Lombard kings precede the ducal year. It is unusual in one other respect: no *intitulatio* precedes the address-clause.[3] I doubt if this is anything more than a copyist's error; but even if it were a feature of the original it would not make the document resemble more closely the private charters of the period. The closest analogies to some of the distinctive phraseology of the dispositive clauses are in the anomalous 'diploma-judgement' of 749, which is one of several reasons for accepting that the Dagarius of 761 and later is the same man as the Dagarius of 745–51.

Private charters written in the duchy of Spoleto after April 761 likewise incorporate the regnal years of the Lombard kings. So do the diplomas of Duke Theodicius (763–73). But this cannot be regarded as evidence of a trend which culminates in the peculiar form of the ducal grant to Rieti in 772. Having admitted the regnal years to the protocol, ducal diplomas of the 760s make no further concession to the forms of private charters; indeed the transfer of the *anno ducatus* to the final *datum*, which is already a feature of Theodicius's first diploma although it is written by Dagarius, brings them more into line with contemporary royal

---

[1] *RF* ii, nos. 42, 43, 44, 47 (one or two Raginfrids?).
[2] *RF* ii, nos. 45, 46. For the ducal signature see Chroust, *Untersuchungen*, p. 153; for the post-774 practice see Manaresi, *Placiti*, i, nos. 2, 3, 5 (*RF* ii, nos. 97, 103, 135).
[3] *RF* ii, no. 48.

diplomas than with contemporary Spoleto private charters.[1] This
is no less a feature of the suspect charter of 772. If in spite of the
difficulties the substantial genuineness of the latter is insisted on,
it is perhaps best regarded as the work of a local notary adapting
his customary formulary to what he supposed to be that of a
diploma in the absence of the duke's regular writers. It is in any
case *sui generis* and cannot be used to throw light on the normal
functioning and character of the ducal writing-office at this date;
to speak, as Professor Toubert does, of a 'slide' in the ducal diplomas
towards the form of the private charter is quite misleading and
directly contradicted by the unbroken tradition evident in
Dagarius's diplomas of 761–7, the Luciarius diploma of June 772,
and the diplomas of the period 774–80.

It may be equally misleading to talk of a *diminutio capitis* of the
personnel of the writing-office in Gisulf's and Theodicius's time.[2]
Admittedly the Stephen who wrote the second notice of judgement
in 761 is probably the notary of that name responsible for a large
number of private charters down to 781; and the fact that the
centre of his notarial activity was Rieti, where the judicial proceedings took place in 761 and where he had a house and other
property, makes it unlikely that he was regularly associated with
the ducal court.[3] It is of no significance, however, that Dagarius
and Luciarius are not recorded as contemporaneously active: and
even if we disregard the Largiarus who is supposed to have written
the Rieti charter of 772, the maximum reduction in the size of the
ducal writing-office would have been from three to two! Moreover,
account must be taken of the *Teudelapus notarius* who in March 773
wrote the notice of a *testimonium* declaring that a disputed donation
had actually been made 'by order of Duke Theodicius'; for in
documents of 776 and 777 Teudelapus appears again as a writer of
ducal documents in association with Dagarius.[4] Indeed, in the
later years of Theodicius the Spoletan writing-office seems once
again to have had a referendary as its head. A reference in a notice

[1] Compare *RF* ii, no. 53 of July 763 with, for example, Chroust, *Untersuchungen*,
tab. 1, no. 28, *RF* ii, no. 51.   [2] Toubert, op. cit., p. 190; cf. p. 189.

[3] *RF* ii, nos. 45 (*iudicatum*), 65, 73 and frequently until 136, predominantly at
Rieti (private charters); 120 of 778, 141 of 786 (property)—the latter when he was
already dead.   [4] *RF* ii, no. 83; Manaresi, *Placiti*, nos. 1, 3.

of judgement of 781 to a *iudicatum* made in the time of Duke Theodicius and deliberately burnt by one of the parties to the current proceedings declares that it had been written *per manum Dagarini castaldii et referendarii*.[1] There is no precise parallel to this remarkable double title, whether in Spoleto documents or elsewhere. It cannot, however, be regarded as either an error on the part of Gregory of Catino or as an idiosyncracy of the notary of the 781 notice—who was writing at the dictation of Dagari(us); for in other *notitiae* of 776–7 as well as in that of 781 when he gave evidence that he had in fact written the destroyed document 'by his own hand', Dagarius is described as *castaldius (gast-)*; and in ducal diplomas of the same years he is *castaldius et notarius*.[2] But of course if the statement 'by his own hand' is taken literally Dagarius's function was not quite that of Andreas before him.

All this does not exclude the possibility of a greater ducal dependence on the king in Pavia in the late 750s and 760s: but it certainly does not demonstrate it. It does not seem possible to use the evolving forms of Spoleto ducal documents to supplement the factual statements of royal diplomas and possibly other texts that can be taken as evidence of a 'crisis' in the Lombard *regnum* and the duchy of Spoleto in the years 770–3. The evidence for a pro-Frankish party in Italy in the last years of the independent kingdom remains much less satisfactory than the evidence for such an element in the Bavarian duchy.[3]

As is well known, in the autumn of 773 a number of leading men

---

[1] Manaresi, *Placiti*, i, no. 5, p. 12 (*RF* ii, no. 135).

[2] Manaresi, *Placiti*, i, nos. 1–3 (*RF* ii, nos. 104, 105, 113). The use of the genitive form *Dagarini* (rather than *Dagarii*) in the post-774 notices of judgement, Manaresi *Placiti*, i, nos. 1–5, is surprising only because it is consistent. *Dagarius* (not *Dagarinus*) represents a Lombardic *Dagari* and in seventh/eighth-century Italy the Latin conjugation of Germanic names in *-ari* was not uncommonly acc.-*arĭnem*, gen.-*arĭni*, etc.: so, for example, in *RF* ii, no. 22 of 749, *Insarenem*—the *Insarius* of *RF* ii, no. 30 of 747; and the familiar *Rotharini*, *-eni* from *Rothari* (Bruckner, *Sprache der Langobarden*, pp. 299–300 and *passim*). I leave open the question whether these are purely learned (notarial) forms or whether they correspond to anything in the current spoken language.

[3] E. Klebel, 'Bayern u. der fränkische Adel', *Vorträge u. Forschungen*, i (1955), 193–208; F. Prinz, 'Herzog u. Adel im agilolfingischen Bayern. Herzogsgut u. Konsensschenkungen vor 788', *Zeitschr. f. bayerische Landesgeschichte*, xxv (1962), 283–311; K. Reindel, 'Bayern im Karolingerreich', *Karl der Grosse: Lebenswerk u. Nachleben*, i, ed. H. Beumann (Düsseldorf, 1965), 220–2, with further references.

from the Spoleto and Rieti regions transferred their allegiance to the pope and secured his confirmation of their own choice as duke, a certain Hildebrand. Not long afterwards he made a grant of property that had hitherto belonged *ad publicum* to the abbey of Farfa: the protocol-date is by reference to the pope, but the unfortunate loss of a leaf from the manuscript Register has deprived us of the eschatocol and therefore of the name of the notary.[1] Both Duke Hildebrand and Abbot Probatus were able to make themselves acceptable to the victorious Frankish king. The post-774 series of Spoletan ducal diplomas begins with two of January 776.[2] They are in almost every important respect written to the same formulary as those of nine or even fifteen years previously. The one difference of substance is a rearrangement of the final clauses: inexplicably, these show a reversion to the form used in Duke Trasmund's time and then abandoned in the time of Duke Lupus, although now with the addition of ducal years. Dagarius's reappearance as a writer of diplomas in March 778, and two further diplomas by the notary Aderis who wrote those of January 776, dated respectively March 776 and May 778, reveal, however, that this archaic form is peculiar to Aderis—who none the less cannot be traced before 776.[3]

The title of *castaldius et notarius* which Dagarius uses in the three diplomas written by him for Duke Hildebrand, all of 778,[4] is presumably intended to indicate a position of seniority among the notaries associated with the ducal court or palace—which it would not be possible to infer from any feature of the diplomas themselves. By contrast Dagarius's superior position, as befitted a man who had served a succession of dukes for more than three decades, is very clear in four surviving notices of judgement from the years 776–81, which in the light of the pre-774 evidence offer no support for the notion of a special 'cancelleria dei placiti'. The three *notitiae* that record proceedings before the duke himself are written *ex dicto Dagarini castaldii* by three different notaries (two of them, Teudelapus and Totemannus, known from other documents); the same form of *scriptum*-clause occurs in the *notitia* of an order given by the duke after judicial proceedings (of January 776),

---

[1] *RF* ii, no. 91.   [2] *RF* ii, nos. 93, 94.

[3] *RF* ii, nos. 104, 96, 116.   [4] *RF* ii, nos. 104, 105, 113.

the notary being the Teudelapus previously referred to.[1] The proceedings recorded in the fourth notice of judgement, of March 779, were before Dagarius himself as representative of the duke in the territory of Valva (a more easterly part of the duchy): the notice is actually written *ex dictatu Dagarini notarii* by the notary Tote-mannus who wrote the *notitia* of 781.[2] The formulary used for these *notitiae* is for the most part identical with that used for similar documents from the duchy in the late Lombard period. Apart from the *ex dictatu* (in place of the earlier *ex dicto*), there is one new turn of phrase which somewhat unexpectedly suggests the influence of the Pavian palace and its notaries: the *scriptum*-clause (the order to the notary to write the notice) is introduced by the words *Unde pro amputanda intentione*. This phrase has not been noticed in earlier documents from Frankish territories and indeed it does not seem to have been used in this particular context in any pre-774 Lombard *notitia*. It is, however, used in a somewhat different context in the famous Siena-Arezzo *iudicatum* of 715 for which a palace notary was responsible; and it is used in the plural in the untypical and awkward conclusion of Charles's so-called 'first Italian capitulary', 'unde qualiter nobis complacuit, presentem deliberationis notitiam pro amputandas intentiones fieri iussimus' etc.—the peculiarities of the text of which I believe must be explained by its having been drawn up by Pavian palace notaries who continued to function after the Frankish conquest.[3]

The notice of judgement of July 781 which marks the final appearance in our texts of both Dagarius and Totemannus is the first from any part of Italy which concludes with an extended witness-list since the early eighth-century Siena-Arezzo judge-ments. It is not difficult to imagine a number of different reasons that might account for this striking innovation; it is difficult to find convincing arguments for any of them. In April of that year Charles had made a formal grant of the Sabina to the pope, and it was eventually implemented some months later, albeit probably in

---

[1] Manaresi, *Placiti*, i, nos. 2, 3, 5; ibid., no. 1. For Teudelapus's first appearance see above p. 16. [2] Manaresi, *Placiti*, i, no. 4.

[3] Schiaparelli, *Cod. Dipl. Long.* i, no. 20 p. 83; *Mon. Germ. Hist.*, *Capitularia*, i, no. 88: this feature of the capitulary is not considered in Manacorda's study of the text, *Ricerche*, pp. 36–43. For *ex dictatu, ex dicto*, see above, p. 8, n. 1.

a modified form.[1] Whatever was conveyed to papal temporal sovereignty, the rights of the dukes of Spoleto over the *publicum* in that region were certainly significantly diminished and there was a sharp decline in the grants made by the dukes of Farfa. Those that were made and survive, together with the Spoletan *notitiae iudicati* from the next two decades, indicate that the years 781–3 constitute a clear break in the history of the ducal writing-office. Hildebrand's two later diplomas, of 783 and 787, were written by *Alefridus diaconus* (*et notarius* in 787).[2] A notice of judgement of 791 was written by the Teudelapus who was already connected with the ducal writing-office in Dagarius's time; but others of 807 and 811 were written by notaries who are the best-recorded of all writers of private charters in the duchy in the early ninth century; Hisemund and Opteram.[3] Whether this conspicuous change is a consequence of the Frankish king's clearer assertion of his authority in the years 779–81, reflected in Hildebrand's case by his recorded presence at Charles's court at Verzenay in 779 and his accompanying the king from Rome to the vicinity of Florence in 781,[4] or of the death or retirement of Dagarius, or of some quite different cause, we shall never know. But unless the Farfa documents preserved by Gregory of Catino convey a wholly false impression, the rise and fall of a distinct ducal writing-office with specialized lay personnel both belong to a period of less than fifty years—a time-span which stretches across major political changes in central Italy and coincides almost exactly with the known notarial activity of one man.

It is unfortunate that we know nothing at all about the background or origins of Dagari(us), except what can be cautiously inferred from his name—which is, of course, Germanic (Lombardic): if he was a man of property at the end of his life he clearly did not give any of it to Farfa. Nor do we know anything about

---

[1] On which the views of O. Vehse, 'Die päpstliche Herrschaft in die Sabina', *Quellen u. Forschungen*, xxi (1929), 121–6 are probably to be preferred to those of H. Müller, *Topogr. u. genealog. Untersuchungen des Herzogstum Spoleto u. der Sabina* (diss. Greifswald, 1930), pp. 1–12, although neither seems wholly correct.

[2] *RF* ii, nos. 137, 144.

[3] Manaresi, *Placiti*, i, nos. 8, 21, 22, 23 (*RF* ii, nos. 154, 184, 204, 197).

[4] *Annales regni Francorum*, ed. Kurze (Hanover, 1895), pp. 52–4; Manaresi, *Placiti*, i, no. 5 (*RF* ii, no. 135).

his fellow-notaries, except for Stephen. The evidence for the latter's property-holding suggests that, like the much more fully-documented Opteram in the next generation, he belonged to the 'middling landowning class' which formed the backbone of the late Lombard and early Carolingian armies, and provided the regular suitors in public courts, the middle ranks of the royal administration, and their counterparts in the church; to this class, whose part in the history of Carolingian Italy and of the Carolingian Empire has attracted far too little attention, notaries of every kind brought a distinctive and important element. For the rest we have to be content with what we can learn from the forms of the documents in the Farfa Register.

Working within the framework of an already-established local notarial tradition, the immediate origins of which are as obscure as they are elsewhere in Lombard Italy because of the almost total lack of seventh-century documents, Dagari and the other notaries and referendary working for the duke of Spoleto evolved appropriate forms and an extended vocabulary for documents of different kinds, which were to have a long history before them. Subsequent modifications of the formulary were usually of a minor kind but none the less clear—although rarely unambiguous in purpose or significance. To some degree certainly, they reflected the political changes which affected the dukes and their territory: but the correlation between political change and changes in diplomatic forms were not at all close nor always what one might expect. The continuation of the practice of omitting (royal or imperial) regnal years from *notitiae iudicati* but not from other types of ducal or private documents throughout the period of Carolingian rule in Italy[1]—which has misled more than one historian seeking to establish the allegiance of the duchy at various dates in the ninth century from the language of protocols and eschatocols—is both a striking example of notarial conservatism and of the perils of trying to infer too much from the forms of individual documents.

D. A. BULLOUGH

---

[1] So still, for example, in Manaresi, *Placiti*, i, nos. 83–6 of 878.

II

English Diplomatic Documents to the End of Edward III's Reign

ALTHOUGH we are often inclined to judge the diplomatic skill of a medieval king by the extent of his success in bringing off advantageous agreements with the leaders of other countries, treaty-making was only one of the two major diplomatic activities of any ruler in any age. The other, often as important and much more frequently exercised, consisted of exchanging with foreign rulers written and oral messages on topics of mutual interest ranging from family matters to affairs of state.

That the kings of England engaged in both types of diplomatic activity long before the thirteenth century is beyond question. From Anglo-Saxon times we have references to trade agreements made by Offa of Mercia with Charlemagne[1] and by Cnut with the king of the Lombards,[2] to a peace treaty between Æthelred II and Duke Richard I of Normandy,[3] and to a number of foreign marriages, those of Æthelberht I of Kent to the Merovingian princess Bertha (late sixth century),[4] of the daughters of Edward the Elder to several continental rulers (early tenth century),[5] and of Æthelred II to Emma, daughter of Richard I of Normandy (1002).[6] Some of

---

[1] *Mon. Germ. Hist., Epist.* iv (*Epist. Karol. Aevi*, ii), no. 100; F. M. Stenton, *Anglo-Saxon England*, 2nd edn. (Oxford, 1947), p. 219.

[2] Gian Piero Bognetti, *Note per la storia del passaporto e del salvacondotto* (Pavia, 1933), pp. 33–4.

[3] *Recueil des actes des ducs de Normandie*, ed. Marie Fauroux (*Mémoires de la Soc. des Antiq. de Normandie*, xxxvi, 1961), p. 22, no. 12 and note 15; Stenton, op. cit., p. 370.

[4] Gregory of Tours, *Historia Francorum*, iv. 26 and ix. 26 (*Mon. Germ. Hist., Script. Rerum Merov.* i, pp. 160, 382); Stenton, op. cit., p. 105; H. G. Richardson and G. O. Sayles, *Law and Legislation from Æthelberht to Magna Carta* (Edinburgh, 1966), pp. 164–5.

[5] R. L. Poole, *Studies in Chronology and History*, ed. A. L. Poole (Oxford, 1934), pp. 115 ff.; Stenton, op. cit., pp. 340–2.

[6] *Two of the Saxon Chronicles Parallel*, ed. C. Plummer (Oxford, 1892–9), i. 134; ii. 182; William of Jumièges, *Gesta Normannorum Ducum*, ed. J. Marx (Soc. Hist. Norm., 1914), p. 69.

these treaties may have been set down in writing, whereas others—for example, marriage alliances—probably were not.[1] We also have unequivocal evidence that letters were sent by Offa to Charlemagne[2] and by various Anglo-Saxon kings to the popes.[3] Besides exchanging correspondence with continental rulers, the Anglo-Saxon kings may have communicated with them by means of oral messages relayed through trustworthy envoys: this second method, occasionally adopted by Charlemagne in his conduct of domestic and foreign affairs,[4] was widely used in western countries, long after the introduction of writing, for communications which were either too lengthy or too confidential to be committed to writing.

The number of diplomatic documents of English origin to have survived from Anglo-Saxon and early Anglo-Norman times is negligible. Before 1100 we only have copies of a few letters sent to the popes.[5] By contrast the twelfth century has left us not only a more numerous and more varied selection of the foreign correspondence which came out of England, but also a fair number of full texts of treaties of almost every kind, half a dozen of which have survived in the original.[6] The correspondence of Henry II

---

[1] On the occasion of the marriage of Edith, Edward the Elder's daughter, to King Otto (I), gospel-books were exchanged between Athelstan (Edith's brother) and Otto: the book given by Otto to Athelstan is now B.M. Cotton MS. Tiberius A ii, which is inscribed '+ ODDA REX' and '+ MIHTHILD MATER REGIS' (f. 24^r); the Gandersheim Gospels, given by Athelstan to Otto are inscribed in a single English hand '+ eadgifu regina. æþelstan rex angulsaxonum et mercianorum' (cf. Ilona Hubay, *Die Handschriften der Landesbibliothek Coburg* (Coburg, 1962), plate 2; I owe this reference to the kindness of Dr. Curt Höfner). The use of the style *rex . . . mercianorum* suggests that a Mercian, possibly Bishop Cenwald of Worcester, whose mission to Germany may have been connected with the marriage, was responsible for this inscription (cf. Plummer, op. cit., ii. 122, 133).

[2] *Mon. Germ. Hist., Epist.* iv, no. 100.

[3] W. de G. Birch, *Cartularium Saxonicum* (1885–93), no. 287; *Journal of the Soc. of Archivists*, iii. 10 (Oct. 1969), p. 535, notes 72–3.

[4] *Mon. Germ. Hist., Legum Sectio* ii, *Capitularia Reg. Franc.* i. 66–7, 225.

[5] Birch, *Cart. Sax.*, no. 287; *Regesta Reg. Anglo-Norm.* i, ed. H. W. C. Davis (Oxford, 1913), no. 134.

[6] P.R.O., Exchequer T.R., Dipl. Doc. 1–3, 5 (*Diplomatic Documents*, i, ed. P. Chaplais (H.M.S.O., 1964), nos. 1–3, 7: A.D. 1101, 1110, 1163, 1197). These four originals of Anglo-Flemish alliances are, technically, the Flemish exemplars, since they were once sealed with the seals of the counts of Flanders and are preserved in England; but as they are chirographs and at least two of them were written by English scribes, they may be regarded as exact duplicates of the English exemplars formerly preserved in the archives of the counts of Flanders. See also Paris, Arch. Nat.,

makes it clear that, by the mid twelfth century, it was not unusual for the king to entrust to the bearer of letters sent to a foreign ruler a supplementary oral message for the addressee's ears; when this was the case, a clause of credence, naming the bearer and asking that he be believed in what he was to say on the king's behalf, seems to have been an essential feature of the letters.[1]

Treaties raised more difficult problems than correspondence, because their various clauses had to be worked out and agreed upon in joint discussions between the two parties concerned. Much of the preliminary work was probably done, not by the rulers themselves, but by representatives appointed by them. Were the English representatives appointed in writing? If so, what sort of writing was it? Was the result of the discussions between the representatives of both sides written down in a document issued in their own names? These are difficult questions to answer for the period preceding the death of Henry II, because all the extant treaties of Henry I's and Henry II's reigns fall into a special category. In all of them the foreign rulers involved had lands which were contiguous to those of the king of England. All are in the form of final agreements, drawn up in duplicate, in the joint names of the two contracting parties, at a meeting which was attended by both and which took place on the 'march' between their respective lands. The two exemplars were sealed interchangeably, the exemplar sealed with the seal of the king of England being delivered to the foreign ruler and vice versa. For further authentication these sealed exemplars were sometimes issued in the form of bipartite chirographs; this was done for the Anglo-Flemish alliances of 1101, 1110, and 1163,

Angleterre I, J. 628, nos. 1–3 (*Layettes du Trésor des Chartes* (Paris, 1909–27), ed. A. Teulet (Paris, 1863–1909), i, nos. 412, 431–2).

[1] *Recueil des actes de Henri II . . .*, ed. L. Delisle and E. Berger (Paris, 1909–27), i, no. 139: Henry II to Alexander III: '. . . latorem presentium fratrem R., in cujus ore mea negotia posui plenius vobis exprimenda, benigne suscipiatis et his que ex parte mea vobis dixerit assensum et effectum exhibeatis . . .'; no. 240: Henry II to Louis VII: '. . . sicut homines mei, quos ob hoc vobis mitto, plenius vobis exponent; quibus, si placet, credatis tamquam mihi super his que vobis ex parte mea dixerint . . .'; no. 287: Henry II to Alexander III: '. . . Et quoniam singula que a nobis dicta sunt et proposita difficile scripto comprehenderentur, transmittimus ad pedes paternitatis vestre clericos et familiares nostros Reginaldum archidiaconum Saresberiensem et Richardum Barre, qui plenius vobis cuncta que hinc inde agitata sunt exponent, quibus in cunctis que ex parte nostra vestre sanctitati proponent fidem indubitanter adhibeatis . . .'.

and also for their renewal by Richard I and Count Baldwin in 1197.[1] During the reigns of Richard I and John several Anglo-French treaties of peace were also concluded on the occasion of a meeting between the kings of England and France, for example at Messina in 1191, between Gaillon and Le Vaudreuil in 1196, and at Le Goulet in 1200.[2] In those instances, the documents exchanged between the two kings were no longer issued in their joint names; they were—like the royal ratifications of the later period—drawn up in the form of individual letters patent, one in the name of the king of England, the other in the name of the king of France. Even after 1200 the kings of England sometimes met another head of state for the purpose of concluding a treaty, but now those occasions were rare. The change seems to have been mainly due to the gradual extension of the theory of representation to diplomatic relations. Once the principle had been accepted that valid treaties could be entered into by proctors duly appointed for that purpose by both sides, meetings between heads of state for the making of treaties had ceased to be necessary, even when their respective lands had a common frontier.

When there was no common frontier, the use of representatives could not be avoided. We know that the lost Anglo-Sicilian treaty of 1176–7 for the marriage of Henry II's daughter Joan to William II of Sicily was the result of negotiations conducted in England by Sicilian *nuncii*, who took oaths on William's soul, and in Sicily by English *nuncii*, who took similar oaths on Henry's behalf.[3] That such oaths could have been taken without written procurations is difficult to believe. In Henry II's reign procurations were used in England for domestic business. In 1184 the prior of Rochester and the twelve monks summoned to Westminster to elect a new bishop were ordered by Henry II to bring along a procuration made out in the name of their chapter ('literas de capitulo vestro patentes de ratihabitione illius eleccionis').[4] Henry II's appointment of William fitzAudelin as lieutenant of Ireland in 1173 was made in the form of a procuration ('. . . Ego quoque ratum habebo

[1] *Dipl. Doc.* i, nos. 1–3, 7.
[2] Ibid., nos. 5–6, 9; *Layettes*, nos. 431, 578.
[3] T. Rymer, *Foedera* (R.C., 1816–69), I. i. 32.
[4] *Memoranda Roll 1 John* (P.R.S. N.S. 21, 1943), ed. H. G. Richardson, p. lxxii.

et firmum quicquid ipse fecerit, tanquam egomet fecissem . . .').[1]
Henry's envoys to Sicily probably had with them a procuration of
the same kind. However, the earliest certain references to English
diplomatic representatives being appointed by letters of procuration belong to Richard I's reign. On 8 July 1193, while Richard was
still in captivity in Germany, William Longchamp and three other
English envoys met Philip Augustus at Mantes and agreed to a
peace treaty between England and France. The treaty issued in
their names states that they had gone to France with Richard I's
letters patent in which it was said that he, Richard, would abide
by the agreement which they would make with the king of France
('ea que ipsi cum ipso agerent et ordinarent ipse rex Anglie rata
prorsus et firma haberet').[2] This is clearly a reference to letters of
procuration such as those which have survived for John's reign.
The four envoys swore that Richard would observe the terms of
the treaty and would send to the king of France his letters patent
ratifying the treaty. The French counterpart, presumably drawn
up likewise *mutatis mutandis*, is lost.

   The use of proctors for the treaty of Mantes was unavoidable on
the English side, since Richard I was a prisoner at the time, but
the Anglo-French truce made on 23 July 1194 between Verneuil
and Tillières was also concluded by proctors, although Richard
was now free and back in France. In this second case the English
exemplar is lost. But there is no doubt that it was issued in the
names of Richard's proctors and that their letters of procuration
were cited in it, in the same way as the extant French counterpart,
made out in the names of the proctors of Philip Augustus, states
that they, for their part, had 'regis Francie litteras patentes de
ratihabitione, videlicet quod quicquid de treugis servandis ordina-
remus ratum haberet et firmum'. In this case, as in the treaty of
Mantes, the agreement specified that each king was to issue letters
patent of ratification, promising to observe the truce and its
provisions.[3]

   From 1199, as a result of the introduction of Chancery enrolments, the number of English diplomatic documents at our disposal

---

[1] *Recueil des actes de Henri II* . . ., i, no. 310.
[2] Rymer, *Foedera*, I. i. 61.   [3] Ibid., I. i. 64.

rises sharply. Now we have the proof that royal messages to foreign rulers were, according to their purport, conveyed in one of three ways: wholly in writing, or partly in writing and partly by word of mouth, or wholly by word of mouth; the third method is attested for the first time in John's reign, although it may have been used earlier. A written message which did not involve any oral communication took the form of letters close without any special features, their dispatch being left to a mere household courier.[1] When, in addition to the written message, an oral one was intended, the letters close were provided with a clause of credence of the type already encountered in Henry II's reign:[2] in this second method both messages were delivered by the same envoy or envoys, whose choice had been determined by the trust which the king placed in them rather than by their social rank; the clause of credence was an assurance to the foreign ruler that the oral message which he was to hear could be trusted as fully as if he had received it from the king's own mouth. If the whole of the communication was to be made orally, the envoy to whom it was entrusted was given letters close of credence pure and simple, which he presented to the foreign ruler on arrival at his court. The following letters were issued in 1213:

Karissimo nepoti suo Othoni Dei gratia illustri Romanorum imperatori et semper augusto, Johannes eadem gratia rex Anglie etc. Mittimus ad vos fideles nostros dominum episcopum Norwicensem et W. comitem Sarr' fratrem nostrum et Willelmum Briwer, rogantes quatinus eis fidem habeatis super hiis que vobis dicent ex parte nostra ad commodum utriusque nostrum. Teste me ipso apud Corff' xxv die julii.[3]

Because letters of credence served only one purpose, that of letters of introduction for an envoy whose mission did not extend

[1] This seems to have been the status of Nicholas Scogernel and William le Chareter, Absalon, and Norman Nevregodman, who carried letters to Rome in 1223–4. See *Rot. Litt. Claus.* (R.C.), i. 578a, 586a, 586b (cf. 542b, 558a, 581b, 584b); *Dipl. Doc.* i, no. 136 and note 5. See also Donald E. Queller, *The Office of Ambassador in the Middle Ages* (Princeton, 1967), pp. 5–6.

[2] See Rymer, *Foedera*, I. i. 104 (to Emperor Otto IV; here the envoys are called *nuncios . . . solempnes*), 114 (to the count of Auvergne).

[3] Ibid., I. i. 114; see also I. i. 120, 124, 137; *CCR, 1227–31*, p. 233. For later letters of credence, see *Treaty Rolls*, i (H.M.S.O., 1956), nos. 214–19, 633–6, etc.

beyond the delivery of one oral message, there was no need for them to be kept by the addressee or for their seal to be preserved intact. This is presumably why throughout the Middle Ages they were usually sealed close, except when they were addressed to several persons, in which case they were sealed patent.[1] It may be objected that many letters of credence of the reign of John and of the first dozen years of Henry III's reign were issued patent, although they were addressed to a single ruler. These letters patent, however, were not ordinary letters of credence. One of them, dated 25 May 1213 and addressed to Count Ferrand of Flanders, states that King John is sending him the earl of Salisbury and four other envoys, adding:

mandantes quod fidem habeatis eis super hiis que vobis dicent ex parte nostra de negotio nostro et vestro, qui ratum habebimus quicquid vobiscum fecerint ad commodum utriusque nostrum.[2]

In letters patent of 28 April 1224 Henry III tells King Louis VIII of France that he is sending him the master of the Temple in England, the prior of Lenton and the chancellor of St. Paul's, London,

quibus fidem habere velitis super hiis que vobis dixerint ex parte nostra de treugis inter vos et nos prorogandis usque ad quadriennium a Pascha anno gracie millesimo ccxxiiij, scituri quod gratum et ratum habebimus quicquid ipsi inde fecerint ex parte nostra.[3]

In other letters patent of 3 January 1225 Henry III informs the duke of Austria that he is sending him the bishop of Carlisle and four other envoys,

ad tractandum vobiscum de negotiis nostris, quibus fidem habere velitis super hiis que vobis dixerint de eisdem negotiis. Nos enim rata habebimus et grata ea que vobis dixerint ex parte nostra et fecerint secundum formam scripti super eisdem conficiendi, cui eorum sigilla fuerint appensa.[4]

---

[1] For example *Rot. Chart.* (R.C., 1837), p. 58*b* (to the envoys of the king and queen of Castile); Rymer, *Foedera*, I. i. 325, 342; *Treaty Rolls*, i, no. 293 (but see no. 409: *et fuit clausa*).

[2] Rymer, *Foedera*, I. i. 113.

[3] *CPR, 1216–25*, pp. 484–5.

[4] Ibid., p. 558; see also ibid., pp. 205, 412.

In these three examples, to which many more, spread over the years 1199–1228, could be added, the mission of the envoys was not only to convey an oral message, but also to negotiate or accomplish something on the king's behalf. All three also state categorically that the king would stand firm by whatever the envoys were to do on his behalf, and the letters of 1225 to the duke of Austria even specify that the English envoys were to make with him an agreement to which they would set their seals. All these are features characteristic of letters of procuration. The combination of a clause of credence with a clause promising ratification (clause *de rato* or *de ratihabitione*) also occurs in English ecclesiastical letters of proxy of John's reign[1] and, thirty years earlier, in the letters by which Henry II notified the Irish people that he had appointed William fitzAudelin as his lieutenant in Ireland.[2] In so far as diplomatic representation is concerned, it is evident that royal envoys arriving at a foreign court with power to negotiate an agreement had to begin by explaining the purpose of their visit, and this could not be better achieved than by delivering an oral message from their master.

By 1228, whenever royal envoys were sent abroad with the double mission of delivering an oral message and negotiating an agreement, it had become customary to issue them with separate letters, one of credence sealed close and one of procuration sealed patent. The change did not affect the form of letters of credence, which remained as it had always been, but the letters of procuration lost their clause of credence, witness the following original of 1228:

Karissimo domino suo et consanguineo Lodovico Dei gracia illustri regi Francorum, Henricus eadem gracia rex Anglie, dominus Hibernie, dux Normannie, Aquitannie et comes Andegavie, salutem et debitum in omnibus servicium. Mittimus ad vos dilectos et fideles nostros nobilem virum Philippum de Albyniaco et Radulfum filium Nicholai senescallum nostrum ad capiendum et firmandum inter vos et nos treugas puras, firmas et rectas, sicut a domino papa Gregorio nono nobis est injunctum. Et nos treugas ipsas pro nobis

---

[1] *The Acta of the Bishops of Chichester, 1075–1207*, ed. H. Mayr-Harting (C.Y.S. 66, 1964), no. 81 and plate.   [2] *Recueil des actes de Henri II . . .*, i, no. 310.

et omnibus hominibus et imprisiis nostris ratas et gratas habemus et firmiter observari faciemus. In cujus rei testimonium has litteras nostras vobis mittimus patentes. Teste me ipso apud Westm' vj die maii, anno regni nostri duodecimo.[1]

By that time the technique of England's diplomatic relations had in all essentials reached the final stage of its evolution, and we may now proceed to study English diplomatic documents in a more systematic fashion, with particular attention to the reigns of Edward I, Edward II, and Edward III.

By the latter part of the thirteenth century the king's written messages to foreign rulers, in other words his foreign correspondence, had become sufficiently diversified to allow classification into types, although these types were often mixed. The letters of credence (*littere de credencia*), which have already been mentioned, were the most common among them. Equally common, but less important from the strictly diplomatic standpoint, were the letters described as *littere de statu* in the formularies of the fifteenth century.[2] Their only purpose was to acquaint the addressee with the state of health of the sender and ask for similar information in return.[3] Such letters were exchanged just as frequently between private individuals of all ranks as between members of royal families.[4]

The *littere recommendatorie* (also known as *recommendaciones* or *littere familiaritatis*)[5] varied widely in contents. Many of them were issued on behalf of one of the king's friends or subjects who was about to embark on a journey to or through a foreign country: some asked the head of state for unspecified assistance (for a grant of 'favour and grace') or for a safe conduct and passage through his dominions,[6] while others, addressed to his relatives or courtiers,

---

[1] Paris, Arch. Nat. J. 655, no. 13: *Layettes*, no. *1967* (cf. *CPR, 1225–32*, p. 214, a slightly different version of the same document).

[2] Bodl. Lib., Ashmole MS. 789, f. 292ᵛ; B.M., Add. MS. 24062, f. 154ʳ (*lettre destat*); *Dipl. Corr. Rich. II*, ed. E. Perroy (Camden 3rd Ser., xlviii, 1933), nos. 35–8, 62, etc.

[3] Rymer, *Foedera*, I. ii. 575; II. i. 251; *Rôles gascons*, ed. C. Bémont (Doc. inédits sur l'Hist. de France, 1896–1906), ii, nos. 681–2.

[4] See *Formularies which bear on the Hist. of Oxford c. 1204–1420*, ed. H. E. Salter, W. A. Pantin, and H. G. Richardson, ii (Oxford Hist. Soc., N.S. v, 1942), p. 485, no. 8.

[5] B.M., Add. MS. 24062, ff. 105ᵛ, 187ʳ; *Dipl. Corr. Rich. II*, no. 51.

[6] Ibid., nos. 143, 233–4; *Treaty Rolls*, i, nos. 476, 492, 556, 567; *CPR, 1225–32*, p. 200.

were requests for good offices on a variety of subjects.[1] A recommendation to the pope and cardinals often amounted to a petition for the promotion of one of the king's clerks or protégés to a bishopric or some other ecclesiastical preferment, or for favours to be shown in a case pending in the Roman curia.[2]

The *littere requisitorie* (or *requisiciones*; in French, *lettres de requeste*) were of a less friendly kind. They were not requests for favours, but demands for redress on behalf of an English subject whose goods had been unlawfully seized abroad or at sea. Their object was to obtain the release of the goods concerned. They often assured the addressee that the same redress would be given to his own subjects, should the occasion arise (which God forbid!), or warned him that, unless redress were forthcoming, the king would have to resort to other measures, which, in the case of depredations at sea, was another way of intimating that the victims would be granted 'letters of marque', allowing them to take reprisals to the value of their loss.[3]

Some miscellaneous letters, which the medieval clerks themselves found difficult to label accurately, can only be described by such meaningless terms as *littere deprecatorie, littere exhortatorie* and *littere regraciatorie*, or even *littere* and *responsiones*.[4] Others display features which are characteristic of several types: among them the letters known as *littere de statu et credencia* are perhaps the most common.[5]

All the letters to which I have referred were normally sent close. The seal used to authenticate and close them was usually the great seal until the second half of Edward I's reign. From that time onwards the most confidential and informal letters were sealed with a smaller seal, the privy seal until 1312, and the privy seal or the secret seal or signet after that year. Letters patent such as

---

[1] *Treaty Rolls*, i, nos. 207–10, 253, 622.

[2] *Dipl. Corr. Rich. II*, nos. 51, 82, 86, 90, 97–8, 110.

[3] B.M., Add. MS. 24062, f. 147ᵛ; Rymer, *Foedera*, II. i. 65–6, 100–1, 110, 133, 206–7; *Dipl. Corr. Rich. II*, nos. 119, 144, 149, 160, 180, 198, 209–10. See G. P. Cuttino, *English Diplomatic Administration, 1259–1339* (Oxford, 1940), pp. 51–2.

[4] For example *Dipl. Corr. Rich. II*, nos. 10, 12, 199, 200; Bodl. Lib., Ashmole MS. 789, ff. 151ʳ–156ᵛ.

[5] Ibid., f. 277ᵛ; *Dipl. Corr. Rich. II*, nos. 182, 249; Rymer, *Foedera*, II. i. 68, II. ii. 770; *Dipl. Doc.* i, no. 403.

safe-conducts for foreign envoys coming to England[1] and protections for English envoys going abroad[2] were not, technically speaking, diplomatic letters; they just happened to be as necessary for the safety of diplomats as they were for foreign merchants wishing to enter the kingdom in time of war and for English officials and captains leaving England for Gascony.

There is ample evidence that, as late as the end of the thirteenth century, secret information was occasionally conveyed under the great seal, but the use of that seal was fraught with security problems. So many Chancery officials were involved in the issue of great-seal letters that the possibility of leakage at home could not be ruled out. It was presumably to avoid this danger that on 20 February 1290 letters connected with Anglo-Norwegian relations were sealed in secret in the chancellor's lodgings and enrolled on a Wardrobe roll instead of a Chancery roll.[3] Precautions of this kind were taken fairly frequently in Edward I's reign.[4] Abroad the size of the great seal was a handicap, because letters sealed with it could not be easily concealed. This problem was particularly serious when delivery entailed a long journey through a foreign country, along treacherous roads which seemed to invite ambush. Smaller and therefore less conspicuous, the privy seal, as early as John's reign, was sometimes substituted for the great seal, 'propter viarum pericula', even on documents relating to purely domestic affairs.[5] The choice of a seal which was closer to the king's person— the privy seal from the thirteenth century, the privy seal, secret seal or signet from the fourteenth—had the additional merit of showing to the recipient that the king took the matter discussed

---

[1] Rymer, *Foedera*, II. i. 68, 73, 85; *Rot. Chart.* p. 103*a*; *CPR, 1225–32*, pp. 244, 246, 323, 380, 436 (cf. 35, 328, 368, 381).

[2] Cuttino, op. cit., pp. 111–12; *CPR, 1225–32*, p. 311.

[3] H. C. Maxwell-Lyte, *Historical Notes on the Use of the Great Seal of England* (H.M.S.O., 1926), p. 26; T. F. Tout, *Chapters in the Administrative History of Medieval England* (Manchester, 1920–33), i. 55 n.; ii. 80 n.; *Calendar of Chancery Warrants* (H.M.S.O., 1927), i. 100. P.R.O., Chancery, Treaty Rolls (C. 76), no. 1 (*Treaty Rolls*, i, nos. 1–102) is unlikely to have been written by ordinary Chancery clerks and kept with the other Chancery rolls: it contains a number of confidential documents and its membrane 3 is endorsed *Secret*'.

[4] Maxwell-Lyte, op. cit., pp. 72–3.

[5] *Rot. Litt. Patentium* (R.C., 1835), p. 155; Maxwell-Lyte, op. cit., p. 20.

in the letters especially to heart.[1] Nevertheless, whatever seal was employed, sending confidential information in writing was always hazardous, since the bearer of any letters, large or small, could be captured on his way, and his documents seized. This was obviously the sort of situation which Henry III sought to avoid when, in March 1229, he sent to the count of Toulouse an envoy in whose mouth he had placed certain matters which, 'propter viarum pericula', he would not commit to writing.[2] Besides, when the information to be conveyed required careful handling, letters were not necessarily the most satisfactory medium, because the meaning of every written word was liable to be twisted or at least misinterpreted by the recipient. Thus in 1317, in connection with particularly delicate questions, Edward II was advised to send to the king of France an oral message rather than a letter, 'quar li Frances pensont trop'.[3] Other matters called for lengthy explanations, which could be dealt with more easily by word of mouth than in writing.[4]

All that was required of the bearer of diplomatic correspondence was diligence and general trustworthiness, qualities which an ordinary courier of the royal household could be expected to possess. When, on the other hand, the king opted in favour of an oral message, much more care had to be taken in the selection of the envoy, who had to be relied upon not only to refrain from revealing any part of his message to unauthorized persons, but also to deliver it as he had received it, without addition or omission. The quality of the person for whom the message was

[1] See P.R.O., Exchequer K.R., Memoranda Rolls (E. 159), no. 97, m. 42d.; Rymer, *Foedera*, II. i. 632.
[2] Ibid., I. i. 194 (*CCR, 1227–31*, p. 233). Compare *Dipl. Doc.* i, no. 175: '... Et quia non esset tutum litteris committere secreta propter viarum pericula, statum et voluntatem nostram vobis refferet viva voce lator presentium litterarum.'
[3] *Gascon Rolls, 1307–1317*, ed. Y. Renouard (H.M.S.O., 1962), p. 581b. Compare P.R.O., Ancient Corresp. (S.C.1), xiv, no. 10 (*Acta Imperii, Angliae et Franciae*, ed. F. Kern (Tübingen, 1911), no. 18): '... Super hoc autem in ore magistri Andree prepositi Werdensis, familiaris clerici vestri, verba nostra posuimus, qui detectius vive vocis oraculo quam interpretis scripture mysterio vobis pandet et exprimet votum nostrum . . .'; S.C. 1, xviii, no. 155 (Avignon, 15 June 1290): '... mentis conceptum clarius verbo exprimitur quam scriptura . . .'
[4] *Recueil des actes de Henri II . . .*, i, no. 287. Compare *Dipl. Doc.* i, no. 196: '... Et quoniam vobis omnia per litteras non possumus explicare, dilectum ac fidelem nostrum . . . duximus transmittendum . . .'

intended as well as what was known of his own preference for some
particular type of envoy also had to be considered. In 1313, for
example, it was reported to the king of Aragon that the French
court was not greatly interested in the exalted status of envoys.[1]
Since the occasion on which this remark was made seems to have
required negotiators, who, as we shall see, had to do a great deal
more than deliver an oral message, it was *a fortiori* true of ordinary
message-bearers. A person of lower rank, familiar with the country
to which he was sent and able to speak the native tongue of its
people, was likely to be a better asset than a bishop or earl without
those qualifications.

Members of the king's council, who had already been sworn not
to divulge the king's secrets, were ideal candidates for the delivery
of oral messages to foreign rulers. So were those confidential
clerks, like Master Philip Martel, to whom Edward I referred as
his *secretarii* and *familiares*, and, to an even greater degree, men like
the notary Master Geoffrey de Eversley, clerk of both Edward I
and Alfonso X of Castile, and the canon of Aachen Master Gerlach
Baumgarten (*de Gardinis*, alias *de Pomerio*), chaplain of Adolf of
Nassau and clerk of Edward I, who enjoyed the confidence of two
kings and could be expected to be loyal to both.[2] According to the
kind of message to be delivered and perhaps to its importance,
sometimes the king sent only one envoy, sometimes two (for
example, a clerk and a knight) or even as many as four or five
(sometimes one bishop and one earl among them), in which case
the letters of credence might contain a quorum clause.[3]

Once the envoy had been chosen, his letters of credence had to
be prepared. This document was important enough: without it
few foreign rulers would have trusted the envoy or believed his

---

[1] *Acta Aragonensia*, ed. H. Finke (Berlin and Leipzig, 1908–22), i–ii, pp. 458–9:
'. . . de magna sollempnitate nunciorum in curia Francie non curatur . . .' Compare
Treaty Rolls, i, no. 613: '. . . dictos militem et clericum quos pro expedicione dictorum
negociorum, que nuncios forsitan solempniores requirerent, ad vestram magnificen-
ciam pro pleniori et secreciori informacione motuum cordis nostri vobis facienda sub
speciali confidencia transmittimus . . .' See also *CCR, 1296–1302*, p. 442.

[2] L. B. Dibben, 'Secretaries in the Thirteenth and Fourteenth Centuries', *EHR*
xxv (1910), 431–3; Rymer, *Foedera*, I. ii. 943, 989; *Treaty Rolls*, i. 180–2, 184,
236, 238–41, 245, 247, 254–6, 260–1; Cuttino, *English Diplomatic Administration*,
p. 42.

[3] *Treaty Rolls*, i, nos. 218, 409, 420, 422, 633–4.

message.[1] More important still, the envoy had to be told what message he was to give to the foreign ruler. This was generally done in the presence of the king's council. In English sources, the envoy's message was known as his *nuncium, credencia, oneracio* or even *instructio* (in French, *message, creance, charge* or *instruction*). All these terms were synonyms, each of them emphasizing one particular aspect of the message; they all referred to the oral message, to the 'credence' announced in the letters of credence.[2]

In so far as the recipient of an oral message was concerned, the letters of credence were a sufficient guarantee of trustworthiness, but the king as sender had also to be reasonably satisfied that his envoy would carry out his mission faithfully, without adding anything to the message or omitting any detail from it. One way of achieving this goal, although it was not absolutely foolproof, was to write down the message before the envoy's departure. The document thus drawn up was in fact a contract between the king and his envoy. Sometimes the written credence contained the exact words to be used by the envoy once abroad. A credence of this type was given to the four envoys sent by Edward I to France to renounce his homage to Philip IV in June 1294:

Nos messages dirrount au roy de Fraunce: 'Nostre seignur le roy Dengleterre, seignur Dirlaunde et ducs Daquitaigne, vous fist homage sur condicion . . . Par ount y lui semble que vous ne lui tenez pas pur vostre homme ne il nentent estre.'[3]

---

[1] See *Bull. de la Commission Royale d'Histoire*, 5th ser., t. iii (Brussels, 1893), p. 308 (for domestic affairs): '. . . un varlet ki navoit ne letres ne mandement por coi i fesist a croire, et li veske ne li vot riens respondre por chu ki nel tenoit nient a message . . .'. Similarly Peter des Rivaux refused to give an answer to Henry III *via* a royal envoy 'quia non tulerat ei litteras de credulitate', but promised to send it through one of his own messengers (P.R.O., Curia Regis Rolls (K.B. 26), no. 115B, m. 1d; I owe this reference to Dr. Patricia M. Barnes). But see Queller, *The Office of Ambassador in the Middle Ages*, p. 113.

[2] *Credencia* (or *creaunce, credence*): S.C. 1/xxxvii, no. 73; P.R.O., Chanc. Dipl. Doc. (C. 47), 30/3/1 and 32/18; *The Gascon Calendar of 1322*, ed. G. P. Cuttino (Camden 3rd ser. lxx, 1949), nos. 302, 400, 412–13. *Nunciacio, nuncium* (or *messagerie, message*): S.C. 1/xxxvii, no. 33; C. 47/27/5/10; *The Gascon Calendar of 1322*, nos. 351, 389, 393; *Speculum*, xvii (1942), 84–5. *Onus, oneracio* (or *charge*): C. 47/29/3/14; *Gascon Calendar*, no. 308; *Antient Kalendars . . .*, ed. F. Palgrave (R. C., 1836), i. 209; B.M. Cotton MS. Caligula D iii, ff. 42, 87. *Instructio* (or *instruction et charge*): Rymer, *Foedera* (Orig. edn., 1704–35), vii. 834; Staatsarchiv Düsseldorf, Urkunde Kurköln, no. 1944.

[3] C. 47/28/5/48–9; 30/6/10; Rymer, *Foedera*, I. ii. 807. For their letters of credence, see *Treaty Rolls*, i, no. 222.

In November 1304 Master Philip Martel, clerk, and William Inge, knight, were also given in their credence the text of the exact speech which they were to make to explain to Philip IV why Edward of Carnarvon had not come to pay homage for Guyenne.[1]

Sometimes, as in the case of the earl of Kent and others envoys sent by Edward II to Charles IV of France on 31 March 1324, the credence took the form of a memorandum which the envoys had to adapt in their own words:

Le counte de Kent et les autres messages qi vount au roi de France, apres ce qils averont saluez le roi et recommendez noz seignurs et dames roi, roine et lour enfantz et mustrez lour estat, le quel bon est, Dieu merci, et le desir qils ount de saver son estat bon, tot primerement prieront amiablement et ove grant affeccion . . .[2]

Another credence, for Anthony Bek and Luke de Tany, sent by Edward I to Philip III of France in July 1281, was a mixture of the two preceding types:

Sire, li roys de Engletere mon seygnur vos pria nad geres par son message pur aver condut de aler en sa tere de Gascoygne . . . Sy le roys de Fraunce respont ke ly plest ke ly roys de Engletere sen entermette de ceste bosoygne, respoygnent e requerent ly message ke il plese au roys de Fraunce . . .[3]

Whichever method was adopted, the principle remained the same: the envoy was not allowed to depart from the text of his message. On 15 April 1280 Edward I sent the following letter to Taillefer de Montausier and Master Geoffrey de Eversley, two envoys already on their way to Spain:

. . . Quia datum est nobis intelligi quod quedam que vobis diximus et injunximus in credencia vestra, quando recessistis a nobis, domino regi Castelle illustri per vos exponenda, per dilectum et fidelem nostrum Galfridum de Genevill' in aliquibus sunt mutata, nos, ne per hujusmodi mutacionem aliquid fiat quod non consonat intencioni nostre, conscribi fecimus in presencia nostra coram nobis quandam cedulam, quam vobis transmittimus presentibus inter-

---

[1] C. 47/27/5/10: *EHR* xxiii (1908), 729. See *Annales du Midi*, lxx (1958), 137, n. 12.
[2] *The War of Saint-Sardos*, ed. P. Chaplais (Camden 3rd ser. lxxxvii, 1954), p. 182.
[3] *Treaty Rolls*, i, no. 170.

clusam, vobis mandantes quod cedulam illam legatis frequenter et eam sic lectam intelligatis diligenter, ita quod extra tenorem ejusdem cedule nichil per vos fiat vel dicatur quod ejusdem tenori contrarium sit vel diversum, et quod verba in eadem cedula contenta nullo modo commutentur, set cum omni cautela et diligencia observentur . . .[1]

Occasionally envoys were given specific permission to say something outside their credence: in such cases they had to speak in their own name, not in the name of the king ('de eux mesmes, nient par lour creance';[2] 'de leur teste demeigne . . . et noun pas par lour creaunce').[3] In this way they expressed their own opinion without committing the king.

From the reign of Henry III until the end of Edward III's reign, English credences were drawn up in the form of bipartite indentures, one half of which was kept by the king and the other half was given to the envoy. At first the indentures were not sealed,[4] but by about 1340 the sealing practice already in use for indentures of military service was probably extended to diplomatic credences as it was to instructions proper: the envoy's exemplar was sealed with the royal privy seal, and the king's exemplar with the envoy's seal.[5] Early in the reign of Richard II the indenture system was abandoned to be replaced by the issue of one single document, normally authenticated by the three royal seals, great seal, privy seal, and signet, to which the sign manual was often added.[6] For some obscure reason, the form of royal wills evolved in the same way: the will of Henry III was in chirographic form, whereas those of Edward III and Richard II were not, being authenticated instead by the three royal seals and the sign manual.[7]

As long as the credence was in indented form, the envoy presumably took his exemplar with him on his mission, so that he

[1] S.C. 1/xiii, no. 149A; no. 149B is the *cedula* mentioned in the letter.

[2] *The War of Saint-Sardos*, p. 182.

[3] C. 47/30/3/1.

[4] S.C. 1/xxxvii, no. 73 (Nov. 1312); C. 47/30/3/1 (June 1333). But see p. 38, n. 3.

[5] Although I have found no original credence for the period 1340–77, the credence was always in the same form as instructions given to proctors; see below. P.R.O., Exch. T.R., Dipl. Doc. (E. 30), no. 1718 (Rymer, *Foedera*, III. i. 22) is partly credence, partly instructions.

[6] The remark made in the preceding note also applies here. E. 30/326 (Rymer, *Foedera* (Orig. edn.), vii. 834) is partly credence, partly instructions.

[7] Rymer, *Foedera*, I. i. 496; III. ii. 1080; Tout, *Chapters*, v. 210 and n. 3.

could learn it by heart and refresh his memory until the time came for him to deliver it orally. This is rather surprising, since, if the envoy was captured, his indenture could be seized just as easily as an ordinary letter which he might have carried. It is even more surprising to find that, after the envoy had surrendered his letters of credence and delivered his oral message, the foreign ruler sometimes insisted on the credence being given to him in writing. In 1340 Benedict XII asked William of Norwich, John Thoresby, and John Offord, Edward III's envoys, to give him their credence in writing, sealed with their own seals.[1] Although the pope's request was complied with on that occasion, the kings of England, unlike the kings of Aragon, tried to resist the practice. In 1354 the duke of Lancaster and the earl of Arundel were specifically instructed not to show their credence or even their letters of credence on some particularly secret matter, unless it were found absolutely necessary.[2] The problem, of course, did not arise when an oral message from the king of England was delivered to a foreign ruler by the latter's own envoy returning home: in this case the credence given to the envoy was automatically surrendered to his master.[3]

The practice of sending envoys with letters of credence and oral messages was not confined to diplomatic relations. It was also frequently adopted in the conduct of confidential domestic business in England and everywhere else in Europe. When the king of England was away from his council, he often communicated with it in this way. In July 1303, for example, Edward I sent John de Drokensford from Perth to his council at York with letters of credence addressed to the chancellor of England and to the chancellor of the Exchequer and with an indented credence in which were set out the various points which he had to explain to them on the king's behalf.[4] Letters of credence for domestic affairs were

---

[1] E. Déprez, *Les Préliminaires de la Guerre de Cent Ans* (Paris, 1902), p. 423.

[2] *Bull. John Rylands Lib.* xv (1931), p. 94.

[3] Staatsarchiv Düsseldorf, Urkunde Kurköln no. 1944: credence (called *instruccio*) given by Henry VI to Arnold de Brempt, envoy of the archbishop of Cologne, returning home (21 May 1439; sealed with the privy seal applied on the face of the document). See also *Speculum*, xvii (1942), pp. 82–4 (April 1304; *sealed* indenture).

[4] P.R.O., Chancery, Parl. and Council Proc. (C. 49), 3/9: J. F. Baldwin, *The King's Council in England* . . . (Oxford, 1913), p. 466. See also E. 159/85, m. 55d; Exch. L.T.R. Memoranda Roll (E. 368), 73, m. 38.

usually issued under the privy seal in Edward I's reign. The credence itself was in indented form until the fifteenth century.

Private individuals also communicated with one another and with the king and his officials by means of letters of credence and credences. This was the method used by the mayor and community of King's Lynn for answering a request of Edward III for an aid at the beginning of the Hundred Years War: the letters of credence and the indented credence of their envoy, John de Cokesford, have both survived in the Public Record Office.[1]

In English sources of the thirteenth and fourteenth centuries those diplomatic envoys whose only mission consisted of delivering a written or oral message were generally described as *nuncii* in Latin and *messages* in French.[2] The word *ambassator* or *ambassiator*, which also occurs in English records of the fourteenth century and especially under Edward III, was generally used to describe a *nuncius* with an oral message.[3] Whatever official designation was correct for him, an envoy whose only diplomatic documents consisted of a credence and a letter of credence could only deliver an oral message or make oral requests and bring an answer back. He was not entitled to negotiate or conclude an agreement or perform any positive act on behalf of his master. For that sort of business, letters of credence were generally regarded as inadequate; they had to be supplemented by letters of procuration. Unfortunately the rulers of Western Europe were not always in full agreement on what constituted a positive act for which a procuration was needed. When, in 1322, an envoy of the king of Aragon went to see Pope John XXII, offering his master's mediation in the dispute between Frederick III and Robert of Sicily, he was told by the pope that such an arduous task required letters of procuration. As the envoy only had simple letters close of credence and a credence (*capitula*), the pope refused to proceed further.[4] In July 1325 an envoy of the king of Portugal arrived in England with letters of credence and an oral message expressing his master's desire for marriage alliances between the royal houses of England and Portugal.

[1] S.C. 1/xxxix, nos. 111, 120.

[2] See, for example, *Treaty Rolls*, i, nos. 214–16; *The War of Saint-Sardos*, pp. 176–81.

[3] Rymer, *Foedera*, II. i. 310–12, III. i. 63, 75, 129.

[4] *Acta Aragonensia*, ed. H. Finke, iii. 411 ff.

Edward II sent him back home with a letter in which he explained that important alliances of this kind could not be discussed without the presence of more *nuncii*; the matter, however, would be favourably considered, if the king of Portugal sent *instructos et solempnes nuncios.*[1] In this instance the necessity of a procuration was not specifically mentioned, but it seems to have been implied by the reference to 'solemn and instructed envoys'. The expression *nuncii solempnes* was generally used, in England and elsewhere, to describe envoys of 'quality' such as bishops and earls (*digniores inter prelatos* and *majores inter seculares*),[2] who were, as a rule, sent as negotiators with letters of procuration, seldom as mere bearers of oral messages with letters of credence and credences.[3] By contrast the words *nuncii simplices* referred to envoys of lower rank, whose normal mission was to convey oral messages and who had 'simple' letters of credence.[4] In other words, the solemnity of a mission was matched by the solemnity of the envoys to whom it was entrusted.

In the thirteenth century it seems to have been the English view that procurations were needed even for the delivery and receipt of diplomatic documents. In 1259 Henry III issued a procuration of this kind for the exchange with Louis IX of documents relating to the peace treaty of Paris,[5] and Edward I followed his example in connection with the Anglo-German alliances of 1294.[6] The need for procurations for the delivery and receipt of diplomatic documents is hardly surprising since the English royal Chancery sometimes insisted on the production of letters of procuration before delivering a document of purely domestic interest. We are told, for example, that the clerks of Edward I's Chancery refused to hand over to the envoy of the Gascon lord of Saint-Pau royal letters granting a pension to his master, on the ground that he had no procuration with him ('pro eo [quod] ille qui petebat

---

[1] Rymer, *Foedera*, II. i. 603.

[2] *Acta Aragonensia*, iii. 354. See *EHR* xvii (1902), 524–6.

[3] Paris, Arch. Nat. J. 918, no. 5: '. . . nuntios nostros sollempnes ad vos duximus transmittendos, quibus etiam potestatem dedimus de pace inter vos et patrem nostrum . . .' (22 May 1240); *Rot. Litt. Claus.* ii. 72*b*; Rymer, *Foedera*, III. i. 151; *Treaty Rolls*, i, no. 206; *Acta Aragonensia*, iii. 342; *Gascon Rolls, 1307–1317*, no. 435.

[4] *Acta Aragonensia*, iii. 318–19, 411 ff.; Rymer, *Foedera*, I. i. 495.

[5] *Treaty Rolls*, i, no. 108.   [6] Ibid., i, nos. 233–4.

pro dicto domino de Sancto Paulo dictam literam non portabat literam procuracionis ab eodem domino').[1]

English records normally give the double title of *nuncii et procuratores* or *procuratores et nuncii speciales* to the envoys sent abroad to negotiate and conclude agreements. They were *nuncii*, like any other envoys, but they were above all *procuratores*, because, unlike all other envoys, they were appointed by letters of procuration and were to transact some royal business on the strength of those letters. Procurations were in England called by various names, *littere procuratorie, procuracio, procuratorium*, or *potestas*.[2] The word *commissio* was sometimes used in the fourteenth century for procurations which were connected with the settlement of disputes with other countries (maritime or border disputes, etc.) and also with the negotiation of treaties; in such cases the king's proctors were sometimes given the title of *commissarii* or *deputati* (*commis* or *deputez* in French) in addition to, or instead of, their normal title of 'envoys and proctors'.[3]

Such important persons as bishops and earls were not sent abroad to negotiate an agreement without some guarantee that their mission had a chance to succeed. Therefore a certain amount of preparatory work had to be done before their dispatch. For truce or peace negotiations the first approach was often made through papal intermediaries. In other cases a common procedure consisted of sending first one or several simple envoys with oral messages, and then, when the ground had been prepared, a delegation of more solemn envoys with power to negotiate would follow.[4] When the business was urgent, a solemn embassy might be sent at once, in which case the purpose of the mission was explained by the solemn envoys themselves, who had been provided for that purpose, in addition to their other documents, with letters of credence and credences. This happened in 1294, when Edward I sent an embassy to Germany and the Low Countries to seek alliances against France.[5] In the case of an embassy sent by

---

[1] S.C. 1/xxviii, no. 81.

[2] *Treaty Rolls*, i, nos. 112, 131, 283–7, 655, 657.

[3] Rymer, *Foedera*, III. i. 47, 74, 140; III. ii. 612, 932; *Gascon Rolls, 1307–1317*, nos. 436–9.

[4] Rymer, *Foedera*, III. i. 151.   [5] *Treaty Rolls*, i, nos. 212–15.

Edward II to the count of Flanders on 26 November 1312, the original credence and copies of the letters of credence and procurations of the English proctors are still extant.[1] The credence gives the exact words to be used by the proctors:

Sire, nostre seigneur le roy Dengleterre desire molt qe bon acord' et bon amour soient toutz jours entre luy et vous et entre ses suzmys et les voz dune part' et dautre. Et vous fait asavoir qe molt li peise de ceo que auscunes choses . . .

The same procedure was repeated many times in the thirteenth and fourteenth centuries,[2] and probably more often than the evidence suggests, because the original letters of credence were not so carefully preserved as procurations by the recipient and many of them, issued under the privy seal, were not copied on the Chancery rolls. However, the essential documents taken abroad by proctors or solemn envoys, those without which they could not act, were their procurations, that is to say their 'full powers'.

From the thirteenth century onwards many English procurations have survived in the original in foreign archives. One of them, issued in 1228, has already been quoted in full.[3] All are in the form of letters patent made out in the king's name and sealed with the great seal in natural wax (rarely with the privy seal), which was appended normally on a tongue, sometimes on a tag. As a rule, diplomatic procurations had a general address, *Omnibus ad quos presentes littere pervenerint, Universis presentes litteras inspecturis*, etc.[4] But some were addressed to the head of state with whom the negotiations were to be conducted,[5] while others, resembling ecclesiastical commissions, were addressed to the envoys themselves.[6] The contents of the procurations varied from one mission to the next: some were more general than others, but in one respect they were all alike. They all contained two essential clauses: one named the envoys,

[1] Rymer, *Foedera*, II. i. 188–9; S.C. 1/xxxvii, no. 73.
[2] *Rôles gascons*, ed. Bémont, ii, nos. 557–9; *Treaty Rolls*, i. 509–10, 581–4, 610–11; 'Some Documents regarding the Fulfilment and Interpretation of the Treaty of Brétigny', ed. P. Chaplais, *Camden Misc.* xix (Camden 3rd ser., lxxx, 1952), pp. 9–10.
[3] Above, pp. 29–30.
[4] *Treaty Rolls*, i, nos. 23–5, 212–13, 266–74, 282–90, 385–90.
[5] Ibid., nos. 368–9, 373–5, 377–8.
[6] Rymer, *Foedera*, III. ii. 943, 1021, 1027.

often giving a quorum, and defined the type of business which they were empowered to transact; in the other, the clause *de rato*, the king promised to ratify what the envoys would do.

It was not unusual for the same envoys to receive a whole series of procurations, each of them dealing with one particular aspect of the proposed negotiations, for example one for the conclusion of a truce, another for the conclusion of a peace treaty, and so on.[1] Sometimes they were given alternative procurations, in the hope that at least one of them might prove acceptable to the other side. Thus the envoys sent to negotiate the marriage treaty between Henry III and Eleanor of Provence in 1235 were in one letter given power to accept a dowry of 20,000 marks from the count of Provence; another procuration mentioned only 15,000 marks, a third 10,000, a fourth 7,000, a fifth 5,000, a sixth 3,000; finally, in a seventh document issued eight days later than the others, the envoys were ordered to conclude the marriage treaty without any payment at all, if the discussions on the dowry resulted in a deadlock.[2] On a number of occasions, the envoys were even supplied with sealed blanks, which they could fill in with whatever type of procuration the situation might demand.[3]

Once the foreign ruler had agreed to begin negotiations, he appointed proctors to represent him. Procurations were exchanged between the two delegations and were not returned, at least when the negotiations were crowned with success. In some cases, for example in the Franco-Castilian negotiations for a marriage treaty in 1294, it was agreed in advance that each side would be given its procurations back, if the negotiations failed.[4]

To make sure that his envoys did not agree to conditions which might prove unacceptable to him the king gave them specific instructions in writing, which were in the form of detailed memoranda defining the limits beyond which they were not allowed to go in bargaining with the foreign ruler's representatives. In their physical appearance and in their method of authentication, the

---

[1] *Treaty Rolls*, i, nos. 639–59.   [2] Ibid., nos. 24–6.
[3] Queller, *The Office of Ambassador in the Middle Ages*, pp. 130–6 and references; see also *Antient Kalendars . . .*, ed. Palgrave, i. 142; *The Gascon Calendar of 1322*, no. 663: 'Commissio vacua, qua non utebatur apud Monstrollium'.
[4] Paris, Arch. Nat. J. 601, no. 27.

instructions of solemn envoys and the credences of simple envoys were identical. Indeed words like *oneracio* or *charge*, *instructio* or *instruction*, were often used indiscriminately to refer to both types of documents.[1] Until the end of Edward III's reign, instructions took the form of bipartite indentures, one exemplar being retained by the king and the other given to the envoys; until 1340 the indentures were unsealed; after that date they were sealed interchangeably, the king's exemplar being sealed with the envoys' seals, and the envoys' exemplar with the king's privy seal. Our earliest original extant is the royal exemplar of the instructions given by Henry III, apparently in 1229, to one of the envoys sent to negotiate a peace treaty with France. It contains five alternative proposals:

Prima propositio: In primis proponatur quod omnes terre transmarine . . . *Secunda propositio sic*: Quod eadem forma servetur . . . *Tercia propositio sic*: Si forme predicte possint emendari per maritagium . . . *Quarta propositio*: Si nulla istarum formarum acceptetur . . . *Item*, si aliqua istarum formarum poterit emendari per denarios . . .[2]

Another original, also a royal exemplar, has a contemporary endorsement which states that 'the other part of this indenture was delivered to the archdeacon of Richmond [one of the English envoys sent to Montreuil to negotiate a peace treaty with France] at Dover on 5 June in the twenty-seventh year' (of Edward I's reign, A.D. 1299). It mentions four alternative proposals:

La volente le rois est que la terre de Gascoigne . . . E si levesque ne sen peusse entremettre personalment . . . E si la busoigne ne se puet mener a nule de ces deus voies . . . E si les choses ne se peussent mener a nule de ces trois voies, si vuet li rois . . .[3]

For reasons even more obvious than in the case of credences, instructions were not to be shown to the other side, at least as a rule.

---

[1] Rymer, *Foedera*, III. i. 153: instructions (*charge*); III. i. 224: instructions (*charge*); III. ii. 943: instructions (*informacion*); (Orig. edn.), viii. 72: instructions (*instruccion et charge*). Compare Staatsarchiv Düsseldorf, Urkunde Kurköln no. 1944: credence (*instructio*).

[2] *Dipl. Doc.* i, no. 215.

[3] C. 47/27/3/25.

Assuming that the procurations had been exchanged without controversy,[1] the negotiations began on the basis of the instructions which the envoys on both sides had been given by their principals. Views were exchanged on the text of the agreement to be concluded. Difficulties often arose which necessitated consultations between the envoys and their principals. This could be done by letters or by oral messages.[2] Sometimes the envoys returned home to seek further instructions and procurations.

It often took many sessions before the two delegations finally reached agreement. When this was achieved, a joint text was issued, the 'articles of agreement' or 'protocol'. In some Anglo-Flemish treaties the articles of agreement were drawn up in the form of bipartite indentures: one exemplar sealed with the seals of the Flemish envoys was handed over to the English side and vice versa; sometimes the two exemplars were sealed with the seals of both delegations.[3] The indenture system seems to have been used mainly for treaties between England and smaller countries whose ruler was not a king.[4] Ordinary letters patent were more usual than indentures: either each delegation issued letters patent in the names of its members, gave it to the other side and received in exchange a similar document;[5] or duplicate sets of the same letters patent were issued in the joint names of both delegations.[6]

Once the articles of agreement had been exchanged, the envoys returned home, and it only remained for the two heads of state to confirm the agreement by issuing a ratification each in their own

---

[1] See G. Digard, *Philippe-le-Bel et le Saint-Siège de 1285 à 1304*, ii (Paris, 1936), 298–9, 301; *Le Moyen Âge*, 4ᵉ sér., vi (1951), pp. 300–2.

[2] *Dipl. Doc.* i, no. 160; *The War of Saint-Sardos*, pp. 129–32.

[3] In the case of the Anglo-Flemish agreement of 1348, the indenture drawn up in the names of both delegations was sealed interchangeably with the *seaulz secrez* of both rulers, not with those of the proctors (K. Fowler, *The King's Lieutenant* (London, 1969), pp. 234–7; J. Froissart, *Œuvres*, ed. Kervyn de Lettenhove (Brussels, 1867–77), xviii. 319–24).

[4] This is not always true: the abortive Anglo-French treaty of London of 24 Mar. 1359 (new style) was indented (Manchester, John Rylands Lib., Latin MS. 404, ff. 59ᵛ–64ᵛ: Froissart, *Œuvres*, xviii. 413–33).

[5] For example, Paris, Arch. Nat. J. 631, no. 12; J. 633, nos. 7 and 33 (English articles of agreement); see *Treaty Rolls*, i, nos. 367, 384, and 393.

[6] For example, Paris, Arch. Nat. J. 634, nos. 6 *bis*, 8, and 9 (English articles of agreement); see *Treaty Rolls*, i, nos. 660–2.

name.[1] This was done by letters patent. From the thirteenth century onwards, English ratifications of truces were sealed with the great seal in natural (white) wax, appended on a tag.[2] Ratifications of alliances and peace treaties—agreements which ranked as perpetuities—were sealed with the great seal in green wax, appended on silk cords.[3] Sometimes the main ratifications were supplemented by separate ratifications of individual clauses. This was done in the case of the treaty of Brétigny-Calais, for which dozens of royal documents were issued on both sides at the end of October 1360.[4]

Secrecy was not the only problem raised by the issue of diplomatic documents. In the more formal letters close, whatever seal was used for their authentication, the wording of the protocol was governed by set rules affecting the order of appearance of title (name and style of sender) and address (name and style of addressee), the choice of the epithets applied to the addressee, and even the greeting. Unless the sender claimed precedence over his correspondent,[5] or meant to be offensive,[6] the address always came first. In the thirteenth and fourteenth centuries the king of England addressed another king as *egregio, excellentissimo, magnifico,* or *serenissimo principi,*[7] a duke or count as *nobili viro.*[8] Feudal relationship between the correspondents was usually noted in the address by the addition of the words *domino suo* or *fideli suo.* For Henry III to have addressed the king of France as *domino suo* in the 1220s, at a time when there were no feudal relations between them, was sheer ineptitude,[9] but to have used the more subtle phrases *domino suo quando ei placuerit* or *domino suo si placet*[10] or *domino*

---

[1] Sometimes the ratifications are in the names of both rulers: see Rymer, *Foedera*, III. i. 178–9.

[2] See Paris, Arch. Nat. J. 631, nos. 13 *bis* and 14; J. 632, no. 24 (English ratifications).

[3] See Paris, Arch. Nat. J. 633, nos. 14 and 16 (English ratifications).

[4] Rymer, *Foedera*, III. i. 518–47.

[5] *Le Moyen Âge*, 4ᵉ sér., xviii (*Livre Jubilaire*, 1963), p. 451, n. 7.

[6] For example, in letters of defiance: see those exchanged between Adolf of Nassau and Philip the Fair in 1294, *Mon. Germ. Hist., Legum Sectio* IV, *Const. et Acta Publica,* iii. 501 (no. 524) and 502–3 (no. 527).

[7] *Treaty Rolls,* i, nos. 155, 159, 172–4, 199–201, 254, 257, 260–2, 618–21.

[8] Ibid., i, nos. 252, 258–9, 404, 413, 422–3, 435–8, 547, 552, 625, 634.

[9] *Dipl. Doc.* i, nos. 44–5, 83.

[10] *CPR, 1216–25,* pp. 412, 484; *Dipl. Doc.* i, no. 234.

suo Deo annuente in proximo[1] when efforts were being made to reach a peace settlement with France may well have been regarded at the time as a shrewd political move. In diplomatic correspondence the normal greeting of the English Chancery (*salutem*) was usually replaced by more courteous phrases, which varied from one addressee to the next: although the fashion changed over the years, a common greeting to send to the pope was *devota pedum oscula beatorum*,[2] to a king *salutem et ad vota successus prosperos ac felices*,[3] and to anyone who was a kinsman or a friend *salutem et sincere dilectionis affectum* (or *augmentum*).[4] Letters close of all types sometimes had a final greeting (valediction), placed between the text and the dating clause, for example *Valete semper*,[5] *Valeat excellencia vestra per tempora diuturna*,[6] or *In votivis successibus Altissimus vos conservet*,[7] or a French equivalent.

Under Henry III the language of English diplomatic documents was almost invariably Latin. Indeed some of those which were written in French appear to have been the work of foreign clerks.[8] In about 1280 French began to be used extensively for documents issued under all seals,[9] although it never superseded Latin, even in letters and treaties relating to French-speaking countries. For countries like Germany, Italy, and Spain, Latin remained the normal language for documents under the great seal, privy seal, secret seal, and signet. Whether French or Latin was used, the literary merits of the documents depended largely on their subject-matter. When the king took a personal interest in the matters discussed in letters close, particular care was taken in their composition. One may quote as a typical example the letter of 27 August 1320 in which Edward II asked Pope John XXII to make Roger of Northburgh a cardinal.[10] The letter was drawn up, presumably

---

[1] *Treaty Rolls*, i, nos. 106–8.   [2] Ibid., i, nos. 226–8, 368, 373, 377–8.
[3] Ibid., i, nos. 618–21, 624, 628–32.   [4] Ibid., i, nos. 622, 625, 634, 637.
[5] Ibid., i, no. 183.   [6] Ibid., i, no. 403.
[7] Rymer, *Foedera*, III. i. 14.
[8] For example, Paris, Arch. Nat. J. 629, nos. 8 and 10 (ratification by Henry III of the Treaty of Paris and confirmation by the baronial council): *Layettes*, nos. 4554–5.
[9] *Treaty Rolls*, i, nos. 165–8, 170–1, 175–7, 188. It is impossible to say whether all these letters were sent under the great seal. For a long letter close sent under the privy seal by Edward I to John, Duke of Brabant, on 15 August 1295, see Brussels, Arch. du Royaume de Belgique, Chartes de Brabant, no. 157.
[10] Rymer, *Foedera*, II. i. 432–3.

in Chancery, on receipt of a memorandum, which is still extant.[1] The memorandum, headed 'A matter on which it has to be written to the pope in a suitable form and in a polished style' (*sub forma competenti et ornate*), gives detailed instructions on the points to be included in the letter: it lists the virtues of Northburgh, all of which had to be 'explicitly mentioned', and again stresses the importance of the stylistic aspect of the letter; the recommendation on behalf of Northburgh was to be *multum ornata*. What the clerk who carried out these instructions understood by the words *ornata* and *ornate* is plain enough from his work. To him elegance in prose-writing meant following the principles of the *cursus* as practised in the papal chancery. His task was not easy, because he had to adhere fairly closely to the text of the memorandum from which he was working, but he succeeded in ending most of his clauses and sentences in a way which would have been acceptable to a papal clerk. Perhaps he made an excessive use of the *cursus velox* (*negóciis | exaudívit, aúribus | intimáre, in memóriam | non veníre, infallibília | cognoscéntes, exsólvimus | sanctitáti, desidériis | supplicántes, ampléxibus | adaugére, ampléxibus | reportámus, in prósperis | adaugéri*); but he also knew the *cursus planus* (*recommendámus | afféctu, deliberatióne | pensántes*), and the *cursus tardus* (*sémper | dignémini, nóvit | sincéritas*).

A close examination of other important letters written to the popes in the thirteenth and fourteenth centuries produces similar results: the long letter 'Venenose turbacionis morbus . . .' sent by Edward I to Adrian V on 8 August 1276 is another example of good prose-writing.[2] Letters addressed to others than the pope, however, were seldom composed with such care; a letter written by Edward III to the doge of Genoa on 22 January 1342 is among the exceptions.[3] Most formal diplomatic documents were, of course, too stereotyped to offer much scope for stylistic refinements, but efforts were sometimes made to preface a treaty with a dignified and well-written preamble.[4]

So little work has been done on the diplomatic of documents

[1] C. 47/27/12/25. [2] *Treaty Rolls*, i, no. 134.
[3] Rymer, *Foedera*, II. ii. 1185. See also N. Denholm-Young, 'The Cursus in England', *Oxford Essays in Med. Hist. presented to H. E. Salter* (Oxford, 1934), pp. 68–103 (especially pp. 88–9). [4] Rymer, *Foedera*, III. ii. 656.

relating to foreign relations that we do not know to what extent each individual European chancery was content to adopt its own domestic practices in drawing up diplomatic documents. In this respect the English Chancery was never absolutely consistent. It seems, however, that in Henry III's reign letters close and letters patent issued under the great seal, for domestic and foreign usage alike, normally ended with the following dating-clause: *Teste me ipso apud N*, day of the month and regnal year. In letters patent the dating-clause was preceded by a corroboration: *In cujus rei testimonium has litteras nostras fieri fecimus patentes.*[1] No mention of the seal was made either in the corroboration or in the dating-clause.

By the 1260s different formulae begin to appear in diplomatic documents. Letters patent of Henry III addressed to Louis IX end with the following clauses: *In cujus rei testimonium presentibus litteris sigillum nostrum fecimus apponi. Dat' London' die dominica proxima post festum sancti Johannis ante portam latinam, anno Domini m°cc° sexagesimo secundo.*[2] In this particular instance the form of the corroboration and the use of the locative (instead of *apud* followed by the accusative) as well as the reference to a religious feast (instead of the day of the month) in the dating-clause, suggest an ecclesiastical draftsman. Although the formulae used for domestic business never went completely out of fashion in documents dealing with foreign affairs, from Edward I's reign the English Chancery normally used in letters patent for foreign consumption a corroboration which referred to the seal, and in letters close and patent a dating-clause in the form *Datum apud N* (or *Don' a N*, in French), day of the month and year of grace, to which was sometimes added the regnal year. Combinations of domestic and foreign formulae also occur. A procuration of Edward III giving several envoys power to make requests to the king of France and discuss them with him ends as follows:

In cujus rei testimonium presentibus sigillum nostrum duximus apponendum. Dat' apud Wodestok' decimo die aprilis, anno regni nostri quarto.[3]

---

[1] *Treaty Rolls*, i, nos. 106–8, 129–30, 132.
[2] Nantes, Arch. Dép. Loire-Atlantique, E. 7.
[3] Paris, Arch. Nat. J. 918, no. 22.

From about 1337 it is often stated, either in the corroboration or in the dating-clause, that the seal used was the great seal:

En tesmoign[ance] des queles choses as presentes nous avons mis nostre grant seal. Don' a nostre ville de Calais le xxiiij jour doctobre, lan de grace mille troiscentz sessante.[1]

Don' par tesmoignance de nostre grant seal a nostre palays de Westm' le xxiiij jour de juyl, lan de grace mille troiscentz soixante et dousze et de noz regnes de France trente et trois et Dengleterre quarrante sys.[2]

It will be noted that in the last two examples the place-name is given as *a nostre palays de Westm'* instead of *a Westm'*, and *a nostre ville de Calais*, instead of *a Calais*. This seems to have been an innovation of the 1340s, but similar formulae also occur in documents of purely domestic interest.

Another peculiarity of English diplomatic documents concerns the royal style. Between May 1259 and April 1260, for example, documents connected with diplomatic relations with France were issued in the name of Henry III as 'king of England, lord of Ireland and duke of Aquitaine', whereas those relating to England and Gascony continued to mention Henry's titles of duke of Normandy and count of Anjou.[3] From 1340 to 1360 documents of domestic interest were issued in the name of Edward III as 'king of England and France and lord of Ireland', but those concerning foreign relations reversed the order of the royal titles ('king of France and England and lord of Ireland'). Sometimes, but not always, these differences in styles were accompanied by matching differences in the seals used. Richard II, who frequently used the titles 'king of England and France and lord of Ireland' in documents sent to the French king, for example in privy-seal letters relating to his marriage to Isabella (24 October 1396),[4] sent on one occasion a friendly letter under the signet to Charles VI, using in this instance the style *R. par ycelle mesme grace roy Dengleterre etc*[a].[5] It is obvious that Richard wished neither to offend his correspondent nor to abandon his

---

[1] Paris, Arch. Nat. J. 638, no. 10.   [2] Paris, Arch. Nat. J. 642, no. 17.
[3] *EHR* lxvii (1952), 251–3.
[4] Paris, Arch. Nat. J. 655, no. 23 *bis*.
[5] *Dipl. Corr. Rich. II*, frontispiece and no. 223.

claim to the French throne; it was left to the recipient to interpret the word *etcª* as he wished.

Needless to say, there are countless English diplomatic documents whose features cannot be explained by what we might call English Chancery practice for foreign affairs. Indeed a large number of them only deserve to be described as English because they are drawn up in the name of an English king or in the names of English envoys. Their diplomatic and even sometimes their handwriting are foreign. Perhaps it is not surprising to find that documents issued in the names of English envoys while they were in France or in the Low Countries display characteristics of diplomatic and hand-writing which belong to those countries. Some letters issued by the bishop of Lincoln and the earls of Huntingdon and Salisbury in the Low Countries in 1337 belong to that category.[1] Nor should we find it strange that documents issued in Edward III's name were drafted and written by clerks of Flanders or Brabant while Edward was there himself in 1338–40.[2] The same could be said of documents issued by Edward I when he was in Flanders in 1297–8.[3] We know that Edward III employed clerks of the city of Ghent in 1339 to write to various Flemish towns, because his own clerks were not conversant with Flemish diplomatic ('quia clerici regis nesciverunt scribere in forma usitata in Flandria').[4] One of these documents written and drafted by a clerk of Ghent has survived in the original. It has no address or greeting and begins: 'Edward par la grace de Dieu rois de France et Dengleterre faisons savoir a tous que . . .'; the corroboration and dating-clause read: 'Par le tesmoignage de cez presentes lettres saiellez de nostre saiel, faitez et donnees a Gand quatuorze jours ou mois de novembre, lan de grace mil trois cens et quarante.'[5] The same foreign features also appear in royal documents dated and sealed in England. Edward I's ratification of the agreement for the marriage of his daughter Margaret to the heir of Brabant (London, 22 January 1279) has a greeting ('saluz e conoistre veritei') and a corroboration ('E pur ceo qe ceo soit ferme chose e estable, en avoms done al avantdit duc e a ses heirs

---

[1] e.g. C. 47/30/8/5. [2] C. 47/28/6/4, 30/8/8.
[3] Paris, Arch. Nat. J. 631, no. 12 *bis*. [4] Tout, *Chapters*, v. 81 n. 7.
[5] Brussels, Archives du Royaume de Belgique, Chartes de Brabant, no. 645.

ces presentes lettres overtes enselees de nostre seel') which make it certain that it was drafted by a clerk of Brabant, although it seems to have been written by an English clerk.[1] The ratification of the treaty of Paris of 1259 by Henry III and its confirmation by the baronial council, both dated at London, were drafted and written by a French clerk.[2] Similar examples of foreign collaboration could be multiplied for the whole of the thirteenth and fourteenth centuries.[3] Some of these anomalies cannot be said to have a great political significance. When, for example, in June 1362, Edward III signed his name (*E. Rex*) with his own hand on full powers for an Anglo-Castilian alliance, he probably did so because he wished to conform to Castilian practice.[4] In other cases, however, such a facile explanation can hardly be correct. It cannot be by accident that the letters by which Edward III appointed, on 16 May 1328, the bishops of Chester and Worcester as his proctors to claim the kingdom of France in his name have a greeting (*salutz et connissance de verite*) and a corroboration which are typical of Flemish diplomatic.[5] By contrast, two letters close addressed one to the leading officials of the city of Bruges and the other to one of its burgomasters, William De Deken, and dated five days earlier are English in every respect.[6] It is worth noting that the letter to Deken is a letter of credence for John de Chidiok, sent with an oral message from Edward III, and that it was the same Deken who was hanged by the French on 23 December 1328 because he had been found guilty of being instrumental in inducing Edward III to claim the French throne.[7] That Deken was somehow connected with Edward's letters of 16 May cannot be proved, but it seems a real possibility.

---

[1] Chartes de Brabant, no. 101.

[2] Paris, Arch. Nat. J. 629, nos. 8 and 10.

[3] Thomas Uvedale, sent to the king of France in Paris in July 1361, paid £2 to Master Jean Caboche, secretary of the French king 'pro informacione et avisamento suo habitis super disposicione et indictamento litterarum, cartarum et commissionum . . .' (P.R.O., Exch. K.R. Acc. Var. (E. 101), 314/15).

[4] Rymer, *Foedera*, III. ii. 657.

[5] Ibid., II. ii. 743.

[6] CCR, *1327–30*, pp. 385–6; Rymer, *Foedera*, II. ii. 742.

[7] H. Pirenne, 'La première tentative faite pour reconnaître Édouard III d'Angleterre comme roi de France (1328)', *Annales de la Soc. d'Hist. et d'Arch. de Gand*, v (1902–3), pp. 5–11.

The famous challenge of Edward III to Philip VI, sent from Chin near Tournai on 27 July 1340, is no less remarkable.[1] The extant original under the great seal again displays all the characteristics of a document drafted and written by a clerk of the Low Countries: the handwriting and spelling (*cyteit, Edeward, eschieuweir, longh, mortaliteit, nobleche, volenteit,* etc.) are unmistakable. There is little doubt that Philip VI and his ministers could have easily identified the clerk's country of origin. It might be suggested that at that time Edward had no English clerk with him, but this does not appear to have been so.[2] Besides, there has survived in the Public Record Office what appears to be an unsealed engrossment of the challenge: this second exemplar, dated at Chin on the previous day (26 July) 'under the privy seal' and possibly intended to be sent close, is in an English hand and in the Anglo-Norman dialect.[3] The initial formulae of Edward's challenge (*Depar Edeward roy de France et Dengleterre et seignur Dirlande,* in the middle of the first line, and the address in the form of an apostrophe, *Philippes de Valoys,* at the beginning of the second line) are modelled on the formulae used by Philip VI in letters close sealed with his *sceau du secret.*[4] Edward as king of France was addressing Philip as his vassal. Any well-informed clerk of Brabant, Flanders, or Hainault would have been acquainted with such formulae and could have drafted and written the challenge: on 3 June 1340 the people of Valenciennes had received from the duke of Normandy a mandate in similar form instructing them to break away from the king of England.[5] No doubt Master Henri de Jodoigne, the notorious and able canon of Cambrai, councillor of the count of Hainault, would have derived a great deal of pleasure from slighting the king of France by writing the challenge himself: at the same time he would have been of service to Edward III, who in 1337 had granted

---

[1] Paris, Arch. Nat. J. 636, no. 12; Déprez, *Les Préliminaires de la Guerre de Cent Ans,* pp. 328–9.

[2] For example, letters patent dated *es champs devant Tournay,* 25 Sept. 1340, are in an English hand (Brussels, Arch. du Royaume de Belgique, Chartes de Brabant, no. 641).

[3] S.C. 1/xxxvii, no. 136.

[4] See R. Cazelles, *Lettres closes . . . de Philippe de Valois* (Paris, 1958), e.g. p. 34, no. 19.

[5] Froissart, *Œuvres,* ed. Kervyn de Lettenhove, xviii, pp. 152–3.

him the handsome yearly pension of 100 gold florins of Florence 'pro bono servicio suo . . . impendendo'.[1]

Once the diplomatic documents which can be ascribed to foreign draftsmen and scribes have been set aside, we are still left with a large number of letters and records of all kinds which were presumably drafted and written by English clerks. The evidence suggests that under Edward I a large proportion of the secretarial work connected with English diplomacy was done by clerks of the Wardrobe. Not only did they draft and write whatever diplomatic letters were sent out under the privy seal, but they also played a considerable part in the drafting and writing of documents issued under the great seal. For confidential letters the role of Chancery was restricted sometimes to affixing the great seal to documents already engrossed, sometimes to translating and engrossing letters which had been drafted in French by Wardrobe clerks.[2] Once the draft had reached Chancery, if the king and Council had second thoughts about the terms of the letter, the necessary amendments were made, not by a Chancery clerk, but by a high official of the Wardrobe. Thus in April 1295 Walter Langton, keeper of the Wardrobe, corrected letters close which were to be sent to Adolf of Nassau.[3]

Routine documents may have been written in Chancery in the normal way, under the supervision of the keeper of the rolls, but the evidence on this point is unsatisfactory. Occasionally payments were made to individual clerks of Chancery or of an unspecified department for the writing of treaties and analogous documents. For example, John de Stow and two colleagues were paid three shillings for writing agreements between Edward I and Count Floris V of Holland in 1295.[4] On 5 March 1361 Edward III ordered payments to be made out of the Exchequer to William de Wynterton, Richard de Graneby, John de Southwell, John de Kirkeby, Robert de Muscham, John Adel, and John de Shippedam, several of whom can be identified as Chancery clerks, for writing documents

---

[1] F. Vercauteren, 'Henri de Jodoigne . . .', *Bulletin de l'Institut Historique Belge de Rome*, fasc. xxvii (Brussels, 1952), p. 482.

[2] P.R.O. Chanc. Warrants (C. 81), 4/365; 6/528, 548, 566; 10/991; 20/1888.

[3] *Treaty Rolls*, i, no. 254.

[4] P.R.O., Exch. of Receipt, Issue Roll (E. 403), no. 96.

relating to the treaty of Brétigny-Calais; similar payments were made to John Bras as spigurnel for the sealing of the same documents, to William de Wynterton for their enrolment, and to William Burstall and John de Derlyngton for making the necessary searches through the Chancery enrolments and writing extracts from them.[1] Payments of this kind suggest that the writing of some diplomatic documents fell outside the normal run of duties of Chancery clerks. Sometimes notaries were employed for that purpose. In October 1288 Master John *Erturi de Cadomo* (or *Cadamo*)[2] accompanied Edward I to Canfranc in Aragon, where he wrote a whole series of notarial instruments relating to the release of the prince of Salerno from captivity: five of these instruments, written and subscribed by him, have survived in the original.[3] He seems to have spent much of the next decade in Edward I's service, writing in particular many documents connected with Anglo-Scottish relations.[4] In August 1334 another notary, Master Henry of Colchester, accompanied the proctors sent by Edward III to Flanders for the settlement of Anglo-Flemish disputes and wrote in notarial form a detailed account of the negotiations which took place in Bruges.[5] John *de Cadamo* was an apostolic notary and Henry of Colchester began his career as notary by imperial authority.[6]

Between 1288 and 1336 many other notaries worked for the king.[7] In diplomatic relations the use of notaries, particularly those appointed in the name of the pope, had an obvious advantage: the instruments which they drew up were deemed authentic

---

[1] P.R.O., Exch. of Receipt, Warrants for Issues (E. 404), 41/21.

[2] He is referred to as *clerico regine* in E. 101/352/14, m. 10. Master John de Cadamo is generally thought, perhaps rightly, to have been English, but his handwriting, his dating habits (e.g. *quarta die exeunte mense octobri*) and his abbreviations (e.g. *Berengaio* and *auctoitate*, both with a superscript *r*) suggest that he received his scribal training in southern Europe, either in Spain or in Italy. See, for example, his notarial instrument in Archives of the Crown of Aragon, Barcelona, Pergaminos, Alfonso II, no. 242.

[3] Barcelona, Arch. of the Crown of Aragon, Pergaminos, Alfonso II, nos. 242, 242 *bis*, 243–5 (I owe these references to the kindness of Professor G. Barraclough).

[4] *Anglo-Scottish Relations, 1174–1328*, ed. E. L. G. Stones (Nelson's Med. Texts, 1965), p. 187 (s.v. 'Caen, John of').

[5] H. S. Lucas, 'Diplomatic Relations between England and Flanders . . .', *Speculum*, xi (1936), 73–85.

[6] P.R.O., Papal Bulls (S.C. 7), 36 (4).

[7] Cuttino, *English Diplomatic Administration*, pp. 135–6.

everywhere (*ubique terrarum*) and were generally accepted as such. Their employment, however, seems to have been of a casual nature and there is no evidence that their work had much influence on the general evolution of English diplomatic documents. In 1336 a notary was for the first time appointed to the permanent staff of Chancery. This was an interesting innovation, which led to important developments under the second holder of the office, Master John de Branketre, clerk of the diocese of Norwich. From 1355 to 1375 Branketre actively supervised the writing of diplomatic documents issued under the great seal. He was directly responsible for the introduction of the short-lived 'visa' and for the substitution of the style of the Nativity for the customary English style of the Annunciation in the dating of diplomatic documents. After a period of twenty years in office, one might have expected Branketre's reforms to have a lasting effect. In fact they all died with him in September 1375.[1]

PIERRE CHAPLAIS

[1] See P. Chaplais, 'Master John de Branketre and the Office of Notary in Chancery, 1355–1375', *Journal of the Soc. of Archivists*, iv. 3 (April 1971).

III

Papal Privileges for St. Albans Abbey and its Dependencies

A FOURTEENTH-CENTURY book of benefactors, richly decorated in the St. Albans *scriptorium*, reveals the existence of 172 papal privileges for the abbey. The greatest benefactor, Adrian IV, is shown with the ring, cup, chasuble called 'Adrian', and the relics of the Theban legion, which he gave to the abbey, while other popes from Calixtus II to Honorius III, together with Adrian I (772–95), are depicted holding letters variously sealed with blue, gold, and silver *bullae*, hanging from green, blue, red, and orange cords.[1] Few of these privileges survive in the original, but ample material from cartulary copies,[2] chronicles, and the papal registers, permits a detailed examination of the privileged position of St. Albans and its dependencies at four different stages. I shall consider successively the early privileges forming the basis of St. Albans' exemption from the bishop of Lincoln, conceded by the papacy between 1122 and *c.* 1180; the report of a visit to the papal curia in 1256–7, when Alexander IV was petitioned to renew the most important of the old privileges and to grant certain indults to accord with St. Albans' changing needs; the fourteenth-century letter-book of Abbot Thomas de la Mare, which includes a detailed discussion by Master Richard de Wymundeswolde of the implications of a privilege granted by Pope Clement III to Abbot Warin; the indults and personal documents of the 1420s and 1430s, the

---

[1] B.M. Cotton MS. Nero D vii, ff. 7–11; the text of the manuscript is printed in W. Dugdale, *Monasticon Anglicanum*, ed. J. Caley and others (London, 1817–30), ii. 218–19.

[2] I wish to thank His Grace the Duke of Northumberland for permission to use the Tynemouth cartulary in Syon House; His Grace the Duke of Devonshire for permission to use the St. Albans cartulary at Chatsworth; and His Grace the Duke of Rutland for permission to use the Belvoir cartularies and connected muniments in his collection.

cost of such documents, the confirmation of elections, and the position of the cells.

I. Amongst English Benedictine houses the great abbey of St. Albans held a unique position throughout the Middle Ages, because of its possession of the remains of Alban, the protomartyr of England. The cult of Alban goes back to the first part of the fifth century, and Bede relates the cure of the sick and frequent miracles at St. Albans in (?)731. Supposedly the tomb was then lost until a miraculous discovery of the relics on 1 August 793. Levison points out that it is unlikely that the tomb was ever lost between 731 and 793, but that King Offa, with whom the legend is connected, may well have erected a new church and shrine there in that year. During Offa's visit to Rome, Pope Adrian I is said to have canonized Alban and granted the abbey some privileges, and it was on this occasion that the king was assumed to have made the celebrated grant of Peter's Pence to the papacy. The rank of St. Albans among the foremost English Benedictine abbeys had thus been established well before the Norman Conquest and, like other abbeys which were important before 1066, it maintained this position thereafter. On 1 August 1129 the fragments of Alban were again translated to a new and more magnificent shrine, and on 25 June 1177 the relics of the newly invented St. Amphibalus, who had allegedly shared martyrdom with Alban, were discovered at Redbourn some four miles away.[1] St. Albans now had a full complement of martyrs, whose blood as it were was used to write the abbey's privileges.[2]

---

[1] For the whole of this paragraph, see W. Levison, 'St. Alban and St. Albans', *Antiquity*, xv (1941), 337–59, esp. 344 and 350–2. 'Amphibalus' was fabricated by Geoffrey of Monmouth, who misunderstood Gildas's account of the cloak in his description of the martyrdom of St. Alban. After 1129 the feast of the translation of St. Alban was celebrated on 2 Aug. because 1 Aug. was another important festival, that of St. Peter ad Vincula.

[2] Cf. C. R. Cheney, 'Magna Carta Beati Thome: another Canterbury Forgery', *BIHR* xxxvi (1963), 11, citing *Patrologia Latina*, ed. J. Migne, ccxv, col. 1048, where Innocent III says that St. Thomas wrote a special privilege for Christ Church 'as it were in his blood'. St. Albans was also associated with St. Oswyn after Robert de Mowbray made Tynemouth priory its dependency, and a bull 'Religione ac pietate' of 1156 ordered the bishop of Durham and his archdeacon to see that the feast of St. Oswyn was observed in the parishes of his diocese (*PUE* iii, no. 111).

The earliest authentic papal document for the house, 'Religione ac pietate', dates from 25 November 1122 and was granted by Calixtus II. It concerns the celebration of St. Alban's feast and grants an indulgence of twelve days to those visiting the abbey within the octave.[1] In conjunction with this grant Calixtus II issued on the same day a solemn privilege 'Ad hoc nos', which granted papal protection to the abbey and confirmed its possessions both past and future.[2] St. Albans' second basic privilege 'Officii nostri nos', which was obtained from Celestine II in 1143, confirmed the previous bull of Calixtus II, took the house under the protection of St. Peter—a special relationship for which it was to pay one ounce of gold to Rome yearly—and granted *episcopalia*, although ordinations were to be undertaken by the diocesan bishop (not by any catholic bishop as at Bury).[3] This, together with Eugenius III's bull 'Pie postulatio voluntatis' of 1147, which specifically detailed the dependencies of St. Albans,[4] laid the foundation of the abbey's privileges before the accession of Adrian IV in 1154, a pope who succeeded to the papacy at a time when papal confirmations were much sought after.

The exact nature of Adrian IV's relationship with St. Albans is obscure. It is unlikely that in his youth he was rejected as a novice in the house, but it is probable that he came from the town or its region and that his father had entered the monastery there.[5] It

---

[1] *PUE* iii, no. 6. In some ways this was a confirmation of an indulgence to all penitents who should come to St. Albans 'ad praedictam festivitatem', which had been issued by Bishop Robert Bloet of Lincoln (*Gesta Abbatum Monasterii Sancti Albani*, ed. H. T. Riley (R.S., 1867–9), i. 92). Adrian IV issued another 'Religione ac pietate' in 1156 (*PUE* iii, no. 102).

[2] *PUE* iii, no. 5 (the last clause of this document is really an abbreviation of no. 6).

[3] Ibid., no. 43. Cf. *The Pinchbeck Register*, ed. Lord F. Hervey (privately printed, 1925), i. 3–4, 19–20 (*PUE* iii, no. 8).

[4] *PUE* iii, no. 68.

[5] The life of Adrian by Boso (in *Le Liber Pontificalis*, ii, ed. L. Duchesne, Bibliothèque des Écoles Françaises d'Athènes et de Rome, ser. 2, no. 3, 2nd edn., Paris, 1955) and the account of William of Newburgh, are to be preferred to that given by Matthew Paris, with whom the story of his rejection originates (*Gesta Abb.* i. 124–32). R. L. Poole in *Studies in Chronology and History* (Oxford, reprint, 1969), p. 293, argues that Adrian had been at the house of Austin canons at Merton before entering the Augustinian community of regular clerks of St. Rufus at Avignon, on the seemingly incontrovertible evidence of the final clause in one of John of Salisbury's letters (*The Letters of John of Salisbury*, ed. W. J. Millor and H. E. Butler, revised C. N. L. Brooke (Nelson's Medieval Texts, 1955), no. 50).

is possible that on his election to the papacy he had taken the name of Adrian in deference to the pope who was held to have canonized Alban, and that he retained a particular devotion to the saint and his birthplace. Although much remains undetermined about Adrian IV, it is certain that he gave to St. Albans a splendid array of privileges, twelve in all, together with similar documents for the cells of Sopwell, Wymondham, Belvoir, and Tynemouth, and that none of these can be deemed forgeries.[1] His two most important bulls for St. Albans—the 'Incomprehensibilis' of 1156 and the 'Religiosam vitam eligentibus' of 1157—were essentially the means by which the abbey secured independence from the diocesan.[2]

Firstly, following these two bulls, the abbey could invite any catholic bishop to conduct ordinations and consecrations.[3] Throughout the medieval period various bishops, some of whom were resident at St. Albans, were called upon to ordain and consecrate, for example the bishop of Down (Ireland) in 1203 and 1214, and the bishop of Lichfield in 1427.[4] A bishop was also necessary to bless the chrism and holy oils, for which Abbot Robert de Gorham alleged the bishop of Lincoln and his archdeacons had taken payment.[5] On Maundy Thursday 1204 Herlewin, bishop of Leighlin,

---

[1] Adrian issued only two (? three) bulls for Bury. Dr. Chaplais has drawn attention to a bull of Adrian IV for Westminster (*PUE* i, no. 69; supposedly based on *PUE* i, no. 21, of Innocent II), which he suspects as a forgery ('The Original Charters of Herbert and Gervase Abbots of Westminster (1121–57)', p. 96 n. 6 in *A Medieval Miscellany for D. M. Stenton*, P.R.S., N.S. xxxvi, 1962). It seems possible to me that 'Religiosam vitam' may have acted as the prototype here to which were added the tell-tale embellishments. The texts of the St. Albans bulls are late, but they cannot be regarded as forgeries on textual grounds, and historically they stood up to immediate scrutiny in the Lincoln case (see below, p. 64). It was St. Albans' good fortune that it did not have to resort to forgeries but was able to get the real thing at a time when written evidence was becoming essential. On this point, see E. Searle, 'Battle Abbey and Exemption: the Forged Charters', *EHR* lxxxiii (1968), 468.

[2] *PUE* iii, nos. 100, 118. 1157 was the date of Battle's first showing of William II's charter confirming ecclesiastical exemption (Searle, op. cit., p. 457).

[3] On monastic exemption in Normandy to 1140, see J.-F. Lemarignier, *Étude sur les privilèges d'exemption et de juridiction ecclésiastique*, Archives de la France Monastique, 44 (Paris, 1937), and for England, see D. Knowles, 'The Growth of Exemption', *Downside Review* l (N.S. 31, 1932), 201–31, 396–436.

[4] 'Annales Sancti Albani a.1200–1214' in *Anglo Normannische Geschichtsquellen*, ed. F. Liebermann (Strasbourg, 1879), pp. 167–8, 171–2; and 'Chronicle of the Reign of Henry VI from St. Albans' in *Annales Monasterii S. Albani a Johanne Amundesham*, ed. H. T. Riley (R.S., 1870–1), i. 15. R. Vaughan, *Matthew Paris* (Cambridge, 1958), p. 15, comments on the residence of John, bishop of Ardfert, and Richard, bishop of Bangor, for periods in the 1240s.   [5] *PUE* iii, no. 105.

who had been a monk of Christ Church Canterbury, consecrated the oil and chrism at the high altar at St. Albans in the presence of Abbot John and the whole convent.[1] Secondly, the abbot and monks could not be summoned to a diocesan synod nor could they be compelled to obey its decrees. Thirdly, the monastery was free from the bishop's excommunication and from general interdicts. Fourthly, the abbot had rights of wearing some or all of the *pontificalia* ('Religiosam vitam' granted mitre, ring, sandals, and gloves, while the reissue of Celestine III added tunic and dalmatic). Fifthly, the monastery was exempt from episcopal visitation and correction, though this privilege was not defined in this specific way until the late twelfth century ('Religiosam vitam' forbade anyone exercising the 'episcopal office', and in 1170 the house was stated to be under no bishop except the pope).[2] Finally, the pope stipulated that in future a profession of obedience should be made only to the Church of Rome. It appears that such professions had been made not to the diocesan but to the metropolitan, until the time of Abbot Richard d'Aubigny, who made his profession to Bishop Robert Bloet of Lincoln.[3] As for the blessing of the abbot, Celestine II's privilege had stated that this should be by the diocesan (place not specified), whereas 'Incomprehensibilis' now stated that it should be by a bishop of their choice, presumably in the abbey church.[4] In 1214 it was Eustace, bishop of Ely, who blessed Abbot William before the high altar at St. Albans.[5]

In 'Religiosam vitam' the area of the liberty of St. Albans was defined with some precision, and the fifteen churches which constituted it are named—St. Peter's, St. Stephen's, and Kingsbury in

---

[1] 'Annales Sancti Albani a. 1200–1214', pp. 167–8.

[2] *PUE* iii, nos. 169, and 170, reissued by Clement III in 1188 (*Chronica Majora*, ed. H. R. Luard (R.S., 1872–83), vi, no. 33) and by Celestine III in 1193 (*PUE* iii, no. 457).

[3] *Gesta Abb.* i. 71–2.   [4] *PUE* iii, nos. 43, 100.

[5] 'Annales Sancti Albani', p. 171. Knowles, 'Growth of Exemption', p. 214, describes 'Incomprehensibilis' as 'a bull of privileges equalling or surpassing that of any other monastic house'. He might have included 'Religiosam vitam eligentibus' with it, which was virtually reissued or confirmed by Alexander III (*PUE* iii, no. 135), Clement III (St. Albans Cart., Chatsworth, ff. 38–9ᵛ; and Small Belvoir Cart., Belvoir Castle Add. MS. 98, pp. 89–91, including 'Incomprehensibilis'), Celestine III (*PUE* iii, no. 459, including 'Incomprehensibilis'), and by Honorius III in 1219 (Large Belvoir Cart., Belvoir Castle Add. MS. 105, ff. 13ᵛ–14ᵛ). The confirmation of Clement III and subsequent reissues I consider to be the 'great privilege', see below, p. 65.

the town of St. Albans, Watford, Rickmansworth, Abbots Langley, Redbourn, Codicote, St. Paul's Walden, Hexton, Norton, Newnham, Barnet (all in Herts.), and Winslow and Aston Abbots (both in Bucks.). This document, too, speaks of the archdeacon who was to administer the liberty on behalf of the abbot, and whose office was filled by monks of the abbey.[1] Besides being lord of the liberty, the abbot of St. Albans was also lord of the hundred of St. Albans. By the fourteenth century the liberty, and consequently the hundred, had grown and had been to some extent rationalized, and by the end of the Middle Ages the liberty contained twenty-six parishes.[2] The early land endowment of St. Albans had established the liberty. Grants had been made to the saint in the remote past; tradition had accorded Offa the position of founder of the abbey's liberties, and Norman kings had confirmed them.[3] Popes, too, had confirmed St. Albans' liberties and possessions in increasingly exact terms, and it was in this now defined area of the liberty that the privileges of exemption from episcopal visitation and control were to be used to the full.

With the death of Adrian IV, the stream of privileges did not cease to flow, and favour continued to be shown by Alexander III, who granted St. Albans some forty-three privileges and in addition important documents for the cells of Binham, Hatfield Peverel, and Hertford, which confirmed their possessions and took them under the protection of the papal see.[4] Alexander also confirmed certain churches to Belvoir and a tithe arrangement with Thetford,

[1] Celestine III's reissue of 'Religiosam vitam' (*PUE* iii, no. 459) actually specifies monks for the office, and it seems likely that they had in fact always filled it. The first occurrence of an archdeacon appears to be in 1129 at the time of the translation of St. Alban. The authority for this is the *Gesta Abb.* (i. 85–6), but there is no particular reason to doubt the existence of a monastic archdeacon before the liberty and archdeaconry were clearly defined.

[2] For an account of the changes, see *VCH, Hertfordshire*, ii. 319 f. For maps of the liberty, see the endpapers of P. Newcome, *History of the Abbey of St. Albans* (1793), and A. E. Levett, *Studies in Manorial History*, ed. H. M. Cam and others (Oxford, 1938); and for the liberty at the end of the Middle Ages, see R. Peters, *Oculus Episcopi* (Manchester, 1963), introduction.

[3] See P. H. Sawyer, *Anglo-Saxon Charters* (Royal Historical Soc., 1968), nos. 136 and 138 (of Offa, probably spurious), and nos. 150–1, 888, 912, 916, 1228, 1235, 1488, 1497, 1517, 1532; and *Regesta Regum Anglo-Normannorum*, ii, ed. C. Johnson and H. A. Cronne (Oxford, 1956), nos. 218a (p. 396), 314c (p. 399), 400a (p. 404), 512, 595, 1203.

[4] The documents for the cells are *PUE* iii, nos. 136, 147, 256.

and upheld the rights of St. Albans over the dependency of Tynemouth against the bishop of Durham, who was attempting to
assert normal diocesan rights by excommunicating the prior of
Tynemouth (a monk of St. Albans), by consecrating chapels and
cemeteries in churches belonging to St. Albans, and by taking
synodalia from their churches.[1] The rest of Alexander's grants fall
into four main groups: confirmations of churches and possessions,
and exemption from paying tithes in certain areas;[2] documents of
protection addressed to influential clerics;[3] confirmation of the
old privileges in the reissue of 'Religiosam vitam' and further
definition of the fact that no one might issue sentences of excommunication or interdict against St. Albans;[4] and a host of documents concerning *episcopalia*, of which the most important was
'Cum vos et' of 1170. This said that no one except a legate might
suspend or excommunicate the priors of St. Albans' cells; that in
the parishes where the abbey did not have episcopal rights it was
to appoint priests and present them to the bishop, who was to
admit them if suitable;[5] that the bishop was not to exact procession
dues within its confines and parishes; and that in abbatial vacancies the prior and chapter of St. Albans might exercise authority
over the dependencies.[6] In parishes where St. Albans did not have
episcopal rights, no one was to build a church or oratory without
the consent of the diocesan and St. Albans,[7] but in proprietary
churches in the liberty the clerics were to be answerable to the
abbot alone in both spiritual and temporal matters,[8] and it was the
archdeacon of St. Albans who inducted, and not the bishop of

---

[1] *PUE* iii, nos. 138, 167, 174–6, 178–81, 184, 190, 203, 239–40, 245, 330, and
332.

[2] Ibid., nos. 152, 168, 171, 255, 326, and nos. 133–4, 205, 246.

[3] Ibid., nos. 177, 191, 206.   [4] Ibid., nos. 135, 165–6.

[5] Further defined in 'Qui ad universorum' of 1171 (ibid., no. 182) and 'Qui pro
defensione', addressed to the bishops (ibid., no. 328) and by Clement III (ibid.,
no. 404).

[6] Ibid., no. 170—confirmed by Clement III in 1188 (*Chron. Maj.* vi, no. 33) and
by Celestine III in 1193 (*PUE* iii, no. 457).

[7] 'Ad officii nostri' of 1173 (ibid., no. 204), confirmed by Celestine III in 1193
(ibid., no. 454).

[8] 'Erga prelatos suos' of 1171–81 (ibid., no. 329) and 'Merito debent dignitatis'
of 1171–81 (ibid., no. 325) and its confirmations of 1188 and 1193 (*Chron. Maj.* vi,
no. 31 and *PUE* iii, nos. 450 and 458), and 'Cum ab ecclesia' of 1173 (ibid., no.
200).

Lincoln's archdeacons.[1] The relationship between these parishes and St. Albans was equivalent to that between St. Albans itself and the pope, who was its only bishop,[2] while the parishioners of its cells were protected from their diocesans to some degree, although only in temporal concerns.[3]

It has been held that Alexander III favoured St. Albans and other great Benedictine houses in their struggles against the bishop. When the Lincoln case opened St. Albans flourished the privileges of Calixtus II, Eugenius III, Adrian IV, and Alexander III.[4] The king demurred to the section of Celestine II's privilege which concerned the vills and liberties of St. Albans, and during the hearing of the case it was obvious that the abbey had stolen a march on the bishop, who could produce no privileges—his cupboard was bare—and who had to fall back on the argument of prescription, that is, the traditional practice of the diocese.[5] It was undoubtedly St. Albans which triumphed in the settlement before the king, his bishops, abbots, and magnates, completed in 1163. For the grant of £10 p.a. the bishop, Robert de Chesney, was forced to surrender his claim over the abbey itself and the fifteen churches of the liberty.[6] It may be asked why the Lincoln party were so slow in pressing their claims before the popes and for that matter before the king. An answer to this seems to lie firstly in the prompt action of St. Albans (when Abbot Robert died on 23 October 1166 the house was more than 600 marks in debt from his efforts),[7] and secondly in the fact that the assumption of powers by the abbot of St. Albans had led to a firmly established jurisdiction at a remote end of the diocese of Lincoln, to the south and east of

---

[1] This may be inferred to have developed from the establishment of the liberty and archdeaconry in or before 1157, see above, pp. 61–2. *PUE* iii, no. 327 'Cum ad tuenda' (1171–81), repeated by Clement III in 1188 (*Chron. Maj.* vi, no. 35) outlines (and the above documents) the duty of the bishop to induct when the abbot and convent had presented to him.   [2] See *PUE* iii, no. 169.

[3] Ibid., no. 172, 'Dilecti filii nostri', confirmed by Lucius III (*Chron. Maj.* vi, no. 27)

[4] See L. F. Rushbrook Williams, *History of the Abbey of St. Alban* (London, 1917), pp. 72–5, for an account of the case.

[5] H. P. King, 'The Life and Acts of Robert de Chesney' (London M.A. thesis, 1955), also gives an account of the case.

[6] *The Registrum Antiquissimum of the Cathedral Church of Lincoln*, i, ed. C. W. Foster (L.R.S. vol. 27, 1931), no. 104, and see also *Reg. Antiq. Linc.* ii (L.R.S. vol. 28, 1933), no. 321 (*Cal. Charter Rolls 1327–41* (H.M.S.O., 1912), p. 149).

[7] Williams, *Abbey of St. Alban*, p. 76.

which lay the powerful diocese of London and the archdeaconry of Middlesex, and the Middlesex parishes of the archbishop of Canterbury's peculiar of Croydon. From 1163 onwards the abbot's rights of exemption from episcopal interference in the liberty were beyond question and, although challenged, the rights of the cells to be extra-diocesan had been clearly declared by the popes. On Easter Sunday 1163 Abbot Robert de Gorham celebrated mass in the abbey church in pontificals and made plain his position as a mitred abbot,[1] and at the Council of Tours in May of the same year he took the first seat among the English abbots—in the words of 'Religiosam vitam': 'sicut Beatus Albanus (Anglorum) prothomartyr esse dinoscitur, ita et abbas monasterii ipsius inter abbates Angliae primus omni tempore dignitatis ordine habeatur . . .'.[2]

II. In 1256 Master William de Sancto Edwardo, clerk, and Brother William de Horton,[3] proctors of St. Albans, set out for the curia with instructions to negotiate for certain documents. There are two accounts of the business which was expedited: the fuller is in the *Gesta Abbatum*[4] which contains two more impetrations and bulls; the other account is in the Wymondham Cartulary,[5] which is considerably more corrupt and was probably taken from another source or perhaps indirectly from the *Gesta*. Firstly the proctors sought the renewal of the 'great privilege', undoubtedly 'Religiosam vitam' as reissued by Clement III, Celestine III, and Honorius III, which they seemingly effected with difficulty.[6] The immediate occasion of their visit, however, was not this, but the desire of St. Albans to appropriate Hartburn church (Northumb.) to

---

[1] *Gesta Abb.* i. 158. The final settlement took place on 8 Mar. 1163, as Foster says, and Easter Sunday fell on 24 Mar. [2] *PUE* iii, no. 118, and *Gesta Abb.* i. 177.

[3] William de Horton occurs as a papal chaplain in 1259 (*CPL* i. 364). He was cellarer of Tynemouth by 1244, was to become (?)prior (*temp.* Hen. III) and finally prior of Wymondham in 1264 (*Chron. Maj.* vi. 90; J. Brand, *History of Newcastle upon Tyne* (1789), ii. 82; and Dugdale, *Monasticon*, iii. 325). His appointment as prior of Wymondham possibly accounts for the copying of these transactions into the Wymondham Cartulary, and the note at the end 'Hec sunt adquisita domini Willelmi prioris de Wymondham' might well refer to him, since he was concerned in the acquisitions, rather than to William of St. Albans, prior from 1257 to 1262.

[4] i. 350–5. [5] B.M. Cotton MS. Titus C viii, ff. 74–5.

[6] Honorius's confirmation of 20 Feb. 1219 appears in the Large Belvoir Cart., ff. 13ᵛ–14ᵛ. Printed in Dugdale, *Monasticon*, ii. 232–3, num. xxi (from the Binham Cart. B.M. Cotton MS. Claudius D xiii); and see *CPL* i. 63 and *Gesta Abb.* iii. 163, and for confirmations by Archbishops Kilwardby and Sudbury (St. Albans Cart.,

go towards expenses on hospitality. On hearing rumours of the death of the rector of Hartburn, Hugh de Florentino, the abbot of St. Albans had presented Robert de Sotingdona,[1] a royal clerk. When the church, which belonged to the cell of Tynemouth and hence indirectly to the abbey, was found not to be vacant after all, the abbot commissioned William de Horton, the cellarer of Tynemouth, to arrange for its future appropriation with Walter Kirkham, bishop of Durham (1249–60). Kirkham agreed that on the death of the present rector two-thirds of the proceeds from the church should go to St. Albans, while the remaining third was to be used for establishing a vicarage. At the time of these transactions Horton himself visited the church of Hartburn, and, on the same occasion witnessing as it happened the sudden death of the rector, took possession of the church despite the presence of armed men. A successful request was made to Sir Hugh Bolebec, to whom the armed men presumably belonged, to surrender the right which he claimed as patron of the church by grant of the abbot and convent of St. Albans.[2] But it was at this point that Master John de Camezano, nephew of the former pope, Innocent IV, and his *auditor litterarum contradictarum*, endeavoured to exchange Wingrave church (Bucks.) for Hartburn.[3] Innocent IV had already promised the appropriation of Hartburn and St. Albans was determined to resist John de Camezano's challenge. John de Camezano now got a mandate to the abbot of St. Augustine's, Canterbury, to act as judge delegate and try the case. The case, perhaps not unexpectedly, was returned to Rome and came before the English cardinal, John of Toledo, to whom the St. Albans proctors, William de Sancto Edwardo and William de Horton, had commendatory

Chatsworth, ff. 53–6). This was confirmed at the petition of King Richard II and St. Albans, by Pope Boniface IX as late as 1395 (*CPL* iv. 516) and by Nicholas V in 1447 (*CPL* x. 353–4).

[1] Robert de Shottindon occurs as a royal justice from 1254 to 1257, when he died at Hertford while on circuit (E. Foss, *The Judges of England* (London, 1848–57), ii. 474, and B.M. Cotton MS. Caligula A xii, f. 58ᵛ).

[2] See *Gesta Abb.* i. 346–9.

[3] For John de Camezano, see P. Herde, *Beiträge zum Päpstlichen Kanzlei-und Urkundenwesen im 13. Jahrhundert*, 2nd edn. (Kallmünz, 1967), pp. 22–4. He was in possession of the church of Wingrave in 1256 (*Les Registres d'Alexandre IV*, ed. B. de La Roncière and others (Bibl. des Écoles Françaises d'Athènes et de Rome, ser. 2, no. 15, Paris, 1895–1959), i, no. 1445).

letters from the king, and also to the royal proctors, Master
Robert de Barro and Master Finatus.[1] Cardinal John's ordination,
dated at Anagni on 10 July 1256, confirmed Hartburn church to
St. Albans but said that St. Albans was to give to John de Camezano
a yearly pension of 25 marks until an alternative benefice of not
less than 80 marks value became vacant.[2] The abbot and convent of
Waltham, St. Albans' conservators, were instructed by Alexander
IV on 23 July of the same year to carry out the sentence.[3] The
church of Wingrave had figured in the history of the appropriation
of Hartburn and now together with Coniscliffe (Durham) it was
to be the subject of further instructions to St. Albans' proctors,[4]
for we read in the account of the curial business that the pope
agreed to the appropriation of these two churches, and that he
issued executory letters about this.[5] The papal document allowing
the appropriation ('Et si ecclesiarum') was addressed by Alexander
IV to St. Albans on 13 January 1257.[6]

A large section of the business naturally concerned further
definition and revitalization of St. Albans' exemption. The pope
stated that obedience from churches, which St. Albans or its cells
held 'in proprios usus', was to be to them and not to the diocesans
of the places where the churches were situated. This was the indult
which was granted on 6 February 1257 by Alexander IV on their

---

[1] *Chron. Maj.* vi, nos. 160–1 (the latter dated 11 Apr. 1256). Henry III had also
written to the pope and to Master John de Camezano on the matter of the church of
Hartburn (ibid., nos. 157–9). The proctors' letters of appointment are dated from
St. Albans on 10 Apr. 1256 (St. Albans Cart., Chatsworth, ff. 51–3).

[2] For Cardinal John of Toledo, see my *Papal Judges Delegate in the Province of
Canterbury 1198–1254* (Oxford, 1971), pp. 24–5. A vicarage was established at
Hartburn by 1260 (*CPR, 1258–66*, p. 96).

[3] St. Albans Cart., Chatsworth, f. 34[r–v] (and see ff. 51–3 for Cardinal John's instrument and account of the case); see also *Reg. Alex. IV*, i, no. 1445.

[4] *Gesta Abb.* i. 350. The monk, William de Sancto Edmundo, seems to have been
part of their number by this time. He had served as a proctor at the curia with
William de Sancto Edwardo as early as 1252. In the September of that year they
received letters of credit for 50 marks (*Chron. Maj.* vi, nos. 108–9). According to the
Gesta Abb. (i. 331) he had been sent to Rome to deal with the Wymondham affair,
while Master William de Sancto Edwardo was to deal with the appropriation of St.
Michael's church Kingsbury (effected in 1252) (St. Albans Cart., Chatsworth,
ff. 45[v]–46, and *CPL* i. 281).

[5] The clause concerning the appropriation of Wingrave and Coniscliffe is missing
from the account in the Wymondham Cartulary but it appears in the account in the
Gesta Abb.

[6] St. Albans Cart., Chatsworth, f. 35. The mandate of induction is in *CPL* (i. 343).

petition.[1] The next concession was a confirmation of the exemption granted by Innocent IV that, contrary to his general ruling in the Council of Lyons of 1245, they should not be forced to answer before ordinaries 'ratione delicti seu contractus'.[2] Two documents from Alexander address St. Albans apparently on this matter, one dated at Anagni on 7 October 1256,[3] the other dated 1257.[4] This exemption went hand in hand with the following one, that neither St. Albans nor its priors should be summoned more than two days' journey from their diocese to make answer in lawsuits which had been initiated by papal letters.[5] The age-old privilege which exempted St. Albans from any adverse decrees or constitutions of legates or *nuncii* was restated in 'Exigentibus vestre devocionis' of 26 October 1256.[6] Finally the abbot of St. Albans was empowered to dispense the monks from any irregularities,[7] the priors of the cells were to enjoy the liberties and immunities of the mother house, and in churches where St. Albans did not have episcopal rights, priests were to be appointed by it, presented to the diocesan, and assigned portions. These priests were to answer to St. Albans in temporal matters and to the diocesan in spiritual matters, according to the tenor of St. Albans' privileges.[8]

A further section of the transactions related to certain indulgences which the pope was asked to grant or confirm. Firstly, he conceded an indulgence of one year and forty days' enjoined penance to all penitents visiting St. Albans on the feast of the Saint and in the following week (eight days). Roughly contemporaneous with this must have been Alexander IV's grant, made on 11 December 1256, of an indulgence but with a lesser period of time (forty days), to

[1] *CPL* i. 341.

[2] c. 1. 6. V. 7, in *Corpus Iuris Canonici*, ed. E. Friedberg, 2nd edn. ii (Leipzig, 1881).

[3] St. Albans Cart., Chatsworth, f. 33ᵛ.   [4] *CPL* i. 344.

[5] See the ruling of Innocent III in the Fourth Lateran Council (c. 28. X. I. 3, in *Corpus Iuris Canonici* ii), and compare a similar undated indult for Bury St. Edmunds from Alexander IV, which refers to a previous exemption for them from his predecessor, Pope Innocent IV (*Pinchbeck Reg.* i. 17–18, and same document on pp. 46–7). This grant was to be valid for five years.

[6] St. Albans Cart., Chatsworth, f. 34.

[7] Ibid., f. 48: a document of Urban IV ('Quia ex apostolica': Viterbo 1 Apr. 1262) is in part a confirmation of this.

[8] See above, p. 63. This application and concession is not included in the account in the Wymondham Cartulary but only in the *Gesta Abb.* (i. 351).

those going to the house of St. Mary de Pré on the feast of the
Blessed Virgin or during the following eight days.[1] The St. Albans
document accords with a later document of Pope Nicholas IV of
17 June 1290 for the house, which granted a similar period of time
to Alexander's.[2] The earliest known grant of this kind to the shrine
had been that of Calixtus II, who had allowed twelve days.[3] Thus
the grant had grown almost thirty-four fold—a sign of the popularity of this kind of document—and by the time of Boniface IX
(1389–1404) a relaxation of seven years and seven periods of forty
days' enjoined penance was made to penitents who visited the
parish church of St. Peter in St. Albans on principal feasts, those of
St. Peter ad Vincula and the Dedication, during the octaves of some
of them, and the six days of Whitweek.[4] A second form of indulgence granted three periods of forty days to those contributing
towards the fabric of the church,[5] and the pope confirmed all
indulgences and remissions which had been granted by archbishops
and bishops 'ab principio mundi usque in hodiernum diem'. These
included one year and forty days granted by the bishop of Sora
(Italy) to those going to the monastery on separate days out of
devotion, or contributing to the fabric, a similar grant from the
bishop of Trebinje in the province of Ragusa, a grant of forty days
from the bishop of Rochester,[6] and of 140 days from the pope
himself.

Another group of documents which were sought concerned
financial exactions. Foremost among these was an indult which
stated that the obligations which had been imposed upon the cells
of Tynemouth and Belvoir by the bishop of Hereford, Peter
d'Aigueblanche, and Master Rostand (Masson), were to be
revoked, since 'one and the same body should not be doubly

---

[1] Dugdale, *Monasticon*, iii. 356–7, num. v.

[2] *CPL* i. 513.

[3] See above p. 59, and *PUE* iii, no. 6 (cf. Bury which was granted twenty days:
ibid., no. 8).

[4] *CPL* v. 276.

[5] Cf. Alexander IV's two grants to St. Mary de Pré (dated 13 Sept. and 23 Dec.
1256) of forty days' indulgence to those helping towards the repair of the buildings
(Dugdale, *Monasticon*, iii. 356, num. iv and 357, num. vi).

[6] Cf. ibid., ii. 236, num. xxiii, a later grant by Thomas of Ingoldisthorpe, bishop
of Rochester—this cannot be before 1283 (see *Handbook of British Chronology*, ed.
F. M. Powicke and E. B. Fryde, 2nd edn. (Royal Hist. Soc., 1961), pp. 247–8).

afflicted'. This doubtless refers to the 1255 mission of the papal collectors who imposed a payment of 500 marks on St. Albans itself, and provoked Matthew Paris to write: 'Alas! For shame and grief! These and other detestable things emanated at this time from the sulphurous fountain of the Roman church.'[1] Money was directly, or indirectly, the subject-matter of some of the other privileges, including tithes. The usual complement concerned possessions—the goods of the monasteries were confirmed and an indult stated that any alienations of land which had been made by their predecessors might be revoked, oaths, pacts, and confirmations notwithstanding. No one from the monastery, without the consent of all or the seals of the convents, was to obligate St. Albans or the priors of the cells to any merchants: nor were they to be compelled to confer benefices or give pensions unwillingly, a reference to reservations[2] and provisions.[3]

Further grants were sought and made to the abbot. He might in future have a portable altar to take about with him, on which he or a deputy could celebrate and administer the sacrament to his household. The date of this grant was 6 January 1257 from the Lateran.[4] It was also requested that the abbot might give solemn blessings after the 'Agnus Dei' outside and through the streets, to which the curial officials replied that the St. Albans proctors unnecessarily sought this privilege, because they already had one which allowed solemn benedictions of all kinds, and no one in a position to object had questioned this.[5]

---

[1] See *Councils and Synods*, ed. F. M. Powicke and C. R. Cheney, 2 vols. (Oxford, 1964), ii, pt. i. 501–3, for the council held at London in Oct. 1255 in this connection; *Gesta Abb.* i. 382–3; and *Chron. Maj.* v. 524, for Matthew Paris's remarks.

[2] Cf. similar indults of Innocent IV, 'Monasterii vestri profectibus' and 'Monasterio vestro quod', dated from Genoa on 1 June 1251, and 'Devocionis vestre precibus', dated at the Lateran on 31 Oct. 1253 (St. Albans Cart., Chatsworth, ff. 45–6^v): presumably it was a confirmation of these.

[3] See canon no. 3 among the decrees of the Council of Lyons (Mansi xxiii) which is obviously referred to in one of the points of petition.

[4] St. Albans Cart., Chatsworth, f. 34^v, and cf. B.M. Arundel MS. 34, f. 13^{r-v}, a later grant of this kind of 1423, and *Gesta Abb.* iii. 437, a grant to Abbot John de la Moote (1396–1401).

[5] Cf. previous documents, the 'Dignum arbitramur et' of Alexander III of 1181 (*PUE* iii, no. 337)—blessing not specifically mentioned here—of Clement III of 1188 (St. Albans Cart., Chatsworth, ff. 37^{r-v}, and B.M. Cotton MS. Nero D i f. 159^v, and *Chron. Maj.* vi, no. 34), and the reissue of 'Religiosam vitam' by Celestine III in 1193 (*PUE* iii, no. 459).

The last section of the curial business, according to the account in the Wymondham Cartulary, concerned the impetration of conservatorial documents, to safeguard all the privileges which had been granted, for a term of five years.[1] The vogue for getting conservatorial documents began during the pontificate of Innocent IV. An example of the appointment of a conservator to protect a particular document is provided in the affair of the appropriation of St. Michael's church, Kingsbury, when the abbot of Waltham was required to see this put into effect in 1252 and to uphold the sentence.[2] The conservatory document provided an insurance cover and became a frequent part of curial business. In all probability the abbot of Waltham (Augustinian, Essex) was one of the conservators who were granted in 1257. He appears as a conservator of the privileges of St. Albans at the end of the thirteenth century in connection with the Datchet case,[3] and in the late fourteenth century as conservator of the privileges of St. Albans and her cells, when he had to deal with certain 'men of Satan' who had assaulted the monks of Tynemouth, burnt their houses and stolen their goods.[4] The abbots of Bury, Westminster, and Reading, are mentioned in the same source as conservators of St. Albans, and it is not difficult to account for their appointment.[5] The abbot of Waltham, though at first sight not the most obvious choice, had much to recommend him. He was only some fifteen miles from St. Albans, not quite so accessible as the prior of Dunstable, but unlike the prior of Dunstable he did not have his own powerful liberty and was therefore obviously more acceptable as a conservator. The requests of St. Albans had thus for the most part been granted and the conservatory letters had been issued, so that the abbey's position was assured, but in point of fact it was St. Alban who proved to be the best conservator of its privileges in the thirteenth century, just as he had been its most powerful advocate with the papacy in the twelfth century.[6]

---

[1] Clause 26 in the Wymondham Cartulary: in the *Gesta Abb.* account it is not placed last.   [2] St. Albans Cart., Chatsworth, f. 46, and *CPL* i. 281.

[3] St. Albans Cart., B.M. Cotton MS. Otho D iii, f. 160.

[4] Tynemouth Cart., Syon House Muns. D. xi. 1, ff. 116ᵛ–118ᵛ.   [5] Ibid., f. 116.

[6] In the fifteenth century the relics of St. Alban were used against dearth, and were allegedly no less powerful in bringing changes in the weather ('Chron. of the Reign of Henry VI from St. Albans', pp. 36, 38, 63).

III. The third part of our investigation concerns Abbot Thomas de la Mare's formulary or letter-book, and in particular the section of that book which records the elucidation by Master Richard de Wymundeswolde of certain doubtful points in the privilege which had been granted in the time of Clement III to Abbot Warin and St. Albans.[1] Abbot Thomas de la Mare, some of whose brilliance and power is captured in the magnificent monumental brass in which he is arrayed in full pontificals and which remains in the abbey today, was elected to rule over St. Albans in 1349. He survived until 1396 and was said to have reached the age of eighty-eight when he died. It is recorded that he entered the monastery in the time of Abbot Hugh of Eversdon (1309–27),[2] was sent by him as a monk to Wymondham and was later appointed prior of Tynemouth, an office which he held by 1340.[3] The documents which are included in the formulary or letter-book range in date from 1342 to 1391, and it is stated that the core of the collection was drawn up in 1382 by Brother William Wyntershulle, chaplain to Abbot de la Mare. The primary interest of the formulary is that it is composed of real documents.[4]

Here the privileges of the abbey and liberty can be seen in operation in the latter part of the fourteenth century. The abbot orders the archdeacon of St. Albans to induct into a benefice in the exempt jurisdiction,[5] and grants him a general commission for absolving.[6] The visitors of the exempt jurisdiction order the archdeacon to cite on their behalf.[7] The abbot seeks chrism from the bishop of London;[8] he grants a licence to William de Saxeby, rector of Bushey (in the exempt jurisdiction), to be absent from his cure for two years;[9] he warns the vicar of St. Peter's in the town of St. Albans to reside.[10] He sends a commission to the bishop of 'Lambrensis' (?Lycostomen, under the patriarch of Constantinople)[11]

---

[1] C.U.L. MS. Ee 4. 20 (Wymundeswolde's section is on ff. 114–18ᵛ).

[2] See *Gesta Abb.* ii. 373.

[3] See Dugdale, *Monasticon*, ii. 197–8, and *Gesta Abb.* ii. 371 ff.

[4] See W. A. Pantin, 'English Monastic Letter-Books', *Historical Essays in honour of James Tait*, ed. J. G. Edwards and others (Manchester, 1933), p. 220.

[5] C.U.L. MS. Ee 4. 20, f. 32ᵛ.   [6] Ibid., f. 35.

[7] Ibid., f. 44.   [8] Ibid., f. 87ᵛ.   [9] Ibid., f. 87.   [10] Ibid., f. 89ᵛ.

[11] Robert, bishop of Lambrensis (1366–94), see *Handbook of British Chronology*, p. 267, and W. Stubbs, *Registrum Sacrum Anglicanum*, 2nd edn. (Oxford, 1897), p. 197.

to come to St. Albans and to confer sacred and minor orders on
17 December 1384.[1] A similar licence to the archbishop of Damascus
from Abbot de la Mare refers to the blessing of chrism, the consecration of altars and churches and the ordination of clerks.[2] The
abbot writes to the bishop of London about an exchange between
the incumbent of Barnet (in the exempt jurisdiction) and the
incumbent of Littleton (Middx.), in the bishop's diocese,[3] and he
collates to the chapel of St. Julian.[4] He notifies the king of the
appointment of a coroner within the liberty.[5] The prior of St.
Albans is granted a commission to visit the priory of Hertford,[6]
and sent to provide a prioress for the cell of Sopwell.[7] Articles of
inquiry are transcribed for use when visiting a monastery,[8] and
the oaths to be taken by the abbot of an exempt monastery and
by the prior of a cell on his appointment are included.[9] Reading
all this, and details about parish churches, deaneries, legal settle-
ments and the ordination of vicarages, one is strongly reminded
of the average diocesan's work.

The section of the book between folios 107 and 119, which
constitutes a separate quire, consists of a section on compositions
between St. Albans and the diocesans of Norwich, Lincoln, and
Durham, a section on portions and the ordination of vicarages, and
the section concerned with the interpretation of Clement III's
privilege for St. Albans. It reflects, therefore, other aspects of
St. Albans' jurisdiction: namely the establishment of the rights of
the mother house and cells *vis-à-vis* the ordinaries and the general
move towards the appropriation of churches, which had happened
in the mid thirteenth century, followed by the ordination of
vicarages and the provision of portions. To find a basis for their
activities, both past and present, the abbots returned to a study
and analysis of some of their early privileges. That Abbot Thomas
de la Mare chose to do so at this time suggests either that certain
rights of St. Albans were under attack, and had therefore to be
established and authenticated, or that the abbot was seeking to
expand his jurisdiction.

[1] C.U.L. MS. Ee 4. 20, f. 49ᵛ.   [2] Ibid., f. 82ᵛ.
[3] Ibid., f. 83ᵛ, and cf. 67ᵛ.   [4] Ibid., f. 59.   [5] Ibid., f. 40.
[6] Ibid., f. 33.   [7] Ibid., f. 35.   [8] Ibid., ff. 71–2ᵛ.
[9] Ibid., f. 73ʳ⁻ᵛ.

Shortly after his election Abbot de la Mare petitioned the pope, Clement VI, for certain grants, firstly that he might present one of his monks to the priory of Tynemouth,[1] secondly that he might appropriate Appleton church in order to send monks to Oxford (the monastery of St. Albans being in financial straits because of the Black Death)[2] and finally that he might have an indult to choose a confessor.[3] According to the St. Albans chronicler, papal claims were made to present to the priory of Tynemouth because the vacancy became known through the promotion of Thomas de la Mare to St. Albans, although the abbot of St. Albans had long had the right of electing the prior of the dependency.[4] This right had been clearly stated in the composition between St. Albans and the bishop of Durham, which was made by judges delegate in May 1247. The abbot was to appoint the prior of Tynemouth (the prior of St. Albans might do so in an abbatial vacancy), to remove him if it was necessary, according to his privileges, and to present him to the bishop of Durham, to whom the prior was to show obedience for his parish churches.[5] The bull 'Religionis zelus sincerae', allowing Abbot de la Mare to appoint, was obtained on 11 August 1349, and thus the rights over Tynemouth were saved, but it was expensive.[6] The second request, which was for the appropriation, was granted saving the rights of the bishop and the archdeacon, and is said to have cost the abbot £200.[7] The effects of the Black Death had made appropriation very desirable and had caused a lack of priests—the subject of two later indults to Abbot de la Mare, dated 28 February 1351 and 7 June 1363. These permitted the abbot to promote monks of twenty to twenty-five years of age to holy orders.[8] Mention has been made of the growing financial

---

[1] *Calendar of Entries in the Papal Registers: Petitions to the Pope, 1342–1419*, ed. W. H. Bliss (H.M.S.O., 1896), i. 172 (hereafter cited as *Cal. Pet.*); and see *Gesta Abb.* ii. 391–2.

[2] *Cal. Pet.* i. 171–2. Nicholas IV had allowed appropriation in 1291 (St. Albans Cart., Chatsworth, ff. 50ᵛ–51), but this presumably had not taken effect.

[3] *CPL* iii. 329 (not in *Cal. Pet.* i. 173 as stated). This is really of no particular note here except that it was granted on the same day as these documents and that this kind of indult was becoming more frequently sought, see below, p. 78.

[4] *Gesta Abb.* ii. 390–4.   [5] C.U.L. MS. Ee 4. 20, f. 108, and *Gesta Abb.* i. 390.

[6] *CPL* iii. 314.   [7] *Gesta Abb.* iii. 386.

[8] *CPL* iii. 383 (St. Albans Cart., Chatsworth, ff. 49ᵛ–50), and *Cal. Pet.* i. 425. See also C.U.L. MS. Ee 4. 20, f. 82. 7 June 1363 is the date of the petition, which is marked 'Granted'.

plight of St. Albans, which Abbot de la Mare attempted to remedy in part by obtaining a perpetual indult to the effect that the abbot-elect need no longer go to the curia for confirmation. This had hitherto been a fruitful source of papal income. In the long term this was a great saving to St. Albans, but immediately it probably added to the abbey's financial difficulties and debts.[1] His abbacy also witnessed considerable discontent from the townsmen, culminating in the Peasants' Revolt.[2] Another challenge to Abbot de la Mare's authority came apparently from within the abbey, from the prior, John de la Moote, who was to succeed de la Mare as abbot in 1396, and who is said to have obtained certain bulls which were to the Abbot's detriment.[3]

These circumstances presumably account for the abbot seeking the opinion of Master Richard de Wymundeswolde, a highly successful English proctor at the papal curia, a D.C.L. in 1338 and an advocate of the curia by 1343. The opinion must have been given by the spring of 1356, for he died early in that year at Avignon. It is interesting that de la Mare chose to employ a famous secular lawyer and not one of St. Albans' monks at Oxford.[4]

The articles of inquiry and Wymundeswolde's opinions were as follows:

(1) whether St. Albans and its priories might be classified as fully exempt. The reply affirmed that there was no doubt on this matter as the words of the privilege definitely showed.

(2) whether the abbot might summon any catholic bishop to celebrate in the monastery or in a church or cell subject to it, without having sought a licence from the bishop of the diocese in question. This point was more open to doubt and therefore more fully argued, the authorities of Hostiensis, Johannes Andreae, and

---

[1] *CPL* iv. 293–4, 517–18; and see below, pp. 80–1. Henceforth St. Albans was to pay the papacy 20 marks yearly for this concession.

[2] See *Gesta Abb.* iii. 285 ff. and 370. In 1357 Abbot de la Mare had obtained a licence to crenellate and in the 1360s a new gateway and walls were erected against the townspeople (*CPR, 1354–8*, p. 574, and *A Guide to St. Albans Cathedral* (Royal Comm. on Historical Monuments, H.M.S.O., 1952), p. 28).

[3] *Gesta Abb.* iii. 463.

[4] See A. B. Emden, *A Biographical Register of the University of Cambridge to 1500* (Cambridge, 1963), and A. B. Cobban, *The King's Hall within the University of Cambridge in the Later Middle Ages* (Cambridge, 1969), p. 54 n. 2 and p. 199 nn. 1 and 12.

others were cited, and it was decided that when a bishop was summoned to a place fully exempt, the diocesan's permission was not necessary.

(3) whether such a bishop might ordain any suitable clerks, who had letters dimissory from their diocesans, or only clerks and monks who were fully subject to the abbot. The bishop might ordain any suitable clerks.

(4) whether, if the bishop ordains those not subject to the abbot, their diocesans might intervene or coerce the bishop in any way. To this it was answered that there could be no coercion because both the place and the ordaining bishop were exempt from the diocesan.

(5) whether priors of priories and cells which were subject to the monastery, not having sought licence from the diocesan in whose diocese they were, might require bishops to celebrate orders in their cells in the same way. Here some definition was needed: it seemed that if it meant that the priors were acting without the licence of the abbot the answer was no, otherwise, with abbatial approval, it was in order.

(6) whether the abbot might institute monks in vacant churches and chapels, which were fully subject, united, or appropriated to the monastery, in which perpetual vicars and secular clerks were usually instituted. It seemed firstly that he could not, because such a right was not specifically conceded, but on the other hand it was not specifically prohibited either and the abbot had definite pontifical powers to change the status of benefices.

(7) whether the abbot might tax, augment, or split up the portions of vicars, when it seemed to him to be a legitimate action. Here it seemed that he might not split up vicarages but that he might augment and tax them.

(8) whether the abbot might authorize exchanges between the incumbents of benefices which were fully subject to him. The authorities of Johannes Andreae and Hostiensis appeared in favour, but against them it was alleged that a dispensation was needed. However, the pope had given pontifical jurisdiction to the abbot and these powers related to jurisdiction and not to episcopal orders.

(9) whether the abbot might unite etc. churches, priories, and cells, over which he had episcopal jurisdiction. First of all it seemed that he might not, because the power was not expressly mentioned in the pope's concession, but on the other hand it might be said that he could, as argued in the answer to question eight.

(10) whether the bishop of the diocese might, without licence of the abbot, ordain those within the jurisdiction of the abbot, and if he should do so whether he would incur a penalty. On the one hand it might be answered in the affirmative, because although they were exempt generally, they were still subject to the bishop to get orders and chrism, but on the other hand there was a negative answer, because the said clerks were like the clerks of another diocese and the bishop could not ordain them without the licence of their superior, in this case the abbot.

(11) whether the abbot might receive *munera* when visiting the cells or priories, and churches, especially when it was the custom, and if he should do so whether he would incur a penalty. It seemed that the abbot might not because the *Decretales* prohibited such tributes and all authorities (Johannes Andreae and the Novels) seemed to agree on this, and there was now a law that he could not receive any gift unless a procuration in money as stated in the *Extravagantes* of Benedict XII, and there was thus accordingly a penalty if he did. But for a solution to this question one had to consider the power of the abbot in the place he was visiting. If he had free administration of the fruits of the place, he might receive *munera*; if, however, he did not have free disposal of the fruits, it did not seem that he could receive gifts at a visitation but only a tax.

(12) whether the abbot might grant general indulgences to those over whom he had episcopal jurisdiction. The answer was in the affirmative, because the abbot had all pontifical rights as stated in the answer to the first point on which there was no doubt.

(13) whether the abbot might make a journey through the province giving solemn blessings anywhere throughout the whole kingdom;

(14) whether a legate *a latere* or his delegate might excommunicate, suspend, or put under an interdict the abbot or monks, without a special licence from the apostolic see;

(15) whether the abbot and monks were bound to keep the decrees of legates of the apostolic see; and finally

(16) whether the abbot might convert churches 'in proprios usus', where he had rights as patron and where the churches were served by secular clerks alone, saving a reasonable delay until provision was made for the priest.

The opinions on the last four points have not survived, if indeed they were recorded, but from the evidence on the other points St. Albans and Abbot de la Mare had reason to be well satisfied with Wymundeswolde's assessment.

IV. From the mid fourteenth century the indult became the most common papal document. The numerous grants of these privileges to individuals reflect the change in social conditions since the period when the abbey as a community had obtained for itself bulls confirming possessions and establishing rights. The most common indults or dispensations were to choose a confessor who might grant absolution enjoining a salutary penance, except in cases which were reserved to the Holy See, or who might give plenary remission to those who were penitent at the hour of their death. Such indults were granted to monks of St. Albans, some of them resident in the cells,[1] and in at least one instance to a nun of St. Mary de Pré,[2] as well as to superiors, including the prior of Tynemouth and the prioress of Sopwell.[3] Many of these were granted by Martin V, a considerable proportion of them in 1423, and it is recorded that the fee was ten *grossi* for an indult for one person and twelve for two persons.[4] Indults to have a portable altar were granted to John Wheathampstead, John Stokes, Adam Thoby, John Langley, and John Hatfield—all monks of St. Albans— between 1415 and 1423.[5] Three of these, Adam Thoby, John Langley, and John Hatfield, acquired indults for confessors at the same time.[6] On 20 October 1423 Martin V issued a general indult

[1] *CPL* iii. 326, 409, 437, 444; iv. 487; v. 42; vii. 307–9, 311, 318, 340, 342; and viii. 36, 432.   [2] Ibid., xii. 701.   [3] Ibid., vii. 307–8.   [4] Ibid., vii. 308–9.
[5] Ibid., vi. 358, 363; vii. 306, 316.   [6] Ibid., vii. 306, 309, 316, 318.

to the abbot and convent of St. Albans allowing them to use portable altars, because some of the monks were frequently called away from the monastery to attend to business in London, while yet others were at the *studium generale* at Oxford.[1] Other indults were sought by monks of St. Albans, who were priests, to receive and retain any benefice, to exchange for similar or dissimilar benefices, to hold a benefice with cure which was normally assigned to secular clerks, and other permutations of these.[2] Sixtus IV granted John, abbot of Wymondham, a dispensation to receive *in titulum* for life, with the said or any other monastery of the same order, any two benefices with or without cure which were customarily held by secular clerks, and to resign them simply or for exchange as often as he pleased.[3] On the same day, 30 January 1481, he dispensed Richard Harman, monk of St. Albans, to receive and retain any benefice.[4]

Details survive of the payments made to procure a general indult to have a portable altar, which was conceded to St. Albans by Martin V on 20 October 1423; for two other indults of the same date to eat meat from Septuagesima Sunday until Quinquagesima Sunday except on days when meat was expressly forbidden, and to let to farm their tithes to laymen;[5] as well as for a confirmatory bull of Eugenius IV of 1431 which confirmed Abbot John's institution of a common chest whose funds might be used in time of need.[6] For the three indults of Martin V, it cost in the one instance 8 and in the other two instances 10 florins for the minute; 3 *bol(endini)* for the charter; for the scriptor 8 and in one instance 10 florins; for the bull (sealing) 22 florins, 8 florins 8 *grossi*, and 11 florins respectively; for the registration, 8 florins and in one instance 10; finally 2 *grossi* for the clerk doing the registration. Additional expenses of 6 *grossi* were paid to the clerks of the lord secretary for writing the minutes. The total sums in English money were as follows: for the

---

[1] B.M. Arundel MS. 34, f. 13 (not in *CPL*).
[2] *CPL* v. 156; vi. 79; ix. 266, 271, 456, 459; xi. 526; xii. 508; xiii (2), 562.
[3] Ibid., xiii (2), 790.
[4] Ibid., and see p. 796 and xiii (1), 156.
[5] B.M. Arundel MS. 34, f. 14. Cf. *CPL* iv. 501, an indult of Boniface IX of 2 Oct. 1395 allowing this. Martin's indult refers to a previous bull of Boniface VIII, perhaps wrongly.
[6] B.M. Arundel MS. 34, ff. 12, 13, 14, 56ᵛ (see also *CPL* viii. 327).

indult about meat eating £7. 14*s*.; for the indult about the leasing of tithes £5. 9*s*. 4*d*.; and for the bull concerning the portable altar £6. 18*s*. 10*d*. In addition to these sums there were other costs since the abbot fell ill with dysentery, while at Rome petitioning, and had to purchase a plenary indulgence, and on his recovery gifts for the pope. The confirmatory bull of Eugenius IV was more expensive and cost £9.[1] The seven bulls which Abbot John de la Moote obtained through his proctor, Master John Fraunceys, between 1396 and 1401, had cost him £44. 6*s*. 8*d*.; Fraunceys received 10 marks and Peter de Bosco, bishop of Dax (France), a payment for his 'benevolence' in the curia, which was almost certainly a 'benevolence' connected with these impetrations.[2]

These amounts were extremely small, however, if compared with one source of expenditure. A decree of the Fourth Lateran Council had stated that the heads of exempt houses were to present themselves in person at Rome for confirmation after election. The first two abbots elected after the decree avoided the trip on the plea of advanced age, but there were still the expenses of proctors to pay, and Abbot John de Berkhamstead made the journey in person in 1291, perhaps to cut the costs.[3] A detailed expense-sheet of money paid out at Rome for Abbot John de Maryns's confirmation in 1302 records an expenditure of 3,000 florins (or 1,250 marks)[4] for obtaining a private audience with the pope—this might be advantageous for the convent but was still expensive—and sums paid out to the examiners, the referendary, the impetrator, the scribe, the papal corrector, the scribe for the second time, the bullators, the registrar, the copiers, and the notaries, for the actual letters and for gifts, bringing a total expenditure of 2,561 marks sterling.[5] The account

---

[1] B.M. Arundel MS. 34, f. 77^{r-v}; and see *Amundesham Annales* i. 149–65, 276, 289–91.

[2] *Gesta Abb.* iii. 436–7, 455–6.

[3] In general, see R. Vaughan, 'The Election of the Abbots at St. Albans in the Thirteenth and Fourteenth Centuries', *Proc. of the Cambridge Antiquarian Society*, xlvii (1954), 1–10.

[4] The editor of the *Gesta Abb.* in the R.S. edition (H. T. Riley) states that this was probably equal to 5000 marks 'as 4 florins are throughout made to equal 1 mark' (ii. 56 n. 4).

[5] *Gesta Abb.* ii. 56–8: printed in translation in G. G. Coulton, *Life in the Middle Ages*, 2nd edn. (Cambridge, 1930), iv. 282. The expenses of Abbot Hugh of Eversdon's confirmation in 1308, the next in the line, were said to be heavy because of his

of the expenditure on his election feast, to which the monastic servants were made to contribute, and at which herons, bitterns, cygnets, peacocks, and sucking pigs were served, is followed by a note of the money borrowed from Florentine merchants presumably to pay for all this.[1] The expenses of Abbot Richard of Wallingford who was at the papal court for confirmation in 1326 were also heavy.[2] Those of Abbot de la Mare in 1349 were detailed as eighty florins for the confirmation documents and 126 florins for the bull which allowed twenty monks to be ordained in their twentieth year.[3] He also took the opportunity of impetrating indults of plenary remission for ten persons, of whom some were his own monks, some seculars, for which he paid 108 florins.[4] In 1382 Abbot de la Mare set in train a process to gain exemption from the requirement that the abbot should visit the curia on election, and supplicated that the abbot-elect should be confirmed in England.[5] Apparently Evesham abbey already had a bull to this effect, and when approached by St. Albans for permission to borrow it, the Evesham monks insisted that it should not leave their abbey but should be copied there.[6] When in 1478 the Benedictine abbey of St. Peter at Westminster sought a similar exemption, they referred to the grants already made to Waltham abbey and to St. Albans.[7]

By the mid fifteenth century one of the most resented rights of the abbot of St. Albans was his power to appoint and remove the priors of dependencies at will, and to post the monks from place to place.[8] Difficult monks had frequently found themselves sent to Tynemouth; at least one monk of St. Albans ended a miserable existence in chains at Binham, and in 1380 the abbot of St. Albans had removed the prior of Wymondham from his office, citing the

lack of Latin and his consequent fear of going to the papal court in person (Vaughan, 'Election of the Abbots', pp. 10–11).

[1] *Registrum Abbatiae Johannis Whethamstede*, ed. H. T. Riley (R.S., 1872–3), ii. 330–3, 335–8, 342–3.   [2] *Gesta Abb.* ii. 186–91.

[3] Ibid., pp. 387–8. For the indult concerning ordination, see above p. 74, and *Cal. Pet.* i. 425. For Clement VI's bull confirming Abbot Thomas de la Mare, see Dugdale, *Monasticon*, ii. 238, num. xxix.

[4] *Gesta Abb.* ii. 388.   [5] Ibid., pp. 146 ff.

[6] Ibid., pp. 160–1; and see *CPL* iv. 293–4, reference to Innocent III's and Urban V's grants to Evesham.   [7] *CPL* xiii (1), 201.

[8] *Gesta Abb.* i. 226. In *c.*1330 the nuns of Sopwell had tried to elect their own prioress but were swiftly thwarted by the abbot of St. Albans (*VCH, Herts.* iv. 423).

privileges which allowed him to do so.[1] The papacy's scheme for
erecting the exempt religious houses *vis-à-vis* the diocesans was no
longer valid in the social context of fifteenth-century society. In
1487 Abbot William Wallingford sought the ultimate mark of
ecclesiastical autonomy for the abbot by asking the pope to endow
him with the episcopal powers of ordination and confirmation. John
de Rothbury, the archdeacon of St. Albans, was dispatched to Rome
to negotiate on his behalf, but the claim was too extreme and on 11
August he returned to St. Albans having been unsuccessful.[2] Even
the powerful mitred abbot of St. Albans, who had within his exempt
area the full jurisdictional powers of a bishop, was not to gain the
sacramental powers which were reserved exclusively to the bishop's
office. Instead of countenancing such proposals for the abbot's
aggrandizement, fifteenth-century popes were prepared to reduce
his authority. Indults were sought by and granted to priors con-
ceding that they should not be removed or recalled by the abbot,
or any other person, without reasonable cause. In 1444 Eugenius IV
granted such an indult to Richard Hall prior of Belvoir;[3] in 1456
Calixtus III confirmed William Albon in his office as claustral prior
of St. Albans (which office was revocable at the pleasure of the
abbot) and stated that he was not to be removed by the present
abbot or his successors;[4] and in 1482 William Dixwell, prior of
Binham, got a similar concession from Sixtus IV.[5] William Somer-
ton, prior of Binham, who sought not to be removed by the abbot
from his post, was arrested on his return from the continent and
his papal letters were seized and given to the abbot of St. Albans—
who 'only knows what the bulls contained'.[6] The extreme authority
of the abbot over his monks was finally flouted in 1448 when, at
the time of Wymondham's erection into an abbey, Nicholas V
granted an indult to Richard Langley, Edmund Shenley, William
Gondred, and William Wubeche, all monks of St. Albans, to transfer

---

[1] Dugdale, *Monasticon*, iii. 309; and *Gesta Abb.* iii. 124, 128.
[2] *Reg. Whethamstede*, ii. 287-9.   [3] *CPL* ix. 453.   [4] Ibid., xi. 88-9.
[5] Ibid., xiii (2), 806. This was really a letter of rectification, because the indult
which Dixwell had got on his election had wrongly stated that Binham was in the
diocese of Lincoln. As prior of Hertford, he is stated to have spent £11. 16s. out of
an expenditure of £90. 10s. on legal and travelling expenses, perhaps applying for
a similar indult (*VCH, Herts*. iv. 420).
[6] Dugdale, *Monasticon*, iii. 350, num. xiii; and *Gesta Abb*. ii. 140.

to the new abbey without licence of the abbot of St. Albans or any other.[1] Two of them, however, seem subsequently to have regretted their act and sought reinstatement at St. Albans.[2]

The priory of Wymondham, which had been founded by William d'Aubigny and put under St. Albans by him, was the first dependency to gain exemption from the overlordship of St. Albans. The bull which constituted it an abbey, named the prior, Stephen London, as first abbot, and declared that the monastery was in future to be subject to the bishop of Norwich and no longer answerable to St. Albans or liable to the annual payment of one mark of silver. The patron was to present to the ordinary the person who had been elected abbot by the convent, and the bishop of Norwich and the abbots of Westminster and Bury were to defend Wymondham against any interference from St. Albans or any other persons.[3] Trouble was not long in developing between Wymondham and its new overlord, the bishop of Norwich. As subject to St. Albans, Wymondham had enjoyed a fair amount of exemption from the diocesan. Now all this was to change. In 1463 Walter Lyhart, bishop of Norwich, excommunicated Wymondham because it had refused to obey his mandate and pay forty shillings annually. He had already, according to Wymondham, snatched the papal letters concerning the exemption from the abbot's hand, had carried them away and was believed to have torn them up.[4] The pope, Pius II, ordered the bishops of Ely and Exeter to inquire into Wymondham's alleged exemption from the bishop.[5] In fact the composition of 1228 had clearly stated that Wymondham was to pay the bishop forty shillings in lieu of visitation.[6]

Three of St. Albans' other dependencies were suppressed, Beadlow in 1428 to provide for the monks at Oxford, Wallingford in 1528 to provide for Cardinal College, and St. Mary de Pré (which

---

[1] *CPL* x. 46 (printed in *Reg. Whethamstede*, ii. 62–3, with additional material on 63–5); and see *Reg. Whethamstede*, i. 137–8 and 146–7, for these and some others from other cells. Cf. the case of Robert Morpath, monk of St. Albans, whom Nicholas V rehabilitated in 1449. He had obtained the perpetual vicarage of Aldworth (Berks.) without seeking a licence from his abbot (*CPL* x. 49).

[2] *Reg. Whethamstede*, ii. 63–4.

[3] *CPL* x. 19–20, and Dugdale, *Monasticon*, iii. 338–9; and *CPL* x. 51. See also *Reg. Whethamstede*, i. 148–52, for an account of the withdrawal.   [4] *CPL* xi. 489–90.

[5] Ibid., pp. 495–6.   [6] C.U.L. MS. Ee 4. 20, f.107.

had been a nunnery since the first part of the fourteenth century) also in 1528.[1] Such suppressions needed the consent of the papacy and documents were applied for to this effect. The authorization of the unification of Beadlow with St. Albans cost the mother house forty shillings.[2] The hospital of St. Julian was annexed to St. Albans in 1505.[3] Of the remaining dependencies Redbourn survived until 1535, Hatfield Peverel until 1536, Sopwell until 1537, Hertford until 1538, and Binham, Belvoir, Tynemouth, and St. Albans itself, until 1539.[4] The old papal privileges had remained powerful enough to prevent the fragmentation of the cells although the hierarchical position of the abbot of St. Albans was challenged when the economic structure of feudal society began to crumble. The relationship between St. Albans and its dependencies had naturally changed since the establishment of the ties in the eleventh and twelfth centuries, and this was reflected in the growing tendency by the late thirteenth and early fourteenth centuries for the cells to seek their own privileges from the papal curia.[5] Yet documents were still issued in the early fifteenth century which spoke of St. Albans and its cells as one entity, although society was no longer tolerant of such a powerful complex.[6] Basically the old privileges remained good until the whirlwind events of 1538–9, which, destroying the old religious houses, destroyed their privileges with them. Against this sort of lightning destruction the privileges and indulgences of the saints and popes were useless, just as the impression of the papal seal, which was fixed to the summit of the tower of the great church of St. Alban, had proved to be ineffectual in the thunderstorms of the early thirteenth century.[7]

JANE E. SAYERS

---

[1] B.M. Arundel MS. 34, f. 33ʳ⁻ᵛ, and Dugdale, *Monasticon*, iii. 277, num. v (the supplication by Abbot John Wheathampstead), 282, num. ix; and 361–2, num. xi. Clement VII confirmed Wolsey's suppression of Wallingford and its annexation to Cardinal College although no mention had been made in the Pope's earlier faculty for the suppression that Wolsey was holding the abbey of St. Albans *in commendam*. The bull, dated 31 May 1528, is P.R.O., Papal Bulls (S.C. 7), 63/14; it is reproduced in Plate 1.

[2] B.M. Arundel MS. 34, f.56, and Dugdale, *Monasticon*, iii. 243.

[3] D. Knowles and R. N. Hadcock, *Medieval Religious Houses* (London, 1953), p. 303.

[4] See ibid. for dates.   [5] e.g., Large Belvoir Cart., f. 12ʳ⁻ᵛ.   [6] Ibid., ff. 19ᵛ–20.

[7] Cf. *Gesta Abb.* i. 313, and Vaughan, *Matthew Paris*, p. 189.

PLATE I

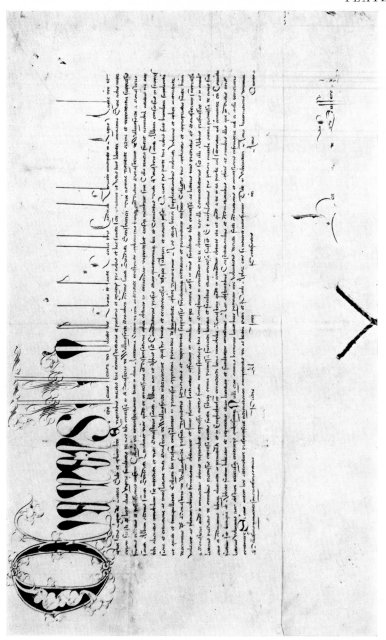

Bull of Clement VII to Cardinal Wolsey, 31 May 1528

IV

The Assizes of Henry II: the Texts

THE texts of the assizes of Henry II survive only in unofficial sources. Some depend on single versions of indeterminate authority. Nevertheless, they have been accepted as largely genuine by Stubbs, Maitland, and many others, both on textual grounds and because they seem to fit what is known from other sources about the development of English law and legal administration in the late twelfth century. In 1963 this was sharply challenged by Mr. H. G. Richardson and Professor G. O. Sayles. They dismissed the received texts of the Assize of Clarendon and the Assize of Woodstock as apocryphal; in the process they questioned the authority of the chronicler Roger of Howden and denounced the editorial methods of Stubbs.[1] They repeated their views in 1966.[2] Their arguments have not received universal assent. Professor Chrimes accepted that the Assize of Clarendon 'was clearly not a piece of legislation nor an instruction actually issued to the courts', but considered that the correction was 'textual rather than substantial';[3] he was followed by Professor Pugh.[4] Mr. Hall seemed to accept the new view, tentatively but without reservation or comment.[5] Lady Stenton, on the other hand, has firmly maintained that the pipe roll of 1166, from which Mr. Richardson and Professor Sayles drew crucial points in their argument, gives the impression 'that the orders of the Assize as it has come down to modern times . . . were being strictly observed'.[6] The views of Mr. Richardson

---

[1] H. G. Richardson and G. O. Sayles, *The Governance of Medieval England* (Edinburgh, 1963), pp. 198–203, 438–49.

[2] H. G. Richardson and G. O. Sayles, *Law and Legislation from Æthelberht to Magna Carta* (Edinburgh, 1966), pp. 88–131.

[3] *Law Quarterly Review*, lxxx (1964), 119.

[4] R. B. Pugh, *Imprisonment in Medieval England* (Cambridge, 1968), p. 4 n.

[5] *Glanvill*, ed. G. D. G. Hall (London, 1965), pp. lv–lviii, 171 n. (page references are to this edition). Cf. *EHR* lxxxiii (1968), 783–4.

[6] *Pleas before the King or his Justices 1198–1212* (Selden Society, 67–8, 83–4, 1952–3, 1966–7), iii, p. liii.

and Professor Sayles depended very much on confronting the texts with the legal practice of the twelfth century as they saw it, and this has determined the framework of much subsequent discussion. The method has its place, but is the less convincing the greater the disagreement on what legal practice was. The present paper is mainly concerned with the texts and manuscripts, for they have not been fully re-examined since Stubbs first printed them.

The documents to be considered are numerous: the Assize of Clarendon 1166, the Inquest of Sheriffs 1170, the Assize of Northampton 1176, the Assize of Arms 1181, the Assize of Woodstock 1184, and several related forest documents of earlier and later date. The texts of all these except the Inquest of Sheriffs appear in the work of Roger of Howden, either in the *Gesta*, or in the *Chronica*, or in both.[1] The texts of two, the Assize of Clarendon and the Inquest of Sheriffs, are contained in the legal collection, Bodleian Library, Rawlinson MS. C. 641. The Inquest of Sheriffs also appears in the chronicle of Gervase of Canterbury. The Assize of Woodstock figures in two versions in a collection of forest records of the sixteenth century, B.M. Cottonian MS. Vespasian F iv, in a fourteenth-century legal collection noted by Mr. Richardson and Professor Sayles, B.M. Additional MS. 5761, and in the Sherwood Forest Book.[2] All except the last two texts were known to Stubbs. The first two sources, Howden and Rawlinson MS. C. 641 are much the most important. The point was thoroughly appreciated by Stubbs when he edited them in his editions of the *Gesta* and the *Chronica*; he was the first to recognize the importance of the Rawlinson MS.[3]

---

[1] I have accepted Lady Stenton's identification of the author of the *Gesta* with Howden. ('Roger of Howden and Benedict', *EHR*, lxviii (1953), 574–82). In working on the texts, I have found nothing to contradict, and much to support, her argument.

[2] *The Sherwood Forest Book*, ed. Helen E. Boulton (Thoroton Society of Nottinghamshire, record series, xxiii, 1965), pp. 59–62.

[3] It should be noted that Stubbs's editorial methods are fully comprehensible once the accession of information to him is properly understood:

(*a*) He presented the texts of the Assize of Northampton and the *prima assisa* of the forest in the body of the text of the *Gesta*.

(*b*) He appreciated that these texts did not match the texts of the Assizes of Clarendon and Woodstock contained in the *Chronica*; he therefore presented these as an appendix to the preface to the *Gesta*. He collated this text of the Assize of Woodstock with the later versions known to him and also included Gervase of

It is immediately obvious that Roger of Howden is the crucial figure in the debate. His work contains all but one of the texts and all the critical variants. It is essential therefore to establish his authority, his *modus operandi*, and the nature and extent of his information. The outline of Roger's life is now well established. He was a secular clerk, parson of Howden from 1173–6 to his death in 1201 or 1202. He was in King Henry II's service by 1174–5 and served in the northern counties as a justice of the forest from 1184–5 to the end of Henry's reign.[1] He went on the Third Crusade; his presence is attested at the siege of Acre.[2] Of his historical work the *Gesta* survives only in secondary versions.[3] Its composition cannot therefore be established with certainty. Except for the annals of 1169–71 which must have been composed after September 1172, it was originally a contemporaneous narrative largely concerned with English history and the fortunes of the Angevin house.[4] In the form in which it has survived, however, it cannot have been completed before 1191 since events of that year are mentioned under the year 1180.[5] This late information is largely concerned with the history of Byzantium and Outremer. It is probable that Roger added it to the original narrative after his return from the Crusade.[6] There is no evidence that any other revision was carried out at this late stage.

Canterbury's text of the Inquest of Sheriffs (*Gesta Regis Henrici secundi Benedicti Abbatis* (R.S. 1867), ii. cxlix–clxiv).

(*c*) He printed the texts of the assizes at the appropriate points in his edition of the *Chronica*.

(*d*) He discovered Rawlinson MS. C. 641 only in the course of editing the *Chronica* (*Chronica magistri Rogeri de Hovedene* (R.S., 1868) ii. xxiii). He printed this version of the Assize of Clarendon along with other legal material as an appendix to the preface of the *Chronica*, ii. ci–cvi.

See also below, pp. 93 n. 4, 97 n. 3.

[1] F. Barlow, 'Roger of Howden', *EHR*, lxv (1950), 352–60. For additional material on Roger, see G. V. Scammell, *Hugh du Puiset* (Cambridge, 1956), pp. 146–8, 256–62.

[2] Doris M. Stenton, 'Roger of Howden and Benedict', pp. 576–7.

[3] *Gesta*, i. xxi–vii.

[4] It may be that it originally ran only up to 1177 since that is where the earliest copy, B.M. Cotton MS. Julius A xi, ends. This problem is not relevant to my argument, except in so far as it concerns the authorship of this section. I have accepted that Howden was the author of this, as of the rest of the work.

[5] *Gesta*, i. xlvi–xlvii, 251–262.

[6] Stubbs, who knew nothing of Roger's participation in the Crusade, suggested a similar explanation (ibid., i. xlvi–xlvii). The intrusion of this information into the text of the *Gesta* confirms Lady Stenton's identification of Howden as the author.

The *Chronica* is more informative. It survives in two manuscripts, B.M. Royal MS. 14 C. 2 and Bodleian Library, Laud MS. 582, which form the original on which all later copies of the *Chronica* and its derivatives depend.[1] Laud MS. 582, covering the years 1181–1201, is composed in various hands and seems to be a working copy. The annal of 1190 must in all probability have been composed before 1194,[2] and demonstrably late information is added throughout only in the margin or at the end of annals. Royal MS. 14 C. 2, running up to 1181, is a fair copy written in a fine bold script. In a *Liber de Legibus Angliae*, included under 1180, a genealogy of the dukes of Normandy is continued down to the death of Richard and the accession of John. Since the rubric to the genealogy states that it ran only to Henry II, it seems likely that the later extension was the work of the copyist. The passage precedes a blank space but is integral with the text; it was probably drawn from the account of Richard's death in the annal of 1199 in the Laud MS.;[3] it establishes that this section of the fair copy was written after that date. The relationship between the two volumes is obscured by the fact that the scribe of the Royal MS. was also chiefly responsible for the Laud MS. to some way through the annal for 1189. However, it is borne out by other indications: the earliest surviving copy of the work, B.M. Arundel MS. 69, itself written before 1213, follows the Royal MS. closely, but the Laud MS. less exactly;[4] another earlier copyist, working *c.* 1225, whose chronicle survives as 'Walter of Coventry', used the Laud, but not the Royal MS.;[5] and the Laud and the Royal MSS. overlap for one folio at the beginning of the annal of 1181.[6] An informal cursive hand appears in both MSS. It is responsible in the Royal MS. for the introduction in the margins of three extracts from Geoffrey of Monmouth and for some verses on the Young King,[7] and in the Laud MS. for minor corrections, many of the rubrics and some extended sections of the text. This hand was still at work in the annals of 1200 and 1201. In all

---

[1] *Chronica*, i. lxxiv–ix, ii. x.   [2] Ibid., iii. 77 n. 2. Cf. *Gesta*, ii. 153 n. 1.
[3] *Chronica*, ii. 239, 241; iv. 84.   [4] Ibid., ii. xi–xii.
[5] Ibid., i. lxxii.   [6] Ibid., ii. 253 n. 1.
[7] The extracts from Geoffrey of Monmouth occur under the years 1066 (f. 51; ibid., i. 113 n. 2), 1100 (f. 73; ibid., i. 157 n. 1), and 1138 (f. 87; ibid., i. 190 n. 9). The verses on the Young King were inserted at the notice of his coronation in 1170 (f. 122ᵛ; ibid., ii. 4–5 n. 3).

probability it is the hand of Roger of Howden.[1] In both volumes space was left at the end of each annal for the entry of later material.[2] Late entries were in fact made, in the Royal MS. in the hand of the main scribe, and in the Laud MS. in various hands including the cursive script attributed to Roger himself.

All the assizes of Henry II are entered in the *Chronica* in the hand responsible for the text of the Royal MS. and the Laud MS. up to 1189. They are integral parts of the text and not late insertions. There is no reason to suppose that they were not written in the order in which they appear or that they were inserted by the scribe in writing the fair copy. In one instance this is demonstrable: the annal of 1184 refers to the Assize of Woodstock included under 1180; if, as seems certain, the annal of 1184 was written before that of 1190, then the Assize of Woodstock must already have formed part of the text when that annal was composed before 1194.[3] It must therefore have been in the exemplar of the Royal MS.

Most of the assizes are preceded by the descriptive titles which are simply the rubrics of Howden's scribe. The texts show some variation in style and reveal no clear diplomatic rules usable as tests of authenticity. They embody instructions to justices, or royal orders or prohibitions, or general instructions on procedure or points of law. However, there is sufficient loose conformity to make it possible to identify a few crucial sections which are unlikely to have formed part of authentic assizes. The most striking instances are where Howden confused a text by introducing a narrative element. Sometimes he described an administrative measure in terms obviously derived from the relevant documents. Sometimes he simply transcribed a text. Sometimes he confused the two methods; here and there he could not resist the temptation, natural enough in a historian who was familiar with the administrative background to his documents, to mix together both text and context.

The *Gesta* refers to four of the texts. The first is the Inquest of Sheriffs.[4] Here Howden made no attempt to present a full text,

---

[1] This was also Stubbs's tentative view (ibid., i. lxxv). His hint that the early copy of the *Chronica*, B.M. Arundel MS. 69, might be annotated in the same hand is incorrect (ibid., i. lxxx).   [2] Ibid., ii. x–xi n. 2.

[3] Ibid., ii. 245–7, 290; iii. 77 n. 2.   [4] *Gesta*, i. 4–5.

but it is clear from his description of the investigation that he had access, directly or indirectly, to the text as it is recorded in Rawlinson MS. C. 641 and the chronicle of Gervase of Canterbury.[1] He drew only on the preamble and cap. 1.[2] He made no errors in incorporating this material into his narrative.

The second of the texts is the Assize of Northampton,[3] the most difficult and controversial of them all. There is no objection to accepting caps. 2–13 as an authentic assize. Cap. 1, however, is quite a different matter. This is in fact an account of the relationship of the Assize of Northampton to the Assize of Clarendon. In several phrases it slips into the form of an historical narrative, most obviously in the title—'Hae sunt Assisae factae apud Clarendone et postea recordatae apud Northamtoniam'—and in the passage 'Et apud Northamtoniam additum est . . .'. These cannot have been part of an official text; indeed in the *Chronica* the title is simply a rubric.[4] The Assize survives solely in the work of Howden. No other text has so far come to light.

The third text, the Assize of Arms, presents fewer difficulties.[5] It contains at least one scribal mistake; as Mr. Richardson and Professor Sayles have pointed out, the 16 marks mentioned in cap. 2 must be an error for 15 marks.[6] It is also possible that the reference to Henry II as 'filius Matildis imperatricis' in cap. 4 represents an interpolation by Howden; he almost invariably described Henry in this manner in noting the regnal year at the beginning of each annal in both the *Gesta* and the *Chronica*. Otherwise the text must stand. The main matter for debate is its date, and here there is no sound reason for doubting the attribution to 1181. The same date is given by Gervase of Canterbury and the Waverley annalist.[7] Howden also noted the Assize of Arms issued by Henry in his continental dominions at the beginning of 1181;[8] he rightly appreciated that this must have preceded the English

---

[1] Stubbs, *Select Charters*, 9th edn., ed. H. W. C. Davis (Oxford, 1913), pp. 175–8.

[2] A curious lapse led Stubbs to think that Howden drew on cap. 9 (*Gesta*, ii. clviii n. 1). He failed to note that cap. 9 repeated the phrases of the preamble.

[3] Ibid., i. 108–11.   [4] B.M. Royal MS. 14 C. 2, f. 156ᵛ.

[5] *Gesta*, i. 278–80.

[6] *The Governance of Medieval England*, p. 95 n. 4.

[7] *The Historical Works of Gervase of Canterbury*, ed. W. Stubbs (R.S., 1879), i. 297; *Annales Monastici*, ed. H. R. Luard (R.S., 1865), ii. 242.   [8] *Gesta*, i. 269–70.

version.[1] The main argument against this date, that no eyre took place in 1181, is beside the point.[2] The Assize can scarcely have been issued before Henry's return to England from Normandy at the beginning of August 1181. If it was issued after the end of September then the references in cap. 9 to judgement by the justices at Westminster in the Michaelmas term must refer to Michaelmas 1182 at the earliest. The pipe rolls record an extended eyre in 1182 and 1183.[3] However, neither these accounts nor those of the eyre of 1176, to which Mr. Richardson and Professor Sayles attribute the Assize, bear any reference to it.

The last text in the *Gesta* is a forest assize placed under the year 1184.[4] This is a brief document prefaced by the statement 'Prima assisa Henrici regis'. There are two possible explanations of Howden's use of this curious phrase: first that he thought that this assize was the first of a series of which later versions were already in existence at the time of writing, and secondly, that the *prima assisa* belonged to an earlier date and that it was entered here in default of the correct text of 1184. There is nothing to support the first explanation; it is incompatible with Stubbs's view that the *Gesta* at this point is largely contemporaneous.[5] The second seems the more likely for Howden altered this text in the *Chronica*. The new text included the old. This may explain his readiness both to accept and then to replace the *prima assisa*.

Howden seems to have had little additional information in the early stages of recasting the *Gesta* as the *Chronica*. He had nothing to say under 1166 of the Assize of Clarendon. Under 1170 he condensed the notice of the Inquest of Sheriffs to a single sentence.[6] He simply repeated the Assize of Northampton under 1176.[7] Under 1181 he also repeated the Assize of Arms with two small additions to the text in caps. 8 and 9;[8] he must have taken these from a

---

[1] Cf. R. W. Eyton, *Court, Household and Itinerary of Henry II* (London, 1878), pp. 237–43.

[2] Cf. H. G. Richardson and G. O. Sayles, *The Governance of Medieval England*, p. 439 n. 3; *Law and Legislation*, pp. 99–100.

[3] *Pleas before the King or his Justices, 1199–1212*, iii. lxv–lxviii.

[4] *Gesta*, i. 323–4.   [5] Ibid., i. xlvi–l.

[6] *Chronica*, ii. 4.   [7] Ibid., ii. 89–91.

[8] Ibid., ii. 261–3. To cap. 8 he added 'nec mercator nec alius ea ab Anglia portet' and to cap. 9 'et de visnetis' (following the numeration of Stubbs's *Charters*, pp. 183–4).

version of the *Gesta* which has not survived or from some other exemplar. By this time, however, he had received a full text of the Assize of Clarendon and the Assize of Woodstock. These formed part of a collection of legal material which he entered under the year 1180. This accession enabled him to replace the *prima assisa* entered in the *Gesta* under 1184 by a reference to the new version already entered in the *Chronica* under 1180.[1]

It is essential to determine the status of this new material. The issue is confused by the printed text in the Rolls Series edition which implies, by the marginal running heads—'Laws of England'—that it was all one and comprised in a *Liber de Legibus Angliae* which Howden included under 1180. This is not so. The *Liber* consisted of the twelfth-century legal text *Tripartita*, a glossary of Old English legal terms, and Glanville. Stubbs did not print the text of Glanville. Nor did he print a crucial sentence with which this version of Glanville and indeed the whole *Liber* ends—'Explicit liber legum Angliae'.[2] The texts of these Assizes are therefore quite separate from the *Liber*. Stubbs himself referred to them as an 'appendix' to the *Liber*;[3] Maitland seems to have appreciated that the material was disparate;[4] and Mr. Hall stated the correct facts, including the *explicit*, in 1965.[5] The authenticity of these texts does not then depend on the *Liber*. It does not even depend in the main on the authority of Howden; all that need be noted is that as a royal official he might well have had access to government records and that he copied and condensed legal texts with reasonable accuracy. It depends in the last resort on the authority of Howden's source, and that has not been identified.[6]

This version of the Assize of Clarendon also appears in Rawlinson MS. C. 641. Stubbs and Liebermann gave this MS. various dates in the late twelfth century.[7] The work falls into three sections.

---

[1] *Chronica*, ii. 289–90.　　　　　[2] B.M. Royal MS. 14 C. 2, f. 274.

[3] *Gesta*, i. lxi; *Chronica*, i. lxxvi. Stubbs was not entirely consistent; he later referred to the whole collection of legal material as a 'legal Appendix' (ibid., ii. xxii).

[4] F. Pollock and F. W. Maitland, *History of English Law* (Cambridge, 1911), i. 163 n.

[5] *Glanvill*, p. lvi.

[6] There are, however, two thirteenth-century versions of the *Chronica* which omit the Assize of Northampton and refer the reader instead to a *liber curialis* (ibid., p. lvi).

[7] *Chronica*, ii. xxiii, xxiv n.; F. Liebermann, *Über die Leges Edwardi Confessoris* (Halle, 1896), p. 124; *Gesetze der Angelsachsen* (Halle, 1903), i. xxxviii.

The first contains the *Leges Edwardi* and other miscellaneous material. The second contains the Assize of Clarendon, the Inquest of Sheriffs, and a version of Magna Carta 1215. The third contains the *Institutiones Cnuti*, the *Leges Willelmi*, and other material.[1] The first and third sections are integral parts of the book; they share the same number of lines and the same early rubrication. The second section is an inserted quire with attached sheets, quite distinct in its handwriting, its rubrication, and the number of lines to the page.[2] At what date it was inserted into the MS. cannot be determined. The first annotations common to all three sections are in a hand of the sixteenth century. The value of the central section is not therefore affected by its later association with a number of legal apocrypha of the early twelfth century. It was not composed as early as the rest of the book. Lady Stenton has suggested a date of *c.* 1220, but since the text of Magna Carta is entered in a different hand the rest may be as early as the reign of John. An earlier date is unlikely.[3]

The collection of material in this section of the Rawlinson MS. is of great value. This version of the Inquest of Sheriffs is the sole source of the 'assize of essoiners', of the provisions concerned with the renewal of actions before the king or his justices, and of chapter 15 of the received text. It omits chapters 2 and 12 of the version in the chronicle of Gervase of Canterbury, but for the rest the two confirm each other, and there is no real doubt that to-gether they come close to an official text.[4] The text of the Assize

---

[1] *Chronica*, ii. xxiv n.   [2] ff. 19–29.

[3] *Pleas before the King or his Justices*, i. 151–3 and frontispiece.

[4] For comment and a reconstruction of the text, including the 'assize of essoiners' see Lady Stenton, ibid., i. 153. Stubbs printed the text of Gervase in *Gesta*, ii. clv-clviii, and in *Historical Works of Gervase of Canterbury*, i. 217–19. He printed the version in the Rawlinson MS. in *Select Charters* (8th edn., 1895), pp. 148–50. The two are collated in *Select Charters* (9th edn., 1913), pp. 175–8, but without indication of detailed variants or the sections not in Gervase. A third version, with the articles in a different order, probably lies behind the terms of inquiry printed in *The Letters and Charters of Gilbert Foliot*, ed. Adrian Morey and C. N. L. Brooke (Cambridge, 1967), pp. 523–4. These omit caps. 9 and 15, but include cap. 14, which is not in Gervase. Stubbs's note on the 'assize of essoiners' in *Chronica*, ii. cvi, is misleading since it refers to the text of the inquest in Gervase of Canterbury, which does not include caps. 14 and 15. For comment on the Inquest of Sheriffs see J. H. Round, *The Commune of London* (London, 1899), pp. 125–36, and V. H. Galbraith, 'Osbert, Dean of Lewes', *EHR*, lxix (1954), 289–302.

of Clarendon is also a good one; Stubbs considered it superior to that preserved by Howden.[1] Moreover, all these texts are associated in the Rawlinson MS. with a variant of an impeccably authentic document, Magna Carta.[2] The collection is concerned with genuine enactments, not apocrypha.

The two texts of the Assize of Clarendon in the Rawlinson MS. and Howden are not directly related.[3] There are, therefore, two independent texts of the Assize derived from early manuscripts in each of which it is associated with other official acts. If the Assize, as we have it, is to be rejected, it must be on strong grounds.

The case for rejection rests on two foundations. First, it is argued that this text of the Assize is inconsistent with the manner of its execution: that it reserved the judgement of criminals to the itinerant justices whereas in fact the work was done by local justices and sheriffs. This argument is far from wholly correct. Moreover, it ignores the possibility of a change in plan, or a failure to match intention by execution. It is discussed below.[4] Secondly, this text of the Assize does not tally with cap. 1 of the Assize of Northampton. Literal acceptance of the one casts doubt upon the other; there is an apparent textual confrontation.[5] Yet it need not necessarily be resolved in favour of the later document. There are two independent texts of the Assize of Clarendon against only one of Northampton. The Assize of Clarendon is textually satisfactory and is associated in both its sources with other assizes. The Assize of Northampton stands by itself, dependent solely on Howden's authority, its text marred in the crucial cap. 1.[6] It does not follow that cap. 1 must be dismissed. By 1176 Howden was certainly in the service of the Crown. He was an expert witness, able to name with complete accuracy the justices who enforced the Assize of Northampton.[7] But he was expert in the events of 1176 not 1166.

---

[1] *Chronica*, ii. xlviii.

[2] This version of the Charter is dated 16 June and has some similarities to that recently discovered by Professor Galbraith, 'A draft of Magna Carta (1215)', *Proceedings of the British Academy*, liii (1967), 345–60. I hope to discuss it elsewhere.

[3] Compare the respective versions of caps. 1 and 2. There are minor variants throughout.   [4] See the Note on the Eyre of 1166, below, pp. 101–6.

[5] For emphasis of this and a reconstruction of the Assize of Clarendon on the basis of cap. 1 of Northampton see Richardson and Sayles, *Governance of Medieval England*, pp. 440–1.   [6] See above, p. 90.   [7] *Gesta*, i. 107–8.

There is not even any evidence that he had a text of the Assize of Clarendon when he entered the Assize of Northampton into either the *Gesta* or the *Chronica*.

However, the confrontation is marginal and explicable. The Assize of Clarendon is concerned solely with murder, robbery, and theft. In 1176 Howden also included arson and *falsoneria*,[1] but in such a manner as to suggest that these two crimes were in some way separate from the others.[2] The justices in eyre in 1166 were certainly concerned with *falsoneria* for men were amerced for failure to proceed. But the two examples recorded on the pipe roll arose from appeal not presentment; this was also true of the single case recorded in 1168.[3] It is only in 1176 that the pipe rolls clearly establish that the procedure laid down in the Assize was applied in this kind of action.[4] Nor does the pipe poll of 1166 record any presentment or indeed any other process for arson. In 1169 the wapentake of Broxtowe in Nottinghamshire was amerced for concealment of such a case;[5] there were similar penalties in 1170 and 1176.[6] Hence it seems likely that *falsoneria* and arson only came within the procedure laid down by the Assize during the decade after 1166.[7] The only evidence strictly contemporaneous with the Assize of Clarendon, Henry II's writ concerning the entry of his justices into the liberty of Durham, confirms this; it refers solely to murder, robbery, and theft.[8]

---

[1] *Falsoneria* included coining, forgery, and falsifying of measures (*Glanvill*, xiv. 7, p. 176).

[2] 'Si quis retatus . . . de murdro vel latrocinio, vel roberia vel receptatione hominum talia facientium, vel de falsoneria vel iniqua combustione . . .'

[3] *Pipe Roll 12 Henry II* (P.R.S., 1888), pp. 67, 120; *Pipe Roll 14 Henry II* (P.R.S., 1890), p. 43. Presentment and appeal were clearly recognized as distinct procedures. See *Glanvill*, xiv. 171 ff. The distinction was made in 1166: in the Nottinghamshire and Derbyshire account Serlo of Thurlaston owed 10 marks 'ut habeat dirationem suam si appellatus fuerit ab aliquo de morte cujusdam unde retatus est' (*Pipe Roll 12 Henry II*, p. 57).

[4] The town of Lewes had to account for receiving men accused of *falsoneria*. Two *falsonerii* were hanged, one in Berks., one in Kent (*Pipe Roll 22 Henry II* (P.R.S., 1904), pp. 135, 203, 211).   [5] *Pipe Roll 15 Henry II* (P.R.S., 1890), p. 66.

[6] *Pipe Roll 16 Henry II* (P.R.S., 1892), p. 33; *Pipe Roll 22 Henry II*, p. 210.

[7] They had certainly come under the procedure of presentment by the time Glanville was written (*Glanvill*, xiv, caps. 4, 7, pp. 175–7). Other actions, not mentioned in either of the Assizes, might be subject to presentment by the 1180s. See Naomi Hurnard, 'The Jury of Presentment and the Assize of Clarendon', *EHR*, lvi (1941), 401–2.   [8] J. H. Round, *Geoffrey de Mandeville* (London, 1892), p. 112.

It also seems probable that there were some changes, perhaps local variations, in the punishment of offenders. The Assize of Clarendon does not lay down that those punished by mutilation should also abjure the realm; cap. 1 of the Assize of Northampton does—after forty days. The Assize of Clarendon provides that those cleared at the ordeal but nevertheless of evil repute should leave the realm within eight days or at the first fair wind thereafter.[1] This relatively loose arrangement did not survive. Cap. 1 of the Assize of Northampton lays down an interval of forty days and allows those going into exile to take their chattels with them. Yet another variant, preserved by Bracton, attaches this provision to the Assize of Clarendon and allows suspects of this kind forty days during which they might seek aid from their friends.[2] Other differences arise from the silence of one Assize on matters covered by the other. The Assize of Clarendon has nothing to say of the penalties of those condemned at the ordeal; cap. 1 of the Assize of Northampton has, because it was aimed at increasing their severity.

These differences are nowhere so wide or so inexplicable as to invalidate either text. Each text is independent of the other; there is no possibility that the Assize of Clarendon is based on cap. 1 of the Assize of Northampton or on its exemplar. True, Howden had the text of the Assize of Northampton when he transcribed the Assize of Clarendon, but no reasonable correlation of the two could explain the independent version of the Assize of Clarendon in Rawlinson MS. C. 641. Neither assize is far removed from current practice.[3] No real difficulty remains if it is allowed that there was

---

[1] Cap. 14.

[2] *De Legibus*, f. 136, ed. S. E. Thorne (Cambridge, Mass., 1968), ii. 383. This seems to be nothing more than a gloss on the provision recorded in cap. 1 of the Assize of Northampton. Bracton's text at this point does not establish that he was quoting directly from a copy of the Assize of Clarendon; if anything, it suggests that he was not. Cf. Richardson and Sayles, *Law and Legislation*, p. 125.

[3] I am unable to follow Miss Hurnard's (op. cit., p. 391) and Mr. Hall's (*Glanvill*, p. 175 n.) interpretation of Glanvill xiv, c. 3: 'Compellitur eciam quandoque rettatus de homicidio legitimam subire purgationem si turba sequente fuerit in fuga comprehensus, et hoc per iuratam patrie fuerit in curia legitime testatum.' Their opinion that this conflicts with the assizes or limits the use of the ordeal seems to strain the sense of the passage. It is surely concerned to ensure that those caught by hue and cry went straight to the ordeal without the presentment of any case other than that they had been taken in flight. It supplements rather than limits the use of presentment by adding a summary process for such cases.

some experiment and development in the decade separating the two, and that cap. 1 of the Assize of Northampton represents an attempt by someone, not in possession of the Assize of Clarendon, to correlate the two and provide a summary of part of the earlier measure. In all probability this person was Howden. In 1176 he had not yet obtained the text of the Assize of Clarendon;[1] he summarized in a similar manner in recording the Inquest of Sheriffs;[2] and one other document which he transcribed reveals a similar interpolation of historical narrative into a legal text. This is the Assize of Woodstock. Cap. 1 of the Assize of Northampton is embellished with the phrase—'apud Northamtoniam additum est . . .'. Cap. 12 of the Assize of Woodstock is embellished with 'Apud Wdestoke rex praecepit . . .'. For this last phrase Howden was clearly responsible. It appears only in his version of the text.

The forest assizes are relatively straightforward. They are three in number: the *prima assisa*, the Assize of Woodstock, and the assize of 1198.[3] Caps. 1–3, 5, and 6 of the Assize of Woodstock repeat the *prima assisa*, and the assize of 1198 repeats the Assize of Woodstock *in toto*. Howden is the earliest authority for the second text and the sole authority for the first and third. The three texts he preserves are independent of each other. The *prima assisa* cannot have been copied from the Assize of Woodstock for Howden was not in possession of the second text when he transcribed the first.[4] Likewise the Assize of Woodstock cannot have been copied from the assize of 1198 for it was already *in situ* in the annal of 1180 when the annal of 1184 was composed.[5] It is equally clear that the later documents cannot have been drawn directly from the earlier; each

---

[1] See above, pp. 91–2.

[2] See above, pp. 89–90.

[3] The *prima assisa* is printed in *Gesta*, i. 323–4. Stubbs already knew of Howden's version of the Assize of Woodstock and he printed it, along with additional chapters drawn from Cotton MS. Vespasian F iv in *Gesta*, ii. clxi–clxiv. He also printed Howden's version of the Assize of Woodstock again collating the additional chapters, in *Chronica*, ii. 245–7, and finally the assize of 1198 in ibid., iv. 63–6.

In printing the Assize of Woodstock in *Select Charters*, pp. 157–9, Stubbs included the additional chapters in brackets and unfortunately simply referred to *Gesta*, ii. clxi. The provenance of the additional chapters was clearly indicated in Stubbs, *Select Charters*, 9th edn., p. 188.

[4] See above, p. 91.

[5] See above, p. 89.

exhibits textual variants peculiar to itself.[1] Howden first served as a justice of the forest in 1184–5. When he wrote the *Chronica* he deliberately replaced the *prima assisa* with a reference to the Assize of Woodstock. Hence the *prima assisa* is best attributed to an earlier eyre, of 1166–7 or 1175–6, for Howden clearly considered the Assize of Woodstock to be the genuine articles of inquiry of the eyre of 1184. It is accompanied in the *Chronica* by apparently authentic articles of the regard.[2] The text of the Assize is corroborated by four other versions, each independent of Howden's text, each containing the preamble announcing that this is the Assize of King Henry son of Matilda made at Woodstock.[3] There are overwhelming reasons for accepting it as authentic.

The forest assizes pose two obvious problems. First, there is an apparent contradiction between cap. 1 and cap. 12 of the Assize of Woodstock. Cap. 1 reasserts the customary punishments for forest offences. Comparison with the *prima assisa* and the articles of 1198 indicates that these included blinding and emasculation; one version of the Assize of Woodstock specifically excludes the provision of sureties.[4] Cap. 12, in contrast, provides that those who commit forest offences shall provide sureties on the first and second occasions, but shall answer with their bodies on the third. The two chapters appear in all manuscripts and were repeated in the assize of 1198. No one from Howden onwards perceived any contradiction. Two explanations seem possible. The first is that at Woodstock in 1184 Henry II ordered a genuine but temporary relaxation in penalties. This is unlikely and is unsupported by the record of the eyre in the pipe roll of 1185.[5] The second is that cap. 1 is concerned with punishment and cap. 12 with process. This seems the obvious

---

[1] The Assize of Woodstock contains seven chapters not in the *prima assisa*. Cap. XI of the assize of 1198 cannot have been taken from cap. 10 of the Assize of Woodstock. Cap. 11 of the Assize of Woodstock cannot have been taken from cap. XII of the assize of 1198. There are numerous minor variants throughout all three texts.

[2] *Chronica*, ii. 243–4.

[3] *Sherwood Forest Book*, pp. 59–62; B.M. Cotton MS. Vespasian F iv, ff. 10, 17; Add. MS. 5761, f. 131ᵛ.

[4] 'non vult quod plegios dant aut in hoc confident . . .' Cotton MS. Vespasian F iv, f. 10ᵛ.

[5] For accounts for chattels of fugitives from the forest law see *Pipe Roll 31 Henry II* (P.R.S., 1913), pp. 167, 171, 207.

explanation, for there is widespread evidence in the pipe roll that
bail was allowed to forest offenders.[1] It matches the procedure of
the thirteenth century whereby those arrested for offences against
the forest, including the venison, might be released on bail pending
trial.[2] One of the later versions of the assize contains additional
chapters which limit this procedure to offences against the vert.[3]
This is not specified in any of the texts of cap. 12. Moreover, a
clumsy insertion in the text of the assize of 1198 indicates that it
also referred to offences against the venison.[4]

The second problem concerns the textual tradition of the forest
assizes. They soon came to carry an accretion of forest regulations
which are not always easily distinguishable from the original
instructions. This occurred at an early date. Howden himself
included in the assize of 1198 a number of notes and memoranda on
pannage, punishment of forest offences, the procedure of the regard,
the charges for assarting, and the digging of ditches, none of which
as they stand can have formed part of this assize or of any other
instruction.[5] Many of them are nevertheless genuine forest customs
and provisions. All the later versions of the Assize of Woodstock
carry accumulations of this kind. The text in the Sherwood Forest
Book includes caps. 14 and 15 of the version in the *Select Charters*.[6]
Of the two versions in Cottonian MS. Vespasian F iv. the first
includes caps. 13, 14, and 15, and the second caps. 14, 15, and 16.
The version in Additional MS. 5761 contains caps. 13, 14, and 15,
along with further material dealing with attachments by foresters
and verderers, destruction of trees and selling of timber, special

---

[1] For amercements *quia non habuit quem plegiavit* and similar forms, see ibid.,
pp. 18, 74, 115, 121, 193, 202, 212, 238.

[2] *Select Pleas of the Forest*, ed. G. J. Turner (Selden Society, 13, 1899), pp. xl–xli.

[3] 'Si quis forestarius invenerit extra dominicum boscum et infra regardum aliquem
prosternantem quercum sine visu aut deliberatione forestariorum aut viridariorum
debet ipsum attachiare per quatuor plegios et per visum forestariorum viridariorum
seu rewardatorum imbreviari et debet poni per sex salvos plegios. Et si alias inveniatur
debent dupplicari eius plegii. Et si tercio corpus eius debet retineri.' Cf. 'Si quis cepit
aliquam feram in foresta sine warranto corpus suum retinendum est ubicunque inveniatur infra metas foreste, et cum captus fuerit non liceat forestarios eum delibe-
rare sine precepto domini Regis vel justiciorum suorum.' (Add. MS. 5761, f. 132ᵛ.)

[4] 'quicunque forisfecerit ei de foresta sua semel de venatione sua, de seipso salvi
plegii capiantur . . .' (*Chronica*, iv. 65).

[5] Caps. XIII–XVII (first sentence), ibid., iv. 65. These additions are entered in the
cursive hand, attributed to Howden.   [6] *Sherwood Forest Book*, p. 62.

inquisitions, control of hounds, reporting of offences, and the use of the hue and cry against forest offenders. The arrangement of these additions may have been determined by different manuscript traditions.[1] The source probably lay in the accumulation of miscellaneous material in the hands of foresters and forest justices. The assize of 1198 demonstrates that this kind of accumulation, represented later by the Sherwood Forest books, was already available for use in Howden's day. This creates a textual problem. If Howden's resources allowed him to blur the distinction between assizes and other forest regulations and so include additional material for 1198, it is also possible that he excluded relevant material in transcribing the Assize of Woodstock of 1184. For this reason caps. 13, 14, and 15 of Stubbs's text cannot be dismissed out of hand. Cap. 16, which probably drew on cap. 10 of the Charter of the Forest and for which there is no authority other than one sixteenth-century version, must be rejected.

This is the only chapter throughout the whole range of the Assizes of Henry II which is certainly apocryphal. The rest stand as genuine attempts to record the actions of government. They can be dismissed only at the cost of abandoning the ordinary standards of textual criticism in favour of views of legal development in the late twelfth century which are at best uncertain and debatable. Some of the texts recorded in the work of Howden reveal initial doubts, as in the *prima assisa*, or interpolated narrative, as in cap. 1 of the Assize of Northampton and cap. 12 of the Assize of Woodstock. But none of this is equivalent to the legal antiquarianism or political distortion characteristic of the real apocrypha of the twelfth century; it is a far cry from the Assize of Clarendon to the London version of *Leges Edwardi*. Howden was simply trying to explain and give the reader the benefit of his knowledge and experience. Neither he nor his contemporaries held a view of law which sharply distinguished the authentic from the apocryphal. An assize was not a charter, an interpolation or comment not a forgery. These

---

[1] The surviving texts contain numerous minor variants and several additions or omissions. There is also some variation in the order of the later chapters. This by itself suggests that the text in Cotton MS. Vespasian F iv, f. 10 is related to that in Add. MS. 5761, f. 131ᵛ, and that in Cotton MS. Vespasian F iv, f. 17 to that in the *Sherwood Forest Book*, pp. 59–62. However, the order is not repeated exactly.

men were beset in their work by the lack of record. If the reconstruction presented above is correct, Howden had no text of the Assize of Clarendon when he recorded the Assize of Northampton and no text of the Assize of Woodstock when he recorded the *prima assisa*. None of the surviving texts may be taken as 'original'. Some, like the forest records or perhaps the Inquest of Sheriffs,[1] may originate in articles used by justices or other officials. The men of Howden's age were not working in the circumstances of the mid thirteenth century when Magna Carta provided a pattern for embodying legislation in royal charter, or even in the circumstances of John's reign when procedural assizes or changes in the law might be announced to the shire courts in letters patent. Their background was both less sophisticated and less formal. That the texts survive imperfectly is understandable. That they survive at all is a tribute not only to the work of Henry II but also to those like Roger of Howden who comprehended its importance.

Note

The Eyre of 1166

There are no judicial records of the eyre of 1166. Financial payments arising from the enforcement of the Assize of Clarendon were put in charge on pipe roll 12 Henry II of Michaelmas 1166. These payments are arranged in two divisions: first, the sums due from sheriffs for the sale of the chattels of those who had failed at the ordeal or fled; secondly, the amercements imposed on individuals and communities by the itinerant justices, Geoffrey de Mandeville, earl of Essex, and Richard de Lucy.

In those accounts in which both entries appear there is usually little difficulty in establishing the relationship between the two. The sheriffs presented accounts for chattels and nothing else. Conversely the records of the judicial proceedings do not normally refer to the disposal of chattels. The two sets of entries are complementary not supplementary and refer to two distinct administrative procedures

---

[1] It may be that Gervase of Canterbury derived his version of the Inquest of Sheriffs from Clarembald, abbot of St. Augustine's, Canterbury, who was a member of the commission of inquiry in the south-eastern counties (*Gervase*, i. 216). Clarembald's successor, Roger, was a monk of Christ Church (Chronicle of William Thorne, R. Twysden, *Historiae Anglicanae Scriptores Decem*, London, 1652, cols. 1815–19).

each pertaining to the same eyre. The one was the sale of chattels; this was the concern of the sheriffs. The other was the imposition of amercements; this was the concern of the justices. They involved separate accounts, the one presented directly by the sheriffs, the other depending on the return of the justices' roll or estreats to the Exchequer. This arrangement was not peculiar to 1166; there was a similar division in the record of the eyres of 1168–9, and indeed it was the usual procedure.[1]

This relationship is clearly established in a number of individual cases. The justices were concerned, among other things, with the amercement of sureties whose charges had fled. In a few instances the name of the fugitive is given; where so he may also appear among those for whose chattels the sheriff accounted. In Norfolk sureties in the hundred of Loddon owed 1 mark for Edwin Balloc;[2] Edwin had fled for the sheriff accounted for 17*s*. 9*d*. for his chattels.[3] In Suffolk the men of Monewden owed 1 mark as sureties of Wigar; Wigar had fled and the sheriff accounted for 3*s*. for his chattels.[4] In Huntingdonshire Terri and the tithing of Hugh Fullo owed 1 mark; Hugh had fled and the sheriff accounted for 9*s*. 7*d*. for his chattels.[5] In Hampshire four tithings were amerced for four named fugitives and the chattels of all four were accounted for by the sheriff; three men were also in mercy for allowing William Hay to escape and the sheriff rendered 15*s*. for William's chattels.[6] These entries put the question beyond serious doubt. The justices were trying the accused under the Assize; the sheriffs were simply rendering account for the chattels of those who had fled or been condemned before the justices. The records could be interpreted as arising from two distinct legal procedures only if it could be shown that the amercement of sureties who were found by the sheriffs or local justices to have failed in their duty, was postponed until the arrival of the justices in eyre. There is nothing to substantiate this. The order in which the information is recorded on the pipe roll is irrelevant to the issue. The sheriff's account usually appears first presumably because it was rendered to the Exchequer first; the submission of the justices had to wait on the return of their rolls or estreats. If the order were to be taken as establishing that local officials conducted an earlier and separate operation which the justices later supervised, it would be difficult to

---

[1] *Dialogus de Scaccario*, ed. Charles Johnson (Nelson's Medieval Texts, 1950), pp. 97–8.   [2] *Pipe Roll 12 Henry II*, p. 31.   [3] Ibid., p. 34.
[4] Ibid., pp. 31, 33.   [5] Ibid., pp. 86, 87.   [6] Ibid., p. 108.

provide an explanation of the Norfolk and Suffolk account where the returns of the justices are entered first.[1] There are even more striking divergencies from the usual pattern. The justices enforced the Assize in Northumberland in 1166,[2] but it was not until Michaelmas 1169 that account was rendered for the sale of chattels for this and earlier years.[3]

Geoffrey de Mandeville and Richard de Lucy visited the eastern half of the realm only; the western limit of their eyre was marked by the borders of Sussex,[4] Surrey, Buckinghamshire, Northamptonshire,[5] Warwickshire, Leicestershire, Derbyshire, Yorkshire, and Northumberland. No visitation was recorded for the whole of the central, western, and south-western counties of the realm or for London and Middlesex. Nevertheless, sheriffs rendered account in these shires for the chattels of fugitives and those condemned by the ordeal. On the Shropshire account it was noted that the sheriff rendered no account for the chattels of fugitives because the Assize concerning them was not held in that county.[6] This exception suggests that the Exchequer had summoned all sheriffs to account and expected them to do so.

These facts suggest three obvious possibilities. First, it could be argued that the sheriffs followed the strict letter of the Assize of Clarendon and that these cases were transferred to the eyre taking place in the eastern half of the country. There is nothing in the accounts to support this and it is inherently unlikely. It can scarcely be assumed that the sheriff of Devon sought out the itinerant justices to deal with the six criminals for whose chattels he accounted.[7] Secondly, it could be argued that the western half of the country was visited by an eyre which is not recorded in the rolls. This again is inherently unlikely. That justices might fail to return their rolls or estreats is possible, but it would go beyond reasonable probability to assume that this occurred in the case of an eyre which also left no other trace in fines or incidental references. Moreover, it is certain that the sheriff of Gloucestershire accounted for chattels in 1166 and equally certain that the eyre enforcing the Assize of Clarendon in that county took place in 1168–9.[8] A third possibility is that the Assize

---

[1] *Pipe Roll 12 Henry II*, pp. 30–1, 33–4.   [2] Ibid., p. 76.
[3] *Pipe Roll 15 Henry II*, p. 132.
[4] For the Sussex account compare *Pipe Roll 12 Henry II*, p. 92, and *Pipe Roll 13 Henry II* (P.R.S., 1889), p. 38.
[5] For the Northamptonshire and Rutland accounts, see *Pipe Roll 12 Henry II*, pp. 65–6; *Pipe Roll 13 Henry II*, p. 116.
[6] *Pipe Roll 12 Henry II*, p. 60.
[7] Ibid., p. 96.   [8] Ibid., p. 79; *Pipe Roll 15 Henry II*, pp. 115–18.

was enforced locally by sheriffs or local justiciars without the intervention of justices in eyre. There can be little doubt that this is what happened. All the sheriffs' accounts in 1166 were headed 'de catallis fugitivorum et eorum qui perierunt in Judicio Aquae'. This was Exchequer common form, and hence it could be maintained that local action was limited to preliminary inquiries by the sheriffs resulting in flights but not trial or punishment of criminals.[1] However, there is some evidence that local action might not be so restricted. The privileges of the Londoners, despite their diminution at the hands of Henry II, were still sufficient to permit the sheriffs to deal with pleas of the Crown;[2] their allowances included charges for putting thirty-four men to the ordeal, mutilating fourteen and hanging fourteen.[3] Municipal privilege may have made these exceptional.[4] No such reservation applies to Wiltshire where the sheriff was allowed 5*s.* for ordeal pits 'for the judgement of robbers', and 20*s.* for payment to the priests who blessed them.[5] There were also pits at Oxford where 3*s.* 6*d.* was allowed for the priest's blessing.[6] It is unlikely that pits dug and blessed were not put to their intended use. They were certainly used in Worcestershire, for there the sheriff accounted for the chattels of an unknown man who had failed at the ordeal and suffered mutilation.[7] In some counties, therefore, the Assize was apparently enforced despite the absence of the itinerant justices.

This seems to undermine the arguments presented above, for if accounts for chattels appear apart from a judicial visitation, then not all the accounts for chattels from those counties which the judges visited need to be related necessarily to their visit. Such logic misleads. Accounts for chattels appear on ten accounts which fail to record a visitation. The number of condemned is stated or may be calculated in nine cases. Oxfordshire totalled 12, Berkshire 11, Gloucestershire 8, Worcestershire 1. The total of condemned for these nine accounts, covering London and nine counties was 54: an average of 6 per account. Of the shires visited by the justices the

---

[1] This is Miss Hurnard's view, op. cit., 403–4.

[2] Henry's charter of 1155 deprived the citizens of their right to elect their sheriff and justice but allowed them to answer pleas of the Crown according to the ancient custom of the city (J. H. Round, *Geoffrey de Mandeville*, pp. 367 ff.).

[3] *Pipe Roll 12 Henry II*, p. 131.

[4] For similar action by the sheriffs of London in later years see *Pipe Roll 14 Henry II*, p. 2; *Pipe Roll 15 Henry II*, p. 170.

[5] *Pipe Roll 12 Henry II*, p. 72.

[6] Ibid., p. 117.   [7] Ibid., p. 82.

lowest returns were 6 for Rutland and 11 for Surrey. Bedfordshire yielded 12, Buckinghamshire 15, Kent 27, Sussex 28, Lincolnshire 30, Norfolk and Suffolk 101. Leaving Yorkshire aside as a special case, the total returns for chattels on eleven accounts covering 17 counties was 363, or 33 per account. The sheriffs of Wiltshire, Worcestershire, Hampshire, and London and Middlesex, failed to match, and the sheriffs of Staffordshire and Devon to exceed, the numbers accounted for by the sheriff of Rutland. This is a startling contrast. It confirms the view that there was no eyre in the western half of the realm; it reinforces the argument that the accounts for chattels and the visit of the justices were intimately related in the eastern half.[1] This relationship was more than a matter of account; it was not the justices' but the Exchequer's task to ensure that sheriffs accounted for the chattels which they had sold. It was a matter of execution; the Assize was enforced much more effectively in those counties which the justices visited; it seems inescapable that the justices were the men responsible.[2]

The evidence for one county, Yorkshire, is altogether exceptional.[3] Most of the amercements returned by the justices for other counties arose directly from the enforcement of the Assize. They are stated to be *pro murdro, pro plegio fugitivi, pro homine sine plegio, pro defalta,* and the like. The Yorkshire return does not fit at all easily into this pattern. It includes some amercements *pro defectu* or *quia defecit* and some *pro plegio,* but none at all *pro murdro.* Much the most frequent entry on the Yorkshire account was *pro placito coronae celato;* there are nine entries of this kind as against one only on the accounts of all the other shires.[4] This suggests that in Yorkshire the justices were following up an earlier enforcement of the Assize. Two entries put this beyond

---

[1] The accounts must be affected to some degree by the distribution of population. This no doubt contributed to the very high return from Norfolk and Suffolk. Population distribution, however, can scarcely account for the sharpness of the contrast between Hampshire (4) and Sussex (28), or Worcestershire (1) and Warwickshire and Leicestershire (32), or generally between west and east. Compare, moreover, the high return for the heavily populated counties of Norfolk and Suffolk (101) with the even higher return for Yorkshire (120) which was less densely populated. On Yorkshire see below, pp. 105–6.

[2] The Gloucestershire accounts are of some interest on this point. The sheriff accounted for the chattels of eight criminals or fugitives in 1166 (*Pipe Roll 12 Henry II,* p. 79). In 1168–9 Guy, dean of Waltham, and William Basset visited the county to enforce the Assize of Clarendon. There were many condemned for whose chattels the sheriff rendered no account. Even so he presented an account for 14 (*Pipe Roll 15 Henry II,* pp. 115–18).   [3] *Pipe Roll 12 Henry II,* pp. 46–9.

[4] Nottinghamshire and Derbyshire (ibid., p. 57).

serious doubt. In Harthill wapentake seventeen men were penalized 'pro quodam homine qui fugit pro alia assisa et rediit et non monstraverunt Justiciis'.[1] It is possible but unlikely that the *alia assisa* was something other than the Assize of Clarendon. Even less doubt arises in the second case: in Birdforth wapentake the soke of Allerton was in mercy for 10 marks 'pro homine quem posuerunt ad aquam sine serviente Regis'.[2]

It seems likely therefore that the Assize of Clarendon was executed in the west without, and in Yorkshire before, the intervention of itinerant justices. It is equally clear that its enforcement was sporadic and ineffective in those counties not visited by the justices. These varied procedures seem to contradict caps. 4 and 5 of the Assize. Nevertheless, the dismissal of the text is not the only possible circumvention of the difficulty. Only the relatively strict divisions of a later age permit the assumption that judgement was restricted to the justices and that the sheriffs were officers of the court and no more. It was still thought necessary in 1215 to lay down that sheriffs should not hold pleas of the Crown.[3] Indeed cap. 1 of the Assize of Clarendon provides that the sheriffs, like the justices, were to make inquiries under the terms of the Assize, and it seems likely that the sheriffs set to work, urged on by the Exchequer.[4] Perhaps something happened to delay or prevent the dispatch of justices to the west; it may be that the death of Geoffrey de Mandeville at Carlisle in October called a halt to the extension of the eyre into the western counties. Perhaps sheriffs simply saw to execution on their own, for the record bears the stamp of character and initiative. The Yorkshire returns are *sui generis*. It is also very striking that the sheriff accounted for the chattels of a hundred and twenty men, more than any of his colleagues. The sheriff was Ranulf Glanville. It may well be that his enforcement of the Assize of Clarendon founded the reputation which was to carry him to the Justiciarship in 1180.

The overriding impression of the pipe roll of 1166 is that officials were ready to experiment and improvise to secure the rapid application of measures against criminals. Administrative elasticity, not textual falsification, is the likeliest bridge between the text of the Assize and the manner of its enforcement.

J. C. HOLT

---

[1] *Pipe Roll 12 Henry II*, p. 48.   [2] Ibid., p. 49.   [3] *Magna Carta*, cap. 24.
[4] The Staffordshire account establishes that some sheriffs had begun to take action before Easter 1166 (*Pipe Roll 12 Henry II*, pp. 60–1).

V

The Early Charters of the Family of Kinninmonth of that Ilk

COLLECTIONS of documents relating to landowners of the middling sort are comparatively rare in Scotland before the fourteenth century, and for the twelfth century are very rare indeed. Such documents tend to survive only where a family had close connections with a church whose own history has been well documented. The small collection presented here is a rare survival of this kind, which throws light on the beginnings of a Fife family of the middle rank and on the cathedral church of St. Andrews with which they were intimately associated.

Twenty years ago, while making a study of the culdees (*célidé*) of St. Andrews, I tried to trace the whereabouts of a notarial transumpt of 1395 whose contents were noted by the eighteenth-century antiquary Walter Macfarlane of Macfarlane.[1] The transumpt was said to contain copies of eleven deeds constituting the earliest titles of the family of Kinninmonth of that ilk.[2] In date, these deeds ranged from the episcopate of Richard, bishop of St. Andrews (1165–78), to the time of Adam of Kilconquhar, earl of Carrick (*c.* 1266–70). Macfarlane also reported a surviving original charter issued by Roger, bishop-elect of St. Andrews (1189–98), not copied in the transumpt but belonging to the same series of titles. When Macfarlane saw these documents they were among the family papers of Sir Alexander Murray-Kinninmond, second baronet,

---

[1] *Genealogical Collections concerning Families in Scotland made by Walter Macfarlane* (Scottish History Society, 1900), ii. 531–4.

[2] I use the spelling Kinninmonth because the estate and lands of Kinninmonth (in Ceres, Fife) are so spelled by the Ordnance Survey. The spelling used by the present representative of the Kinninmonths of that ilk, the earl of Minto, is Kynynmound. Macfarlane used the form Kinninmond. The name is Gaelicized Pictish and means 'head of white hill' (W. J. Watson, *History of the Celtic Place-Names of Scotland* (1926), p. 402).

representative, through his father and mother respectively, of the families of Murray of Melgund and Kinninmond (or Kinninmonth) of that ilk. Sir Alexander died without issue in 1736, and the Kinninmonth descent eventually devolved, again through marriage with an heiress, upon Sir Gilbert Elliot of Minto, fourth baronet, afterwards first earl of Minto, who died in 1814. His senior direct descendant is the fifth earl. Unfortunately, Lord Minto was not able to help me to trace the Kinninmonth charters in 1951, and in a paper on the St. Andrews culdees published in 1952 I was forced to make do with Macfarlane's tantalizingly inadequate abstracts.[1] In 1958, however, the Minto Papers were acquired by the National Library of Scotland, and in July 1968, while working through an inventory prepared by the library's department of manuscripts, I at last came across an item which, from the tell-tale date 1395, seemed to correspond to Macfarlane's notes. To my great delight, Minto Charters 212 proved to contain the very documents reported by Macfarlane, although his notarial transumpt turned out on inspection to be a fragile paper roll on which a sixteenth-century clerk unskilled at transcribing fourteenth-century Latin texts had copied the notary's formal transumpt in an unpleasing secretary hand. Next to this roll lay the original charter of Bishop-elect Roger of St. Andrews, and in the same bundle were a considerable number of later medieval and sixteenth-century deeds anent the barony of Kinninmonth, which Macfarlane had used to construct his genealogy of the family.

The interest of these documents derives from several features. In the first place, as already mentioned, the Kinninmonths of that ilk, although of knightly rank, were in their beginnings, and always remained, gentry of the middling sort, never rising to the level of the greater baronage and never acquiring any considerable possessions or standing outwith their own county of Fife, or even outwith their own district of East Fife. But because of their association with the cathedral church and diocese of St. Andrews, the Kinninmonths are very much better recorded by documents of an early date (i.e. before 1300) than most, if not all, families of comparable status; especially if one considers families which, like the Kinninmonths,

---

[1] G. W. S. Barrow, 'The Cathedral Chapter of St. Andrews and the Culdees in the Twelfth and Thirteenth Centuries', *JEH* iii (1952), 23–39, especially 30–2.

have had a continuous existence over nearly six and a half centuries. Although—or perhaps because—they were of middle rank, the Kinninmonths could boast a surprising number of leading figures in the Scottish church. Two bishops of St. Andrews, Robert (1127–59) and John 'the Scot', who held the see temporarily and uneasily in the 1180s, had some close connection with the family. Matthew, bishop of Aberdeen (1172–99), was a brother of the founder of the family; and later members included John Kinninmonth, bishop of Brechin (1298–1322 or later), and two more bishops of Aberdeen, Alexander Kinninmonth I (1329–*c.* 1343) and Alexander Kinninmonth II (1356–80).

A second point of interest lies in the fact that the ancestors of the family and their collateral kinsmen formed one of those quasi-ecclesiastical clans which were such a familiar feature of the larger churches, especially the cathedral churches of the eleventh, twelfth, and even thirteenth centuries, not only in Scotland but very widely in western Christendom. In order to strike root effectively, such clans usually needed to produce at least a couple of bishops and enough clerical members to fill most of the greater offices and dignities of the church. Meanwhile, lay members of the clan could be appointed to leading secular offices serving the church and its ecclesiastical dignitaries. These laymen were normally infeft in lands belonging to the church. They were thus placed in a somewhat ambivalent position in relation to the church, half dependents, half patrons and protectors. This relationship seems often to have characterized the larger ecclesiastical communities, which although they were well endowed and influential were always vulnerable and anxious.[1] The position of the Kinninmonths and their kinsmen

[1] Evidence of their anxiety is provided by the letter of Pope Lucius III, dated Velletri, 28 Mar. (1182), addressed to the bishop of St. Andrews and the remaining bishops, the abbots, priors, archdeacons, deans, and all prelates appointed in the kingdom of the Scots. The pope commands that as often as they may be requested, the addressees are to do justice upon malefactors living in their parishes and dioceses who have done harm to the prior and canons of St. Andrews by plundering their property. Divine service is to be suspended wherever the priory's stolen goods are detained, and the addressees are to denounce as excommunicate all who have laid violent hands upon the canons or lay brothers of the priory until, armed with testimonial letters from the addressees, they present themselves before the papal curia (*Liber Cartarum Prioratus Sancti Andree in Scotia* (Bannatyne Club, 1841), p. 111). 1182 seems the correct year, since Pope Lucius was receiving a distinguished

at St. Andrews was all the more striking because the church itself formed an Augustinian priory served by a prior and convent of canons-regular. On the other hand, the see of St. Andrews had a quasi-primatial character as the premier episcopal office in the Scottish kingdom, and as such it was far too important to be left alone and independent by the Crown.

Other features possessed by this collection of documents are that it contains the only surviving charter of infeftment (*anglice*, enfeoffment) issued by the culdees of St. Andrews (No. 2); includes no fewer than four acts of King William the Lion (Nos. 4, 6, 8, 9) previously known only from Macfarlane's abstracts; and contains a bull of Innocent III for a relatively obscure layman (No. 11). In addition, the documents throw a little more light upon the household of the bishops of St. Andrews and on the domestic arrangements of the cathedral priory.

The starting-point for the genealogy of the Kinninmonths of that ilk seems to be provided by a certain Michael, recorded only as the father of Simon son of Michael, a contemporary of Kings David I and Malcolm IV, and a landholder in Fife.[1] Simon son of Michael and his son Alan may be regarded as the ancestors of the Kinnears of that ilk, an East Fife family who were benefactors of the hospital at St. Andrews and of the cathedral priory,[2] and also of Balmerino Abbey.[3] Alan son of Simon was still living in the period 1189–98.[4] The Simon 'of Kinnear' who gave Torkedlock (in Logie) to Balmerino Abbey *c.* 1230–40 was either his son or his grandson.[5] This Simon was succeeded by his son Simon,[6] from whom the descent of the Kinnears of that ilk may be traced

---

Scottish mission in March of that year (*Annals of the Reigns of Malcolm and William, Kings of Scotland,* ed. A. C. Lawrie (Glasgow, 1910), pp. 242–5).

[1] *Early Scottish Charters prior to 1153,* ed. A. C. Lawrie (Glasgow, 1905), no. 267 (for the hospital at St. Andrews); *Regesta Regum Scottorum,* ed. G. W. S. Barrow and others (Edinburgh, 1960–   ), i, no. 138.

[2] *Liber S. Andree,* pp. 212, 292.

[3] *Liber Sancte Marie de Balmorinach* (Abbotsford Club, 1841), no. 39.

[4] *Liber S. Andree,* pp. 149–52. For Alan son of Simon, also called Alan brother of Matthew (archdeacon and bishop), cf. ibid., pp. 126–7, 137, 212–18, 244, 306–7, 324–5; *Registrum Episcopatus Aberdonensis* (Spalding and Maitland Clubs, 1845), i. 10.

[5] *Liber . . . de Balmorinach,* no. 39.

[6] *Liber S. Andree,* p. 292.

reasonably clearly.[1] In addition to Alan, Simon son of Michael seems to have had three other sons: (1) Matthew, who was archdeacon of St. Andrews from *c.* 1150 to 1172, when he was elected and consecrated bishop of Aberdeen;[2] (2) Odo, who first appears as marischal of Bishop Arnold of St. Andrews (1160–2)[3] and then as dapifer or seneschal, sometimes explicitly 'of the bishop', in the time of Bishops Richard and Hugh (1165–88) and of Bishop-elect Roger (1189–98);[4] and (3) Simon, described as Archdeacon Matthew's brother and appearing among clerical witnesses in the period 1160–72,[5] recorded as Bishop Matthew's archdeacon and brother after 1172[6] and more commonly occurring simply as archdeacon of Aberdeen.[7]

Although Odo may be regarded as the first of the Kinninmonths of that ilk, the connection between his family and the estate itself went back to the time when his brother Matthew was archdeacon of St. Andrews. Bishop Robert, who had been (with King David I) a principal founder of the cathedral priory in 1144, and who died in 1159, had granted to the canons the lands of Kinninmonth, with a toft in Kilrymont, by a charter dating 1147–53.[8] By a further charter, the bishop had granted the canons the toft on which had been built the house of Archdeacon Matthew in Kilrymont, with three crofts by the Kinness Burn 'of the tenure of Kinninmonth'.[9] That these all formed part of a single estate seems clear from subsequent confirmations to the priory of 'Kinninmonth with the whole shire,

---

[1] It looks as though the John and William 'de Kuere', of the county of Fife, whose homage is recorded in 1296, were members of the family of Kinnear (*Calendar of Documents relating to Scotland*, ed. J. Bain (Edinburgh, 1881–8), ii. 204, 209). The homage of Sir John of Kinnear is recorded in 1304 (ibid., no. 730, misdated).

[2] Matthew's earliest appearances in record seem to be *Charters*, ed. Lawrie, nos. 225, 228, 256, all *c.* 1150. For Matthew's possessions while archdeacon, cf. *Regesta Reg. Scot.* i, no. 120 (= *Liber S. Andree*, p. 200). For his career as bishop, see J. Dowden, *The Bishops of Scotland* (Glasgow, 1912), pp. 99–100.

[3] *Liber S. Andree*, p. 127.

[4] Ibid., pp. 134, 136, 141, 175, 180, and elsewhere (time of Bishop Richard); pp. 147, 149 (time of Bishop Hugh); pp. 45, 152, 153 (time of Bishop-elect Roger). Odo was still alive in the year 25 Mar. 1195–24 Mar. 1196 (ibid., p. 323).

[5] *Liber S. Andree*, pp. 127, 133, 179.

[6] *Liber S. Thome de Aberbrothoc* (Bannatyne Club, 1848–56), i, no. 85.

[7] *Liber S. Andree*, pp. 239, 299; *Chartulary of the Abbey of Lindores* (Scottish History Society, 1903), no. 3.

[8] *Liber S. Andree*, p. 125. The original is National Lib. of Scotland MS. Adv. 15. 1. 18, no. 12, in which the spelling Kininmuned is used.   [9] *Liber S. Andree*, p. 124.

together with one toft in Kilrymont'.[1] Moreover, Kinninmonth with the toft in Kilrymont had been granted to Archdeacon Matthew by the bishop and by Prior Robert and the convent in charters which, though now lost, were confirmed by King Malcolm IV.[2]

No. 4 below is a royal confirmation of another lost charter whereby the prior (Walter, Robert's successor) and convent of St. Andrews granted to Odo, brother of Matthew, bishop of Aberdeen, Kinninmonth by its right marches, with the whole shire of Kinninmonth and with the toft in the burgh of St. Andrews, to be held in feu and heritage of the prior, canons, and house of St. Andrews, for all service pertaining to the house, for an annual rent of two merks. No. 7 is the charter by which G[ilbert] the prior and the convent of St. Andrews regranted these lands, now listed in detail, to Odo's son Adam. This charter also granted to Adam the hereditary seneschalcy in the household and lands of the priory. Since Adam's father is sometimes called 'steward of the bishop', it may be thought that it was not until his son had succeeded him, in the 1190s, that the tenant of Kinninmonth changed from being bishop's to priory's steward. But it seems rather more probable that at first Odo had served both bishop and priory as steward, and that under Bishop Hugh (1178–88) he took office solely as the priory's steward, holding Kinninmonthshire in return for this service. From this time on we find other stewards serving the bishops: Henry,[3] William[4], and Hugh (of Nydie?).[5] And the great quarrel between the king and the priory over the disputed election of 1178, which lasted for the best part of a decade, would be quite enough to account for the separation.

The central figure in the St. Andrews election dispute was Master John 'the Scot'.[6] His election to the see by the prior and canons in

---

[1] *Liber S. Andree*, pp. 131, 143, 145.   [2] *Regesta Reg. Scot.* i, no. 120.

[3] *Liber S. Andree*, pp. 147, 149; *Liber Ecclesie de Scon* (Bannatyne and Maitland Clubs, 1843), nos. 41, 50; *Registrum de Dunfermelyn* (Bannatyne Club, 1842), no. 98.

[4] *Liber S. Andree*, p. 152 (of very rare occurrence).

[5] Ibid., pp. 45, 154, 156, 260, 319, 329, 353; *JEH* iii. 26 n. 5.

[6] Walter Bower's version of Fordun's *Scotichronicon* (ed. W. Goodall (Edinburgh, 1759), i. 350–1) has a circumstantial story that 'Master John called the Scot', despite his by-name, was English by birth, having been born in the village which is called 'Podoth' in the county of Chester. I am deeply grateful to Mr. John Dodgson for

1178 was rejected by King William, who succeeded in having his own chaplain Hugh elected and consecrated instead. John the Scot is to be identified with Master John, nephew of Bishop Robert who died in 1159, and styled in one document Bishop Robert's chancellor.[1] Master John, sometimes called 'Bishop Robert's nephew' but more often simply 'the bishop's nephew', was obviously one of the leading clergy of the church of St. Andrews in the time of both Bishop Robert and Bishop Richard.[2] Under these descriptions he disappears from record after 1178. From this year onwards, however, there is abundant record of Master John the Scot. Compelled to abandon his claim to St. Andrews, although duly consecrated to that see in 1180 in the presence of four bishops and with the consent of five,[3] Master John held the next-senior Scottish see of Dunkeld from 1183 until his death in 1203.

As well as being Bishop Robert's nephew, Master John was also nephew of Matthew, bishop of Aberdeen, previously archdeacon of St. Andrews under Bishop Robert and his two next successors. It was, indeed, Bishop Matthew who consecrated John the Scot to St. Andrews in 1180.[4] Within a few days of the ceremony, the king had driven both John and his uncle Matthew furth of Scotland, and had even had the bishop of Aberdeen's houses burned down.[5] Other friends and kinsmen were also banished or put in peril. Three of them, named in letters sent to the king of Scots by Pope Urban III in 1186,[6] were Aiulf, dean of Christianity of Lothian, Odo the seneschal, and Roger of 'Fedic' or 'Fedich'. Aiulf, who is very well recorded in the period from *c.* 1150 to the date of the papal letters,

advising me that 'Podoth' is most probably a phonetically rendered form of one or other of the Cheshire villages called Budworth, most likely Little Budworth. This village is not far from Tattenhall, and it may be noted that Bishop Matthew of Aberdeen had a dependent named William de Tatenell who may have taken his surname from Tattenhall (*Registrum . . . Aberdon.* i. 13).

[1] *Liber S. Andree*, p. 126.

[2] Ibid., pp. 124–5, 134, 136, 139–41; *Registrum de Dunfermelyn*, nos. 90, 91, 94, 97; *Liber Cartarum Sancte Crucis* (Bannatyne Club, 1840), no. 19 and Appendix II, no. 4; *Liber S. Marie de Calchou* (Bannatyne Club, 1846), nos. 420, 448.

[3] *Chronica Magistri Rogeri de Houedene*, ed. W. Stubbs (R.S., 1868–71), ii. 210.

[4] Ibid., ii. 212; *The Chronicle of Melrose*, ed. A. O. Anderson and others (1936), p. 43.

[5] *Gesta Regis Henrici Secundi* ('Benedict of Peterborough'), ed. W. Stubbs (R.S., 1867), i. 265.

[6] *Chron. Houedene*, ii. 312, 313: 'clerks, friends, and kinsmen' of the bishop of Dunkeld.

was probably the Aiulf who had been chaplain to Bishop Robert.[1]
Odo the seneschal was, of course, Bishop Matthew's brother. Conceivably, he was also John the Scot's father, for the personal name
John was borne by Odo's grandson and by later Kinninmonths.
But as far as our evidence goes, John might have been a son of Alan
son of Simon, or of an unrecorded daughter of Simon son of Michael.
It is hardly possible that Bishop Robert and Bishop Matthew were
brothers, for the former was already an old man in 1156,[2] three
years before his death, while the latter survived until 1199. Conse-
quently, we must infer that either a daughter of Simon son of
Michael married a brother of Bishop Robert,[3] or that Alan or his
brother Odo married a sister of Bishop Robert. As for Roger 'of
Fedich', it seems clear that he was the Roger who held the lands of
Feddinch (in Cameron, south of St. Andrews) as a tenant of St.
Andrews priory in the time of Prior Walter.[4] Roger had a son
Richard to whom Feddinch was confirmed by Prior Gilbert,[5] and
it will be noted that No. 10 below, dating 1198–9, was witnessed
by Richard 'of Feddinsche'. It is not certain that Roger used the
name Feddinch in the form of a surname, and what relationship,
if any, there was between him and the bishops Matthew and John
is unknown. A Roger of Wilton, sometimes called Roger the knight
of Wilton, is recorded in association with Matthew both when he
was archdeacon and when he was bishop of Aberdeen,[6] but it is
doubtful whether he was identical with Roger of Feddinch.

---

[1] J. Raine, *The History and Antiquities of North Durham* (London, 1852), Appendix,
nos. 447–8, charters of Bishop Robert in which Aiulf (Aulfus) is styled chaplain;
probably earlier in date than other charters of the same bishop where Aiulf is styled
dean. References to Aiulf as dean are too numerous to be listed here: they have been
collected in D. E. R. Watt, *Fasti Ecclesiae Scoticanae Medii Aevi* (Scottish Record
Society, 1969); and cf. G. W. S. Barrow, 'A Twelfth-Century Newbattle Document',
The Scottish Historical Review, xxx (1951), 44 (A.D. 1170).

[2] *Annals*, ed. Lawrie, pp. 24–5.

[3] Presumably not the bishop's uterine brother Robert, parson of Tynninghame
and afterwards a canon of St. Andrews (*Chronicles of the Picts: Chronicles of the Scots*, ed.
W. F. Skene (Edinburgh, 1867), p. 193).

[4] *Liber S. Andree*, p. xxv, no. 3. Walter was prior from 1160 probably to *c.* 1196.

[5] Ibid., p. xxv, no. 2. Gilbert was prior for only a very short period, *c.* 1196–8. A
Matthew de Feding' witnessed a charter granted to St. Andrews priory in 1266
(ibid., p. 109), while a Matthew de Kynynmond witnessed no. 14 below.

[6] Roger of Wilton witnessed *acta* of Bishop Arnold of St. Andrews, *Liber S. Andree*,
pp. 127 (anent Archdeacon Matthew), 128; *acta* of Bishop Hugh, ibid., pp. 147, 149;
a confirmation by King Malcolm IV, in company with Archdeacon Matthew; and

Odo, recipient of five of the charters printed here, seems to have died about 1195. There is ample record of his son and heir Adam, who on occasion used the surname 'of Kinninmonth'[1] and received six of the charters in this collection (besides figuring largely in two others). Elias of Kinninmonth, appearing in documents of the 1220s, was evidently a younger son of Odo.[2] Sir Adam, living presumably at 'Kinninmonth where the hall is',[3] survived until the episcopate of David Bernham, bishop of St. Andrews (1240–53), but he seems to have died during this period, and was succeeded by his son and heir John. John in turn had been succeeded before the date of No. 14 (?1266–70) by Elias of Kinninmonth, to whom the lands of Balgrummo in Scoonie were granted by Adam, earl of Carrick. Elias of Kinninmonth and his son Odo witnessed a confirmation by William Comyn, provost of the chapel-royal of St. Mary of the Rock, St. Andrews, dating *c.* 1290.[4] Odo of Kinninmonth, a tenant of the bishop of St. Andrews in the county of Fife, did homage to Edward I of England in 1296,[5] and in 1303 Adam of Kinninmonth served as a juror on an inquest into the lands of Bruckly (in Leuchars) and Nydie (in St. Andrews), Fife.[6]

a grant by King William I dated at St. Andrews, ibid., pp. 203, 228. Roger the knight of Wilton witnessed two *acta* of Matthew as bishop of Aberdeen, ibid., pp. 298–9 (respectively with Odo the steward and 'Adam our nephew', i.e. Odo's son). But presumably this Roger of Wilton was the man of that name who witnessed several acts of King William, and despite a probable connection with the county of Fife it seems unlikely that he was identical with the Roger who held Feddinch.

[1] *Liber . . . de Aberbrothoc*, i, no. 169 (1226–31); *Liber S. Andree*, pp. 271–2, 273; and cf. no. 12 below.

[2] *Calendar of the Laing Charters 854–1837*, ed. J. Anderson (Edinburgh, 1899), no. 6; *Registrum Honoris de Morton* (Bannatyne Club, 1853), i, Appendix, no. 1.

[3] A terrier of St. Andrews priory lands composed *c.* 1212–20, of which only an execrable copy survives (B.M. Harleian MS. 4628, pp. 240 et seq.), lists first among 'Terrae quas Adam filius Odonis tenet de eis', 'Kininmuneth ubi aula est'.

[4] *Cal. Laing Charters*, no. 15.

[5] *Cal. Docs. Scot.*, ii. 205 (Eude de Kyn[ne]muth'). Note also that in 1291 Odo de Kinemuthe had letters of presentation to the church of St. Santan in Man (ibid., p. 130). On the occasion of the St. Andrews parliament of Mar. 1304, King Edward I's Wardrobe was twice accommodated at Durie (in Scoonie, just south of Balgrummo) in houses belonging to Eudo of Kinninmonth (ibid., iv. 475).

[6] Ibid., no. 1350.

SUGGESTED PEDIGREE OF THE EARLIEST KINNINMONTHS

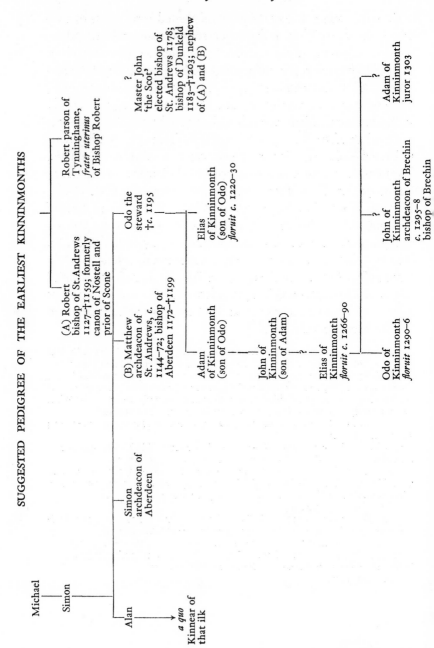

APPENDIX

Of the fourteen documents printed here in chronological order, the originals of only three are extant:

No. 5 is among the Minto Papers at the National Library of Scotland, in a bundle bearing the class mark Minto Papers, Charters Box 212.

No. 12 is also in the National Library, among the Denmylne Charters (MS. Adv. 15. 1. 18, no. 20).

No. 13 (and Plate 2) is in H.M. General Register House, Edinburgh (Scottish Record Office, Register House Charters, no. 27).

The remaining documents (nos. 1–4, 6–11, 14) are taken from a sixteenth-century copy on paper of a notarial transumpt of 1395, which is also preserved in the same bundle of Minto Papers as No. 5 above.

In editing the three originals the scribes' punctuation and use of capitals have been retained; in the remainder, punctuation is editorial, and the use of u and v has been modernized. Letters omitted by marks of contraction or suspension are shewn in italics. In the paper copy, the protocol and eschatocol of the notarial transumpt are given as follows:

In dei nomine amen. Anno a nativitate eiusdem millesimo tricentesimo nonagesimo quinto, indictione sexta ac die vicesimo mensis Octobris pontificatus sanctissimi in Christo patris ac domini nostri Domini Benedicti divina providentia pape octodecimi [*sic*] anno secundo. In mei notarii publici ac testium subscriptorum presentia constitutus, potens dominus Eliseus de Kynnynmound dominus eiusdem quasdam evidentias et cartas bene et integre sigillatas, sanas, integras, non rasas non abolitas nec in aliqua sui parte vitiatas, et omni prorsus vitio et suspitione carentes, formas que sequuntur continentes presentavit, quas per me notarium infrascriptum publicum legi fecit, quarum tenores sequuntur in his verbis.

Post quarum quidem evidentiarum et cartarum lecturam, dictus Eliseus a me notario publico requisivit ut dictas suas evidentias et cartas sub manu publica redigerem, propter diversa pericula, viz. ignis et aque vel huiusmodi iminentia [*sic*] in futurum. Acta fuerunt haec apud Cuprum in Fyff, sub anno, die, indictione et mense quibus supra, presentibus honestis viris fratre Johanne de Dunbar, priore fratrum capelle beate Catherine iuxta Cuprum, Willelmo de Ferny, Wilelmo Ydel, Johanne de Arous, Wilelmo filio

Roberti burgensibus de Cupro in Fyff, et pluribus aliis testibus ad premissa vocatis specialiter et rogatis.

Sic subscribitur.

Et Ego, Nicolaus Allattes, clericus Sancti Andree dioc*esis*, publicus auctoritate apostolica notarius, premissis in omnibus et singulis dum ut premittitur agerentur et fierent, una cum prenominatis testibus presens fui, eaque sic fieri vidi, audivi, publicavi et in hanc publicam formam redegi signoque meo solito signavi, rogatus et requisitus in testimonium omnium premissorum. Subscryvit (?)

1

Richard, bishop of St. Andrews, grants to Odo his steward Auchtermoonzie and Lordscairnie (in Moonzie, Fife), in feu and heritage, as freely as any land in Scotland is held by any knight, for an annual rent of 40s., payable at Whitsun and Martinmas (1172–8).

Ricardus dei gracia ecclesie beati Andree minister humilis, universis sancte matris ecclesie filiis, clericis et laicis, salutem. Sciant presentes et futuri nos dedisse et concessisse et hac carta nostra confirmasse Odoni dapifero nostro Uchthirmonsyn et Karnyn, cum rectis divisis suis et asiamentis et libertatibus, tenend*as* sibi et heredibus suis in feodo et hereditate de nobis et successoribus nostris, adeo libere, quiete et honorifice sicut aliqua terra in tota Scotia ab aliquo milite quietius, liberius et honorificentius tenetur et possidetur. Reddendo nobis et successoribus nostris[1] annuatim quadraginta solidos, xx scilicet solidos ad pentecosten et viginti ad festum sancti Martini. His testibus, A. archid*iacono* Laodon*ie*, Waltero archidiac*ono* de Sancto Andr*ea*, A. decano[2] Laodon*ie*, Roberto fratre episcopi, Johanne nepote Roberti episcopi, Roberto de Perth', Alexandro et Wilielmo capellanis episcopi, Rogero de Listoun', Galfrido clerico de Cunynghame,[3] Rogero capellano, Magistro Benedicto, Magistro,[4] Ricardo clerico archidiac*oni*, Hugone [pincerna],[5] Guidone marescaldo, Aldredo pistore.

Heading: 7. Carta de Octhirmonsyn et Karnyn

Comment: Date is later than the election of Matthew, formerly archdeacon of St. Andrews, to the see of Aberdeen; he was consecrated on 2 April 1172. He was succeeded in the archdeaconry by Master Walter of Roxburgh. The

---

[1] MS. repeats last three words.　　[2] MS. *deacono*.
[3] *Sic*; read *Tinynghame*.　　[4] Blank in MS.
[5] Blank in MS.; *pincerna* conjectural.

archdeacon of Lothian was Andrew (1164–*c.* 1184); the dean of Lothian was Aiulf. Geoffrey, clerk of Tynninghame, East Lothian (a church belonging to the bishops of St. Andrews), witnessed *acta* of Bishop Richard (Raine, *North Durham*, Appendix, nos. 454–6, 460, 461). For Hugh the butler, see *Liber S. Andree*, pp. 134–6, 138–41. Between 1189 and *c.* 1196, Prior Walter and the convent of St. Andrews granted land to Hugh the butler, evidently in the burgh (St. Andrews Univ. Library, MS. 30276).

Auchtermoonzie is the present Moonzie. The Cairnie referred to here was evidently Lordscairnie in Moonzie parish, distinguished from Myrecairnie, Hillcairnie, Newcairnie and Murdocairnie, all in Kilmany. In the 'Golden Charter' of 1479–80 these lands appear as Auchtermoonsie and Barclais Cairnie (George Martine of Claremont, *Reliquiae Divi Andreae* (1797), p. 115).

2

Gilchrist, the abbot, and the convent of the culdees of St. Andrews grant to Odo, brother of the bishop of Aberdeen, Kinkell and 'Pethsprochyn' and Peekie (?), free of exactions save for a rent annually of 32 melae of cheese, 32 melae of barley and a one-year-old pig: besides the forinsec service due to the king (1172–c. 1196; probably 1172–8).

Universis sancte matris ecclesie filiis, tam clericis quam laicis, Gillechristus Abbas de Sancto Andrea de Kyldeis, eiusdem quoque loci conventus, salutem. Sciant tam posteri quam presentes nos dedisse et concessisse et hac carta nostra confirmasse Odoni fratri Episcopi Aberdonensis et heredibus suis in feodo et hereditate Kynkel cum rectis divisis et Pethsprochyn et Petkennum[1] cum rectis divisis et pertinenciis aliis, liberas et omni exactione quietas, excepto quod singulis annis redditus[2] est iis xxxij melas casei et xxxij melas hordei et unum porcum unius anni, excepto forinseco servitio quod ad regem spectat. His testibus, toto conventu eiusdem loci, Matheo Episcopo de Aberdon', Waltero priore de Sancto Andrea, Comite Duncano, Nes filio Wilielmi, Maduchyn et Gyllechrist filiis Machasal,[3] Roberto de Cambun,[4] Adam de Syres, Willelmo de Hoddum', Gilemichel filio Fogan', Malcolmo filio Gilmychel.

Heading: 4. Carta de Kynkel, Pethsprochyn et Petkennun[1]

Comment: According to a mid twelfth-century account of the church of St. Andrews (*Chron. Picts-Scots*, p. 188), the culdee community numbered

---

[1] For *Petkennin.*
[3] Or *Machasat.*

[2] *Sic*; for *reddendum?*
[4] *Sic*; for *Camboc?*

thirteen, *per successionem carnalem*, holding a little inferior property communally but their better property individually. David I intended this community to be absorbed by the Augustinian priory, founded in 1144 (Lawrie, *Charters*, no. 233); but it was still distinct in the reign of Malcolm IV (*Liber S. Andree*, p. 203); and Ewin the abbot, presumably a predecessor of Gilchrist, witnessed a charter of Bishop Richard dating 1165–9 (ibid., p. 133). Madethin and Gilchrist, sons of Methuselah, witnessed charters of Earl Duncan of Fife and Walter lord of Lundin (ibid., pp. 242–4, 264). Fogan may be an error for Sogan; Soen *dux* occurs in a St. Andrews context in 1128 (ibid., 117).

Pethsprochyn is unidentified: it appears as 'Petsporgin' in an agreement of *c.* 1198 between Prior Gilbert and the culdees (ibid., p. 318), associated with Kinkell and 'Petkennin', probably Peekie, beside the Kenly Burn, at the eastern end of St. Andrews parish.

For comparable rents measured in *melae* of cheese, barley (and malt), and in pigs, cf. ibid., pp. 43, 117, 317.

3

Richard, bishop of St. Andrews, confirms to Odo his steward Kinkell, 'Pethsprochyn' and Peekie (?), to be held of the culdees of St. Andrews (1165–78, probably 1172–8).

Ricardus dei gracia Sanctiandree humilis minister, universis sancte matris ecclesie filiis, clericis et laicis, salutem. Sciant tam posteri quam presentes nos concessisse et hac carta nostra confirmasse Odoni dapifero nostro in feodo et hereditate Kynkel et Pethsprochyn et Petkeynun cum rectis divisis suis et pertinenciis et asiamentis, tenen*dum* sibi et heredibus suis in feodo et hereditate de kyldeis de Sancto Andrea, liberas et quietas ab omni exactione et consuetudine excepto redditu de kyldeis de prenominatis terris debito, sicut supra[1] chyrographum[2] inter eos factum testatur. Testibus, Waltero priore de Sancto Andrea, Roberto fratre episcopi, Johanne nepote Roberti episcopi, Roberto de Perth, Alexandro, Albino capellanis, Galfrido de Cunyngham,[3] Hugone [pincerna],[4] Willelmo Marescaldo,[5] Gamello ostiario, Ricardo camerario, Elia de Wedalia, Aldredo pistore.

Heading: 5. Confirmatio.

Comment: The chirograph referred to has not survived, but this confirmation was presumably later than No. 2. William the marischal (*marescaldus*)

---

[1] *Sic.* [2] Added above line. [3] *Sic*; read *Tinyngham.*
[4] Blank in MS.; *pincerna* conjectural. [5] MS. *Mascaldo.*

witnessed an act of Bishop Richard (*Liber S. Andree*, p. 141). Wedale (now Stow) in Midlothian belonged to the bishops of St. Andrews. Gillis (Gill' Iosa) of Wedale witnessed an act of Bishop Richard (Raine, *North Durham*, Appendix, no. 454), and is known from another record (*Liber Sancte Marie de Melros* (Bannatyne Club, 1837), no. 112, and appendix to preface, p. ii); but Elias of Wedale is otherwise unknown, and the name may be a miscopying of, or alternative for, Gillis.

4

King William I confirms to Odo brother of Matthew, bishop of Aberdeen, Kinninmonth (in Ceres, Fife), by its right marches, with the whole shire of Kinninmonth and the toft in the burgh of St. Andrews, as is contained in the charter of the prior and convent of St. Andrews, for an annual rent of two merks for all service due to their house. St. Andrews (1189–95).

Wilielmus dei gracia Rex Scotorum, Episcopis, Abbatibus,[1] baronibus, Justic*iis*, vice*comitibus*, prepositis, ministris et omnibus probis [hominibus][2] totius terre sue, clericis et laicis, salutem. Sciant presentes et futuri me concessisse et hac carta mea confirmasse Odoni fratri Mathei Episcopi de Aberdoen' Kynninmon' per rectas divisas suas et cum omnibus iustis pertinentiis suis et cum tota syra de Kynninmonth et cum tofto in burgo Sancti Andree, sicut in carta prioris et conventus ecclesie Sanctiandree apostoli continetur. Tenen-*dum* sibi et heredibus suis in feodo et hereditate de Priore et canonicis et domo Sanctiandree. Reddendo inde singulis annis duas mercas[3] pro omni servitio ad predictam domum pertinente, ita libere et quiete, plenarie et honorifice, sicut carta inde confecta testatur, salvo servitio meo. Testibus, Hugone Cancellario meo, Roberto de Aula,[4] Comite Duncano, Malcolmo filio eius, Adam de Syres, Henrico Revel, Alano filio suo, Henrico medico, Hugone clerico. Apud Sanctum Andream.

Heading: 2. Confirmatio.

Comment: The prior referred to was no doubt Walter (1160–c. 1196), but his charter to Odo has not survived. Hugh (of Roxburgh) became King William's chancellor in 1189; royal acts began to be dated by the day of the month in the earlier part of 1195; those without this form of date after 1195 are very rare.

[1] *comitibus* omitted.   [2] *hominibus* omitted.   [3] *Sic.*
[4] *Aula* written over other letters, probably for *Quenci*.

5

Roger, bishop-elect of St. Andrews, confirms to Odo the steward Auchter-moonzie and Lordscairnie with their right marches, as in the charter of Bishop Richard (1189–c. 1195).

Omnibus Sancte matris Ecclesie filiis · Roger*us* dei gr*ati*a Electus Sancti Andr*ee* · salutem. Nouerit uniuersitas uestra nos concesisse 7 presenti Carta confirmasse Odoni senescaldo Vhctredmunesin 7 Karnin cum rectis diuisis suis 7 aisiamentis 7 libertatibus tenendas sibi 7 heredibus suis in feudo 7 hereditate de nobis 7 successoribus nostris adeo libere · quiete · 7 honorifice ⸴ sicuti continetur in carta predecessoris nostri Ric*ardi* pie memorie venerabilis Episcopi · reddendo nobis 7 successoribus nostris annuatim quadraginta sol*idos* · viginti scilicet sol*idos* · ad Pentec*osten* · 7 viginti ad festum Sancti Martini. Hiis Testibus · Waltero priore Sancti Andr*ee* · eiusdemque loci conuentu · Magistro Ran*ulfo* officiali · Magistro Willelmo de Hal' · Magistro Johanne de Legr' · Marchisio de Aubinn' · Alexandro 7 Johanne Capellanis · Radulfo clerico · Magistro Adam · Roberto capellano de Pert' · Henr*ico* Trutanno · Hug*one* Senescaldo · Johanne de Bereford' · Buthou' · Gospatric filio Baucan · Aldredo pistore · GilleAndr' le bracur · Radulfo Coco · 7 Gamel hostiario · Ricardo de Legr' · 7 pluribus aliis.

No endorsement.

Description: This original measures 7·1″ (18 cm.) × 4·5″ (11·4 cm.). Foot folded, with two slits for a seal tag, which survives. The seal is missing. It is in a decorative court hand written with a thin, sharply-cut pen. Ascenders and descenders are exaggerated; the long s, which is used initially, medially, and often finally, is especially exaggerated.

Comment: Roger, brother of the earl of Leicester, was elected bishop of St. Andrews in 1189; Master Ranulf was certainly his official by 2 February 1194 (Raine, *North Durham*, Appendix, no. 462), but had most probably been official well before this date. He became archdeacon of St. Andrews before 6 June 1199. Master John of Leicester became archdeacon of Lothian probably in 1200. Marchisius de Aubigny, at one time Bishop Roger's chaplain, became a canon of Lincoln Cathedral, holding the prebend of Clifton (*Registrum Antiquissimum of the Cathedral Church of Lincoln*, iii, ed. C. W. Foster (L.R.S.,vol. 29, 1935), nos. 872, 912).

Buthou' is probably for Buathach, father of Baldwin, 'the Scot', son of Buathach, who witnessed an agreement of 1199–1209 (*Liber S. Andree*, p. 329). Buathach 'of Inchmurdo' witnessed an agreement of 1198–9 (ibid.,

p. 319); Inchmurdo near Kenly belonged to the bishops of St. Andrews and in the thirteenth century was much in use as an episcopal residence. An earlier Buathach (Budadh) had been one of the leaders of the force which formed the bishop of St. Andrews' contribution to the 'common' or 'Scottish' army (*exercitus episcopi*) in 1128 (ibid., p. 117). Gospatric may have been the son of Balsan, who witnessed a charter of Bishop Robert (Raine, Appendix, no. 446). Although most of the bishop's menial servants—Aldred the baker, Gamel the doorward, Ralph the cook, and others—are otherwise well known, this seems to be the sole occurrence in surviving record of Gillandres the brewer.

6

King William I confirms to Adam, son of Odo the steward, the grant made to Odo by Gilchrist, the abbot, and the convent of the culdees of St. Andrews, as in No. 2. Forfar (c. 1194).

Wilielmus dei gratia Rex Scotorum, Episcopis, Abbatibus, Comitibus, Baronibus, Justic*iis*, vic*ecomitibus*, ministris et omnibus probis hominibus totius terre sue, clericis et laicis, salutem. Sciant presentes et futuri me concessisse et hac carta mea confirmasse Ade filio Odonis Senescald*i* donationem illam quam Gilchrist' abbas et conventus kyldeorum de Sancto Andrea [fecerunt][1] predicto[2] Odoni dapifero nostro[3] de Kynkel et Petsprochyn et Petkynninn. Tenen*dum* sibi et heredibus suis de predictis kyldeis et ecclesia eorum, per rectas divisas suas et cum omnibus ad predictas terras juste pertinentibus, in feodo et hereditate, ita libere et quiete, plenarie et honorifice, sicut carta prefati abbatis et conventus kyldeorum testatur, salvo servitio meo. Testibus, Comite Duncano Justic*ia*, Ricardo de prebenda clerico meo, Philippo de Valon*iis* camerario, Malcolmo filio Comitis Duncani, Wilielmo Cumyn, Wilielmo de Haya, Umfrido[4] de Berk', Dauide de Haya, Philippo de Lundyn, Adam de Lundin', Rogero de la Kernel. Apud Forfar.

Heading: 6. Alia confirmatio.

Comment: Presumably this was given after Odo's death; but before the dating by day of the month began to be added to royal acts, in the first half of 1195. Philip de Valognes did not succeed Walter of Berkeley as chamberlain much before 1194.

[1] Blank in MS. followed by *nostro*; *fecerunt* conjectural.
[2] MS. *predilecto*.   [3] *Sic*.   [4] MS. *Umfy^n*.

7

Gilbert, the prior, and the convent of St. Andrews grant to Adam, son of
Odo their steward, Kinninmonth with the whole shire, viz. the three Magasks,
'Inchcalk', Ladeddie, 'Incherech', 'Ballechodyn', in feu and heritage, for an
annual rent of two merks, payable at Whitsun and Martinmas. On the death
of Adam and his heirs a relief of one merk shall be paid. Adam and his heirs
shall have the hereditary seneschalcy in the household and lands of the priory as
fully as any steward most fully has his office in the whole county (provincia)
(c. 1196–8).

Omnibus sancte matris ecclesie filiis, Gilbertus dei gracia prior ecclesie
Santiandree et totius eiusdem ecclesie conventus salutem et orationes
in Christo. Sciant tam posteri quam presentes nos dedisse et hac
carta nostra confirmasse Ade filio Odonis Senescaldi nostri et heredibus suis Kynninmonth cum tota syra, scilicet tres Magaskes, Inchcalk, Ledochyn, Incherech, Ballechodyn, cum omnibus rectis divisis
suis et omnibus pertinentiis et asiamentis, tenen*dum* sibi et heredibus
suis in feudo et hereditate, libere et quiete ab omni servitio et consuetudine ad nos pertinente. Reddendo nobis annuatim duas mercas,[1]
unam ad Sancti Martini festum, alteram ad Pentecostes. Decedente
autem iamdicto Adam et succedentibus heredibus suis singuli dent
unam mercam[2] in relevio. Ipse etiam Adam et heredes sui succedendo
habebunt senescalciam in domo nostra et in terra nostra, in feodo et
hereditate, et omnia nostra ad eandem pertinentia, sicut aliquis
Senescaldus melius et plenius in tota provincia habet. Testibus, M.
Episcopo Aberdonense, Johanne Episcopo Dunkeldense, Comite
Duncano de Fyff, Comite Gilberto de Strathern,[3] Comite Gilchristo
de Mar, Malcolmo filio comitis Duncani, Adam fratre comitis,
Willelmo[4] de Haya, Adam de Syres, Henrico Revel, Magistro
Rann*ulfo*, Willelmo de Hales.

Heading: 1. De Kynninmond.

Comment: Gilbert seems to have been prior only from *c.* 1196 to 1198. According to George Martine of Claremont, Kinninmonthshire comprised Kinninmonth itself, Baldinnie, Over and Nether Magask, Arnydie and Lambies
(*Reliquiae Divi Andreae*, pp.177, 181). 'Inchcalk' and 'Incherech' seem to be lost.
Baldinnie appears to be the modern form of the place called Ballemoedunegin
in the terrier of *c.* 1212–20 copied in B.M. Harleian MS. 4628, f. 240 et seq.

---

[1] *Sic.*   [2] *Sic.*
[3] MS. *octhen'*.   [4] MS. *Willielmi*.

I have not located Ballechodyn, which does not appear in *Liber S. Andree*. East of Over and Nether Magask or Magus is Magus Muir, famous as the scene of the murder of Archbishop Sharp of St. Andrews in 1679.

8

King William I confirms to Adam, son of Odo the steward, the grant made in No. 7. Forfar, 10 March (1196–1204).

Wilielmus dei gratia Rex Scotorum, Episcopis, Abbatibus,[1] baronibus, Justic*iis*, vice*comitibus*, prepositis, ministris et omnibus probis hominibus totius terre sue, clericis et laicis, salutem. Sciant presentes et futuri me concessisse et hac carta mea confirmasse Ade filio Odonis Senescalli donationem illam quam Prior et conventus Sanctiandree patri eius et ei fecerunt de tota terra de Kynninmond, cum tribus Malgask*is* et Inchcalc et Ledethyn et Incherech Ballechodyn, per rectas divisas suas et cum omnibus iustis pertinentiis suis, et de uno integro tofto in burgo Sanctiandree. Tenendum sibi et heredibus suis in feodo et hereditate de predicto priore et canonicis et domo Sanctiandree. Reddendo inde iis singulis annis duas mercas[2] pro omni servitio ad ipsam domum pertinente, ita libere et quiete, plenarie et honorifice, sicut carta predicta[3] prioris et canonicorum testatur, salvo servitio meo. Testibus, Comite Duncano, Philippo de Valon*iis* camerario meo, Malcolmo filio comitis, Wilielmo de Haia, Wilielmo Cumyn, Philippo de Lundin, Rogero de la Kernel. Apud Forfar, decimo die Martij.

Heading: 3. Alia confirmatio.

Comment: Dating by the day of the month began to be used in royal acts in the spring of 1195, when the king, suffering and then convalescing from a serious illness, was in the neighbourhood of Stirling and in the Tweed valley. Malcolm succeeded his father Earl Duncan in 1204, probably in the first half of the year.

9

King William I confirms to Adam, son of Odo the steward, the grant made to him by Malcolm son of Malpatric of the lands of Denork and 'Corlkelly' by their right marches, in feu and heritage, as Malcolm's charter bears witness, saving the king's service. Forfar, 13 March (1196–1204).

Wilelmus dei gratia Rex Scotorum, Episcopis, Abbatibus, Comitibus, baronibus, Justic*iis*, vice*comitibus*, prepositis, ministris et omnibus

---

[1] *comitibus* omitted.   [2] *Sic.*   [3] *Sic.*

probis hominibus totius terre sue, clericis et laicis, salutem. Sciant presentes et futuri me concessisse et hac carta mea[1] confirmasse Ade filio Odonis Senescald*i* donacionem illam quam Malcolmus filius Malpat*rik*[2] ei fecit de terra de Dunork et Corlkelly[3] per rectas divisas suas, cum omnibus aliis justis pertinentiis suis. Tenen*dum* sibi et heredibus suis de predicto Malcolmo et heredibus suis, in feodo et hereditate, ita libere, quiete, plenarie et honorifice, sicut carta predicti Malcolmi testatur, salvo servitio meo. Testibus, Comite Duncano, Ricardo de prebenda, Philippo de Valoniis camerario meo,[4] Wilielmo de Haya, Malcolmo filio fratris episcopi,[5] Matheo clerico. Apud Forfar, decimo tertio die Martij.

Heading: 9. Carta confirmationis de Dunork et Torlkelly.[6]

Comment: Denork is at the north-west corner of Cameron parish. From an important agreement of *c.* 1212 between Prior Simon of St. Andrews and Master Patrick, master of the schools of St. Andrews (*Liber S. Andree*, pp. 316–18) it appears that Denork was divided into two parts, 'Dunorc Auiel' and 'the other Dunorc which Adam son of Odo holds'. 'Corlkelly' or 'Torlkelly' is unidentified; the only extant name in East Fife which seems at all similar is Carlhurley, in Largo parish.

Between 1189 and *c.* 1196 Prior Walter and the convent bought land from Master Malpatricus which they granted to Hugh the butler (St. Andrews Univ. Library, MS. 30276): Malpatricius, or Master Malpatricus, witnessed *acta* of Bishop Richard and other contemporary deeds (*Liber S. Andree*, pp. 133, 137, 259–60), and his son Malcolm witnessed an agreement of 1198–9 (ibid., p. 319).

Matthew of Aberdeen, clerk of the lord king, witnessed a charter of Earl David, King William's brother, dating 1202 or 1203 (*Chartulary . . . of Lindores*, no. 3).

10

Roger, bishop of St. Andrews, confirms to Adam son of Odo, the steward, Auchtermoonzie and Cairnie, as in No. 1 (1198–9).

Omnibus sancte matris ecclesie filiis Rogerus dei gracia ecclesie Sanctiandree humilis minister, salutem et benedictionem. Noveritis universitas vestra nos concessisse et presenti hac carta confirmasse Ade filio Odonis Senescald' Uchtirmonsyn et Karnyn cum rectis

---

[1] MS. *nostro*.
[2] MS. *Malpack* with mark of suspension.
[3] *Sic.*
[4] MS. *nostro*.
[5] Perhaps supply *comitis Duncani* after *filio*; thereafter a name has possibly been omitted.
[6] *Sic.*

divisis suis et asiamentis et libertatibus. Tenen*das* sibi et heredibus suis in feodo et hereditate de nobis et successoribus nostris, adeo libere et quiete, plenarie et honorifice, sicut continetur in carta predecessoris nostri Ricardi pie memorie venerabilis episcopi. Reddendo annuatim nobis et successoribus nostris quadraginta solidos, xx ad pentecosten et viginti ad festum Sancti Martini. Testibus, Matheo Aberdon*ensi* episcopo, Magistro Ranulfo officiali, Magistris Wilelmo de Hal*es* et Johanne de Leic', Adam de Syres, Hugone Senescaldo, Roberto Aberdon*ensis* ecclesie decano, Wilelmo et Waltero capellanis Aberdon*ensis* episcopi, Matheo et Michaeli clericis eiusdem episcopi, Ricardo de Feddinsche, Stephano clerico de Perthe et Wilelmo filio eiusdem.

Heading: 8. Confirmatio.

Comment: Roger was consecrated bishop of St. Andrews on 15 February, 1198; Matthew, bishop of Aberdeen, died on 20 August, 1199.

11

Pope Innocent III confirms to Adam, steward of the canons of St. Andrews, the properties of Kinninmonth, Auchtermoonzie and Cairnie, Kinkell, 'Petsprochyn' and Peekie (?), and Denork and 'Corlbelly'. Lateran, 25 March, 1200.

Innocencius episcopus servus servorum dei, dilecto filio A. Senescaldo canonicorum Sanctiandree in Scotia, salutem et apostolicam benedictionem. Justis petentium[1] desideriis dignum est nos facilem prebere assensum, et vota que a rationis tramite non discordant [effectu][2] prosequente[3] complere. Eapropter, dilecte in domino fili, tuis justis postulationibus grato concurrentes assensu, Kynninmond cum omnibus pertinentiis suis, sicut continetur in carta prioris Sanctiandree, et Uchtirmonsyn et Carnyn cum omnibus pertinentiis suis, sicut in carta continetur episcopi R. Sanctiandr*ee*, Kynkel et Petsprochyn et Petkennyn cum omnibus particulis suis, sicut continetur in carta Abbatis Kyldeorum Sanctiandr*ee*, Dunork et Corlbelly[4] cum omnibus particulis suis, sicut continetur in carta Malcolmi filii Malpat*ri*k,[5] sicut juste et pacifice possides, devotioni tue auctoritate apostolica confirmamus et presentis scripti patrocinio[6]

---

[1] MS. *justum arbitrium.*   [2] Omitted in MS.
[3] MS. *prosequentes.*   [4] *Sic.*
[5] MS. *Malpack* with mark of suspension.   [6] MS. *proximo.*

communimus, inhibentes ut nulli omnino [1]hominum liceat[1] hanc
paginam nostre confirmationis infringere vel [ei][2] ausu temerario
contraire. [3]Si quis autem[3] hoc attemptare presumpserit, indignationem
omnipotentis dei et beatorum Petri et Pauli apostolorum eius [4]se
noverit incursurum.[4] Dat' Lateran' viij Kalend' Aprilis, pontificatus
nostri anno tercio.

Heading: 10. Confirmatio istarum a Curia Romana.

Comment: For 'Corlbelly', unidentified, see comment on No. 9.

12

*William (Malvoisin), bishop of St. Andrews, confirms to William son of
Lambin, at the request of Adam of Kinninmonth, the ploughgate of land,
namely Balrymonth, which Adam holds for the term of his life from the prior
and convent of St. Andrews; to be held of Adam for the term of his life for an
annual rent of one merk, payable at Martinmas and Whitsun (1209-28)*

Will' · dei *gratia* Episcopus Sancti Andre*e* · Omnibus has literas
uisuris uel audituris eternam in domino Salutem. Nouerit uniuersitas uestra nos ad peticionem Adam de Kinigmund concessisse · et[5]
Hac karta nostra confirmasse Will*elmo* fili*o* Lambini et heredibus suis
illam carucatam terre Scilicet Balrimund quam prenominatus Adam
tenet in uita sua de Priore et Conuentu Sancti Andre*e*. Tenend' sibi
et Heredibus suis de predicto Adam quamdiu[6] idem Adam de Kinigmund uixerit · reddendo inde annuatim prenominato Adam unam
marcam argenti medietatem ad festum sancti Martini et medietatem
ad Pentecosten. Quare uolumus ut predictus Will*elmus* fili*us* Lambini
et heredes sui habeant teneant et possideant predictam terram de
Balrimund cum omnibus ad predictam terram iuste pertinentibus
quamdiu prenominatus Adam de Kinigmund uixerit · ita libere et
Quiete · plenarie et honorifice sicut karta Adam de Kinigmund
testatur. Hiis Test*ibus* Magistro Laur*entio* Archidiacono Sancti
Andre*e* · Petro et Edwardo Capellanis nostris · Johanne de Hautewise ·
Geruasio de Neafle · Magistro Stephano · Magistro Michaele ·
Galfrido de Neafle · Petro de Driburc Clericis nostris · Willelmo de
Wiuile · Malco *mo* iudice · et multis aliis.

No endorsement.

[1-1] MS. *huius* m̄e *in* (?).   [2] Omitted?
[3-3] MS. *et quasi auctoritate.*   [4-4] MS. *sanctis videat mensuram.*
[5] Here and throughout the scribe uses a crossed tironian sign.
[6] Written as two words.

PLATE 2

Charter of John Kinninmonth (probably *c.* 1240)

Description: This original measures 7·3″ (18·5 cm.)×4·5″ (11·5 cm.). Foot originally folded, with single slits for tag, but no tag or seal remains.

It is written in the well-known hand in which the great majority of the later acts of William the Lion are written, probably the hand of the royal clerk Gilbert of Stirling, who became bishop of Aberdeen in 1228. A number of other *acta* of Bishop Malvoisin are also in this hand (e.g. National Library of Scotland, MS. Adv. 15. 1. 18, no. 14).

Comment: Master Laurence, official of St. Andrews, became archdeacon in 1209. John 'de Hautewise' is otherwise recorded as John of Haltwhistle, a well-known clerk of Bishop Malvoisin. William son of Lambin, a burgess of St. Andrews, witnessed a charter of Bishop Roger (*Liber S. Andree*, p. 45) and he and his brother Andrew witnessed, with the provosts of St. Andrews, an agreement of 1212 (ibid., pp. 315–16) whose witnesses should be compared with those above. In the terrier of *c.* 1212–20 (B.M., Harleian MS. 4628, f. 240 et seq.), there seems to be a reference to this transaction in the words 'quod abscondit Ballerimuned', referring to Adam son of Odo.

13

(Plate 2)

John son of Adam, son of Odo, announces his consent to the sale made by his father in his presence to the prior (John White) and convent of St. Andrews of the land lying between St. Leonard's Hospital on the one side and the road leading to the watercourse flowing to the 'abbey' on the other side, with the buildings (a solar) constructed upon it (1240–c.1250).

Omnibus Christi fidelibus presens scriptum visuris vel audituris · Johannes filius Ade filii Odonis Salutem Eternam in domino. Nouerit Vniuersitas vestra me venditioni illius terre que iacet inter hospitale Sancti Leonardi ex una parte · et viam que ducit ad aquam decurrentem ad abbaciam ex altera cum edificiis in ea constructis ? quam fecit Adam pater meus Priori et Conuentui Sancti Andree spontaneum prebuisse Consensum De cuius terre precio Dicti Prior et Conuentus Domino A. patri meo in mea presencia plenarie satisfecerunt. Vt autem hec mea Ratihabitio perpetue firmitatis Robur optineat ? iuramento corporaliter prestito Renunciaui omni petitioni hereditatis et patrimonii quantum ad dictam terram. Et iuri cuilibet ecclesiasticum forum vel ciuile Contingenti pro me et heredibus meis in perpetuum. Obligaui etiam me dicto iuramento Dictam Terram cum Edificiis in eadem Constructis et construendis Dictis Priori et Conuentui pro me et heredibus meis in perpetuum Warantizaturum secundum quod plenius continetur in Carta patris mei quam dicti

Prior et Conuentus habent de dicta Terra. scilicet de pena et dampno et sumptibus et interesse Restaurandis. In cuius rei Testimonium presens scriptum sigillo meo Roboratum Dictis Priori et Conuentui duxi Concedendum. Testibus Domino D*aui*d dei gr*ati*a Episcopo Sancti Andr*ee* · Domino M*a*l*colmo* Comite de Fif · Domino Ad*a* archi-di*acono* Sancti Andr*ee* · Magistris Hugone dei Melleburn*e* · Willelmo de Cuningham · Waltero de Mortuo Mari · Adam de Malcaruest*on* et Domino P*atricio* de M*ukard* · Clericis Domini Episcopi · Johanne de Blabok · Germano fil*io* Leuing · Ragnulfo Hem · Laurencio · Simone · Willelmo Mirihild · Lambino fil*io* Andr*ee* · Lambino fil*io* Egidii · Burgensibus Sancti Andr*ee* · et multis aliis.

Endorsed: De solario quondam \ Ade filii / Odonis de elem' Sancti Leonardi (hand contemporary with text).

Description: This original measures 7·2″ (18·4 cm.)×6·2″ (15·9 cm.). Foot folded, with tag and seal extant. Seal elliptical with ear of corn (?) inside a knot pattern. Legend: IOHANNIS . . . INMV . . . (see comment). It is in a handsome, rounded court hand written with a broad pen. There is some light decoration of the horizontal stroke of the crossed tironian sign for *et*, and of certain capitals.

Comment: Date: after the consecration of David Bernham, 22 January 1240; before Abel of Gullane succeeded Adam as archdeacon of St. Andrews, *c*. 1250.

This document must be read in conjunction with *Liber S. Andree*, p. 281, a simultaneous notification by Adam of Kinninmonth that he has sold certain land and buildings to the prior and convent of St. Andrews in return for 40 merks which they have made available to him for his great and pressing business. The endorsement on this document shows that the property was essentially a two-storey house standing on the land of St. Leonard's Hospital. Prior John, named in Adam's deed of sale, was John White, prior from 1236 to 1258, who is said to have restored the fortunes of the priory (*Scotichronicon*, i. 368). In 1841, the legend on the seal read S. IOHANNIS DE KININMVND (*Liber S. Andree*, p. xviii n. 5).

14

Adam of Kilconquhar earl of Carrick grants to Elias of Kinninmonth and his heirs his whole land of Balgrummo in the shire of Scoonie (in Scoonie, Fife), for his homage and service, to be held as freely as Adam son of Odo ever held it; performing the forinsec service due to the lord king, and, to the grantor, the

---

¹ *de* inserted above line.

third part of a knight's service for all secular service and demand. The grantor
warrants the land to Elias against all men and women (c. *1266–70*).

Omnibus Christi fidelibus hoc scriptum visuris vel audituris, Adam
de Kylleconnech Comes de Carrick salutem in domino. Noverit
universitas vestra me dedisse, concessisse[1] et hoc presenti scripto
meo confirmasse Helie de Kynnynmond et heredibus suis de me et
heredibus meis totam terram \ meam/[2] de Balgormak in syra de Scony
pro homagio et servitio, per rectas divisas suas, cum omnibus iustis
pertinenciis suis et asiamentis dicte terre pertinentibus vel pertinere
valentibus. Tenend*am* et habend*am* de me et heredibus meis sibi et
heredibus suis tam libere, quiete, plenarie et honorifice, cum pratis,
pascuis, moris, marresiis, stagnis, molendinis, petariis, aquis, viis
et semitis, et in omnibus aliis asiamentis predicte terre pertinentibus, sicut Adam filius Odonis illam terram aliquo tempore liberius,
quietius et honorificentius tenuit aut possedit. Faciendo forinsecum
servitium domini nostri Regis quantum ad dictam terram pertinet et
mihi et heredibus meis ipse et heredes sui tertiam partem servitii
unius militis, pro omni servitio seculari, exactione et demanda. Ego
vero predictus Adam comes et heredes mei predicte Helie et heredibus suis prefatam terram cum omnibus iustis pertinentiis suis et
libertatibus et asiamentis prout superius dictum est contra omnes
homines et feminas warrantizabimus et in perpetuum defendemus.
In cuius rei testimonium presens scriptum sigilli mei munitione
roboravi. Hisce[3] testibus, Domino D*a*vid de Lochor, Domino Wilelmo
de Valoniis, Domino Radulpho de Lascell', Domino Alexandro de
Blar, Magistro Adam de Malcarstyn, Wilelmo de Ferslay, Alexandro
de Sproustoun, Ricardo de Nydyn, Matheo de Kynnynmond et
multis aliis.

Heading: 11. De Balgormak.

Comment: Adam of Kilconquhar, descendant of a twelfth-century earl of Fife,
became earl of Carrick on his marriage, c. 1266, to Marjorie, daughter and
heir of Neil, earl of Carrick. Earl Adam died at Carthage in 1270 while on
St. Louis' crusade.

G. W. S. BARROW

---

[1] MS. *concesse*.   [2] Added above line.   [3] *Sic*.

VI

The Organization of Material in Medieval Cartularies

AT some time, everyone who works on medieval charters is drawn to ask questions about the structure of the cartularies from which so many of his documents must be derived. What systems of classification and arrangement were used in monastic cartularies? What indications are there that the compilers of cartularies had what might be called an 'archive sense'? Did they see only the contents of their documents, or had they some awareness of the documents themselves? The range of answers which such questions will produce depends largely upon the number and type of cartularies with which individual scholars are familiar.[1] The purpose of this paper is to see what answers may be forthcoming from a moderate cross-section of cartularies and registers, many consulted for other purposes, and some examined with this immediate inquiry in mind. It would be easy to amass long lists of examples, each with its own footnote, but such a collection would be more impressive than useful. The method adopted for this paper is to cite representative examples of different types of cartulary, and to concentrate upon more detailed analysis of a small number of cartularies of special interest.

Archive sense, an appreciation of documents for their own sake, and an understanding of the shape of any particular archive, are not essential for the compiler of a register or a cartulary. That can be a clerical exercise, a job for the conscientious administrator who is not alarmed by the bulk of documents to be handled. His purpose may often be imposed from without. If his intention is to preserve letters,

---

[1] One who, like Miss Major, has collected *acta* from cartularies covering the whole of England, will have a wide range of reference. In building up her collection of Langton's *acta*, she drew upon more than seventy cartularies (*Acta Stephani Langton*, C.Y.S., vol. l, 1950).

the nature of his compilation is defined in advance, and he may be both exclusive and selective. Perhaps he values letters for their style, and he will then produce a collection of literary interest;[1] or, if he is concerned with examples from which to choose the appropriate draft at need, he will produce a formulary.[2] If his intention is to collect leases, issued by his community,[3] or rents due to his house,[4] this will define the type of register which he compiles. A *Liber de Cartis Pensionum*, containing forty-four charters concerning pensions[5] is one of the smaller registers at Lincoln Cathedral, while the nuns of Shaftesbury maintained a cartulary 'intended apparently as a register of rights, privileges etc. given and conceded rather than of title-deeds'.[6] Another fairly obvious method of organizing material was to consider the use made of revenues from the estates in question, and to build up registers relating to different monastic offices. At Bury St. Edmunds the monks kept a series of volumes relating to the estates of the cellarer, hostiller, infirmarer, pittancer, sacrist, and cook.[7] Walter of Frocester, abbot of St. Peter's, Gloucester, was responsible for new registers of deeds, drawn up after 1393.

[1] *The Letters of Arnulf of Lisieux*, ed. F. Barlow (Camden 3rd ser., vol. lxi, 1939), and *The Letters of John of Salisbury*: vol. i, *The Early Letters* (1153–1161), ed. W. J. Millor, H. E. Butler, and C. N. L. Brooke (Nelson's Medieval Texts, 1955), are two convenient examples. Dom Adrian Morey and C. N. L. Brooke have much of value to say in *Gilbert Foliot and his Letters* (Cambridge, 1965), especially in Chapter II, pp. 8–31.

[2] See W. A. Pantin, 'English Monastic Letter-Books', *Historical Essays in Honour of James Tait*, ed. J. G. Edwards, V. H. Galbraith, and E. F. Jacob (Manchester, 1933), p. 213. *The Letter-Book of William of Hoo Sacrist of Bury St. Edmunds 1280–1294*, ed. Antonia Gransden (Suffolk Record Society, vol. v, 1963), began as a formulary and was expanded into a more general and personal collection. It is unique as a letter-book drawn up by a monastic obedientiary.

[3] 'The Little Cartulary' of St. Bartholomew's Hospital is such a collection of leases (G. R. C. Davis, *Medieval Cartularies of Great Britain* (London, 1958), p. 69, no. 618). Dr. Davis's catalogue is an indispensable work of reference. Much of what I have to say is based upon my own use of and acquaintance with a variety of cartularies, and where I have used a cartulary in print or in manuscript I have not given any reference to Dr. Davis; I have acknowledged him whenever I have used material from his catalogue without consulting a manuscript.

[4] B.M. Cotton MS., Vespasian A xxii, ff. 60–129, is a register of custumaries and rentals of Rochester Cathedral Priory (Davis, op. cit., p. 93, no. 821).

[5] *The Registrum Antiquissimum of the Cathedral Church of Lincoln*, vol. ii, ed. C. W. Foster (L.R.S., vol. 28, 1933), p. xxxi. The volume also contains accounts *sede vacante*.

[6] Davis, op. cit., p. 100, no. 885. The MS. is B.M. Harley 61.

[7] The MSS. are listed conveniently in Davis, op. cit., pp. 13–17, and D. C. Douglas, *Feudal Documents from the Abbey of Bury St. Edmunds* (London, 1932), pp. xix–xxvii. Douglas has detailed comments on some of these registers.

The allocation of the convent's estates is shown in detail in a series
of registers now bound in two volumes. One section deals with the
monastery's churches[1] and in a second register the material was
divided according to the ten offices of the abbey, the sacrist, the
almoner of Standish (Glos.), hostiller, sub-almoner, master of the
works, chamberlain, refectorer, infirmarer, master of the chapel of
St. Mary, and precentor.[2] At another Gloucestershire abbey,
Winchcombe, a similar allocation is reflected in the divisions of
Liber B of the *Landboc* of that house.[3] Very rarely, documents relating to a particular class of people have been preserved in a separate
register. The *Carte Nativorum* of Peterborough abbey is the outstanding example, consisting as it does of 'the title deeds of
properties of men who were themselves villeins of the abbot of
Peterborough or possessed bond land held of the abbot, or for some
other reason were compelled to surrender their charters or have
them registered by the abbot's officials.'[4] When the canons of
Malton (N.R. Yorks.) used the rubrics *Nativi* and *De Nativis* to
describe one section of their cartulary, the term had a different
meaning, for they had brought together in one group all the charters
recording grants of villeins and their families to the priory.[5]

The intention common to almost all medieval cartularies was the
preservation of title deeds to lands, rights, and revenues, and by far
the easiest way was to organize these deeds on a topographical
basis. The compilers thought in geographical terms and were concerned with estates and tenements. The content of the document
was all-important, and manor and vill provided an easy form of
reference. Sometimes, as with the cartulary of Healaugh priory, 'the

[1] Gloucester Cathedral, Dean and Chapter Library, Register A, ff. 76–178. An
edition of this is planned for the Record Section of the Bristol and Gloucestershire
Archaeological Society. Part has been made available in print in very brief form in
A. T. Bannister, *The History of Ewias Harold* (Hereford, 1902), pp. 48–61. The Registers
and the deeds on which they are based have recently been catalogued: Isabel M.
Kirby, *The Diocese of Gloucester: a Catalogue of the Records of the Dean and Chapter including
the former St. Peter's Abbey, Gloucester* (Gloucester, 1967), ii. 1–22.
[2] Gloucester Cathedral, Dean and Chapter, Register B.
[3] *Landboc sive Registrum Monasterii de Winchelcumba*, ed. D. Royce, 2 vols. (Exeter,
1892–1903).
[4] *Carte Nativorum*, ed. C. N. L. Brooke and M. M. Postan (Northants. Record
Society, vol. xx, 1960), p. xii.
[5] B.M. Cotton MS. Claudius D xi, ff. 235ᵛ–237ᵛ.

system of arrangement, if any, is somewhat difficult to determine
. . . items follow a very erratic course.'[1] Often, rubrics are, by
modern standards, very inadequate. The Cirencester cartularies
were not easy to use until a modern editor provided guidelines.[2]
The cartulary of Easby priory is introduced by the laconic rubric
'Hec sunt carte et confirmaciones ecclesie Sancte Agathe', and
place-names are used as running rubrics, either at the head of each
folio, or in the margin. Occasionally the compiler was more expan-
sive and allowed himself *Kerpby incipit* or *Hudeswel' incipit*.[3] In the
Healaugh cartulary there are no folio headings, but vills are named
in the margin.

What is at first sight a simple topographical arrangement may
hide more complex features. The cartulary of Spalding priory, for
instance, includes a long section organized by place-names, but
within each place-name there is also a chronological arrangement.
By grouping together the 'acquisitions' of successive priors, the
compiler has illustrated the gradual build-up of the priory's fenland
possessions.[4] Another Fenland cartulary, which displays a similar
complexity hidden by a topographical arrangement, is the Goxhill
Leiger Book.[5] The Goxhill family acquired possessions by marriage
into the Oyry and Pointon families, and sections of their Leiger
Book consists of part of the archives of these families.

A topographical arrangement was rarely satisfactory, for there
were always some types of document which deserved special
attention. Papal documents, royal charters, and agreements of
various kinds had particular value, and the simplest deviation from
a topographical plan was to provide special sections for such documents. There can be no doubt that, as a class of documents, final
concords were treated with great respect. If evidence were needed
of their popularity, it could be provided in abundance from the

[1] *The Chartulary of the Augustinian Priory of St. John the Evangelist of the Park of
Healaugh*, ed. J. S. Purvis (Yorks. Arch. Soc., Record Series, vol. xcii, 1936 for 1935),
p. vi.

[2] *The Cartulary of Cirencester Abbey Gloucestershire*, ed. C. D. Ross, 2 vols. (1964).

[3] B.M. Egerton MS. 2827, ff. 2, 171, 190.

[4] B.M. Harley MS. 742, ff. 2–320. This forms section four of the cartulary. Section
five is also included in Harley 742, while sections one to three are in volume i of the
Spalding cartulary, B.M. Add. MS. 35296.

[5] Peterborough Cathedral, Dean and Chapter MS. 23. An edition is in preparation
for the Lincoln Record Society.

cartularies in which they are transcribed in separate groups. The Easby cartulary has a small number of special sections, each with its rudimentary rubric:[1] *Fines*; *Confirmaciones*; *Priuilegia incipiunt.* Royal charters received rather less prominence in this cartulary, for the canons were more keenly aware of the immediate importance of charters issued by the founder's kin. There is a long section devoted to the *Carte Alanis constabularii et heredum suorum,* and another which brought together charters of the counts of Britanny and of Henry I and Henry II, with the rubric, *Comites H. Rex.*[2] The canons of Bridlington arranged their cartulary topographically, and a long section dealing with estates in Holderness, though treated as one unit, was carefully sub-divided by place-names. They used special sections for *confirmaciones ecclesiarum* and *confirmaciones regum,* which they also described as *libertates* and *privilegia.*[3] Rubrics for individual documents were very brief, but they have some interest because they were, for the most part, descriptions of the documents and not identifications by place-name: 'quieta clamacio j bouate et seruicii ij bouatarum cum pertinenciis', or 'finalis concordia de sex bouatis terre', these are the characteristic formulae.

Another Yorkshire cartulary, from the Gilbertine priory at Malton, represents a sustained attempt to deal with the complexity of material at the compiler's disposal. It is divided into seventy sections, mostly on the basis of a section for each place-name, but in fourteen sections the writer has tried to deal with documents which do not fit in easily elsewhere. Privileges, royal charters, founder's kin (in this case the Vescy family), and episcopal charters were simple to organize. A section headed *De Nativis* brought together charters recording the grants of villeins and their families to the priory. The almoner's charters, agreements, *obligaciones,* leases for the term of a single life, and corrodies, were followed by detailed statements of accounts for the years 1244 to 1257. Only at this point did the energy and application of the copyist flag, for he drew up columns to continue his accounts down to 1260, but left them blank.[4]

---

[1] B.M. Egerton MS. 2827, ff. 261, 282.   [2] Ibid., ff. 152, 321.
[3] B.M. Add. MS. 40008, ff. 2^v, 229, 323.
[4] B.M. Cotton MS. Claudius D xi, ff. 178, 228^v, 232, 235^v, 262, 264, 274^v. For the section *De Nativis* see above p. 134. There are also signs of strain in the Kirkstead

One of the most successful attempts at the organization of a large mass of material on a topographical basis is to be found in the cartulary of the Fenland monastery at Thorney, the Red Book drawn up in the fourteenth century.[1] The abbey's estates lay in a number of shires, and the compiler divided his material into nine parts, six of which were devoted to estates in different counties.[2] Where the monks had considerable possessions in a single shire, such as Huntingdon, Cambridge, and Lincoln, the shire was given a separate section. In other cases, where the abbey's possessions were more limited, shires were grouped together. So, estates in Northamptonshire and Rutland and Warwickshire are included in part three, and part six covers Bedfordshire, Hertfordshire, and Norfolk. The compiler worked to a careful plan and he knew in advance precisely what range of material was to be included in each section of his cartulary. He provided an elaborate *incipit* for each part. Part two dealt with Huntingdon, and its contents were described in these terms:[3]

Comitatus Huntingdon'   Pars Secunda

Hic incipiunt carte et scripta de terris et tenementis ac redditibus pertinentibus ad ecclesiam Sancte Marie et Sancti Botulphi Thorneye in comitatu Huntendone.

cartulary (B.M. Cotton MS. Vespasian E xviii). This is a composite volume, the earliest parts of which date from about 1200, and which has been described as 'a cartulary of early date and competent workmanship' (Sir Frank Stenton, *Documents Illustrative of the Social and Economic History of the Danelaw* (1920), p. 103). There is a section for *cyrographa perpetua in curia domini regis facta*, which contains the texts of forty-two concords. A useful system of cross-reference was designed to make it easier to use the cartulary, with such phrases as *post cartas de Vlseby* and *post cartas de Lyndewode* as guidelines. A sustained attempt was made to provide indices of charters for the whole collection, some of which were contemporary, while others were added later. There is one index for a section of charters which were not, in the event, transcribed, and this has the rubric *superhabundantia cartarum*. Was this merely a means of indicating that transcripts were unnecessary, or can we see the monk responsible for that part of the work flinging up his hands in despair? (For the cirographs, f. 211ᵛ, and for the last index, f. 213.)

[1] C.U.L., Add. MSS. 3020, 3021. Miss Major made use of charters from the Thorney cartulary, together with material from the Easby, Bridlington, Spalding, and Crowland cartularies, for a paper on 'Conan Son of Ellis, an Early Inhabitant of Holbeach' in *Reports and Papers of the Architectural and Archaeological Societies of the County of Lincoln and the County of Northampton*, vol. xlii (1936), pp. 1–28.

[2] The remaining three sections are devoted to royal charters (part one), fines and compositions (part seven), and papal and episcopal charters, with material described as *De gestis abbatum* (part nine).   [3] C.U.L., Add. MS. 3020, f. 41.

This could be matched by a similar *incipit* for Lincolnshire in part five,[1] but for Middlesex, in part seven, something more explicit was necessary:[2]

Hic incipit pars septima huius libri in que continentur scripta et munimenta diuersarum terrarum et tenementorum in villis de Enefeld' Edelineton' et Totenham in comitatu Middelsex que dominus Willelmus de Iakele quondam abbas de Thorneye sua industria a diuersis hominibus strenuissime adquisiuit. Dominus Vmfridus de Boun comes[3] Hereford' de cuius feodo singulis tenencium existunt de sua gracia ratificauit vniuersa et in puram elemosinam confirmando perpetuauit.

Where three shires were treated in one part, he could add, at the end of his general rubric, 'Et in primo ad Northampton' incipiendum est.' It is a neat, well-turned phrase.[4]

It needs but a cursory reading of this cartulary to see that the compiler was completely master of his material. Not only the estates and the documents relating to them, but the means by which they were acquired were matters of immediate concern to him. He can provide useful sub-headings. He notes the charters which relate to Yaxley (Hunts.),[5] and within that group, the charters about the lands, tenements and rents which Richard de Grauele obtained for the annual observance of his anniversary.[6] There is a rubric for the vills which are not part of the demesne of Thorney abbey in Huntingdonshire, Sawtry, Folkeworth, Stilton, Chesterton, Orton Longueville, Orton Waterville, Botolph Bridge, and Grafham.[7] In a different way, marginal references indicate which of the abbey's obedientiaries has an interest in particular estates, the almoner, cellarer, cook, precentor, sacrist, and pittancer, while other estates are ascribed to the hospital at Yaxley. The compiler is aware of changes in tenure. John, son of Thomas Pecok, of Wigtoft (Lincs.) quitclaimed to Thorney two tofts in Sutterton (Lincs.), and at the foot of the folio the compiler could add that later, in the time of Abbot Odo, these were held by a certain Peter

---

[1] C.U.L., Add. MS. 3021, f. 244. [2] Ibid., f. 345.
[3] MS. *Domino Vmfrido de Boun comite.* [4] C.U.L., Add. MS. 3021, f. 285.
[5] C.U.L., Add. MS. 3020, f. 42ᵛ. [6] Ibid., f. 54.
[7] Ibid., f. 77. Botolph Bridge is in Orton Longueville.

Dabbel of Sutterton for his lifetime, at an annual rent of 3*s.* 4*d.* He gives the reference to the deed which provides this information, 'et hoc per scriptum conuentuale quod xlv^m intitulatur'.[1] Again, he records the grant of a small tenement in Bedfordshire, given to Thorney by Walter son of Fromund, and he adds the information that this Walter was the father of Ralph the chaplain and that he had held the estates which, later, Ralph gave to the abbey.[2] A certain John son of Robert received a grant of land in Bolnhurst (Beds.), but the relevant charter is followed by a note that this tenement has been taken into the abbot's hand, since John is the abbot's villein.[3] This range of knowledge could be illustrated from every section of the Red Book.

There is a thorough, and in the large majority of cases, accurate, system of cross-reference, which demonstrates clearly the compiler's grasp of his material. It also emphasizes that his interest was primarily in 'his book'. Often and again he will give a reference to documents which relate to the charter or agreement in question, and with equal frequency he can direct a reader to another section of his book. That it is, in the end, his volumes and not the original documents which are of primary importance can best be seen from the long *incipit* which he provided for the part dealing with Cambridgeshire. There, he writes of the charters and muniments issued by the bishops of Ely, together with those of the archbishop of Canterbury and other bishops. Two *acta* he cites in particular, one issued by Hervey, bishop of Ely, in 1128, the year of the dedication of Thorney, and the other a confirmation issued by William, archbishop of Canterbury. The reason for reciting these is that the correct series can thus be maintained in his book ('ut huius operis recta series obseruetur').[4]

But what of the men who thought, not of places, but of documents, and who organized their cartularies by reference to the way in which the muniments of their house were stored? At Glastonbury the deeds seem to have been stored in one or more vaults, and when

[1] C.U.L., Add. MS. 3020, f. 252, nos. 44, 45.
[2] Ibid., f. 303^v, nos. 26, 27.   [3] Ibid., f. 322, no. 73.
[4] Cambridge section, part 3, f. 1 (ibid., f. 166). Perhaps the most interesting episcopal charter is a final concord issued in 1237 in the court of Hugh, bishop of Ely, before Bishop Hugh and the itinerant justices of the bishopric of Ely (f. 174^v, no. 33).

the Great Cartulary was drawn up its arrangement was dominated by the groups in which the documents were kept.[1] For the most part the Glastonbury archive was organized topographically. The editor of the Newnham cartulary could discern the canons' archive storage from their use of duplicate entries in their cartulary, and especially from one rubric which said that a deed 'remains in the treasury of the house of Newnham among the charters of Harrowden and Fenlake'.[2] At Sawley abbey, the Cistercians arranged their cartulary by press-marks, in twelve divisions, *casae cartarum*.[3]

Without question, the Great Cartulary of the canons of Lanthony is a particularly fine example of a cartulary arranged by pressmarks. It runs to two volumes, written *c.* 1350, and it is beautifully produced.[4] A striking feature is that the compiler was aware, all the time, of the original documents which he was transcribing, and in his scale of values they were more important than the cartulary he was drawing up. In a long prologue he stated precisely what he proposed to do, and where he found his material. The priory's charters were stored in *scrinia*, one for each manor or group of manors, and each had its special *signum*.[5] This determined the form of the cartulary, for the compiler copied his charters *signum* by *signum*. His prologue begins: 'Iste prologus subsequens facit mencionem de omnibus munimentis prioris et conuentus Lanth' iuxta Glouc' de maneriis et locis suis. Et memorandum quod quodlibet manerium habet signum suum per se sicut plenius patet inferius . . .' There follows a list of twenty-eight sections, and at the end the

---

[1] *The Great Chartulary of Glastonbury*, ed. Dom Aelred Watkin, vol. i (Somerset Record Society, vol. lix, 1947), p. xii.

[2] *The Cartulary of Newnham Priory*, ed. J. Godber (Bedfordshire Historical Record Society, vol. xliii, 1963), pt. i, p. vii; pt. ii, p. 350.

[3] *The Chartulary of the Cistercian Abbey of St. Mary of Sallay in Craven*, ed. J. McNulty (Yorks. Arch. Soc. Record Series, vol. lxxxvii, 1933). They used very brief rubrics for only five of the twelve presses, e.g., *incipit octava casa cartarum*.

[4] P.R.O., Chancery Masters' Exhibits (C. 115), vols. A 1 and A 2.

[5] C. 115/A 1, f. 5. At first sight there is a strong similarity between the arrangement of this cartulary and the cartulary of another Augustinian house, Darley abbey. There, the late thirteenth-century cartulary is arranged in sections A–P, but the scheme is not maintained consistently, and it does not appear to be organized by press-marks (*The Cartulary of Darley Abbey*, ed. R. R. Darlington (Derbyshire Archaeological Society, 1945), 2 vols.; see especially i, pp. lxxv–lxxix). For another elaborate arrangement by *signum* and number, cf. the Dover cartulary (see below, p. 149).

description continues 'Quequidem munimenta in diuersis scriniis sunt posita et titulata ut patet supra et inferius plenius patebit. Et quodlibet munimentum habet super se signum suum scriptum et eciam numerum suum scriptum sicut scribitur in registro. Et sic per scrinium et signum titulata et numerum superscriptum inuenies munimentum.' A brief check-list of place-names for each section is given, and after this there is an elaborate index of charters for sections I to XXV. There is then a blank folio, and it would appear that the final three sections of the index for sections XXVI to XXVIII were never written. Initially these indices are very full, with each entry written on a separate line, and with some cross-references noted very briefly. Before long the writer begins to search for means to reduce the scale of his task. He noted, not the individual entries, but blocks of related charters. In section V he could refer to the charters of Alexander son of Sewein and others 'per xxxvij munimenta', and the same device was used with increasing frequency as the index continued. Section XX, containing documents relating to Gloucester was undoubtedly difficult to plan and to summarize. The index is laconically brief: entries run consecutively, with no attempt to begin each entry on a fresh line, and blocks of related deeds, ranging from a small group of thirteen to a large group of seventy-seven, were obviously welcomed with relief. The indexer grew intensely weary of his task before he abandoned it.

The cartulary itself was carefully written, and where necessary, neatly corrected. The large majority of charters have individual rubrics, but the rubricator did not number his charters as consistently as the prologue would suggest. Long runs of deeds were left unnumbered, and at a later date the numbers were added in a cursive hand in the margin, though even this was not carried through consistently. It was not part of the plan of this cartulary to provide general rubrics for each section, but the compiler made an exception for section XX.[1] A space was left for a general rubric which was never added, and some attempt was made to assist the

---

[1] Section VI caused some difficulty. The compiler left a blank folio, and at the head of the next folio he transcribed charter no. 6 of his sequence. He then filled in charters 3–5, but nos. 1 and 2 were never entered. The result is an unusually untidy mixture of entries and spaces, but a general rubric does not seem to have been intended.

reader as he explored this complex division. One rubric indicated a series of leases and agreements relating to tenements, shops, and curtilages in Gloucester 'traditis per priorem et conuentum Lanthonie tempore diuersorum priorum ad terminos vite et annorum et in excambium . . .', and there were two very uncharacteristic rubrics *pars borialis* and *pars orientalis Glouc'*. A fourth heading heralded a series of charters relating to shops and tenements which Walter de Boyfeld' and his wife had given to the canons.[1]

This compiler did not think in geographical terms. No matter how many places were covered in any section, he moved from one group of charters to another without giving any indication of a change. He was dominated by the archive arrangement of his muniments. He would not copy a charter in the wrong sequence, even if it was directly relevant to the estate with which he was dealing. A rubric and a few lines of the document will be followed by a short comment. In one case the charter is not given in full because it will be found elsewhere, and the abbreviated entry is not given a number because, as the writer says, it occurs on another folio where the number agrees with that of the charter.[2] A quitclaim of the earl of Warwick, relating to Hempstead (Glos.) is only given in part since it does not run in the proper sequence of numbers and it appears elsewhere in the right place.[3] In yet another instance, the compiler had to omit a charter, and when he left a space for the missing document he was careful not to use the number which should be assigned to that deed.[4]

The Great Cartulary of Lanthony, then, was a collection of transcripts for regular use, but it was also a faithful reflection of the collection of charters in the canons' archive. This is demonstrated most clearly by the system of cross-reference adopted in this cartulary. A small number of charters issued by the founder and his kin

[1] C. 115/A 2, ff. 113, 137, 148, 161.

[2] C. 115/A 1, I [no. 89a]. 'Cuius carte copia non hic tota scripta est quia inferius cum aliis cartis et copiis eandem materiam tangentibus numero cxxiij. Et copia non hic currit in numero quia ibidem videlicet inferius et sic numerus concordat ibidem cum carta.'

[3] C. 115/A 1, I [no. 113a]. 'Non currit hic in numero quia superius numero lj cum aliis cartis diuersorum comitum de Warewyk' eandem materiam tangentibus scripta est et sic ibidem copia cum quietaclamantia concordat in numero.'

[4] C. 115/A 1, VII, no. 34 is followed by a blank space of nine lines, after which comes no. 36.

were of particular importance.[1] Some, especially a series of confirmations, were transcribed at the beginning of section I, but they were also appropriate at the beginning of other sections. The compiler's technique here was simple. He cited part of the charter, or repeated the relevant passage from a confirmation, and he provided a directive so that those who used his work could easily find the full text. His reference was then complete, but he went further, and provided a statement of where the charter itself could be found. A typical entry reads:[2] 'Cuius copia inuenies supra in Lanthonia inter alias copias cartarum M. de Boun ad hoc signum I et ad numerum xviij et cartam inuenies in scrinio de Lanthon' per idem signum et numerum.' Where, with the Red Book of Thorney, the emphasis is always on 'this book', with the Great Cartulary of Lanthony the emphasis is on the charter and the archive order.

Another cartulary which demonstrates a similar sense of the importance of the archive as a whole comes from Canterbury.[3] It is a composite volume, with sections drawn up by different compilers at intervals in the thirteenth century. The compiler of the earliest part could note that some documents were still to be found, while others were lost. The writer of a later section matched the number of his transcripts with those on the dorse of his charters, and noted when he was entering documents in more than one place. Where the originals were no longer available in the archbishop's treasury he copied documents from earlier registers.[4] In that respect he resembles the compiler of Glastonbury's Great Cartulary, who could note when he was obliged to work *per copiam*.[5]

This Canterbury cartulary (Lambeth MS. 1212) is a timely reminder that many volumes, as they now exist, are composite volumes, the work of several compilers. Even when one man can be seen to be responsible for a whole cartulary, there may be a

---

[1] These were charters issued by Miles of Gloucester, his sons and daughters (see David Walker, 'Charters of the Earldom of Hereford, 1095–1201', *Camden Miscellany XXII* (Camden 5th ser. vol. i, 1964)).

[2] C. 115/A 1, f. 50. This is a charter of Margaret de Bohun on the first folio of section II.

[3] The MS. is Lambeth Palace MS. 1212, which I have not seen. For the dating of different sections see K. Major, *Acta Stephani Langton*, pp. 158–9, amended by F. R. H. Du Boulay, *The Lordship of Canterbury* (1966), p. 5.

[4] Du Boulay, op. cit., pp. 4–6.

[5] *The Great Chartulary of Glastonbury*, i, pp. xii, 10, 15; ii, pp. 342–4.

calendar, a table of contents, or an index added in a different hand, while rubrics may be by yet another writer.[1] It is never easy, in those circumstances, to determine how far these elements may be part of a single unified scheme. Many indices are contemporary, and to single out particular instances like those which occur in the cartularies of Cirencester (Glos.), Leominster (Herefs.), and St. Guthlac's, Hereford, is merely to illustrate the commonplace.[2] Kirkstead (Lincs.) raises complex problems since some of the indices in this cartulary are contemporary and others were added later.[3] Some cartularies were provided with this apparatus long after they were written. The cartulary of Aconbury (Herefs.) was produced late in the thirteenth century, and its index was added in the fifteenth century.[4] Many cartularies were, of course, continued, sometimes with new sections added on a considerable scale, and sometimes with various additions made in haphazard fashion.[5] Rarely, it is possible to see a single continuator carrying on along the lines laid down by the original compiler.[6]

The immediate occasion for compiling a cartulary can sometimes be seen. Often, new registers were necessary to keep up to date, especially with changes in the tenure of estates and tenements. A cellarer's cartulary from Bury St. Edmunds, begun in 1265-6, 'bears all the marks of having been in daily use', and it has been described as 'the sort of record that one would expect a rent-collector to keep'. Another Bury register was drawn up by John of Lakenheath because of the loss by theft of some of the abbey's registers and

[1] Marginal annotations, of course, could be still later additions, but these are divorced from the compiler's original intention, and are a reflection of the way in which a particular volume was used by other members of the house in question.

[2] *The Cartulary of Cirencester Abbey*, i, pp. xiv, xv, 1; Leominster, B.M. Cotton MS. Domitian A iii, which may be compared with the cartularies of its parent house, Reading abbey, each of which has a contemporary table, B.M. Egerton MS. 3031 and Harleian MS. 1708; St. Guthlac's, Balliol College, Oxford, MS. 271, ff. 11-15ʳ. An edition of this cartulary is in preparation. I particularly like the tables in the Dieulacres cartulary, in the William Salt Library at Stafford, which consists of a roll with a table, followed by transcripts of charters, on both the *verso* and the *recto*.

[3] B.M. Cotton MS. Vespasian E xviii. The separate parts were brought together, and the provision of indices completed after 1259 (Davis, op. cit., p. 58, no. 519).

[4] P.R.O., Exch. Augm. Off. Misc. Book (E. 315) 55, a neat little MS. with a substantial calendar at ff. 1-12, and a table of charters at ff. 13-16.

[5] e.g. Kirkstead and Canterbury (Lambeth MS. 1212) for the first type, and Cirencester for the second.

[6] The Red Book of Thorney is a particularly good example.

muniments in riots in 1327, and similar riots in 1381 left further gaps in the monastery's archives.[1] Pride of achievement, leading to the desire for a well-written copy of a cartulary already in existence, may sometimes be suspected. This seems to be the explanation of the two cartularies of Bradenstoke priory, one written in a series of hands of the fourteenth century, and the other produced by a single writer a little later.[2] At Chester additions were made to a cartulary written early in the fourteenth century, and about one hundred years later a copy was made of this volume, incorporating the additional material in the proper place.[3] Elsewhere reorganization is the explanation. In the fifteenth century the canons of Lanthony reorganized their cartularies. A new chest had been made for documents relating to tenements in Gloucester, and in 1440 a new cartulary was drawn up, based on the original deeds, some stored in the new chest ('in novo scrinio ponenda'), and others in the old chest ('in veteri scrinio ponenda').[4] For this volume the canons were able to produce a list of deeds drawn up by Richard Steymus, and copied for this purpose by Robert Cole *rentarius* and John Machyn *coquinarius*. The chief interest of this list is that it was provided with an elaborate system of references to copies available in older cartularies. In 1449, when Richard Steymus was responsible for another new cartulary, a different method of arranging the material was

---

[1] R. H. C. Davis, *The Kalendar of Abbot Samson* (Camden 3rd ser. lxxxiv, 1954), p. xlix. The cellarer's cartulary is P.R.O., Duchy of Lancaster, Misc. Books 5 (D.L. 42/5), begun in the time of H. de Hospitali and W. de Beccles, cellarers (Davis, *Medieval Cartularies*, p. 15, no. 108).

[2] Ibid., p. 10, nos. 66, 67. I know the later of these two cartularies, B.M. Stowe MS. 925.　　　　　　　　　　　　　　[3] Ibid., p. 27, nos. 229, 230.

[4] C. 115/A 6. Reorganization seems to have been responsible for at least one of the cartularies of Durham (Davis, *Medieval Cartularies*, p. 39, no. 330). The situation at Lanthony is reminiscent of that which Richard Empson discovered at Luffield priory in 1496. There, in St. Mary's chapel, was a chest containing 'the evidences concernyng the landes of the said house', consisting of many deeds and of a cartulary drawn up some twenty years earlier (G. R. Elvey, *Luffield Priory Charters*, vol. 1 (Bucks. Record Society and Northants. Record Society, Joint Publication, 1968), p. ix). Lanthony had a much larger archive, with many chests in use. The cathedral priories had well-developed archive storage. It is tempting to discuss the arrangements at Canterbury, where the archbishop's records were kept in the treasury in the cathedral and then in St. Gregory's priory, in *vasa* (I. J. Churchill, 'The Table of Canterbury Archbishopric Charters', *Camden Miscellany XV* (Camden 3rd ser., xli, 1929), especially p. vii). The monks kept their archives in files, hampers, chests, desks, and linen sacks (*Hist. MSS. Com., Ninth Report*, Appendix, pp. 74–5; Du Boulay, op. cit., p. 6).

used, and there is surprisingly little indication that he had handled any documents on that occasion.[1]

The patronage under which cartularies were made is sometimes explicitly stated, and in many other cases it is indicated by the fact that a register was identified by the name of a particular individual. The earliest English cartularies, from Worcester cathedral priory, show the concern which Bishop Wulfstan (1062–95) had for the records of his see at the end of the eleventh century.[2] In the last decade of the fourteenth century, Abbot Walter of Frocester was supervising the reorganization of the registers of St. Peter's, Gloucester,[3] while at Meaux (E.R. Yorks.), Abbot Thomas Burton was responsible for one cartulary as well as for the chronicle of his house.[4] Of the two cartularies of Godstow, one was 'made at the charge and labour of Alice de Henley, prioress', while the second, a remarkable compilation since it was written in English, was produced by a 'well wyller' of the same abbess.[5] A late, but very interesting example, is the inventory of documents 'begun, 1500, by Alexander Katour, sacristan, for Abbess Margery Twynyho at the advice of her brother Christopher, steward of the abbey, and completed after her death in 1505'.[6] In many instances a compilation has been identified by the name of the abbot or obedientiary for whom it was drawn up. Bury St. Edmunds and Peterborough each have a series of volumes identified in this way, sometimes by the name of the compiler, but more often by the name of abbot or officer.[7] Before 1450, Abbot William Curteys was responsible for a

---

[1] Where A 6 was arranged by press-marks, A 4 and A 5 were drawn up on a topographical basis. A 5 was known to the canons as the Gloucester Book, and contained deeds relating to tenements, rents, and services in Gloucester. The first volume of this cartulary, A 4, dealt with possessions held elsewhere.

[2] N. R. Ker, 'Hemming's Cartulary', *Studies in Medieval History presented to Sir Maurice Powicke* (Oxford, 1948), pp. 49–75, and especially p. 63.

[3] See above, p. 133.

[4] Davis, *Medieval Cartularies*, p. 74, nos. 654, 659, 660. An example from a secular foundation is to be found at Chichester, where Bishop William Reade (1369–85) was responsible for four registers (ibid., p. 28, nos. 235–8). These, and the following two examples are taken from Davis; I have not had occasion to use the records of these houses.

[5] Ibid., p. 52, nos. 462, 463.

[6] Ibid., p. 101, no. 887.

[7] Bury is notable because its muniments were eventually recorded in a series of registers devoted to the office of different obedientiaries, and no attempt was made to keep an up-to-date general cartulary (ibid., p. xii).

group of registers which still bear his name.[1] At Peterborough fourteen volumes are associated with individual members of the house:[2]
John of Threckingham, Henry of Pytchley junior, Robert Swaff-
ham, Abbots William of Woodford (1295–9) and Godfrey of Crowland (1299–1321), Abbot Adam of Boothby (1321–38), Walter of
Whittlesey,[3] John of Achurch[4] who produced a Great Book and a
Little Book, Henry of Pytchley,[5] Abbots William Genge[6] (1396–
1408) and John Deeping (1409–38), George Fraunceys the sacrist,
whose name is linked with two volumes, Roger Bird,[7] and William
Morton the almoner.[8] A fifteenth register is now identified by its
contents as the *Carte Nativorum*.[9]

Authorship is less frequently indicated. The second of Worcester's
early cartularies is still known by the name of its compiler, Hemming.[10] At Bradenstoke, the writer of one cartulary can be identified
only by his initials, T. de M.[11] Robert de Doddeford, clerk, transcribed a Ramsey cartulary,[12] and Stephen Green is known as the

---

[1] For a list of the Bury registers, ibid., pp. 13–17. For Curteys see nos. 99–104, 129, 130.

[2] The names are listed in chronological order. This Peterborough run is certainly the best I know. Six of the cartularies are still in the custody of the Dean and Chapter of Peterborough Cathedral, and are now splendidly housed, with photostats of manuscripts to be found elsewhere, collected by W. T. Mellows. For details, ibid., pp. 86–9, nos. 754–73, and *Henry of Pytchley's Book of Fees*, ed. W. T. Mellows (Northants. Record Society, vol. ii, 1927), pp. xxv–xxxvii.

[3] Whittlesey Mere (Hunts.).

[4] Thorpe Achurch (Northants.).

[5] His book of fees was edited by W. T. Mellows; see n. 2 above.

[6] Mellows habitually preferred the form *Gyenge*.

[7] Bird's book covers the reign of two abbots, Richard of Ashton (1438–71) and William of Ramsey (1471–96).

[8] *The Book of William Morton*, ed. W. T. Mellows (Northants. Record Society, vol. xvi, 1954).

[9] *Carte Nativorum*, ed. C. N. L. Brooke and M. M. Postan (Northants. Record Society, vol. xx, 1960). The first part of the cartulary consists of the *carte nativorum*, ff. 1–87.

[10] B.M. Cotton MS. Tiberius A xiii; *Hemingi Chartularium Ecclesie Wigorniensis*, ed. T. Hearne, 2 vols. (Oxford, 1723); see also N. R. Ker, 'Hemming's Cartulary', pp. 49–75. The compiler of the thirteenth-century cartulary of Worcester remains un-known, though the identity of the prior, William de Bedford, for whom he did the work can be inferred (*The Cartulary of Worcester Cathedral Priory (Register I)*, ed. R. R. Darlington P.R.S., N.S. vol. xxxviii, 1968, p. xii).

[11] B. M. Stowe, MS. 925, f. 24. At the end of section cvi of the index there occurs the bidding 'orate pro anima fratris T. de M. qui hunc librum scripsit.'

[12] *Cartularum Monasterii de Rameseia*, ed. W. Hart and P. A. Lyons (R. S. 1884–94), i, p. x. I have noted a monk of this name active on one occasion (ibid., iii. 321).

writer of an inventory at Fountains in 1509.[1] To be told incidentally in a rubric that the Missenden cartulary was written by Robert de Welwes, and that it was completed on 20 February 1330/1, is an unexpected and rare detail.[2] At Bury, in the fourteenth century, a register was drawn up by John of Lakenheath whose care of the abbey's muniments brought upon him the hatred of the townspeople of Bury St. Edmunds. When riots broke out there in 1381, and the abbey was attacked, the muniments were plundered and John was put to death.[3] Occasionally writer and patron can be seen together. The *Secretum Domini* of Glastonbury, attributed to Brother Thomas de Lamport, was drawn up for Abbot William de Monington,[4] while at Furness, in 1412, a cartulary was written by John Stell for Abbot William de Dalton.[5] At Lanthony, the work of reorganizing the cartularies of the house is especially connected with Richard Steymus, under the patronage of Prior John Garlande, but at Lanthony something more than mere names emerges. The canons had possessions in Ireland which played an important part in the economy of their house, and the deeds relating to Ireland were stored separately in their archives, and had been registered in separate divisions in the Great Cartulary.[6] In 1408, an Irish cartulary was compiled by Adam Elmeley and William Temset *procuratores dicte domus in Hibernia*.[7] A generation later Prior Garlande was at work. In 1440 a new cartulary was drawn up, by Richard Steymus and two other canons, Robert Cole and John Machyn, and it is clear that Cole and Machyn were doing routine copying rather than compiling a volume on their own initiative. Nine years later Steymus was responsible for another large cartulary.[8] It is not too much to see a small staff working on the records of Lanthony, with Richard Steymus as the canon who knew his archive in detail, and with Cole and Machyn in a subordinate position.

[1] Davis, op. cit., p. 48, no. 422.

[2] *The Cartulary of Missenden Abbey*, ed. J. G. Jenkins, pt. i (Bucks. Arch. Soc., Records Branch, 1938), pp. ix, 36.   [3] *Kalendar of Abbot Samson*, p. xlix.

[4] *The Great Chartulary of Glastonbury*, i, p. xi.

[5] Davis, op. cit., p. 48, no. 428.

[6] C. 115/A 2, sections XXVII and XXVIII.

[7] C. 115/A 8. *The Irish Cartularies of Llanthony Prima and Secunda*, ed. E. St. John Brooks (Irish MSS. Com., 1953), p. 1.

[8] C. 115/A 6, followed by A 4 and A 5.

To see a group of men working on the muniments in this way is unusual. The clearest parallel comes from an earlier century. In 1372, Robert de Welle and John Whitefelde, with the support of their subprior, Thomas of Canterbury, and at the expense of their prior, John Newenam, set out to compile a cartulary for their house, Dover priory. The loss of some muniments had caused the monks embarrassment. Fire, enemy raiders, decay, and neglect had all played a part in the disruption of the priory's archive, and the two monks were determined that all the muniments still surviving should, through their many vigils and labours, be entered into the new cartulary in due order.[1] Each chest containing charters was given a letter as its *signum*, and each charter a number, and these were written in the margin of the cartulary and on the dorse of each document. Where no reference was cited in the volume, the reader was to understand that the original had been lost and the text supplied from a copy. The compilers were conscious that they were working for posterity. In their earnest effort to impress those who might use the cartulary, they drafted a long and exhaustive account of their motives and intentions, and of the plan of their volume. It is not easy to assess the quality of mind, nor the technical proficiency of such men, but it is clear that the two monks of Dover, like the compilers of the Lanthony cartularies or of the Canterbury cartulary (Lambeth MS. 1212), were unquestionably archivists with a deep understanding of the collections in their care and a genuine concern for the preservation and use of the material in their custody.

It is both natural and appropriate, in the context of this present volume, to turn by way of conclusion to Lincoln Cathedral and its records, and, in particular, to a cartulary which was planned but never written. When he was working on the edition of the *Registrum Antiquissimum* of Lincoln, Canon Foster saw superimposed upon his manuscript the design for a new cartulary. The *Registrum Antiquissimum* is a composite volume consisting of an early section compiled

---

[1] 'omnia munimenta nostra jam habita prout multis vigiliis et laboribus potuimus presenti volumini sub scrineis titulis et locis expressis duximus inserenda.' The cartulary is Lambeth Palace MS. 241. For the preamble see C. R. Haines, *Dover Priory* (Cambridge, 1930), pp. 490–1. The same two writers were responsible for a cartulary for the neighbouring hospital of St. Bartholomew, a dependent house of their priory (Davis, op. cit., p. 37, no. 314).

about 1225, and material added about 1260. Then, at the end of the thirteenth century, 'the manuscript was subjected to a careful and drastic redaction with a view to the making of a new cartulary'. The redactor provided a table of contents, and indicated how the documents should be rearranged and what new material should be added. In fact, his plan was never carried out. It gave Canon Foster great pleasure to identify the redactor who knew his archive so intimately as John de Schalby, who had been registrar to Bishop Oliver Sutton from 1282 to 1299, and, almost certainly, to Bishop John Dalderby until 1308.[1] He died, not far short of the age of eighty, in 1333. As he finished the first volume of the splendid edition of the *Registrum Antiquissimum*, now nearing completion under Miss Major's hand, Foster thought especially of Schalby 'who classified, transcribed and helped to preserve the archives, and showed an eager desire to record what he had seen or had been able to discover'. His purpose was clear, 'that those who were living as well as those who were to come, might have certain knowledge of the past which is needed for the wise administration of the church of Lincoln'.[2] What John de Schalby was doing in the rich collection of Lincoln, other custodians were doing, perhaps on a much smaller scale, for the archives of their own houses, often valuing the documents for their own sake, and, in some cases at least, finding enjoyment in the care and use of their records.

DAVID WALKER

[1] *The Registrum Antiquissimum of the Cathedral Church of Lincoln*, vol. i, ed. C. W. Foster (L.R.S. vol. 27, 1931), pp. xxxi–xxxiv. Schalby can now be seen much more clearly with the edition of Sutton's register; *The Rolls and Register of Bishop Oliver Sutton, 1280–1299*, ed. Rosalind M. T. Hill (L.R.S. vols. 39, 43, 48, 52, 60, 64); the introduction to vol. iii (L.R.S. 48, 1954) is particularly useful.

[2] Foster, op. cit., i, p. xlviii.

VII

The Registration of Deeds of Title in the Medieval Borough

ENROLLED deeds are among the earliest of English borough records, and they make up a substantial part of our material from the medieval town. They are interesting not only for what they say about properties and those who held them, but also as records of a kind that is rare in England. The customary usages of boroughs are well known to have varied from the forms of the common law but seem often to be only crude archaisms. The registration of conveyances, a precaution against loss and fraud so commonplace as largely to have escaped comment by historians of the town, represents one of the most striking differences between the rules of those privileged urban communities and the ordinary law of the land.

Elsewhere, copies of deeds were made only by the initiative of religious houses and, less commonly, of secular lords, in cartularies, private registers of which nearly 1,400 examples survive from medieval Britain.[1] It might seem a short step from a private duplicate to a public copy, but in England it proved, outside the towns, a long and devious road. There were attempts in the sixteenth century to have conveyances registered,[2] but nothing effective was done until the West Riding Deed Registry was set up by an Act of 1704.[3] The principle was extended to the East Riding in 1707,[4] to Middlesex in 1708,[5] and to the North Riding in 1735,[6] but there was no general registry until 1862,[7] and no provision for the compulsory registration of titles until Lord Halsbury's Land Transfer Act of 1897.[8] Even today the Act has

---

[1] G. R. C. Davis, *Medieval Cartularies of Great Britain*.
[2] See below, p. 154.   [3] 2 & 3 Anne, c. 4.   [4] 6 Anne, c. 62.
[5] 7 Anne, c. 20.   [6] 8 Geo. II, c. 6.   [7] 25 & 26 Victoria, c. 53.
[8] 60 & 61 Victoria, c. 65. See also W. S. Holdsworth, *A History of English Law*, xv (London, 1965), 184–6, 192.

been applied only to four counties and a score of county and municipal boroughs.

In the Middle Ages, there was provision for the official recording of deeds when it was wanted: indeed, parties to a conveyance who wanted their transactions underwritten or formally recorded had a choice of procedures. The king, for a consideration, would inspect and confirm a private charter, and it could then be entered upon the charter rolls.[1] Private contracts could also be enrolled on the dorse of Chancery's close rolls, without confirmation, a practice that was popular enough to survive the use and registration of letters-close themselves. Beyond those devices, the courts at Westminster would establish and record an indefeasible title by means of the final concord or fine, a device always available to genuine litigants, but decisively associated from the end of the twelfth century with fictitious actions, designed to convey land.[2] The fine survived upon its merits to the nineteenth century, but it had a rival in the boroughs, where from the earliest appearance of judicial records the courts registered transactions in land, and as the thirteenth century progressed, the deeds of title that ordinarily testified to them.

The existence of such records in the medieval boroughs is well known, but they have attracted comparatively little attention.[3] They seem in that setting to lack the intrinsic interest of administrative records: to be, in short, mere compilations of second-hand material. Cartularies have a unifying theme; the registers in town were records of many men's transactions, yet never of all. Freedom of devise made escheats difficult to enforce in the boroughs, and although registration was a sensible precaution, it was never made mandatory. With the king's dues, including burgage ground-rents, subsumed by the annual farm, there was no over-riding interest, like that of the lord in a manor, to insist upon a record of every change of title to every tenement. Faced with a choice between an arbitrary collection of transcripts, and the substantial private

[1] S. J. Bailey, 'Thirteenth-century conveyancing from the Charter Rolls', *Cambridge Law Review*, 1961, pp. 200–22, a paper which includes an interesting discussion of the attestation of deeds in courts.

[2] The literature of the final concord is very large, but the best general account is probably still that in F. Pollock and F. W. Maitland, *The History of English Law*, 2nd edn. (Cambridge, 1923), ii. 94–105. See also p. 179 below.

[3] Pollock and Maitland, op. cit., ii. 413 and note.

collections of original deeds that have survived, the student of town history, and still more the student of diplomatic, has some good reason to regard the transcripts as the less consequential. Enrolled deeds lose much of their original interest: their scripts are reduced to uniformity; they have no seals; their texts are often truncated. Those who search them are more likely to follow the descent of individual properties, the fortunes of particular families, than to consider the circumstances of their enrolment. Yet every record has its peculiar claim to attention, its own diplomatic.

The enrolment of deeds in boroughs is usually discussed, in general terms, in association with final concords. Borough courts, like others, licensed and attested final concords of their own,[1] but there is another and more striking connection. The final concord made at Westminster endured, despite its specialized and formidable procedure, because it conferred an absolute title, and in particular because it enabled a married woman to join her husband in alienating property without the suspicion—or, at least, without justifying any subsequent allegation—of constraint. There was always a danger in joint alienations that the wife would subsequently claim, or reveal, that her husband's wish had not been her own. Purchasers might have to buy off the widow of their feoffor in a second transaction. No ordinary protestation carried conviction; no ordinary deed, however, carefully drawn, was proof against the widow's disclaimer. If, however, a married woman renounced her title and claim to dower in a private examination before the king's justices, then she renounced it for ever.

The only other conveyance to carry such assurance of finality was a deed regularly enrolled in a borough court. By a custom general in the free boroughs[2] a married woman could assure the magistrates in private that the alienation in which she had joined her husband was made *spontanea voluntate sua*, and her disclaimer, when enrolled, gave the donee a title secure from claims 'nomine dotis, seu liberi banci, sive aliquo alio jure'. The provision was a necessary one, for borough custom often took a generous view of

---

[1] E.g. *Dover Charters and other Documents*, ed. S. P. H. Statham (London, 1902), pp. 428–30.

[2] *Borough Customs*, ed. M. Bateson (Selden Society, 18, 21, 1904–6), ii. 115–19.

dower, and the custom of free bench, in its simplest form the enjoyment of her late husband's chief dwelling-house until she remarried, gave the widow an additional lien upon the marital property. Real estate was the commonest form of investment in towns, and much depended upon its being freely disposable. Medieval burgesses enjoyed the unique privilege of devising land by will, and their heirs came of age when they could satisfy simple tests of commercial knowledge and acumen:[1] the free alienation of joint property, and an assurance of the recipient's title, was a natural complement to those privileges. It is for that reason that when Tudor governments tried to secure the registration of acts of bargain and sale, a policy the failure of which had a long and peculiar effect upon the English practice, or practices, of conveyancing, the enrolment of deeds 'according to the laudable usages and customs of the boroughs' was exempted from the scope of the acts.[2] Such deeds were specifically described as 'in nature of fines . . . whereupon women *covert* have been used to be examined', because that was their most striking characteristic, but the free borough's charters gave them an exclusive jurisdiction over pleas arising within the town. A deed duly acknowledged in their courts and entered as of record, especially when sub-tenants were brought to attorn to their new landlords as part of the transaction, gave as secure a title to properties there as a regular fine could afford.

Although the ordinary association of final concords and customary enrolment in the boroughs assumes the primacy of the fine, the usage in the towns deserves study on its own account. Whatever their origins, such registrations of title not only catered in a satisfactory way for the peculiar needs of the medieval burgess, but remained useful, and therefore lasted, until the seventeenth and eighteenth centuries. In their time they rescued a large number of transactions of which we should otherwise have lost trace. They also afford us evidence, beyond that of the ordinary records of pleas, of the workings of borough courts, and thus of an important body of medieval administrative practice. Numbered as they are among

---

[1] *Borough Customs*, ii. 157–60.
[2] 27 Henry VIII, c. 16; the exemption of enrolled deeds in London and other towns was reiterated in 34 and 35 Henry VIII, c. 22.

the oldest of our town records, they have much more than their antiquity to recommend them.

The witnessing of title is one of the oldest functions, perhaps indeed the primary function, of the borough court. We have an early reference to its principle in a celebrated passage in *Liber Eliensis*, which shows the men of Cambridge claiming that transactions bargained before them, like those witnessed by the men of Ipswich, Norwich, and Thetford, needed no pledges for their completion.[1] That claim was made at the end of the tenth century, but the principle is timeless. Whether we think of a court's authority as inherent in the community, or delegated by some sovereign power, its judicial competence rests upon its knowledge of its suitors and their transactions. The modern court scrutinizes witnesses and their evidence, the *jurati* of the grand assize and the possessory assizes attested in court to the facts, but in the earliest days the court weighed what the court itself knew. It was both private wisdom and public policy for men to secure witnesses to their dealings, and there could be no better body of witnesses than the common tribunal.

The borough court's cognizance of sales, exchanges, and it may even be, inheritance, was therefore no by-product of its written record, but rather the foundation of its jurisdiction. Written records, however, gave permanence to the common memory, and it is natural to find evidences of title among the earliest matters committed to writing in the boroughs.[2] The oldest surviving record of the kind appears to be a roll from Wallingford, now in the Berkshire Record Office.[3] A single narrow membrane, $5\frac{1}{4}$ inches wide by 20 inches long, it is headed 'Rotulus [de] captione terrarum [?in] Wallingeford anno xvj regni regis Henrici filii Johannis regis' [1231–2]. It is therefore a few years later than the earliest dated court roll there (1229) and the Wallingford taxation rolls, which begin in 1227, but like them it is a notably early example of a specialized record. It bears thirty-three blunt and tightly-written entries, the first of which reads:

[1] *Liber Eliensis*, ed. E. O. Blake (Camden 3rd ser., xcii, 1962), p. 100.
[2] G. H. Martin, 'The origin of borough records', *Journal of the Society of Archivists*, 2 (1960–4), 149–50.
[3] Berkshire Record Office, W/RTa. 1.

Johannes de Stanford capit et emit in feodum et hereditatem v sol. et ij d. redditus de Cristiano Lorimero Oxonie, tenendum et habendum sibi et heredibus suis de predicto Cristiano et heredibus suis in perpetuum, reddendo inde annuatim sibi et heredibus suis ij d. et dominis feodorum xviij d. ad festum Sancti Michaelis pro omni servicio. Pro hoc autem captione et emptione dedit predictus Johannes predicto Cristiano j marcam et uxori sue j anelum aureum coramam[1] Burg [imoto].

The subsequent entries, which refer in sixteen instances to messuages, and in the others to rents, market stalls, threshing floors, and land, vary that form only in details, but usually specify the parishes in which the properties lie.

The substance of these jottings is evidently the names of the parties concerned, some identification of the property, the consideration involved, and the services reserved to the grantor and the lord of the fee. The first entry is more laconic than most; the *ij d.* of the rent has been interlined, and it may be that the rent is a composite one arising from several properties. Ordinarily the clerk notes the parish, and quite often abuttals and the names of previous tenants. With these matters witnessed by the court, public knowledge of the transaction was complete. There is no reference at this stage to written deeds, nor is there in the similar notices of conveyances which occur in some of the early Burghmote rolls,[2] although there are deeds of this period in the archives in which the lists of witnesses open with the magistrates and end *toto Burgimoto*.[3] What is more remarkable at first sight, given the detail in which the transfer is noted, is the absence of any reference to seisin, but it appears that *captio* is to be read in that sense. The second and only other surviving roll in this early series is headed 'Rotulus de seisinis terrarum in Wallingeford anno regni regis Henrici xxxvij° tempore G. de W[?alingeford] et Johannis le Hyne prepositorum' [1252-3].[4] If *captiones* stand for *seisine*—and the second roll uses *capere* in its entries in the same manner as, though more literately than, the first—then what the court was witnessing was a conveyance in the fullest meaning of the term.

---

[1] *Sic.*
[3] W/RTb. 1-30.

[2] Berks. Rec. Office, W/JBa. 3, 5.
[4] W/RTa. 2.

There are, however, some other differences between the first and the second rolls for us to note, besides the explicit use of the word *seisin* in the title. The second is a more neatly written and a more literate record than the first, better arranged although it is written on a smaller membrane. It is also, in at least two of its seven entries, paraphrasing written deeds. The change can be seen in the first transaction, which is described in the following terms:

Johannes Doget cepit in feodo et hereditate de Rogero le Tannor unum mesuagium cum pertinentiis suis quod iacet inter mesuagium quod aliquando [fuit] Godwini filii [–]ernaldi et tenementum Humfridi le Tannor in parochia Sancti Luciani, habendum et tenendum sibi et heredibus suis inperpetuum, reddendo inde annuatim Galfrido de Chauser et heredibus suis ad festum Sancti Michaelis unum obulum, et michi et heredibus meis dicto die unum obulum, pro omnibus rebus et secularibus demandis. Et dedit in gersuma decem solidos. Teste Burgemoto.

The phrase *michi et heredibus meis* can only have come from a written instrument; it occurs in the same place in the second entry, but the remaining five follow the conventions of the first roll. If there were more examples it might be tempting to suggest that these small slips distinguished those transactions, or some of them, which were evidenced by written deeds from those performed orally. As it is, two examples out of forty would be an improbably small proportion of deeds to oral conveyances at a date which, though respectably early for borough records, is relatively late as the development of private deeds is reckoned. What these rolls do show is that the clerks at Wallingford established a distinctive system of registering titles, as soon as they established conventions at all, and one in which written deeds were of secondary importance.

The manner in which conveyances were recorded showed the recipient of the property as the leading party, and established the terms of the transaction, including the premium exchanged. Husbands and wives alienated property together, but there is no reference to disclaimers by the wives, although the first entry of all, by chance, shows a purchaser giving the seller's wife a ring, in addition to the *gersuma* for the property. Inducing a married woman to accept a consideration of that kind to engage her consent and underline her part in the transaction, was a device sometimes employed outside the boroughs, but one which would have the less force where there was a customary procedure for registering her assent and renunciation. With the record so sparing of its words, and the ways of individual buyers and sellers of property so various, we cannot be sure of the implication of the act, but the property was probably one held jointly.[1] One other family transaction on the first roll occurs when the purchaser of a messuage and stall immediately transferred the property or part of it to his daughter. The first conveyance attested, 'idem Jacobus dedit predictum mesuagium Matilde filie sue coram burgmote'. That was that.

We find a different pattern of registration in the records of the city of London, where the rolls of deeds and wills presented in the court of husting begin in 1252. That great series, which is also the oldest regular record of a court in the city, is based from the beginning upon written instruments, although the form of enrolment changes during the first fifty years in a way that lays increasing emphasis upon the wording of the documents. The rolls, which extend in continuous series from the later years of Henry III's reign to the reign of George I, and are still in use as a register of corporation deeds, are probably best known as the source of the testaments calendared by R. R. Sharpe.[2] The *Calendar* begins in 1258, but there are in fact references on the first roll to two testaments offered for probate in 1252, the first of which was noted in the margin but not entered on the roll, and the second referred to by way of introduction to a conveyance by the executors.[3] Although the two classes of document run together, however, the wills are greatly outnumbered by the deeds, of which some 3,000 had been registered by the end of Edward I's reign.

The first hustings roll has no general title beyond the heading 'Annus tricesimus septimus', and there is nothing about its regular

[1] For some similar transactions, see M. de W. Hemmeon, *Burgage tenure in medieval England* (Camb., Mass., 1914), p. 145. The presents offered to heirs suggest that there was sometimes a speculative element of insurance in the device.

[2] *Calendar of wills proved and enrolled in the Court of Husting, London, 1258–1688*, ed. R. R. Sharpe, 2 vols. (1889–90): the work is an outstanding example of an intelligent digest.

[3] Corporation of London Records Office, Court of Husting, Deeds and Wills, [roll] 1/4.

and neatly-written entries to suggest innovation. On the other hand, the fact that the width of the membranes used increases between the first and the fourth rolls from 6¼ to 9½ inches, a size maintained until there was further enlargement to 11 inches in the early fourteenth century, might suggest some change about this time which would account for the preservation of the rolls from the 1250s. A marked and sustained increase in the number of registrations at that time, for example, perhaps even the regular addition of testaments, may have imposed a larger size and uniformity upon a record kept more casually in the first half of the century. It is noticeable that although the first few rolls in the series cover irregular periods between one year or less, and five years, a pattern of one substantial roll each regnal year is established by the first decade of Edward I's reign. The larger rolls attain lengths of seventy and eighty feet, and bear up to two hundred entries, but the chancery style of stitching, with the membranes attached head to tail, persists well into the fourteenth century despite its inconvenience in documents of that size. Although the rolls appear to have been made up at the year's end, the course of the entries varies, running sometimes continuously on the face of several or all the membranes, and sometimes alternately on the face and the dorse.

The entries are elaborate, well-written, and carefully set out. They begin with the date of the court, and the names of the mayor, sheriffs, and chamberlain at the first court of the regnal year. The names of other notables present are given when the court had such public business as the assizes of victuals before it, and when the city was in the keeping of the constable of the Tower, Hugh fitz Otto, in 1269, the names of the bailiffs and aldermen were recited as an earnest of the citizen's hopes.[1] The usual form of the entry reports that the recipient of the property appeared before the court 'et fecit legere quandam cartam'. On occasions the deed is produced by the grantor, particularly deeds made 'in libera potestate viduitatis sue', but the pattern is not entirely clear. Grantors whose status or age might be challenged presumably presented their own deeds, but so did others whose legal competence seems indisputable, and who

---

[1] Hustings rolls, 4/31. The leading citizens assembled for the court at Rogationtide, 1254, are also noted: 1/32.

may have performed the ceremony in the recipient's absence. The recital that follows describes the grantor as present in court, if his presence is not already explicit, and follows the wording of the deed closely through its clauses as far as *habendum et tenendum*. The names of witnesses are not given in the earliest rolls, and the summary usually ends 'sicut in carta de feofamento quam dictus A. fecit predicto B. plenius continetur', a formula which survives into the period when the whole text of the deed seems to have been reported. It is clear, however, that so much of the deed as is recited is transcribed, with such necessary changes as *sua* for *mea* and *nostra*, rather than paraphrased, and that for reasons which anyone who has abstracted large numbers of documents will readily appreciate.

The grantor is not usually said to have acknowledged his deed formally, a ceremony made explicit in other towns, but he was ordinarily present, and the court took elementary precautions against misrepresentation. There is a blank space on the first roll with the marginal note 'Memorandum de carta quam Willelmus de Dunolm fecit legere in qua nullum sigillum fuit appensum'. The implication is that the clerk expected the deed still to be validated, but it was not presented again. What is made explicit, however, is the grantor's renunciation of title, his status, when any formal testimony such as proof of age is required, and a married woman's renunciation of her rights, whether in dower, in property held jointly, or in property of her own inheritance. Disclaimers—'quicquid in dicta terra . . . habuerunt, vel habere potuerunt et debuerunt, cum omnibus pertinentiis in longitudine et latitudine et rebus cunctis'—are made effective by the wife's attestation with which the entry ordinarily ends. 'Et M. uxor G. predicti in predicto Hustengo spontanea voluntate sua remisit, forisaffidavit, et quietumclamavit dicto H. totum jus et clamum quod habuit vel habere potuit vel debuit nomine dotis seu liberi banci sive aliquo alio jure in predictis terris [*etc.*] in perpetuum', or 'extra se et heredes suos in perpetuum'. The words and the order of the phrases vary slightly over the twenty years of the first five rolls, but the substance is unchanged. The disclaimer is usually marked *forisaffidatio* in the margin, and it is that ceremony as much as the details of the conveyance that gives the entry its substance.

In that sense, the early hustings rolls, despite the deeds and the texts of the testaments on which they draw, are registers of transactions. Unlike the Wallingford roll of *captiones* they point to the existence of a written deed and refer specifically to its contents, but they take an even view of the evidentiary charter and of the ceremonies that attach to it, excluding, however, the livery of seisin itself.

That omission cannot be explained, as it can in Wallingford, by a form of words, because seisin is specified on certain rare occasions. The first is an unusual transaction in 1254, when a widow presented a deed made by her son four years earlier, granting her land in Distave Lane. The son's *ligia potestas*, presumably his age at the time of making the deed, was attested by the alderman of the ward, *et per visnetum*, and the deed was enrolled. The widow thereupon gave the property, *et carta sua confirmavit*, to an elder son of her first marriage, 'et carta de dimissione sua cum plenaria seisina eidem in dicto hustengo liberavit.'[1] The only other references to seisin occur in a similar context, but coupled with the delivery of earlier title deeds. They seem always to refer to sales of property by executors, who usually present their own deeds for enrolment: their status, like that of widows and young heirs, might be subject to scrutiny.

In the thirteenth century, the edited text of the deed is embedded in that narrative material. If we turn to the fourteenth-century rolls, however, we find them simple transcripts of deeds, with only the date of the court by way of introduction, and the barest reference to renunciations and attornments noted after the text. The marginal note *examinata* appears, and, as the surviving originals show, the fact of enrolment is now endorsed upon the deed.[2] That the medieval deed of feoffment is evidentiary and not dispositive, that the unique importance of seisin made the deed unnecessary, and at best only a reinforcement of title, are familiar themes. The process by which a register of titles became a register of deeds has a larger significance than the documents themselves.

The conveyances recorded in the Hustings Court are for the most part sales of messuages or *managia*, of *terre* with houses, shops, and other buildings, and of rents. Many of the properties are large,

---

[1] Hustings rolls, 1/37.   [2] e.g., Deeds box 9, no. 10.

and some complex. William Eswy, whose testament was enrolled in 1259, instructed his executors to sell his *sokagia*. A few weeks later the executors presented a deed which shows Eswy's estate to have included two sokes, to one of which was attached the advowson of St. Bartholomew's the Less.[1] In other transactions, rents arising from several properties are specified, or the sub-divisions of tenements are described in detail. The deeds involved were elaborately drawn, and they must have been read in full. Every entry appears to be based upon a written instrument of some kind, even when what is recorded is the composition of an action in the city courts. It seems to have been the practice to procure a private deed when one of the parties ceded a title in dispute; there are a number of such *scripta* and *carte* enrolled, of which only one is distinguished as a chirograph, and that says nothing to suggest that it was prepared under the court's direction, like a final concord.[2] Most of these documents arise from actions on writ of right, but a grant of two marks' rent in 1261 composed an action on possessory assize—'ratione mortis antecessoris in Gilhalla Londonie'.[3]

The most unusual transaction registered is probably one of 1260 in which a husband and wife entered separate deeds assigning a *capitale managium*. The husband 'recognovit per cartam suam ibidem lectam quod vendicavit, concessit, assignavit, forisaffidavit, ac eciam carta sua confirmavit [*etc.*]', a variation of the ordinary formula that might indicate a quitclaim rather than an ordinary alienation. The abstract of his deed is then followed by a note of his wife's: 'Et Cristina uxor predicti Fabiani spontanea voluntate sua per quoddam scriptum ibidem lectum remisit, quietumclamavit, et forisaffidavit totum jus et clamum quod ei ratione dotis maritagii seu aliquo alio modo unquam accidere poterit de managio cum suis pertinentiis, et hoc per impressionem sigilli sui confirmavit'. 1260 is a fairly late date for a deed executed and sealed by a married woman, and there was a more effective means of achieving its end readily available in the court. Perhaps Christina had a will of her own.[4]

---

[1] Hustings rolls, 2/36; his will is 2/22, Sharpe, *Calendar*, 1, p. 1.

[2] 2/87.   [3] 2/169.

[4] 2/136. Pollock and Maitland, op. cit., ii. 412, mention some earlier examples, including one of 1223 made in the county court at Gloucester.

Interspersed among the transfers of property and the smaller number of leases for terms of years there are a few other documents, remarkable for their rarity rather than for their kind. A recognizance of a debt of 50 marks was registered in 1260 to be repaid by Easter 'sub unaquaque pena in predicto scripto contenta'. In 1269 there is a more elaborate recognizance of 240 marks owed for transactions in Bordeaux and London, pledging the debtors' 'bona mobilia [et] immobilia presentia et futura'. In Edward I's reign such bonds were recorded in the letter-books, and an ordinance noted there shows that even after the statute of Acton Burnell the citizens preferred an informal and adaptable procedure for registering recognizances of debt. The implication of the ordinance and the evidence of the letter-book and *Liber Horn* is that bonds were acknowledged before the city chamberlain, in his house upon occasion.[1] In Henry III's reign they were evidently enrolled, if not more casually, then with less emphasis, than were conveyances. Individual creditors seem to have been moved only rarely to seek the security of the hustings roll.

References in the early hustings rolls to the advantages of registration are rare, but a note of a chirograph making a family settlement ends 'et ad maiorem securitatem et testimonium recordata fuerunt omnia supradicta in predicto Hustengo et ex utraque parte concessa.'[2] The rest of the entries underline the principle, but there is even in that comment an uncertainty between the record which is the court's roll and the testimony which the court exists to bear. The distinction cannot be drawn clearly until the deeds are allowed to speak for themselves.

The change from abstract to engrossment is neither the result of a sudden innovation in policy, nor a gradual and orderly transition from reporting to transcribing. The first document to be copied in full is a royal grant by letters patent to Richard of Exmouth, king's serjeant, of freedom from tallage, prises, and other demands upon his lands, rents, and goods. It was sealed in 1259, but was not brought to the hustings court until November 1271.[3] Its engrossment then was no doubt a tribute to its origin, but it was produced

---

[1] Hustings rolls, 2/153 (50 marks); 4/37 (240 marks); *Calendar . . . of Letter-book A*, ed. R. R. Sharpe (1899), pp. iv, v, and 26.   [2] 2/151.   [3] 4/116.

at the same court as a royal charter and a deed involving another royal grant. The charter is an *inspeximus* and confirmation, not entered on the charter roll, of a grant by the Lord Edward to Iterius Bochard, then a clerk in his service and later a clerk of the king's household. The dating-clause of Edward's charter has been abbreviated to the year 52 Henry III, 1267–8, but as it granted a house in St. Mary Aldermanbury, confiscated from Thomas fitz-Thomas, formerly mayor of London and then Edward's prisoner, the occasion is clear enough. It was confirmed by Henry on 1 November 1271, eight days before it was produced in court, and like Richard of Exmouth's letters patent, represents some final tidying of the confiscations and claims of the confused years in London after Evesham and Kenilworth.[1]

Richard had received houses in Southwark, and wished to secure his privileges in the city. The next entry on the roll is a private quitclaim, abstracted in the usual way, but it is followed by a deed produced by Pontius de Mora, a royal merchant and agent, which again relates to a royal grant, and is transcribed in full.

The deed is an attornment by Stephen Heyn as tenant of a house granted by the king to Pontius de Mora. The property was formerly held by John Reynger, a royalist, but whether or not it had been disputed in the war its new owner evidently felt some anxiety about it. Pontius was a Gascon, a royal clerk, merchant, and agent, and although Henry accounted him a denizen, he had his anxieties. He was also a substantial creditor of the royal household, and was no doubt intent upon securing what he had in hand.[2]

Later in 1272, Pontius appeared again in the hustings court, and assured his title by a more elaborate procedure. On this occasion he produced a royal letter addressed to the mayor and sheriffs, describing John Reynger's bequest of his houses in St. Thomas's parish to his executors to sell, the king's inspection of the testament, the executors's delivery of the property to the king for 350 marks, a substantial sum, and the king's subsequent grant of the property to Pontius. The letter ends 'et ideo vobis mandamus quod

---

[1] Hustings rolls, 4/117. For Bochard as a royal agent, see *CPR, 1266–72*, pp. 596, 639.

[2] 4/119. There are numerous references in *CPR, 1266–72* to Pontius as the king's and the queen's clerk. For a note of Henry's debts to him, see ibid., p. 715.

carta nostra predicta quam sibi super hoc fieri fecimus in pleno
hustengo vestro Londonie legere irrotulari et firmiter teneri
faciatis'. Pontius produced the charter, and the clerk duly enrolled
both documents *verbatim*, and followed them with another, a deed
made by the executors, acknowledging receipt of the 350 marks, 'de
quibus protestamus nos bene esse pacatos', and discharging all
claims upon the king, Pontius, and his heirs.[1] No title is ever beyond
challenge, but as a Gascon in the London of 1272, Pontius had done
all that he could.

The precedent set in these months was not immediately taken
up, but marks the beginning of a long process. The fourth roll, the
first with a general heading, is labelled 'Rotulus cartarum lectarum
et testamentorum probatorum in plenis Hustengis Londonie, anno
regni regis Henrici filii regis Johannis L^{mo} ij^o et tercio'. In
Edward I's reign the clerks began to add warranties, witness lists,
and then dating-clauses to their abstracts, passages that do not
conform grammatically to the narrative of the entries, but empha-
size the documents behind them ever more strongly. By the 1280s
the rolls are headed, sometimes after the name of the mayor, *Inro-
tulacio cartarum et testamentorum*, running on to the date of the first
court, and that convention is accompanied by occasional *verbatim*
transcripts.

The literal transcripts are infrequent at first, but not arbitrary.
They record deeds with a fiduciary or conditional element: com-
mitments to pay for property by instalments, leases for terms of
years. The convention in opening clauses that often distinguishes
the dispositive *carta—Sciant omnes per presentes—*from the *scriptum*
used for quitclaims and contracts—*Omnibus Christi* (or *Universis
Christi*) *fidelibus ad quos presens scriptum pervenerit*—is marked in these
rolls before 1300. Whether a document is called *carta* or *scriptum* in
the margin (and so far as the distinction can be maintained, though
a *scriptum* may be referred to as a *carta*, *carte* are not called *scripta*) it
appears for more than a decade that if it is enrolled *verbatim* it will
begin with a pious invocation and refer to itself as a *scriptum*. The
practice persists until the last years of the century, when from 1298

[1] Hustings rolls, 4/160–2. The king's grant to Pontius is on the Charter Roll,
2 Jan. 1272 (*Cal. Charter Rolls*, ii. 179).

deeds of all kinds are enrolled in full, and testaments either in full or *verbatim* so far as they concern the testator's lay fee. The abstract has become a copy, one which in the late fourteenth century is presented without introductory matter, the court's cognizance being recorded on the dorse of the deed.

The course of events in London is suggestive. We cannot now be certain when the enrolments began, but they constituted a substantial record by the middle of the thirteenth century. Their chief purpose was to provide a record of title, and extraneous matters, such as records of debts and privileges, were most sparingly admitted to the rolls. The testaments added nothing in particular to the roll; it certainly cannot be argued that any pressure of competition from the ecclesiastical courts moved the city, or other towns with such records, to transcribe testaments before deeds. The first impulse at London to recite the whole deed came from the anxieties of individuals who, with royal support but uncertain allies in the city, sought an extra measure of security as the turmoil of Henry III's later years died down.

From that beginning, we could reasonably expect the events of Edward I's reign to reinforce any interest that the clerks and their clients felt in an exact record. Edward's preliminary inquiries into abuses and usurpations, the *Quo warranto* proceedings, the anxious and continuing concern with precision in the statutes, all emphasized the importance of the written word and its literal meaning.[1] The ordinances of Acton Burnell and the Statute of Merchants may have provided an additional model for enrolments, but they derived from a practice already established in the towns, and if they influenced the towns' practice at all in that matter it was to sharpen rather than shape their procedure.[2]

In the free boroughs at large enrolments of deeds of title and of wills were records of some importance. In Ipswich, where they were called, as they were in some other East Anglian towns, recognizances of free tenement, they were first concentrated during Edward I's reign on to a single membrane of the great court roll, and then

---

[1] D. W. Sutherland, '*Quo Warranto*' *Proceedings in the Reign of Edward I* (Oxford, 1963), pp. 111–29.

[2] T. F. T. Plucknett, *The Legislation of Edward I* (Oxford, 1949), pp. 138–44.

kept as a separate record.[1] The deeds were more often abstracted than transcribed as late as the 1320s, but thereafter were copied verbatim. In the meantime the recognizance roll had inspired a separate roll of pleas of abatement, like the London assize of fresh force, and these, though recording a possessory action, came to be regarded as conferring a title.[2] In the fourteenth century, taking recognizances and recording probate of testaments, together with such associated business as witnessing proof of age and hearing the disclaimers of married women, were regarded not as functions of the great court, but as the business of a petty court of recognizances, which could assemble for that business alone.[3] There was a similar concentration of the record at Great Yarmouth, and also at Norwich, where the roll of deeds and wills is the earliest of the regular city records.[4]

Registers of that kind were distinct from municipal cartularies, and it seems to have been unusual to associate the deeds of corporate properties with those of private individuals. Where such cartularies were kept, similarly, they were reserved for public muniments, like the White Book and the lost Domesday Roll of Dublin.[5] In some towns, however, enrolled deeds were entered or recopied for convenience in codices, where corporation business might be entered more or less haphazardly beside them. The Great Red Book of Bristol and the Red Register of King's Lynn are probably the most celebrated examples of such books, but there were many others.[6] Hythe has the remains of a substantial paper register

[1] G. H. Martin, 'The Records of the Borough of Ipswich to 1422', *Journal of the Society of Archivists*, I (1955–9), pp. 89–90.

[2] Ibid., p. 90; G. H. Martin, *Early Court Rolls of the Borough of Ipswich* (University of Leicester, Occasional Papers of the Department of Local History, 5, 1954), pp. 34, 44.

[3] Ipswich and East Suffolk Record Office, Ipswich recognizance roll, 11–12 Edward III, m. 2 recto.

[4] *Handlist of the Archives of Great Yarmouth*, ed. P. Rutledge (National Register of Archives, 1965), pp. 8, 9; *The Records of the City of Norwich*, ed. W. Hudson and J. C. Tingey (Norwich and London, 1906), i. 224–58.

[5] *Historical and municipal documents of Ireland, 1172–1320*, ed. J. T. Gilbert (R.S. 1870), pp. x–xi, 280–4. There are deeds in Trinity College Library, Dublin, which are endorsed as enrolled in the Domesday (J. G. Smyly, 'Old Latin deeds in the Library of Trinity College', *Hermathena*, 67 (1946); 69–72 (1947–8); 74 (1949)).

[6] *The Great Red Book of Bristol*, ed. E. W. W. Veale, 5 vols. (Bristol Record Society, 2, 4, 8, 16, 18, 1931–53), has excellent editorial matter, including a learned discussion

which was in use from the middle of Edward III's reign, and the Burwarmote Book of Lincoln begins in Edward II's.[1] During a general revision of its administration and archives in the later fourteenth century, Colchester began to keep a list of wills proved in the borough oath book, together with details of leases of town lands, but private deeds, which were entered on the general court rolls as they were presented, were not included.[2]

The White Vellum Book of Scarborough is an interesting example of a medieval register which continued in use as a record of title into the seventeenth century. After a confusion of private transactions, town leases, and civic ordinances of the late fourteenth and the fifteenth centuries, it was used to register conveyances, and particularly those involving disclaimers by married women, from the 1580s to 1641. Part of another volume, now kept with the White Vellum Book, continues the record to 1646.[3]

The White Vellum Book emphasizes the continuing importance of tenurial custom in the boroughs, and also the enduring convenience of a simple and inexpensive form of local registration. In the context of town history, the first point seems the more substantial, but it is an instance of a rational uniformity in borough customs rather than, as is more usual, of a marked and bewildering variety. It is arguable that the wives and daughters of burgesses enjoyed a status that was privileged by comparison with that of other women, and if the procedures by which their rights were defined and maintained were standardized by pressure from the common law, there was little disposition or occasion to allow the contagion of liberty to spread outside the towns. Within the walls, however, the relative longevity of women and their capacity for business when they were allowed to exercise it, combined to make them valuable members of the community. The customs that protected their interests, however imperfectly, gave reassurance and promise to a harsh and

of conveyancing in the first volume. For Lynn, see *The Red Register of King's Lynn*, ed. H. Ingleby, 2 vols. (King's Lynn, 1919–22).

[1] *Hist. MSS. Com. Fourth Report* (1874), part 1, pp. 436–8; J. W. F. Hill, *Medieval Lincoln* (Cambridge, 1948), p. 291.

[2] *The Oath Book or Red Parchment Book of Colchester*, ed. W. G. Benham (Colchester, 1907).

[3] I. H. Jeayes, *Description of documents contained in the White Vellum Book of the Scarborough Corporation* (Scarborough, 1914).

constricted society. It is not inappropriate that they should have encouraged an administrative procedure that was in advance of the rules of the common law.

The largely self-contained world of the boroughs preserved their customs and privileges, but diminished their value as an example to the rest of society. It would seem, from one of the few indications that we have of royal policies toward the towns, that in the fourteenth century the common lawyers looked askance at the custom of registering conveyances by married women in the borough courts. Bristol took the unusual step, in its petition for the charter that it received from Edward III in 1373, of asking for a clause permitting the registration of deeds, including those acknowledged by married women upon a confidential examination in the Guildhall. The charter, one of the series that year which among other privileges conferred the status of a county upon Bristol, duly affirmed the principle that charters and writings acknowledged and enrolled in the Guildhall should be of record to all, with the force of writings enrolled in Chancery, but explicitly excluded those by married women. Against that restriction, there was a further provision, for which the burgesses had not asked, that the mayor and sheriff in the Guildhall court should have cognizance of any writ sued out for the purpose of levying a fine, so that final concords made before them there, and duly certified and paid for at the Exchequer, should rank with fines levied at Westminster. The apprehension that the burgesses had entertained about the security of their custom was evidently justified, although it is not clear why they felt it necessary to agitate the matter in their petition. What is clear is that the attempt to impose the common law practice was a failure; there was, indeed, some suspicion of fines compounded in the town, and perhaps a preference for the customary deed. The result was that with its ordinary power of registering deeds and proving testaments explicitly confirmed by charter, Bristol was able to reassert its traditional practice.[1]

The terms of Bristol's charter opened the court's register to all who had deeds to acknowledge, *mulieribus maritatis exceptis*, when the property in question lay within the town, its suburbs, and

[1] *Great Red Book of Bristol*, i. 220–1.

precinct. The privilege of enrolment could only apply to tenements within the court's jurisdiction, and whilst those who acquired other properties might envy the ease with which titles within the towns could be protected, we should not expect them to seek to share the privilege. There is, however, a fragment of evidence to show that the advantages of enrolment were appreciated outside the boroughs.

In 1343 a quitclaim was produced in the borough court at Ipswich by a canon of Butley, an Augustinian house near Orford. It was made by Robert, son of Gilbert of Dedham, and released the advowson and patronage of the church of Dedham, in Essex, to the prior and convent of Butley. Robert was present and acknowledged the deed, which was enrolled on payment of the customary fee of 2s.[1]

Behind the transaction lies a confused but interesting piece of manorial history. Dedham was a manor of the Stutevilles, lately escheated to the crown and granted by Edward III to Robert Ufford, earl of Suffolk.[2] Robert of Dedham's father was a small freeholder and socager, tenant of an estate which later became known as the manor of Overhall.[3] Robert himself was a busy and probably unscrupulous man, who had been committed to Newgate the year before on a charge of conspiring to murder, and who subsequently earned a general pardon for his service with the army in France.[4] He had evidently been tempted, perhaps by the recent uncertainties over the lordship of the principal manor, to appropriate the advowson of the parish church, and so round off his modest estate with the dignity of patronage. The advowson, however, had been granted some time since to Butley Priory which had appropriated the living, and at a low point in Robert's fortunes he was induced to give up his claim—a claim that can never have rested upon much beyond impudence. He had no heir, and the less reason therefore to persist in his ambitions.[5] When he abandoned them, Butley evidently looked for some greater publicity for his renunciation than its own cartularies afforded, and pitched upon the borough court at Ipswich.

[1] Ipswich recognizance roll, 16–17 Edward III, m. 2d.

[2] *Early Yorkshire Charters: (ix) The Stuteville Fee*, ed. C. T. Clay (Yorks. Arch. Soc., Record Series, extra series, 7, 1952), p. 65.

[3] P. Morant, *The History and Antiquities of the County of Essex* (1768), ii. 246–7.

[4] *CPR, 1340–3*, p. 585; *1345–8*, p. 503.

[5] Morant (ii. 247) confuses Robert as the tenant of Over Hall in 1349 with his father, Gilbert (see *CPR, 1348–50*, p. 145).

Dedham is in Essex, and the diocese of London, but Butley is in Suffolk and Ipswich was its nearest substantial town. It seemed a pity not to use its amenities. The following year Butley had another deed enrolled at Ipswich, this time a quit-claim to land in Glemham, near Saxmundham, and made by a chaplain with no obvious connection with the borough.[1] If Butley's innocuous experiment had been imitated elsewhere, the registration of titles in boroughs could have made, by example, a larger mark on the general practice of conveyancing. As it was, the later confusion between the privileges of incorporation and parliamentary representation constricted the enfranchisement of towns, and the concurrent, if not concomitant, development of industry outside their jurisdiction diminished the absolute importance of transactions in real estate in all but the largest commercial centres. Just as the borough probate of wills remained the only breach in the privileges of the ecclesiastical courts, so the registration of deeds survived largely unnoticed by a society which, though not indifferent to the towns, supposed itself affected by only one of their political functions. It is interesting that the first act setting up a land registry was secured by the West Riding of Yorkshire, the one division of the county with no anciently enfranchised borough among its towns, and that the second, which excluded the city of York, was specifically said to be supported by the inhabitants of Hull. When the Act for the North Riding was prepared, Scarborough made an unsuccessful attempt to obtain exemption from its provisions on the grounds that they would deprive the borough of an ancient privilege.[2] The protest went unheeded, but the principle of registration was not extended to other counties, and by the time that the first steps towards effective general registration were taken the law of property, like the towns themselves, had undergone substantial, though by no means complete, reform.

The peculiar development of the common law, with its insistence upon personal affirmation from personal experience, and the rituals of seisin, exalted physical presence and oral testimony above the

---

[1] Ipswich recognizance roll, 17–18 Edward III, m. 3 recto.
[2] Scarborough Town Hall, Corporation records, A. 4, Minutes and orders, 18–29 Oct. 1734. I am obliged to Miss S. C. McIntyre for the reference.

written word. There was no room for a notarial tradition either in the courts, or in those administrative practices that were modelled by the common law. Yet although secular records in medieval England were memoranda and aids to reflection rather than sworn texts, their use demanded new skills and determined new attitudes. As records of title moved from mere notes of enfeoffment to abstracts of the deeds that the transactions came to entail, the importance of the document grew irresistibly. The ceremony that surrounded its acknowledgement remained important, but the evidence of the rolls, and especially those of the hustings court, suggests that the transcript of the deed came to imply the ceremony, just as the record of the ceremony had once implied the existence of the deed.

We cannot say from the bald transcripts of the fourteenth-century enrolments in the husting, or from the absence of any reference to seisin in the more elaborate records of recognizances at Ipswich, that the copy, any more than the original deed, conferred a title, or that the ceremony of seisin was unimportant. To do so would be to disregard the whole practice of the courts and the unanimous voice of the law's commentators. What we must notice is that the boroughs perfected and defended for several centuries a custom that ran outside one of the strictest rules of the common law—that a husband could not bar his wife's claim to dower in an alienated property, unless she joined him in levying a fine—that they did so as a natural consequence of the extraordinary freedom with which their inhabitants disposed real property, and that in the process they laid an emphasis upon literal transcription, that pointed the way to a much later, and more painfully-contrived, refinement of the rules of conveyance.

The interest of the enrolled deeds is much wider than that which attaches to their texts. The conventions of enrolment, the patterns of abbreviation, like that which brought the warranty into prominence in the hustings rolls between 1275 and 1285, tell us succinctly what the clerks thought important. Lists of witnesses in private deeds are often regarded as conventional gestures after the thirteenth century, but the clerks at Ipswich throughout the whole series of their rolls recorded the names of those who witnessed the deed as carefully as those of the *probi homines* in whose presence it was rehearsed and recorded. These are matters which the volume of the evidence challenges, rather than invites us to explore. The value of the deeds themselves needs little urging, except perhaps to observe that the variety and detail of the testaments proved in borough courts have enabled them to overshadow the deeds, to which they must appear, in their context, as of secondary importance. Burghal probate was a privilege carefully asserted, but when we examine the conveyances amid which the bequests were recorded, we have to doubt whether the procedure could have been refined as it was without the sustained example of the enrolled deeds.

The whole significance of these documents is very great; they are a fund of riches, upon which we have drawn very lightly. Like the rest of our borough records, they offer us knowledge of an energetic and articulate community with whose contrivances we are still familiar, but they differ from the other material in the special demands that their form makes upon, and the rewards that they offer to, the student of diplomatic.

G. H. MARTIN

VIII

The Making of the Declaration of Arbroath

THE palladium of Scottish nationality for those who require for it a historical foundation is called the 'declaration of Arbroath'—a diplomatic euphemism in a country anxious not to slip into the religious divisions of another northern Province. This document is in form a supplication to the pope dated at the monastery of Arbroath on 6 April 1320 from eight earls, thirty-one barons (all named) 'and the other barons and freeholders and whole community of the realm of Scotland'. It relates briefly the history of the nation of Scots which lived 'in freedom and peace' until attacked by the English. Freed again by Robert I, rightfully king, the writers would nonetheless expel him if he subjected them to the English, for they fight only for freedom (a famous passage, lifted from Sallust). The pope is asked to urge the English king to 'leave us Scots in peace who live in this poor little Scotland beyond which there is no dwelling place at all'; he is urged to see that English attacks on Scotland are an excuse for not going on Crusade and that unless he refrains from favouring their side he endangers his own soul as well as the Church and the protagonists. The writers commit their cause to God. This document has come to occupy in Scotland a position somewhat like that of Magna Carta in England even though it treats of national liberty, not of liberties, and in 1970 has enjoyed the treatment thought appropriate to a 650th anniversary:[1] at Arbroath municipal dignitaries in full regalia sat down to pray in the pools of rain which had gathered in their seats while they stood to hymn; the postal authorities gave their own fivepenny lesson in diplomatic, depicting an abbot in mass vestments and mitre seated at an altar writing the declaration while five barons stand quizzically by. But the Scottish Record Office has also mounted an invaluable special exhibition and

---

[1] The *Daily Mail* explained to its readers that the document was produced by Robert T. Bruce and the Bishop of Arbroath.

the writer owes a special debt of gratitude to the Keeper of the Records for abetting the study of the original, a fragile relic, which is the basis of this paper; its purpose is to bring some material evidence to bear on the speculation as to how the declaration was drawn up.[1]

In another place the writer has tried to show the circumstances for which the petition was written.[2] In 1317 John XXII had pressed for an Anglo-Scottish truce but his letters and legates were given short shrift because they did not acknowledge Robert I as king. Already he claimed that the Scottish barons would not allow him to compromise on this issue—he could only agree with their letter (unfortunately lost) to the legates. The pope made the necessary concession but the Scots immediately broke the papal truce by seizing Berwick, the last *terra irridenta* which had long eluded them and which was worth a cursing. It duly came but not until the end of 1319 did the papacy proceed to stronger measures, summoning 'Robert Bruce' and four bishops to the curia in person or by proctors before 1 May and threatening further penalties. These bulls were issued presumably at English instigation after an attempt to retake Berwick had failed ignominiously, and they must have arrived about the time of the conclusion of a two-year truce in December 1319. Robert I had to stave off papal censures, and to secure some diplomatic backing for the concessions which would have to be extorted from the English if the forthcoming peace negotiations were not to be futile. For these reasons he despatched to the curia not proctors to answer a case but postmen, a minor Scottish baron and a knight, apparently French but otherwise unknown, with three letters, from himself, from the bishop of St. Andrews and from the earls and

[1] The declaration has been printed many times, and is likely to be most readily accessible to a reader in *Source Book of Scottish History*, ed. W. C. Dickinson, G. Donaldson, and I. A. Milne (either edition). For a diplomatic text and a full study of the printed editions, see Sir James Fergusson, *The Declaration of Arbroath* (Edinburgh, 1970), with a photograph of Tyn. The same photograph has also been published in 1970 by H.M.S.O. as *The Declaration of Arbroath, 1320, Facsimile and Translation*. But it is essential to refer also to the two earlier engravings: (i) James Anderson, *Selectus Diplomatum et Numismatum Scotiae Thesaurus* (Edinburgh, 1739), no. li; (ii) *Acts of the Parliaments of Scotland* (Edinburgh, 1814–75), i. 474–5 and *National Manuscripts of Scotland* (1867–71), ii, no. xxiv.

[2] A. A. M. Duncan, *The Nation of Scots and the Declaration of Arbroath* (Historical Association pamphlet G 75, 1970).

barons. The two former are lost, the third is the declaration of Arbroath, but the papal reply to each is known, dated 16 August (to the king and to the bishop) and 28 August (to the barons).[1] The Scottish letters had, however, been received at the curia by 29 July, the date of a bull to Edward II in the terms requested by the declaration of Arbroath and employing a variation of some of its terminology.[2] There has been discussion of the use of the *cursus* in the declaration of Arbroath and other state documents of the reign;[3] it was of course particularly apposite to the declaration which requested the issuing of papal letters and thus provided phrases quotable in those letters. More germane to the present discussion, however, is the date at which the letters were received at Avignon. This can hardly have been much later than, say, 25 July, and from other evidence it cannot have been much earlier than 16 June.[4] Allowing about eight weeks for travel from Scotland (the time from England seems to have been four to six weeks), a date of dispatch for the three Scottish letters in late May seems indicated. The date of the declaration of Arbroath, 6 April, is very early for such dispatch, and poses the first of several problems associated with the document.

According to Barbour, after the relief of Berwick in September 1319 (I paraphrase) 'when the king had been there a while he sent for masons far and near and had built ten foot high the wall round Berwick town. Then he took the road to Lothian with his following.'[5] Royal documents are dated at Arbroath in October, Dunblane and Scone in November,[6] and at Berwick only from 8 December.[7] The truce was made there on 22 December;[8] on 7 January an English

[1] *Vetera Monumenta Hibernorum et Scotorum Historiam Illustrantia*, ed. A. Theiner (Rome, 1864), nos. ccccxxxi–iii.

[2] Ibid., no. ccccxxx.

[3] Lord (T. M.) Cooper, *Supra Crepidam* (London, 1951), pp. 48–54; or his *Selected Papers* (Edinburgh, 1957), pp. 324–8.

[4] *Vetera Monumenta*, no. ccccxxvii.

[5] *The Bruce*, ed. W. M. Mackenzie (1909), pp. 321–2.

[6] *Registrum Honoris de Morton* (Bannatyne Club, 1853), ii, no. 22; *Miscellany of the Spalding Club* (Spalding Club, 1841–52), ii. 316; *Liber Ecclesie de Scon* (Bannatyne and Maitland Clubs, 1843), no. 130.

[7] *Charters and other Writs illustrating the History . . . of Aberdeen*, ed. P. J. Anderson (Aberdeen, 1890), nos. vii, viii; *Reg. Morton*, ii, no. 23.

[8] *Calendar of Documents relating to Scotland*, ed. J. Bain (Edinburgh, 1881–8), iii, no. 681.

safe-conduct was issued for an embassy of twelve to go to Edward II on unspecified business, perhaps to collect his oath to adhere to the truce.[1] If they went it was before the end of January when he left York. It would seem likely that the rebuilding of the walls began after 22 December and ran on at least until the spring of 1320 but more probably for a year or more; an aid to cover the expense was collected at some time during 1320 to which Melrose abbey reluctantly contributed, apparently in November.[2] Barbour's statement fits with the suggestion of the dates of royal charters that the king was at Berwick early in 1320 on at least some occasions; after December a letter patent was dated there on 2 February 1320.[3] On 13 March a dispute between Dunfermline abbey and two small freeholders was settled at Newbattle abbey by six arbiters, two of them barons in the declaration,[4] and on the following day the bishop of St. Andrews, an earl and four leading barons witnessed a resignation to the king at the same place.[5] Royal documents were dated at Berwick on 25 and 26 March,[6] but on 31 March, Easter Monday, a long royal charter of liberties to the burgh of Berwick was dated at Newbattle.[7] The resignation of 14 March was later described by chancery as made 'in pleno consilio nostro apud Neubotill coram regni nostris nobilibus',[8] while the charter of 31 March undoubtedly represents a special Easter court, housed in a monastery, like the Christmas courts at Coupar Angus in 1316 and Newbattle in 1317.[9] All four bishops summoned to Avignon and three earls (an unusually high number) witness this charter

---

[1] *Foedera*, ed. T. Rymer (R.C., 1816–69), ii. 412; this is a safe conduct for five knights (three, and possibly four (? Seton) are in the declaration), four clerics (of whom Wautier de Gauwaye is Walter de Twynham), and three valets.

[2] *Registrum Magni Sigilli Regum Scotorum*, ed. J. M. Thomson and others (Edinburgh, 1882–1914), i, Appendix 1, no. 17.

[3] *The Blackfriars of Perth*, ed. R. Milne (Edinburgh, 1893), p. 10, no. xi.

[4] *Registrum de Dunfermelyn* (Bannatyne Club, 1842), no. 352.

[5] *Reg. Morton*, ii, no. 24, reading *decimo nono* for *decimo [quinto]* (National Library of Scotland, MS. 72, f. 64ᵛ).

[6] *Genealogical Collections . . . made by Walter Macfarlane* (Scottish History Society, 1900), i. 48; G. Mackenzie, *Writers of the Scots Nation* (Edinburgh, 1708–22), iii. 211.

[7] *Percy Chartulary* (Surtees Society, no. cxvii, 1911), pp. 437–40.

[8] *Reg. Morton*, ii, no. 25.

[9] *Liber Sancte Marie de Melros* (Bannatyne Club, 1837), no. 382; J. Anderson, *The Oliphants in Scotland* (Edinburgh, 1879), Appendix, no. 1.

of 31 March. The same large gathering is presumably represented by a royal charter of his family lands to Douglas dated the following day, Berwick 1 April 1320, and witnessed by the bishop of St. Andrews, an earl and four rarely occurring barons, one of whom is in the declaration, another of whom was the panetar evidently (as we shall see) scratched from it.[1] No document other than the declaration is dated 6 April, but a private charter records another resignation to the king at Liston, a few miles on the other side of Edinburgh from Dalkeith on Friday after St. Ambrose.[2] In 1320 this feast fell on Friday 4 April so the resignation presumably took place on 11 April. Liston was a manor of the bishop of St. Andrews who was again present; subsequently this resignation was described as taking place 'in presencia nobilium' when the lands were conveyed to Newbattle abbey,[3] and it was therefore a postscript to the council.

On 17 April a letter of protection for Arbroath abbey was issued under the great seal dated at Berwick.[4] This document, following common form and probably issued 'of course', is no indication of royal presence but presumably only of the great seal and, one would normally assume, of the chancellor, Bernard, abbot of Arbroath. Its effect was similar to that of an English writ of peace in bringing proceedings against the abbey to a halt in a lower court[5] and it must have been sought by the abbot-chancellor. It is one of a number of surviving original royal writs to Arbroath and its appearance is suggestive: the seal tag is broader than on any other writ of similar size and much broader than most. It is also short, without the fold or knot which was buried (otherwise invariably, so far as I can tell) in the seal and without a tail hanging from the seal. The writing is formal and rather spiky, while in the top line initials (Robertus, Omnibus and Sciatis) there are parallel dividing lines with dots in the segments and some other doodles. This is not a hand found in other documents of 1320 but some seven years later it becomes quite common and is published in the facsimile of the indenture of

---

[1] *Reg. Magni Sigilli*, i, no. 77; ibid., Appendix 1, no. 35.
[2] *Registrum S. Marie de Neubotle* (Bannatyne Club, 1849), nos. 53–7.   [3] Ibid., no. 58.
[4] *Liber S. Thome de Aberbrothoc* (Bannatyne Club, 1848–56), ii, Appendix, no. vii; Scottish Record Office, Register House Charters (RH. 6), no. 86B.
[5] A. Harding, 'Medieval Brieves of Protection', *Juridical Review* (1966), 115–49.

1328 renewing that of 1326;[1] it continues after Abbot Bernard was succeeded as chancellor by Master Walter de Twynham in 1328, and in my view is most likely to be his hand, for he was named as one of the ambassadors to go to England in January 1320 and so was at court about this time. This unusual letter patent is evidence that the great seal had been entrusted by the chancellor and his clerk or clerks to a temporary deputy who remained at Berwick with it, perhaps to issue credentials or safe conducts for negotiations with England.

On 4 May Chancery resumed its activities at Arbroath with a charter to Kilwinning abbey.[2] On 6 May lands resigned at the Newbattle council on 14 March were granted to Sir James Douglas and another major grant was issued to him.[3] (A charter of his family lands had been dated 1 April at Berwick.) On 20 May the lands resigned at Liston on 11 April were granted to Newbattle abbey.[4] The month's gap between the beginnings of these conveyances and their completion is noteworthy, though unfortunately we do not have other fully documented examples to show how typical such a delay would be; it can only be said that business was held over from Newbattle in March for completion and engrossment at Arbroath in May. The engrossments contain witness lists but these cannot be taken as evidence of presence at Arbroath; of the two grants to Douglas on the same day one has four earls (three witnesses at Newbattle), the other none. While such lists can be tested at other times to show that a magnate absent in England, Ireland, or the Continent does not appear, the details of how they were constructed are not recoverable, and it is therefore possible, indeed probable, that the 'witnesses' to these engrossments were names carried forward from the effective transactions in the king's presence a month or more before. This indeed is the nub of the matter: the usual doubts about the significance of place-dates as evidence of whereabouts are multiplied in the case of the frequent royal documents ostensibly from Arbroath by the association of the

[1] *Acts Parl. Scot.*, i. 483; *Nat. MSS. Scotland*, ii, no. xxvii.
[2] *Vetera Monumenta*, no. dii.
[3] *Reg. Morton*, ii, no. 25; W. Fraser, *The Douglas Book* (Edinburgh, 1885), iii, no. 288; ibid., no. 12 (of the same date though undated).
[4] *Reg. Neubotle*, no. 58.

chancellor with that place. In the absence of a series of enrolments such as is familiar to the English historian, we can only test one hypothesis about chancery practice against another and accept as a model those possibilities which become probabilities through their congruence with each other.

The model to which we can work would begin at a great council at Newbattle in the second half of March 1320 when reconstruction measures on Berwick were already under consideration or even in course. The council may have granted the aid for this purpose and may have been responsible for an undated proclamation offering a burgage and house, or burgage and 100*s*. to anyone willing to settle in B[erwick] within forty days.[1] But it is also likely to have discussed the prospects for peace with England and relations with the pope, the four bishops under summons to Avignon being present; a démarche at the curia by letters from king, bishop, and barons was planned. Early in April (before the 11th, but not necessarily before the 6th) the king, his chancellor, and his great seal parted company, the king to Liston, the seal to Berwick. The chancellor was at Arbroath early in May when the great seal returned there; presumably he had been there for three or four weeks and his business had been the letters to the pope. The text of the declaration of Arbroath was produced by the government; it is closely paralleled in 1301 when there was a papal claim that Edward I should argue at the curia his case to be superior lord of Scotland. Unable to admit papal jurisdiction but unwilling to defy the pope, the English king had drawn up a strong rebuttal of the claim in the name of his barons which was sealed partly at the Lincoln parliament and partly by being sent round absent barons.[2] An elaborate historical account of Anglo-Scottish relations (not admitting papal jurisdiction) was then drawn up as the king's reply and the two documents were probably sent to Boniface VIII. When the English barons said they would not permit their king to admit papal jurisdiction, their intransigence was a convenience for Edward I, not otherwise notable for being pushed into Scottish ventures by

[1] Edinburgh Univ. Lib., MS. 207, f. 143ᵛ.
[2] F. M. Powicke, *The Thirteenth Century* (Oxford, 1953), p. 705 and literature cited there.

his barons. In the same way Robert I had pleaded baronial intransigence to papal legates in 1317, and the royal, episcopal, and baronial letters of 1320 served the same functions, when the king could not admit the pope's right to summon him for making war against England. He thus wrote about a number of specific grievances and asked that the process against him be revoked. The general message, the real justification of Robert I's behaviour, that the Scots were struggling against English aggressors and that the pope should constrain the English to peace, and not the Scots, was put in the baronial letter. The declaration of Arbroath was in a sense an alibi provided for himself by Robert I, an alibi for having ignored the papal truce and the process begun against him.

A draft of the declaration is represented, as Sir James Fergusson has shown, by the text [Sc] in the fifteenth century *Scotichronicon* of Walter Bower; it lacks the name of three senders and gives to another the office of panetar which he did not hold—the name of the true panetar, Sir Andrew Moray, must have been deleted at an earlier draft. The office was removed before the text of the surviving original [Tyn] was written. There was also a slight tightening up of Latinity between Sc and Tyn: 'non enim propter gloriam *belli* . . . pugnamus set propter *leges paternas et* libertatem solummodo . . .' in Sc lost the italicized words in Tyn. In the date the regal 'apud monasterium nostrum' in Sc, a slip which betrays the chancery origin of the document, was corrected in Tyn. The latter, however, is by no means perfect, omitting several words necessary for the sense or demanded by the *ars dictaminis* and found in Sc. A third text [Av] was sent to the curia and is now lost; the papal reply echoes it faithfully enough to show that it resembled Tyn but without its errors; although this reply names only the earls and three officers of state 'and many others' as senders of the declaration there is no reason to think that Av contained different names from Tyn.[1]

Although a file copy, neither intended to be sent, nor sent, Tyn is a sealed original.[2] It is $19\frac{1}{4}$ inches (49 cm.) broad and $22\frac{1}{2}$ inches (36·3 cm.) deep with a fold $1\frac{3}{4}$ inches (4·7 cm.) deep. The sides and

---

[1] On all this see the excellent and full account (of which only the main points are indicated here) in Sir James Fergusson, *The Declaration of Arbroath*.

[2] Scottish Record Office, SP13/7, 1320, at Tyningham during the seventeenth and eighteenth centuries, whence Tyn.

top of a frame within which the text is written were ruled drypoint[1]
as was normal chancery practice, but writing lines seem also to
have been ruled; the hand is court hand identifiable in many, probably in most, surviving original Robert I documents earlier than
1327; the script of Av was doubtless more formal. Although the
text has been combed for many purposes, there seems to be no
account of the sealing of Tyn by which we can judge whether the
declaration was sealed at an assembly, sent round the country, or
validated in some other way.

In principle there were to be three rows of seals and above each
slit on the fold was written the name of the sender whose seal was
to be appended. These names and seals were to be in the order
in which they occur at the beginning of the letter. There are,
however, departures from this scheme which can only be explained
by itemizing the seals. It should be noted that many tags survive
only as short stumps and that it is usually no longer possible to be
sure whether a seal was or was not appended to a long tag.

First row:[2]

1. S. comitis de Fyf. Tag, no seal, but Anderson's engraving
   shows that this seal was appended in the early eighteenth
   century.
2. S. comitis Morauie. No tag or seal.
3. S. comitis Marchie. Tag and seal in red wax.
4. S. comitis de Stratheryn. Tag and seal in red wax. The
   nineteenth-century engraving shows that below the earl's
   seal was that of Alan Moray in green wax (no. 40 below),
   now lost.
5. S. comitis de Leuenax. Tag and seal in red wax. Below this
   seal is the trace of
6. a seal in green wax, and below this on the tag: Alanus de
   Kalantyr.
7. S. comitis de Ros. Tag, no seal.
8. S. comitis Cathanie. Tag bearing no sign of seal in red wax
   but with seal of

[1] The side margins are approximately 3 cm. (left) and 2·7 cm. (right) broad.

[2] In this list the first words, if Latin, are as written on the fold or, occasionally, on the tag. S. = sigillum.

9. John de Inchmartin in green wax; the nineteenth-century engraving shows his name on the bottom end of the tag, now gone.

10. S. comitis Suthirlandie. Tag, no seal.

11. S. Walteri Senescalli Scocie. Tag, no seal.

12. W. de Soules. Tag, no seal, but the nineteenth-century engraving shows his seal appended in red wax.

13. S. Jacobi de Duglas. Tag, no seal.

14. S. Rogeri de Moubray. Tag and seal in red wax.

15. S. Dauid de Brechyn. The name Brechyn is written over an erasure, presumably Graham. Tag, no seal and almost certainly never bore a seal.

16. S. Dauid de Brechyn. An attempt has been begun to alter Brechyn to Graham (whose name should be here, see no. 50 below) and then given up. Tag and seal in red wax of Brechin's wife.

Second row:

17. S. Ingerammi de Umfrauill. Tag and seal in red wax.

18. S. J. de Meneteth. Tag, no seal.

19. S. Alexandri Fraser. Tag and seal in red wax.

20. S. Gilberti de Haya. Tag and seal in red wax.

21. S. Roberti de Keth. Tag bearing no sign of seal in red wax but on the tag the words

22. Alexandri de Lamberton with his seal in green wax.

23. S. Henrici de Sancto Claro. Tag, no seal.

24. S. Johannis de Graham. Tag, no trace of Graham's seal but the words

25. Thome de Meneris and his seal in green wax.

26. S. Dauid de Lindesay. Tag, no seal.

27. S. W. Olifaunt. Tag and seal in green wax.

28. S. Patricii de Graham. Tag, no seal, nor is his seal on the document despite several commentators who have taken no. 30 as his.

29. S. J. de Fenton. Tag, no trace of Fenton's seal but the words

30. T. de Morham and a seal in green wax which (as the nineteenth-century engraving shows) is Morham's.

31. S. W. de Abernithy. Tag, no seal.
32. S. Dauid de Wemys. Tag, no seal.
33. S. W. de Montefixo. Tag, no seal.
34. No name. Tag bearing words Roger Mouaut, no seal.
35. No name. Tag, no seal.
36. S. Fergus de Ardrosan. Tag, no seal.

Third row:

37. S. Eustachii de Maxwell. Tag, no seal.
38. S. W. de Ramesay. Tag, no seal.
39. S. W. de Monte alto. Tag, no seal.
40. S. Alani de Morauia. No slit or tag. The seal was on no. 4 above.
41. S. Douenaldi Cambel. Tag bearing once three seals, the first, presumably Campbell's, now gone, but leaving traces of green wax.
42. Seal of Edward de Keith in green wax on the same tag.
43. Small seal in green wax, legend reading in nineteenth-century engraving S. MARTINI . . . BEL (? Cambel) on the same tag.
44. S. J. Cambrun. No slit, tag, or seal.
45. S. Reginaldi le Chen. Tag and seal in green wax.
46. S. Alexandri de Seton. Tag and seal in green wax.
47. S. Andree de Lescelyn. Tag, no seal.
48. S. Alexandri de Straton. Tag, no seal.
49. No name. Tag, no seal. Placed rather high and under no. 31 above.
50. Tag and seal of David de Graham in green wax (displaced from slit at 15 or 16) above.
51. In a fourth row tucked before and below 45, tag and seal of John Duraunt in green wax.

It is quite clear from the original that the first two rows of names were written first, and the slits for them cut. The second row of slits slipped and sagged towards the middle out of alignment with the names so that when the third row of names was written, no. 45 was written round the tag of 26; there was no room to put slits under the names 40, 44, and the seals were put elsewhere, while the slit follows the name in the case of 45, 46, and 47 instead of being underneath it. Thus the seals of the first two rows were appended before the third row was prepared. If the names of senders only are taken into account and additional seals ignored it is clear that the intention was to use red wax at least as far as the eighteenth name (no. 20) and that from the twenty-third name (no. 27) they were to be in green wax. It is curious that the change should take place in the middle of a row, but explicable if Tyn follows Av which had not three but two rows of seals, the top row in red ending with the nineteenth name, the marshall, whose seal is absent (or perhaps with the twentieth) and the second row having twenty green seals (or perhaps nineteen). This view implies not haphazard sealing of a round robin but programmed sealing of fair copy (Av) and file copy (Tyn) in a central office; and a comparison of Tyn with an original of the 1301 English letter (made possible by their simultaneous exhibition in Edinburgh in 1970) shows a marked contrast between the mottled and varied seals on the English letter (a round robin) and the absolutely uniform two waxes of Tyn. The latter cannot have been a round robin.

The names Brechin and Graham in the text were reversed by oversight on the fold, and an attempt was made to correct them and then abandoned. Graham's seal was thus ousted from its red placing and relegated to the corner below where it was put in green wax; when this happened some attempt was still being made to match the seals exactly to the names in the text—indeed the unfinished correction represents the first abandonment of that purpose —and to preserve the hierarchy of two colours borrowed from Av, i.e. before the third row of slits and seals was appended to Tyn. With this third row came a further abandonment of the original purpose when names were written but some seals put elsewhere, as though it were realized that a file copy did not have to meet the scrutiny of the papal curia. Then came the seals, at least eleven of them, of those who were not named as senders. These are appended in three ways, through additional slits (34, 35, 49, 51), through slits prepared for others (9, 22, 25, 30), and on tags already bearing their correct seals (6, 42, 43) and it would seem logical that the first or second of these was tried before recourse was had to the others. These expedients represent the total abandonment of a plan suited to, and needed for, Av alone; since there was little point in adding eleven seals to Tyn unless they were also on Av, we may conjecture that they made an altogether neater show, perhaps as a third row, upon it.

There is reason to believe that many of the missing seals were once appended, for the eighteenth-century engraving shows one of them (no. 1) and thirty-nine circles to represent others. The document was subsequently badly treated and a heavy loss is understandable. However, the seals of the three northern earls were probably (one certainly) not appended and their names represent aristocratic weight to impress the pope. Three other earls (Moray, Fife, March) were at Newbattle on 31 March and with a fourth (Strathearn) witness a royal charter dated at Arbroath on 6 May: their seals could have been in the chancellor's custody in the intervening period. The seal of the remaining earl, Lennox, was accompanied by that of a Stirlingshire laird (nos. 5, 6), and it would seem possible that he brought the earl's seal to chancery; a similar explanation would fit nos. 41 and 43, and the use of the seal of Brechin's wife—he would not part with his own. Moreover, the apparent placing of two important barons, Cheyne and Seton, towards the end of an obvious hierarchy should give us pause; the Sc text shows that they were placed thus in a draft so they are not late additions. In the circumstances they must be the synonymous heirs of, and representing, their baronial fathers. Since Seton the father was steward of the king's household, his omission is notable but could be explained by his need of his own seal. A similar explanation for the brothers, nos. 21 and 42, seems rather weaker. When three names were added to the draft, already dated Arbroath 6 April, at least one name, the panetar, had already been deleted from it, perhaps because Alan Moray had brought his seal in lieu.

It would seem that like Topsy the list of senders growed, and with a few exceptions what determined the names in it when Tyn and Av were written was the availability of their seals; the exceptions were names (e.g. the marshall no. 21) kept in because their seals were expected or hoped for, but the absence of other obvious names is most simply explained by a decision to go ahead before their seals arrived. It has already been suggested that the chancellor may have kept some 'red-rank' seals from the time of the Newbattle council. But others must have been sent for and brought to Arbroath in person or by deputy, and this process cannot have been a matter of a few days or even a week: the need to let these seals go again would explain the decision to finalize the list of senders, write the documents, and append the available seals. It would also explain the addition of supernumerary or makeweight late-arriving seals. It is impossible to put a strict timetable upon the various stages but a preliminary list is likely to have existed by the end of March when the panetar was at court. When the Sc draft was made it already bore the date 6 April yet the text and names of senders were revised before Tyn and presumably Av were drawn up and given the same date. It follows that while the genesis of the declaration lies before 6 April, its final form must be somewhat, and could well be much, later in the same month or even early in May. There was in fact no need to finalize the sealing of the declaration until the other two letters were also ready—and that of the king required the great seal. Since the great seal seems to have returned to Arbroath early in May, in the course of which month other business begun in March and early April was completed, May is also the most likely time for the final drawing up of the royal letter to the pope and the baronial letter could be as late. Why the date 6 April was chosen for the latter is unknown and conjectures that it represents the first draft or the sending for seals are incapable of proof. But there was some point in retaining 6 April since it gave to the letter the appearance of being a timeous reply to the papal summons of Robert I and his bishops for 1 May. It is significant that the pope in accepting Robert I's letter and offer of due reverence found in the letter an excuse for its lateness: 'in eadem subiuncto quod super eo quod citius ad nos tuos nequiveras nuncios propter impedimenta in eisdem expressa litteris destinare, nec invenires quos mitteres, excusatam habere tuam innocentiam dignaremur.'[1] This is a convenient if somewhat lame explanation for a difference in date between the royal and baronial letters. In fact, since they were part of the same démarche and since neither had point without the other, they are likely to have been synchronous or nearly so.

To sum up, it is argued that the idea of the declaration was

[1] *Vetera Monumenta*, p. 209b.

conceived at a large council at Newbattle in March 1320 and that the text was drafted about 6 April 1320 by the chancellor at Arbroath but not finalized till later, being dispatched in May. The seals were to be appended (to both the surviving original and the lost text sent to Avignon) in concordance with the names of senders but this plan was changed because, it is suggested, seals were not made available by all the named barons, while some supernumerary ones were available. This explains why the method of sealing shows irregularity although the seals themselves are uniformly in two colours of wax. The document was produced by the government for its own diplomatic—some might say propaganda—purposes, and there is no necessity for or even likelihood of the putative *convocatio* of magnates at Arbroath attributed to the declaration by a chronicler a century later.[1]

A. A. M. DUNCAN

[1] *Chron. Bower*, ii. 275. I should like to express my indebtedness to my colleague, Professor E. L. G. Stones, who very kindly gave me a number of references to barons' letters to the pope.

IX

The Records of the Bishop's Official at Ely: Specialization in the English Episcopal Chancery of the Later Middle Ages

IN the twelfth century the archdeacons of the newly created diocese of Ely claimed to have inherited from their predecessor Henry, archdeacon of Huntingdon and Cambridge, a well-established tradition of independent action, which virtually excluded any judicial or administrative action by the bishops of the see. At intervals during this and the next two centuries the bishops resisted this interpretation of archidiaconal powers, but without permanent success, for Ely was a wealthy see, its bishops were very often royal clerks, and their long absences allowed the archdeacons to re-establish themselves after every check. At last a long series of clashes in the late fourteenth century resulted in the defeat of the archdeacon, in a composition forced upon him by a former bishop of the see who had become archbishop of Canterbury.[1] Briefly, this composition finally awarded to the bishops the custody of all vacant benefices within the diocese, ordinary jurisdiction, without intervention by the archdeacon, in the whole of the Isle of Ely and in the three Cambridgeshire deaneries of Camps, Chesterton, and Barton, and testamentary jurisdiction in the same area.[2] For the future the bishop and his representatives would have undisputed control of a much larger share of the diocesan administration and the bishop's leading representative, his official, would be of primary importance there. It is with this official, and particularly with the records of his activity, that this paper is concerned.

Interest in the subject of ecclesiastical administration was first

---

[1] Margaret Aston, *Thomas Arundel* (Oxford, 1967), pp. 83–133.
[2] C. L. Feltoe and E. H. Minns, *Vetus Liber Archidiaconi Eliensis* (Cambridge Antiquarian Society, octavo series, xlviii, 1917), pp. 180–95.

aroused by the publication in 1880 of Paul Fournier's important work on the medieval episcopal official in France. There have been since that time a number of studies of the officiality in individual German, Swiss, and Belgian dioceses, an edition of a Paris consistory court book has appeared, and Edouard Fournier, in two works on the vicar general in the French church, has added much to his namesake's original observations.[1] Meanwhile, in England, a few scholars began to make tentative studies of the officials and their consistory courts, and of the origins of episcopal administration. Professor Major's own work on the *familia* of Stephen Langton, and Professor Cheney's study of English episcopal chanceries, have laid the early foundations for this work, while Professor Hamilton Thompson's unrivalled knowledge of the episcopal records of the fourteenth and fifteenth centuries enabled him to publish a general survey of great insight, of the working of the later administration.[2]

Since 1945 a few studies have been made of the administration of individual dioceses, and it is becoming increasingly clear that superficial similarities in the names of officials and of their books may mask entirely different forms of administration. Every diocese seems to have an official, who presides over a court known as a consistory, but in many cases the official shares responsibility for the rest of the work of the diocese with officials variously known as sequestrators, or commissaries, who sometimes merely look after vacant benefices, but more often are also concerned with the probate of wills. Then there are in some cases commissarlies general, who prove wills and correct the faults of the laity, in the course of 'tourns' rather similar to the later visitation circuit. At

[1] P. Fournier, *Les Officialités au Moyen Age* (Paris, 1880); E. Fournier, *Les Origine du vicaire général* (Paris, 1922), *L'Origine du vicaire général et des autres membres de la Curie Diocésaine* (Paris, 1940); C. Petit, *Registre des causes civiles de l'officialité de Paris, 1384–7* (Paris, 1919); L. Carlen, 'Zum Officialat von Sitten im Mittelalter', *Zeitschrift der Savigny-Stiftung, Kanonische Abt.*, vol. xlvi (1960), pp. 221–38; L. Carolus-Barré, 'L'organisation de la juridiction gracieuse à Paris dans le dernier tiers du XIIIᵉ siècle', *Moyen Age*, t. lxix (1963), pp. 417–35. I am very grateful to Mr. David Smith, who has drawn my attention to recent European work on the officiality.

[2] Kathleen Major, 'The *Familia* of Archbishop Stephen Langton', *EHR*, xlviii (1933), 529–53; *Acta Stephani Langton*, ed. K. Major (C.Y.S., vol. 50, 1950); C. R. Cheney, *English Bishops' Chanceries, 1100–1250* (Manchester, 1950); A. Hamilton Thompson, *The English Clergy and their Organisation in the Later Middle Ages* (Oxford, 1947), pp. 40–71.

Worcester, the sequestrator acted as commissary general; in Hereford, Bath and Wells, and Rochester the commissary also did the
sequestrator's work; in York and Durham a sequestrator general
seems to have been the principal diocesan administrator beside the
official.[1] The larger diocese of Lincoln had its own special problems,
which Professor Morris has elucidated for the earlier period, and
which Mrs. Bowker considers below. Here the sequestrator of each
archdeaconry had very marked importance and power as early as
the pontificate of Oliver Sutton, and occupied a position of influence
second only to that of the official in the diocese as a whole. Eventually he was known as the bishop's commissary.[2]

Generalization about episcopal administration in England
would obviously be somewhat dangerous, and the situation is
not simplified by the almost complete absence of records of the
administration of most of these functionaries. There are plenty of
mandates showing for what *ad hoc* business they were used at
different times, but very few detailed commissions showing what
the regular work of a commissary, a sequestrator, or even an official,
should be. The official, it is true, has his authority in the canon law,
and such of his records as have survived have generally been held to
demonstrate that he presided over the court in which contentious
litigation brought to the bishop's judgement was heard.[3] There
seems to be little evidence for the exercise of the so-called gracious
jurisdiction, the use of the court as a place of record for agreements,

[1] R. L. Storey, *Diocesan Administration in the Fifteenth Century* (St. Anthony's Hall
Publications, no. 16, York, 1959); R. M. Haines, *The Administration of the Diocese of
Worcester in the first half of the Fourteenth Century* (Church Historical Society, 1965),
Calendar of the Register of Wolstan de Bransford, 1339–49 (H.M.C. Joint Publication
no. 9, with Worcs. Hist. Soc., 1966); R. W. Dunning, 'The Wells Consistory Court
in the Fifteenth Century', *Proc. Som. Arch. and Nat. Hist. Soc.*, vol. 106 (1962),
pp. 46–61; Maidstone, Kent Archives Office, DRB/Pwr/1, Rochester will register
1440–53, containing miscellaneous court records; Hereford, diocesan records, office
court books, 1 and 2.

[2] C. Morris, 'The Commissary of the Bishop in the Diocese of Lincoln', *JEH*, x
(1959), pp. 50–65; other material relating to the thirteenth-century sequestrator
appears in D. M. Owen, 'A Lincoln Diocesan Book', *Lincs. Architectural and Archaeological Soc. Reports and Papers*, vol. x (1963–4), pp. 138–47, and *Rolls and Register of
Bishop Oliver Sutton*, ed. R. M. T. Hill, vol. 6 (L.R.S., vol. 64, 1969), pp. 2–3.

[3] C. E. Woodruff, 'Notes from a Fourteenth Century Act Book of the Consistory
Court of Canterbury', *Archaeologia Cantiana* 40 (1928), pp. 53–64; *Registrum Hamonis
Hethe diocesis Roffensis*, ed. C. Johnson (C.Y.S., vol. 49, 1948), pp. 911–1043; C. Morris,
'A Consistory Court in the Middle Ages', *JEH*, xiv (1963), pp. 150–9.

declarations, and the like, which formed so conspicuous a part of the activity of the official of Paris, yet most of the known earlier *acta* of English episcopal officials seem to be connected with this sort of business and there is no doubt that it continued to play an important part in their activity. Remarkably little is really known as yet about the way in which testamentary jurisdiction was exercised before the fifteenth century, for it has left few traces, except in the records of clergy and magnates' wills in the episcopal registers, before that period.[1] We have seen that some evidence exists for the functions of the sequestrator in the diocese of Lincoln, and a notebook of the canon lawyer who was official of Winchester and archdeacon of Totnes in the late fourteenth century, John Lydford, which Miss Joan Sinar found among the Exeter diocesan records, and which the present writer is editing for the Devon and Cornwall Record Society, reveals how much more than a presiding judge the official could become, even in a large diocese.

Special conditions, such as those in Canterbury, or the mere smallness of some dioceses, like Rochester, make it likely that the official, or whoever presided in the consistory, performed many functions which can never be thought of as strictly judicial, even though they may be recorded among the acts of the consistory. His office became, in fact, an amalgam of official, sequestrator, and commissary, as they appear to have developed in larger dioceses. The situation in Ely is of this nature, and the need to concentrate offices in the person of the official was intensified there, in the late fourteenth century, by the need to counteract the archdeacon's official, who had usurped, or perhaps always performed many of them in the past. As a result, the episcopal official began to perform in his consistory, or in association with it, many administrative acts which were duly recorded in its records. This is a development which is of more than antiquarian interest, for it seems to explain the curious form of record which appears, in the seventeenth and eighteenth centuries, in Ely and elsewhere, and which includes in a

---

[1] For an appraisal of the present state of knowledge, see M. M. Sheehan, *The Will in Medieval England* (Pontifical Institute of Medieval Studies, Studies and Texts 6, Toronto, 1963), pp. 164–76. For the later period there is much information in the introduction to vol. ii of *The Register of Henry Chichele*, ed. E. F. Jacob (C.Y.S., vols. 42, 45–7, 1937–47).

single volume sequestrations of benefices, *caveats* in testamentary causes, and marriage licences.[1] Such a volume might well involve the cataloguer and user of such records in serious problems of classification, and while this is not the place for a detailed discussion of the difficulties and dilemmas of the archivist cataloguing ecclesiastical records, it is not inappropriate, in a volume of studies intended to honour the author of a pioneer handlist of diocesan records, to draw attention to some of the administrative and historical factors which help to create these problems. Failure to recognize the existence of these special factors led Alfred Gibbons, who produced in 1891 the first catalogue of the Ely diocesan records, to bury in arbitrary classes of visitation and court books the records of diocesan synods, and to ignore the evidence of the machinery by which the Reformation changes were implemented in the diocese.[2]

The early history of the officiality in Ely is as obscure as in most other dioceses. It seems certain that Hugh, the bishop's official ('Hugo officialis episcopi') who witnesses an act of Bishop Eustace (1197–1215), is in fact the same as Hugh the official of the archdeacon ('Ricardus archidiaconus Eliensis', 'Hugo officialis eius').[3] The same difficulty of interpretation attaches to Mr. Robert of Ewerby, who appears as official of Ely among the witnesses of three charters of Bishop John of Fountains (1220–5).[4] Mr. John of Caen is described by Hugh of Northwold as 'our official' in two acts earlier than 1245, again without any certainty that he is not the archdeacon's official.[5] None of these officials has yet been found performing judicial functions, but Dr. Donald Logan has recently shown that Hugh of Balsham's first official, Roger Leicester, was certainly doing so about 1258.[6] Balsham's second official, Alan of Ruckland,

---

[1] An example of this type is the first Rochester muniment book, Kent Archives Office, DRB/Am 1, 1683–1717.

[2] A. Gibbons, *Ely Episcopal Records, A Calendar and Concise View* ... (Lincoln, privately printed, 1891); D. M. Owen, 'Synods in the Diocese of Ely', *Studies in Church History*, vol. iii, ed. G. J. Cuming (Leiden, 1966), pp. 217–22, and 'The Reformation in the Diocese of Ely', *Papers read to the Colloque d'histoire ecclésiastique de Cambridge*, 1968.

[3] C.U.L., Ely Dean and Chapter, charter 60; Ely Diocesan Records (E.D.R.) G/3/28, f. 92ᵛ.   [4] E.D.R. G/3/28, ff. 94ᵛ, 95.

[5] Ibid., ff. 101, 101ᵛ; G/3/29 (Liber R), f. 224.

[6] F. D. Logan, *Excommunication and the Secular Arm in Medieval England* (Pontifical Institute of Medieval Studies, Studies and Texts 15, Toronto, 1968), p. 27 n. 12, citing P.R.O. C. 85/66/7.

appears in two cases where he is plainly acting as vicar general during the bishop's absence, in 1269 and 1272.[1] When William of Louth became bishop in 1290, the seal of the officiality was in existence and Guy, the bishop's official, was applying it to a series of acts recording the settlement of disputes in which he had acted as arbitrator, between 1290 and 1295.[2]

The earliest surviving episcopal register of the diocese, that of Simon Montacute, for the years 1337–45, contains a few references to the official John of Clipsham, when he is acting as a special commissary of the bishop, in disputes relating to the Chancellor of the University of Cambridge, and in the sequestration of the benefices of defaulting incumbents. It also mentions an advocate of the consistory, and the seal of the officiality.[3] There is evidence from the next episcopate, that of Thomas Lisle, that the official was engaged in visitation and clerical discipline, for in 1352–3 he imposed a money penance, which was collected on his behalf by the sacrist of Ely, on the vicar of Whittlesey St. Andrew.[4] Nevertheless, Lisle's register, like that of his predecessor, suggests that for general administration the bishops were relying almost entirely on the official of the archdeacon or the prior of Barnwell. Thus, the archdeacon's official was used as an agent in the levy and collection of clerical subsidies and the return to the archbishop of the names of alien incumbents, while the prior presided over the synod and received oaths of obedience.[5] The relative position of official and archdeacon's official, and the predominance of the latter, is well displayed in two instances. In 1340 a royal writ ordered a search of the records of Bishop John of Hotham's time to be made, for information about a divorce cause. The bishop's return says that the bishop's and archdeacon's registers have been searched without success, but Mr. John of Tydd, 'commissary of the spiritual jurisdiction of the archdeacon', 'exhibuit nobis quasdam cedulas inventas ut dicitur in quadam cista archidiaconi predicti in quibus

---

[1] J. W. Clark, *Liber Memorandorum Ecclesie de Bernewell* (Cambridge, 1907), pp. 172–3. Professor Cheney has pointed out to me a further reference to Ruckland in E.D.R. G/1/3, f. 148 (1272).

[2] *Liber . . . de Bernewell*, pp. 210, 212–18.

[3] E.D.R. G/1/1 Montacute, f. 92.

[4] F. R. Chapman, *The Sacrist Rolls of Ely* (Cambridge, 1907), ii. 151.

[5] E.D.R. G/1/1 Lisle, ff. 1ᵛ, 8, 8ᵛ.

scribitur quod divorcium celebratum extitit inter partes infra-
scriptas set quia harum cedularum alique non sunt sigillate nec
integre set in tantum corrupte quod propter corrupcionem perlegi
non poterunt ullo modo'.[1] This all sounds a little amateurish and
unsatisfactory, but no mention is made of any records of the consistory, or the official. It is equally significant that although, since
the legislation of the papal legate Otto for the English Church in
1237, archdeacons and lesser judges had been discouraged from
hearing matrimonial causes, the archdeacon of Ely was plainly still
doing so.[2] The second incident occurred during the long absence
at the papal court, terminated only by his death in 1361, of Bishop
Lisle, a time when no doubt the archdeacon and his official improved
all their opportunities. A royal writ addressed to the vicar general
of the diocese, who would be presumed to act in the bishop's
absence abroad, ordered him to sequestrate the goods of a vacant
benefice, a duty which had certainly been performed by the episcopal official in Montacute's episcopate. The writ was returned by
Thomas of Wormenhale, official and commissary general of the
archdeacon, who had acted 'because there is no such vicar general'.[3]

The encroachments of these absentee years were no doubt too
palpable to be tolerated and it seems likely that they must have
provoked a reaction in the following episcopates. Certainly there
is a marked effort to reassert and redefine the powers of the episcopal
official, and to reorganize his administration and its records in a
more professional manner. There is not much sign of activity
against the archdeacon during the next two episcopates, those of
Simon Langham and John Barnet, which cover the years from 1362 to
1373, but this may be only because the episcopal registers are
wanting. Certainly the consistory was active again before Barnet's
death, for in 1372 Thomas of Wormenhale, who by this time was
episcopal official, was recorded as twice, in the single year 1372,
admitting and swearing advocates to plead there.[4] It seems very
much as if a rather weakened and depleted organization was being

---

[1] E.D.R. G/1/1. Montacute, f. 92.

[2] F. M. Powicke and C. R. Cheney, *Councils and Synods* (Oxford, 1964), i. 255.

[3] *Calendar of Miscellaneous Inquisitions*, iii (H.M.S.O., 1937), pp. 126–7; E.D.R.
G/1/1 Montacute, f. 73, Lisle, f. 82; for Lisle's career see *Dictionary of National Biography*, xxxiii. 343.   [4] C.U.L., Add. MS. 3468, f. 94ᵛ.

revivified. With the episcopate of Thomas Arundel (1373–88) a determined effort was made to combat the archdeacon, to control his official and limit his jurisdiction, and to strengthen the hand of the episcopal official. Mrs. Aston has traced the course of the dispute in great detail, and there is no need to retell the story here, but it is necessary to remember that the principal engagements were fought in the episcopal consistory, and that organization of its sessions and systematic record of its activities seems to have been a by-product of the struggle to reassert episcopal authority.

The earliest commission of an Ely official is recorded at the beginning of Arundel's register, when Nicholas Roos was empowered to hear and determine all cases, both of instance and office, which belong to the bishop's jurisdiction, to correct and punish his subjects, to sequestrate benefices, prove wills, and approve administrations of intestates, to receive oaths of obedience, and to celebrate the diocesan synod.[1] This mixture of judicial and purely administrative functions is unusual and is clearly intended to strengthen the episcopal machinery to counteract the archidiaconal encroachments, particularly in the matters of sequestrations, probates, and the synod. Earlier episcopal officials in Ely and elsewhere may have performed some or all of these acts, as special commissaries, at various times, and we have seen that the Lincoln functionary known as sequestrator or commissary was always particularly concerned with sequestrations and probates, but no evidence has as yet been found to show that the official was required, in any other diocese than Ely, to do this work. Nor is there much evidence that earlier officials had received comparable powers, but the pattern was now laid down for future commissions of the officiality. Richard le Scrope and John of Newton who followed Roos in 1375 and 1379 respectively, had identical commissions, and Newton's commission was renewed on the same terms in 1388 by Arundel's successor John Fordham.[2] It is true that during this episcopate the official usually shared any specially assigned duties with a commissary, but there is no specific commission for him, and he appears to be no more than the official's deputy. Thomas Bourchier briefly introduced a slightly different procedure in 1445, when, on the same day, he commissioned

---

[1] E.D.R. G/1/2, f. 1.　　　　[1] Ibid., ff. 11ᵛ, 30ᵛ; G/1/3, f. 3ᵛ.

a commissary general to correct and punish his subjects, and to deal with probates, administrations, sequestrations, and pensions, and an official, who was to proceed in all cases belonging to the bishop's jurisdiction, in deprivations of clerks, augmentations of benefices, appointments of penitentiaries and the celebration of the diocesan synod.[1] This division of functions, which Bourchier may have known and imported from his previous diocese of Worcester, was short-lived, and his successors William Gray and John Alcock (there is no register for Morton's episcopate) reunited the two offices, so that by 1500 the officials of Ely had an almost continuous tradition of some hundred and twenty years of administrative activity in the consistory court.[2]

Reference has already been made to a record of admissions of advocates to practise in the consistory court, and the volume in which this occurs, University Library Cambridge Additional MS. 3468, the Black Book of Ely, is an important testimony to the reorganization of the Ely consistory. It is a collection of miscellaneous quires of various dates, which were apparently put together in the early fifteenth century. The first gathering of twelve leaves contains a calendar, written in a thirteenth-century hand and much rubbed and thumbed. The second gathering, eight leaves in all, consists of early fifteenth-century copies of various ecclesiastical statutes. This is followed by a copy of the Arundel composition of 1401, written fairly soon after it was concluded, and taking up two gatherings, of sixteen leaves, two blank sides in which are filled with copies of the statutes of the consistory. Gatherings five and six, of sixteen leaves in all, contain an office for the synod, and a copy of the Ely synodal statutes, all written in a mid fourteenth-century hand, and showing signs of heavy use. This section is followed by six gatherings, of forty-seven leaves, taken up by a copy of the taxation of Pope Nicholas for the diocese, various financial memoranda and metropolitical statutes, and the names of advocates and proctors admitted to practise in the consistory in the late fourteenth century. This whole section is written in the same hand or hands as the consistory court register discussed below. The volume is completed by three later gatherings, of whiter parchment than the

[1] E.D.R. G/1/4, ff. 2 and 2ᵛ.   [2] E.D.R. G/1/5, ff. 1ᵛ, 50ᵛ; G/1/6, ff. 5, 61ᵛ.

rest, which contain a series of entries, including proctors' names, of the sixteenth, seventeenth, and eighteenth centuries. The last record of a proctor is dated 1708, at which date the volume was presumably still in official custody. Francis Blomefield handled it, and perhaps even acquired it, in 1728, and William Cole wrote his name in it in 1752 and may also have owned it. If, when Cole saw it, the book was still in the consistory court records, it no doubt escaped, like the consistory register, after the sudden death of the deputy registrar, Thomas Higgins, in 1760.[1]

The whole of the Black Book has traces of Mr. Robert Foxton, notary public, who was scribe and registrar of the consistory during Arundel's episcopate.[2] His hand, for example, makes lavish and elaborate annotations on the calendar, of the dates of Easter between 1375 and 1410, the death of Mr. Nicholas Roos, official of Ely, in September 1375, the coronation of Pope Urban VI, in April 1378, and similar outstanding anniversaries. He makes a few verbal corrections and annotations on the copy of the synodal statutes, he, or his clerks, actually copy the decrees of Archbishops Winchelsey and Reynolds relating to tithes and church furniture, and the whole of the Pope Nicholas taxation for the diocese, and it is he who enters the names of advocates admitted to the consistory in the years 1372–5. Since Foxton's entries on occasion cross the boundaries between two gatherings it seems likely that the present format had already been reached when he wrote, and that he, or one of his masters, prepared the volume for use by the officers of the consistory soon after 1401.

Perhaps the most important single item, from the point of view of the consistory, is the set of articles for the conduct of advocates and proctors in the consistory of Ely, which is found on f. 35. This follows the text of the statutes of the consistory, to which the advocates admitted by Mr. Richard le Scrope during a full meeting of the clergy of the diocese, which had been called to elect proctors

---

[1] I am very grateful to Mr. H. L. Pink and to Dr. A. N. L. Munby, for helping me to elucidate the history of this manuscript, which figured in John Meyrick's sale in 1806, and was there purchased by Richard Heber, at whose sale in 1836 Sir Thomas Phillipps acquired it (Phillipps 8121). It was sold to C.U.L. in 1898. For the dispersal of 1760 see D. M. Owen, 'Ely Diocesan Records', *Studies in Church History*, vol. i, ed. C. W. Dugmore and C. Duggan (1964), 176–83.

[2] For Robert Foxton, see A. B. Emden, *A Biographical Register of the University of Cambridge to 1500* (Cambridge, 1963), p. 241; Aston, op. cit., *passim*.

in convocation, on Saturday 24 January 1377/8, were required to swear obedience.[1] In the Black Book version there are three additional statutes concerned with the maintenance of episcopal jurisdiction. A parallel set of statutes, using almost identical words, except where the interests of the archdeacon require small verbal adjustments, was entered in the *Vetus Liber Archidiaconi* in the early fifteenth century,[2] and it is difficult to avoid the conclusion that the appearance, or perhaps reaffirmation of the statutes, marks a conscious attempt, made in Arundel's time, to organize the episcopal consistory on a professional basis, which also influenced the rest of the legal community in Cambridge. It is conceivable that a document copied by the antiquary Thomas Baker for Browne Willis, 'ex Registro Veteri Eliensi, f. 43' relating to the system of sequestrators in the diocese of Lincoln, may be associated with the same period of reform and reorganization, but the evidence is as yet too tenuous for this to be established.[3]

The chief evidence for the reorganization of the consistory and the episcopal administration is the register of the consistory itself (E.D.R. D/2/1). Although the inscription on the first folio of the manuscript, 'Registrum primum causarum consistorii Episcopi Eliensis de tempore Thome de Arundell' is perhaps a later addition, there is no evidence that any earlier register was ever made. It is equally significant that at the end of the register the scribe has written 'Quere proximum consistorium in libro secundo registri causarum' as if this were indeed the first of the series. We have seen that no consistory court records were searched for evidence of a divorce cause in 1339, and presumably none existed. Arundel's own register contains mention of the quire of episcopal visitation, and there was a register of corrections made during the vacancy after the death of John Barnet (1373)[4] but nothing suggests that earlier records of this type were retained. Occasional official acts such as the Barnwell compositions made by the official Guy, have

---

[1] E.D.R. D/2/1, f. 62ᵛ, printed in Aston, op. cit., pp. 407–8.
[2] Feltoe and Minns, op. cit., pp. 164–5.
[3] Mentioned by Morris, 'The Commissary . . .', p. 53, n. 7. I am very grateful to Dr. D. M. Barratt for verifying and amplifying this reference for me in Bodleian MS. Willis, 39, f. 285. The reference is to B.M. Add. MS. 9822, f. 27, where the document is copied in a late fifteenth-century hand, as Dr. G. R. C. Davis informs me.
[4] E.D.R. G/1/2, ff. 12ᵛ, 19.

been preserved in a copy, and an original from the time of Arundel himself survives in the muniments of Corpus Christi College.[1]

The register thus begun to record the official's activity, under what seems to be an entirely novel commission, is a remarkable document. It consists of twenty gatherings, carefully numbered, each of eight leaves. The whole is fairly written, in two, or at most three hands, with the signature of the registrar Robert Foxton, at the lower right hand corner of each *recto*, a running head of the year date and the official's name, marginal titles, and a pagination in Roman numerals slightly later in date than the text hands. The gatherings are stitched and toggled into a limp parchment cover which appears to be of the same date as the volume itself and is lined with linen. It has been adorned with two shields of arms still bearing traces of colour and has had an imposing appearance. The volume opens with a copy of the official's commission, which is followed immediately by a record of the taking by the archdeacon, before the official, of an oath of obedience to the bishop. Then there is a 'congregacio cleri pro obediencia prestanda', with a full record of the names of the clergy taking part in the two sessions in Cambridge and Ely. A chronological record of the formal judicial sessions of the consistory, which cover the period 21 March 1373/4 to 28 February 1381/2, now begins. Each session has its heading: 'Acta coram nobis . . . in ecclesia . . . die . . . anno domini predicto. Et agendum in ecclesia . . . coram . . . die . . .' (see Plate 3). Between the formal sessions non-judicial business was entered more or less chronologically, but without formality, as it might be in an episcopal memoranda register.

The strictly judicial record is, for the most part, a brief note of the cases heard at each session, with a memorandum of the stage each had reached and of the next date assigned to its hearing; it is, in fact, what is later known as an 'assignation book'. At the end of many sessions, however, there are full narratives, often with transcripts, of libels, depositions, and sentences, of many matrimonial and tithe causes which seem to have been heard separately, either by the official or by one of his deputies, outside the regular meetings

---

[1] I am grateful to Mrs. C. P. Hall for knowledge of this document, of which a sixteenth-century copy is entered in a formulary, E.D.R. A/6/1, p. 53.

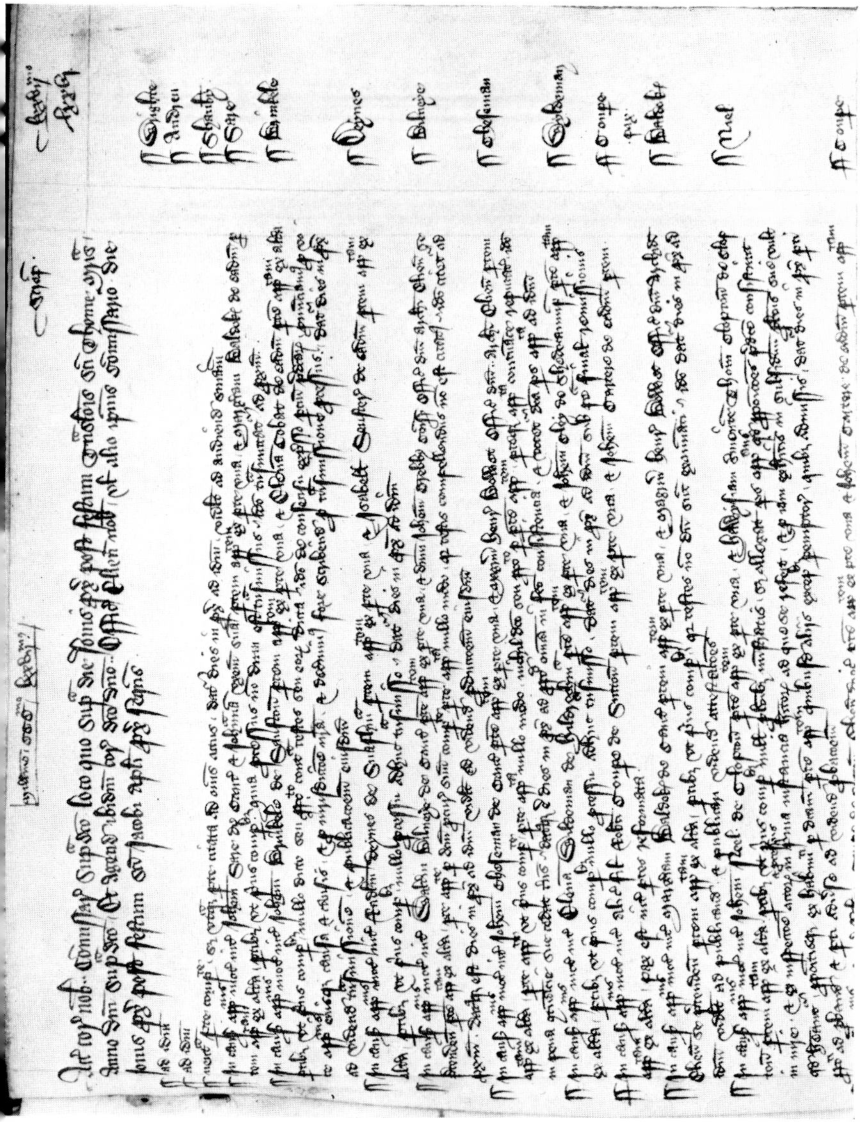

PLATE 3

Act book of the
Official of Ely,
9 July 1377

of the consistory. Many of the cases, especially in the earlier sessions, are appeals from judgements given in the archidiaconal court and they doubtless result from the determination of the episcopal administration to weaken the hold of the archdeacon. Many, though by no means all, of the cases are brought by one party against another, that is, they are instance cases and there is so little of the correction business resulting from visitation that separate registers must certainly have been kept for it, although a certain number of office cases promoted by third parties were heard in the consistory. Moreover, the business produced by sequestrations and the assignment of 'curators' for delinquent or inefficient incumbents seems to have been treated as if it were office business, with formal investigations made by the official in a legal form. A hundred years after this time the official was certainly conducting visitations, for the only surviving consistory record for the medieval period, after the register, is a so-called will register, for the years 1460–80, which consists largely of records of *capitula generalia*, or visitations, of the official in the deanery of Wisbech, in the blank spaces of which a number of wills were copied at a slightly later date.[1] Records of this nature can be paralleled in Hereford, Bath and Wells, and Rochester, at much the same period, and Brian Woodcock has described the court in circuit, with much the same effect, in Canterbury.[2]

The rest of the material contained in the register, outside the regular sessions, falls into several different sections. There are firstly the records of synods, celebrated sometimes by the official himself, sometimes by the prior of Barnwell, which are noted in their appropriate chronological place. Closely related to these entries are the records of the assemblies of clergy in which the proctors for convocation and the provincial councils are elected.[3]

[1] Cambridge University Archives, probate records, consistory, Liber B. I am grateful to Miss H. E. Peek for facilitating access to this and other volumes in her care. Some of its contents were published by W. M. Palmer in *Proc. Cambridge Antiquarian Soc.*, 39 (1938), pp. 69–75.

[2] See p. 191, nn. 1 and 2; B. L. Woodcock, *Medieval Ecclesiastical Courts in the Diocese of Canterbury* (Oxford, 1952), p. 33.

[3] f. 127ᵛ: 'comparens coram nobis Officiali Eliensi in ecclesia Sancte Marie extra Trumpitongates Cantebr' clerus Eliensis diocesis ad eligendum duos procuratores sufficientes.'

Then there are various acts connected with the probate of wills: probates, administrations, appointments of tutors for heirs who are under age, exhibition and approval of executors' accounts. One entry of a probate executed in St. Mary's church at Ely by a commissary, on 17 September 1376, records that a copy of the will, and an inventory of the goods of the deceased, was deposited with the bishop's registrar; no other reference has been noted to the accumulation of probate files.[1]

There remains a series of administrative acts performed by the official on the bishop's behalf, in connection with the clergy of the diocese. These were sequestration of benefices on the death or incapacity of the incumbent, appointments of curators or coadjutors, monitions to incumbents and parochial chaplains to reside, examinations of the titles of new incumbents before administering the oath of obedience to them. Besides this the official scrutinized and licensed the questors who came to the diocese to collect money, investigated the accounts of charities, and received the payments of pensions due to the bishop.

This first surviving record of the Ely consistory is no more than a combination of court act book and general memoranda register, but it is a stage on the way to a much more intensive specialization of record, and by the time the consistory records reappear this has been partly achieved. There are many gaps, which can be attributed to the eighteenth-century dispersals, but certain main lines of development can be discerned. From the early sixteenth century there is a series of call books and journals of the diocesan synod, for the years 1506–51, 1570–83, and 1604.[2] The first of these contains entries relating to sequestrations and suspensions of clerks, an order to repair a rectory house, payments of pensions, and elections to convocation. These seem clearly to record in a single register the exercise of most of the official's functions which relate to the clergy. Some part of the official's probate business was by this time also recorded in a separate series of registers. It seems likely that at first only the clergy wills and those from the three 'official's' deaneries were proved at Cambridge, while those of the two Ely parishes and the deanery of Wisbech were dealt with in the course of the official'

[1] E.D.R. D/2/1, f. 51ᵛ.   [2] E.D.R. B/2/1, 7, 19.

visitation. The earliest surviving will register which contains copies of the wills proved, that is, Liber A, which covers the years 1449 to 1460, relates only to this part of the diocese, and the wills copied into the second register, which is, as we have seen, primarily a visitation record, covers only the same area. The appearance of this latter volume suggests that systematic record keeping had not yet been achieved, at least in this department of the consistory. Meanwhile the wills proved at Cambridge during the same period were presumably recorded in the same rather slipshod fashion, in consistory registers now lost, along with all records of tuitions, *caveats*, and litigation resulting from disputed wills. The first sign of increasing specialization is the third will register, Liber C, which contains copies of wills proved throughout the official's jurisdiction in the years 1478 to 1486, and is the first of a continuing series. Annual bundles of original wills have survived from 1503, and presumably there were at one time parallel series of administration documents and inventories from the same period.

Meanwhile, traces of the records of the official's purely judicial activity may be seen in a series of registers of depositions and *responsa personalia* in instance causes which begins in 1532 and continues to the end of Richard Coxe's episcopate in 1581,[1] in two survivals from a parallel series of assignation books,[2] and in odd examples from two sets of office court books, one for the county and the other for the Isle.[3] The official's visitation and correction records are difficult to distinguish from this last series, and, after 1549, they appear to have given way to the episcopal visitation books, in which the official's only business was with the hearing of correction cases which had not been summarily dealt with by the visitor.[4]

The most notable innovation of the sixteenth century was, however, in the introduction of a miscellaneous administrative register for the official's non-judicial acts. The later medieval bishops of Ely had at various times of absence from their diocese appointed one or

[1] E.D.R. D/2/2, 3, 4, 6, 7, 11.
[2] E.D.R. D/2/3a, 12.
[3] E.D.R. D/2/8, 9, 10a; B/2/20.
[4] e.g. E.D.R. B/2/4, Bishop Coxe's 1564/5 visitation, where the episcopal visitation which took place in September 1564 was completed by proceedings based on the presentments which were heard by the official between November 1564 and January 1565.

more vicars general, who performed for them such administrative functions as did not fall under the official's commission: institutions to benefices, elections, and installations of the heads of religious houses, returns of royal writs, and the like. As early as 1348 Lisle did this, setting up a commission of three vicars, consisting of the chancellor, the official, and the rector of Trumpington.[1] At the same time the bishops continued to appoint a chancellor, who occasionally acted as the bishop's special commissary in complicated transactions like the decreeing of an appropriation,[2] but whose other functions are now lost beyond recall. A large part of the routine administration of the diocese which was outside the official's competence still fell to the bishop himself, despite the existence of these officers, whenever he was in the diocese, and the later registers of Gray and Alcock record many such acts.[3] It was only, in fact, when the volume of business caused by any one type of act became so great that the bishop and his immediate entourage could no longer easily deal with it, that it was delegated to some one else. This, it seems was what happened to marriage licences, which were infrequently granted in the fifteenth century, but appear in far larger numbers during the next century, and are, in consequence, passed over to the official, who is by this time variously styled, official, chancellor, commissary general, and even vicar general. At the same time the official was entrusted with the issue of licences for schoolmasters, curates, and catechists, to which the demands of the Reformation had given great prominence. As a result further reorganization of the records of the officiality took place, and there were begun, in 1563, general licence registers which, until 1600, included administrations, tuitions, caveats, sequestrations and licences for marriages, curates, schoolmasters, and catechists, and which were in part the descendants of the first consistory register.[4]

The long interregnum in the diocese of Ely after the death of Richard Coxe, from 1581 to 1600, seems to have brought to an end many of the more individual features of diocesan administration. The synods virtually disappeared, the licence registers were restricted to marriage licences, the deposition registers vanished to

[1] E.D.R. G/1/1, Lisle, f. 17.   [2] E.D.R. G/1/3, f. 208.
[3] E.D.R. G/1/5 and 6.   [4] E.D.R. G/2/18 and 19.

make way for the more usual 'court files', and although the omni-competence of the official appeared to grow, his records were increasingly sub-divided and formalized. The end of the story comes in the evidence given by Isambard Brunel on 3 April 1876, before a select committee of the House of Lords on the Ecclesiastical Offices and Fees Bill.[1] He was, he told the committee, chancellor of the diocese of Ely which 'comprised the two offices of official principal and vicar general'. Of his duties as official principal, by the time he was speaking there remained only the faculty jurisdiction; as vicar general he granted marriage licences through his surrogates, took fees for sequestrations, visited the churchwardens of the Isle, performed acts connected with consecrations, presided at the diocesan synod when proctors in convocation were elected, performed various functions related to clergy discipline and dilapidations, and 'acted as general adviser to the bishop'. Brunel was a self-conscious antiquarian, yet it is not hard to see in the duties he describes the line stretching back to the first consistory register.

DOROTHY OWEN

[1] *Parliamentary Papers 1876*, xxvi. 272–311.

X

The Reliability of Inquisitions as Historical Evidence

MEDIEVAL and later inquisitions can seldom be taken at their face value, and recent research has begun to explain why. Firstly, many inquisitions *post mortem*, and others, contain information which clearly could not have been provided, as is always stated, by the jurors, but must represent a compromise acceptable both to the presiding official and to the heir of the tenant-in-chief or other interested party;[1] and in these circumstances earlier inquisitions were often recopied verbatim, with their inaccuracies perpetuated or, through miscopying, made increasingly bizarre.[2] Secondly, in many inquisitions the facts were made to fit into stereotyped patterns. The artificial nature of many 'proofs of age' is the best example of this,[3] followed by the highly stylized form of inquests into homicides committed in self-defence.[4] Thirdly, especially in

---

[1] For inquisitions *post mortem* see especially C. G. Crump, 'A Note on the Criticism of Records', *Bull. John Rylands Library*, viii (1924), 140–4; C. D. Ross and T. B. Pugh, 'Materials for the Study of Baronial Incomes in Fifteenth-Century England', *Economic History Review*, 2nd ser. vi (1953–4), 186–9. Miscellaneous Inquisitions are discussed in reviews in *EHR*, lxxxi (1966), 149; lxxxiii (1968), 385; *History*, N.S., xlix (1964), 344–5. The Miscellaneous Inquisitions seem usually to have repeated the details of inquisitions *post mortem* in respect of lay lands, but to be more accurate for ecclesiastical estates.

[2] This is particularly obvious in the aberrant forms of place-names shown in the indexes of the printed calendars. See, for example, the index of *Calendar of Inquisitions post mortem* (H.M.S.O., 1904–), xv, under Belluton, Birdbrook, Bowden (Little), Burton Coggles, Catfield, Disley Stanley, Fawton, Netley, Rushall, Wacton, and Walton. The forms of these names which begin with a hopelessly wrong initial letter are most likely the result of the miscopying of considerably earlier documents.

[3] See notes and reviews in *EHR*, xxii (1907), 101–3, 526–7; xxix (1914), 323–4; xxxii (1917), 454; lii (1937), 537; lv (1940), 328; lxxii (1957), 110.

[4] See the close similarity of all such inquests in *Calendar of Nottinghamshire Coroners' Inquests, 1485–1558*, ed. R. F. Hunnisett (Thoroton Soc., Record Ser., xxv (1969)), nos. 7, 13, 16, 50, 63, 64, 71, 74, 78, 80, 86, 111, 116, 138, 139, 155, 159, 166, 177, 200, 250. Likewise the 'opprobrious words' spoken during quarrels and leading to injury or death came regularly to be reported as 'thou art a knave' (e.g. ibid., nos. 323, 334). They are unlikely to have been so unimaginative or so mild.

the fifteenth century, juries were sometimes packed, or persuaded or coerced by the person officiating to return a certain verdict; and other verdicts were influenced by local politics, the jurors fearing some faction or lord, or hoping for some favour.[1] Finally, other jurors were anxious to mitigate the severity of their verdicts, either to help their locality to avoid a penalty or to save a man's property or honour. Thus coroners' juries preferred verdicts of misadventure to suicide, and often undervalued deodands and the lands and chattels of felons.[2]

A few inquisitions are known to be untrustworthy because they were challenged and traversed,[3] while the survival of conflicting evidence throws doubt upon others.[4] But in most cases it is impossible today to discover whether any of the influences listed above applied and therefore to assess the accuracy of the returns. Worse still, there is a further serious complication in that nearly all inquisitions survive only in the form of 'fair copies', if not copies of copies. The purpose of this paper is to show what distortions can result from this—distortions which can rarely be guessed and allowed for when the fair copy alone survives. The following examples are from coroners' inquests, but the lessons to be learned from them are of far wider application.

Among the many coroners' rolls handed in to King's Bench when it sat at Lincoln in Easter term 1396 were those of Thomas de Horncastre and Nicholas de Werk,[5] who had been Lincoln city

---

[1] For examples see R. L. Storey, *The End of the House of Lancaster* (London, 1966), pp. 26, 55–6, 144–5, 174, 192, 225, 227.

[2] R. F. Hunnisett, *The Medieval Coroner* (Cambridge, 1961), pp. 30–4; *Cal. Notts. Coroners' Inquests*, pp. vii–ix. For an interesting case of a coroner's jury being accused of deliberately disguising a suicide as murder by fictitious persons, see J. Miller and K. H. Rogers, 'The Strange Death of Edward Langford', *Wilts. Arch. & Nat. Hist. Mag.*, lxii (1967), 103–9.

[3] See P.R.O., Placita in Cancellaria (C. 43 and C. 44), *passim*. For a very interesting example of a fraudulent proof of age being successfully challenged, see *Cal. Inquisitions p.m.* xi. 611; xii. 96. It is discussed by L. B. Larking, ' "Probatio Aetatis" of William de Septvans', *Archaeologia Cantiana*, i (1858), 124–36. I am grateful to Mr. L. C. Hector for drawing my attention to this case.

[4] *EHR*, lxxxi. 149; lxxxiii. 385; Ross and Pugh, op. cit., 187.

[5] R. F. Hunnisett, 'The Medieval Coroners' Rolls', *American Journal of Legal History*, iii (1959), 336–8; P.R.O., Coram Rege Roll (K.B. 27) 540, fines and forfeitures, mm. 8, 11d.

coroners earlier in Richard II's reign. The first entry on Horncastre's roll reads:[1]

Inquisicio capta apud Lincoln coram Thoma de Horncastr' uno
coronatorum domini regis in civitate Lincoln die martis proximo
post festum Sancte Trinitatis anno regni regis Ricardi secundi
tercio super visu corporis Willelmi de Berughby thressere indictata
de felonia[2] defuncti in prisona castri Lincoln per sacramentum
Johannis de Baldon Simonis de Brynkill Johannis Strynger Willelmi de
Howton Thome Cassaundr' Johannis de Kelsey Ricardi de Seuerby
Johannis Bakerr Roberti de Muston Johannis de Nesfeld Johannis de
Banbury et Johannis Rudyerd juratorum qui dicunt super sacramentum suum quod predictus Willelmus obiit confessus morte
naturali et non alio modo in prisona predicta die et anno predictis;
et quod nulla habuit terras seu catalla etc.

This would seem an unremarkable inquest but for the existence of
the following case on Werk's roll:[3]

Inquisicio capta apud Lincoln coram Nicholao de Werk coronatore
domini regis civitatis predicte die mercurie proximo post festum
Sancte Trinitatis anno regni regis Ricardi secundi tercio super visu
corporis Willelmi Trescher de Beroghby defuncti in prisona castri
Lincoln per sacramentum Johannis de Baldon Simonis Brynkyll
Johannis Strynger Willelmi de Howton Thome Cassaundr' Johannis
de Kelsey Ricardi de Stylby Johannis Baker Roberti Muston Johannis
Schefyld Johannis de Banbury et Johannis Rudeard qui dicunt super
sacramentum suum quod predictus Willelmus obiit confessus morte
naturali et non alio modo; et quod nulla habuit terras seu catalla.

Neither inquest by itself would arouse any suspicions, but considered together they pose many questions. They must both relate
to the same death, but we do not even know whether the deceased
was a thresher named William de Berughby or a man of unknown
occupation named William Trescher of Barrowby. It is inconceivable that two inquests were really held by two different coroners
on two successive days, firstly because the death occurred in gaol,
and coroners were particularly reluctant to hold inquests in gaols,

---

[1] P.R.O., Coroners' Rolls (J.I. 2), 87, m. 1.
[2] *indictata de felonia* is interlined, which probably accounts for the wrong ending
of the first word.   [3] J.I. 2/80, m. 1, sixth entry.

where plague and other diseases were rife;[1] and secondly because the juries are exactly the same.

They are the same despite two apparent differences, Richard de Seuerby and John de Nesfeld on Horncastre's roll occurring as Richard de Stylby and John Schefyld on Werk's. Horncastre's forms are probably correct. Stylby could hardly be misread as Seuerby, but the opposite is very possible when Seuerby is written, as on Horncastre's roll, with the usual 'er' sign,[2] the down stroke of which could easily join the top of the second minim of the 'u', as it almost does on the roll. The name would thus appear to end 'ilby', and it is understandable that the 'Se' should then have been misread as, or even deliberately improved to, 'St'. This argument apart, Seuerby, being derived from Sewerby in Yorkshire, is an inherently more likely surname. Similarly Nesfeld was probably the other juror's name. A capital 'N', like that on Horncastre's roll, can easily be misread as 'St' or 'Sc',[3] and 'sf' (with a long 's') as 'ff'. One 'f' was dropped, but that is not significant, and an 'h' added, probably as a deliberate improvement to produce a better form of what must have been a more widely known name, although both Sheffield and Nesfield are Yorkshire places.

In addition, Horncastre's roll alone gives the date of death and states that the deceased was indicted for felony, but it would be unwise to conclude from all this that his version is more likely than Werk's to be completely genuine. Inquests into deaths in gaol always need to be treated more cautiously than most: neither coroner may have held a formal inquest and no jury may ever have sat.[4] If so, it is the more understandable that both coroners should claim and enrol it. But it is more likely that in the hasty flurry of enrolment which took place after the announcement of the visitation of King's Bench, the version on the Lincoln coroners' files was entered on one of the rolls, was not cancelled and so came to be

[1] *The Medieval Coroner*, pp. 35–6; *Cal. Notts. Coroners' Inquests*, pp. iii–iv.

[2] As illustrated in C. Johnson and H. Jenkinson, *English Court Hand . . .* (Oxford, 1915), part I, p. 59.

[3] Compare illustrations 7 and 9 of the capital 'N' with most of those of the ligature 'st': ibid., pp. 33, 48.

[4] *Cal. Notts. Coroners' Inquests*, pp. iii–iv; W. Kellaway, 'The Coroner in Medieval London', *Studies in London History presented to Philip Edmund Jones*, ed. A. E. J. Hollaender and W. Kellaway (London, 1969), p. 81.

enrolled again.[1] As will be seen later, the officiating coroner was not always named in individual items on coroners' files, and this, together with the scrappy nature of most files, could easily explain how two varying copies of the same inquest could have been made on the rolls of two different coroners. An equal possibility is that two versions of the case were on the files, one being copied on to Horncastre's roll and the other on to Werk's. That this is a real possibility is proved by a study of the only inquests for which items from a coroner's file and the enrolled versions both survive.

Robert Waver, a member of a well-known Warwickshire family which held lands mainly in Knightlow and Hemlingford hundreds,[2] had two periods of office as a Warwickshire coroner, and his roll,[3] which was handed in to King's Bench when it sat at Coventry in Trinity term 1387,[4] consists of two sections, one for each period. At that time there was normally one coroner for each of the four Warwickshire hundreds,[5] and the cases on the first two membranes of the roll all relate to Hemlingford hundred, except for one which concerns Arley, a detached part of Knightlow hundred, while those on membrane three all relate to Knightlow hundred. The Hemlingford cases range in date from 5 February 1365 to 13 May 1367 and the Knightlow ones from 30 October 1372 to 4 June 1373. On 26 October 1367 a writ issued for the election of a new Warwickshire coroner in place of Waver because he was 'insufficiently qualified',[6] which must mean that his lands were in Knightlow and not in Hemlingford hundred. He was presumably re-elected, for the correct hundred, shortly before 30 October 1372, and he was replaced again by a writ of 10 May 1373, this time because he was sick and aged.[7]

The inquests from his second period of office were probably enrolled first. With one exception they are in chronological order.

---

[1] For other results of the lack of time for proper enrolment at such times or of the panic the visitations caused, see *Am. Journ. Leg. Hist.* iii. 99–100, 118–19.

[2] *VCH Warwickshire*, iv. 36–7, 254; vi. 177, 189–90.   [3] J.I. 2/184.

[4] *Am. Journ. Leg. Hist.* iii. 344–5; K.B. 27/505, fines and forfeitures, m. 2d.

[5] *The Medieval Coroner*, pp. 135–6. In the inquest on J.I. 2/184, m. 1, schedule, Waver is called 'the king's coroner in Hemlingford hundred'.

[6] *CCR, 1364–8*, p. 362.

[7] *CCR, 1369–74*, p. 501.

Their number and fairly regular spacing in time (nine in just over seven months, two even being held after the issue of the writ for Waver's replacement) suggest that they could well be complete. Of the earlier inquests the nine on membrane one are in chronological order and are also probably complete for the period they cover (February to September 1365), but there is then a gap of four and a half months before the first case on membrane two. The first seven inquests on that membrane run in chronological order for just over seven months, for which period they are probably complete, but the eighth and last was held after a space of four months, while the dorse of membrane one contains the beginning of another which was held after a further interval of four and a half months. Yet it was not for another five and a half months that the writ for Waver's first replacement was issued.

There are two possible interpretations of these facts. One is that during the last year of his first period of office Waver held only three inquests—the two last mentioned, and a third which was unlikely to have been enrolled in any event because it was returned into Chancery. It resulted in a pardon in November 1367[1] and was probably held shortly before Waver's replacement. But this interpretation is improbable, despite Waver's disqualifications, in view of his obvious conscientiousness earlier and in his second term, even when sick and aged. The true explanation must be that there was insufficient time to enrol all his inquests. This is supported by the fact that the last case on the dorse of membrane one was left unfinished, presumably when it was realized that it contained an error. Instead, the relevant membrane from Waver's file was sewn to membrane one. It was probably intended to hand in with the roll the other pieces on the file which had not been enrolled, but in the rush six inquests which had already been enrolled were erroneously substituted for them.[2] They all derive from Waver's second period of office and all have *Knyht'*, for Knightlow hundred, written at the top, where the other piece has *Huml'*, for Hemlingford. These headings are in a different hand from the body of the cases and were probably added during the sorting of Waver's file, preparatory to enrolment. In support of the theory that the six Knightlow

---

[1] *CPR, 1367–70*, p. 42.　　　　[2] They are now J.I. 2/255/8.

membranes were handed in erroneously, they are cancelled, presumably because enrolled, whereas the Hemlingford one is not.

These two features which contrast with the Hemlingford inquest, their heading and their cancellation, are almost the only things that the six Knightlow membranes have in common. Physically they have no uniformity: the cases were obviously written on whatever pieces of parchment or paper came to hand, irrespective of size and shape. More vitally, they vary enormously in form and lay-out. Most important, there are great differences between each case as recorded on the file and as enrolled. Before the significance of all this can be discussed, it is necessary to study each inquest, making a detailed comparison of the file with the roll. To facilitate this, both versions of all six cases are printed in an Appendix in the order of their enrolment; and there follows here a case-by-case description of the appearance, form, and presentation of the file inquests and a summary of the most important points arising from a comparison with the enrolled versions.

Case 1

In the file this inquest is written on the top half of a piece of parchment varying in width between 7½ and 9 inches (19–23 cm.) and from 9½ to 10½ inches (24–26·5 cm.) long. Written upside down from what is now the foot is a half-erased list of jurors in two columns. All their names can be distinguished with the help of ultra-violet light, under which Plate 4 was taken. They were the jurors of the last of Waver's enrolled Knightlow cases.

Case 1 itself is handsomely written in a single paragraph, apparently by the clerk who wrote Waver's roll. Its form is one which is quite common in coroner's inquests and it is used, with occasional minor variations, throughout Waver's roll. This usually begins 'Inquisicio capta coram . . . apud . . . die . . . super visu corporis . . . per sacramentum [names of twelve jurors] qui dicunt super sacramentum eorum quod'.[1] There then follows the verdict, introduced by the words *contigit apud* and followed by this sentence: 'Et hoc presentant predicti xij juratores iiij^{or} villatarum de . . .' The phrase

---

[1] The date of the inquest is sometimes given before the place: e.g. in Case 3.

super visu corporis . . . is omitted from the file version of Case 1, where the other *super* is replaced by *per*, while in the final sentence *xij* is omitted from the roll and *de* from the file, but these are small details of no significance.

The exact form of the usual ending of inquests on the roll is: 'Et hoc pres' predicti xij jur' iiij^or villat' de . . .' It is clear from two entries that the enrolling clerk meant *villat'* to represent *villatarum* and that he thus thought of the twelve jurors as the representatives of the four townships.[1] *Villat'* is therefore extended to *villatarum* in the Appendix. But there are good reasons for thinking that what he should have written was: 'Et hoc presentant predicti xij juratores et iiij^or villate de . . .' To say at the end of each inquest that 'the said twelve jurors present this' is unnecessary because the verdict is earlier introduced as what the twelve 'say upon their oath'; and to begin the final sentence with *Et* suggests that it contains additional information. Moreover, if the twelve were the representatives of the townships, the natural place to mention this would be immediately after their names. On the other hand, it is quite reasonable that the verdict of the twelve should be followed by a note that both they and the townships made the same presentment. That this is what should have been written is proved by other cases in Waver's file, particularly Case 3, and also by some of the entries on other Warwickshire coroners' rolls compiled at the same time.[2]

The form of both versions of Case 1 is identical and the two verdicts are substantially the same, with the facts related in virtually the same order. Nevertheless, there are a few differences other than the minor ones already noticed. The juror named William Offechirch of Princethorpe in the file is replaced on the roll by William Cochel. The roll names the finder of the body much earlier than the file and, unlike the file, gives his occupation. According to the file

---

[1] The two entries are the last complete case on m. 1d, which ends: 'Et hoc presentant predicti juratores predicte ville sine aliis villatis quia nulla villa interponit eis'; and the third case on m. 2, which ends: 'Et hoc presentant dicti juratores iiij^or villatarum de Arleye et trium villatarum circumstancium'.

[2] The inquests on many of them end in the same way as Waver's, but one roll has some which end: 'Et hoc presentant predicti juratores et iiij^or villate de . . .' (J.I. 2/185, m. 1); another has inquests ending: 'Et hoc presentant [*predicti* in one case only] xij juratores et homines iiij villatarum de . . .' (J.I. 2/188, m. 4); and a third has some ending: 'Et hoc presentant predicti juratores et decennarii iiij^or villatarum de . . .' (J.I. 2/189, m. 1).

the body was found at Princethorpe, whereas the roll says that it was at Stretton Wood in Stretton on Dunsmore—a place which throughout is called just Stretton in the file by contrast with the roll. In the file the deceased is said to have been struck to the heart with a knife worth 1*d.* with which the township was charged, but the roll merely says that he had divers wounds. The file states only that the slayers were unknown, but the roll calls them thieves and strangers who immediately fled. Finally, the finder's sureties and the four townships are both named in a different order on the roll from that of the file.

Case 2

In the file this is written on a piece of parchment measuring about 5½ inches (14 cm.) across and 4 inches (10 cm.) long. It consists basically of two columns of jurors. Twelve are listed down the right side and bracketed together in pairs, each pair being marked *jur'*, for *jurati*. Eight tithingmen are in a column on the left. They are bracketed by townships and are all jointly bracketed to the word *jurati*. The verdict, which is very brief, is written beneath the names of the tithingmen. The dominant position of the lists of jurors, the general lay-out, the brackets, and the cancellation combine to give the membrane a very scrappy appearance.

This is one of several cases in the file which prove that there were two separate juries at Waver's inquests: the twelve, presumably freemen of the hundred, and the representatives of the townships, who seem normally to have been tithingmen.[1] The verdict is not

---

[1] For coroners' juries generally see *The Medieval Coroner*, pp. 13–19. The representatives of the townships are normally described in Waver's file as *dec'*, *des'*, or *decen'* of townships, which can equally well be extended as *decennarii* or *decenne*. But they are described at the end of Case 3 in the file as *predicti des'*, which can only be extended as *desennarii*. This confirms that these jurors were tithingmen (head men of tithings) and not just ordinary members 'of tithings'. Without this piece of evidence the same conclusion might have been reached, although more tentatively, from two considerations. First, the only two jurors described as *decen'* in Case 6 are at the head of the panel and slightly separated from the others, which suggests that they were local officers and not just members of the tithing. Secondly, it is reasonable to assume that tithings would normally have been represented by their tithingmen rather than by one or two ordinary members. Similarly the five jurors in Case 4 described as *francipleggii* of townships were almost certainly themselves the frankpledges, meaning the capital pledges or tithingmen (see W. A. Morris, *The Frankpledge System* (New York,

only written below the tithingmen: it is also introduced by the words 'Idem decennarii dicunt quod . . .' The twelve freemen are merely named. On the roll, however, the verdict is that of these twelve, while the case ends, unusually wearily: 'Et hoc presentant predicti juratores iiij^{or} villatarum de Rokeby etc.' Rugby is the first of the four townships of the tithingmen in the file. Many of the twelve are spelt differently, the following showing the greatest variations:

File	Roll
Henry of ye Grene	Henry atte Grene
John Melewart	John Muleward
Ralph Westone	Geoffrey de Weston
John Ricardessone	Richard son of Richard (*filii Ricardi*)

The verdicts vary far more. File and roll agree on the hour and day of the fatal blow, although the file omits the regnal year; but the file seems to imply that the death occurred then, whereas the roll specifically states that it was three days later. Only the roll gives the date of the inquest, names the coroner, describes the felon as 'of Rugby', calls the case a felony and says that the hue and cry was raised, that the felon fled and had no chattels, and that the deceased had the last rites of the Church. The other main variations are in the Christian name of the deceased, which the file gives first as *Jilia* and then as *Jiliana* and the roll consistently calls *Juliana*, and the weapon, which according to the file was a knife called a 'broche' worth 18*d*. whereas the roll calls it a baselard and does not give it a value.

Case 3

In the file this case is well written on a piece of parchment roughly $11\frac{1}{2}$ inches (29 cm.) wide and 5 inches (12·5 cm.) long. It is in two sections. The first and longer begins with the finding of the bodies, introduced by the words *Accidit apud,* and continues: 'Inquisicio inde capta coram . . . super visu corporum . . .' There then follow the jurors' names and their verdict. This is a perfectly good form of

London, etc., 1910), p. 103), rather than ordinary members 'of the frankpledge' in its corporate sense.

coroner's inquest, although different from that of Case 1 and those on the roll. Also, the jurors are not the twelve freemen of the hundred but ten tithingmen of four townships. The second paragraph reads: 'xij juratores [named] qui dicunt super sacramentum suum quod predicti desennarii quo ad presentacionem bene et fideliter presentant.' This proves even more conclusively than the last case that there were two separate juries.

By contrast, the roll as usual gives the verdict of the twelve with the normal ending concerning the four townships, which are the same and in the same order as those of the tithingmen. There are some differences between roll and file in the spelling of the jurors' names, notably:

File	Roll
John Thenale	John de Thornhale
Robert Jelion	Robert Julian
William Irishman	William Irysh

The coroner is called Robert Wouere, the king's coroner, in the file, and Robert de Waure, one of the king's coroners in Warwickshire, on the roll; and the file names the first finder's sureties as John Westwale and John Bont, but they appear as John Webbe and Robert Blont on the roll. File and roll differ considerably on dates, both in amount of information given and in terminology, as the following table shows:

	File	Roll
Date of inquest	Not given	Saturday after Epiphany 46 Edward III
Date of finding of bodies	Friday the morrow of Epiphany 46 Edward III	Not given
Date of deaths	*in nocte Epiphanie domini*	Friday after Epiphany *noctanter*
Form of regnal year	*anno regni regis Edwardi tercii a conquestu xlvj^{to}*	*anno regni regis Edwardi tercii post conquestum xlvj^{to}*

Similarly the verdicts, although substantially the same, with the facts in much the same order, are very differently worded. The following are the outstanding examples:

	File	Roll
The vessel	*parva navicula*	*limbus*
The event causing the deaths	*saltat in predictam naviculam*	*saltavit ad eos*
[The vessel] overturned	*jusum vertit*	*subvertebat*
Manner of deaths	*Sawer se ipsum demersit et* [the other two] *similiter; et nuli alii inde male creditur*	[all three] *ceciderunt in dictam aquam unde submersi sunt*

Only the roll states that the first finder raised the hue and cry. The most surprising discrepancy, however, is that according to the file 2*s*. 1*d*. was found with the bodies, for which information the roll substitutes the fact that the boat was appraised at 3*s*. 4*d*. with which the abbot of Stoneleigh was charged as the king's deodand.

Case 4

In the file this case is unique in that it is written on a piece of paper, measuring approximately 6½ inches (16·5 cm.) across by 6 inches (15·5 cm.) long. Seventeen jurors are named in a column down the left, the first five described as frankpledges, meaning tithing-men,[1] and bracketed by townships, and the rest bracketed in pairs. The verdict is written to their right, beginning beneath the frank-pledges and in line with the first of the final twelve jurors. All this, together with the cancellation of the verdict and the fact that one word and one longer passage are struck through and rewritten differently, the single word as an interlineation, makes this inquest look very untidy.

The verdict is introduced by the words 'Isti duodecim homines jurati presentant . . .', which, together with its position, strongly suggest that it is the verdict of the final twelve and that they were the freemen of the hundred, the five frankpledges having, as usual, made a separate presentment. On the roll, however, the verdict is given as that of twelve jurors, who were the five frankpledges (not so described) and seven of the file's final twelve, and the inquest ends

[1] See above, p. 214, n. 1.

with the normal sentence about the four townships, which are the same and in the same order as those of the frankpledges, although the spellings differ. Some of the twelve common jurors are very differently spelt, especially:

File	Roll
William of Kuchene	William Ofthe Cuchene
John Creste	John Cosse
John Bynley	John de Bilneye
John Harry	John Harrys

Both verdicts are brief, especially that in the file, but there are still many differences. The coroner is named only on the roll, while the information concerning dates is utterly different, as follows:

	File	Roll
Date of inquest	Not given	Tuesday before the Purification
Date of finding of body	Not given	Monday before the Purification at vespers
Date of death	Monday before the Purification *circa noctem*	Not given

The first finder and his sureties are even more discrepant than the jurors:

	File	Roll
First finder	John Potatden	John Porter
Sureties	Davit of Braundone	David de Braundon
	Walter Argent	Walter Forgo

But the main difference is that whereas the file begins with the statement that the deceased was drowned in a river between Monks Kirby and the prior's meadow called Stocwelmed (this meadow having been substituted during the writing of the verdict for Brokhurstmede, which is deleted), the roll begins by saying that the first finder found the body while crossing a river near Brochurstmede. The finder is not named until the end in the file. Only the roll states that nobody was suspected and that the hue and cry was raised.

Case 5

In the file this is on a piece of parchment about 8½ inches (22 cm.) wide and 6½ inches (16·5 cm.) long. It is well written and has the same two paragraphs as Case 3. The first begins *Contigit apud . . .*, and the verdict is that of six tithingmen of four, or possibly five, townships, but otherwise the form is identical with that of Case 3. The second paragraph, introduced by the word *Juratores* in the margin, merely names the twelve freemen. The roll has the verdict of the twelve with the usual ending concerning the townships.[1] The four townships on the roll are Stretton on Dunsmore, Princethorpe, Bubbenhall, and Frankton, while those of the tithingmen are Princethorpe, Bubbenhall, Ryton on Dunsmore, and Frankton. The discrepancy was almost certainly caused by the first tithingman being described as Thomas Randolf of Stretton, tithingman of Princethorpe. Stretton and Princethorpe were both copied as townships and Ryton was omitted. Some of the twelve are spelt differently in the two versions, while there are three more serious variations, namely:

	File	*Roll*
2nd juror	William Prynsthorp	William Cochel
3rd juror	William Marchel	William Smyth
11th juror	Robert Dunes	Robert Anneys

The last is understandable since the contemporary capitals 'A' and 'D' are often very similar,[2] and there is a similar discrepancy in the surname of the finder's first surety, who is David Denes in the file and Robert Anneys on the roll. The other two cannot be the same names differently copied, and it is interesting to compare the second juror with the juror of Case 1 who is called William Offechirch of Princethorpe in the file and William Cochel on the roll.

The coroner is called Robert Wouere, king's coroner, in the file and Robert de Waur', one of the king's coroners in Warwickshire, on the roll, which is again reminiscent of Case 3. So is the relative amount of information given about dates:

---

[1] The word *predicti* is omitted, but that is not significant.
[2] Compare illustrations 8 and 11 in *English Court Hand . . .*, part I, p. 4, with nos. 11 and 18, ibid., p. 13.

	File	Roll
Date of inquest	Not given	Wednesday after St. Ambrose
Date of finding of body	Tuesday after St. Ambrose	Not given
Date of blow	the said Monday (*sic*) after St. Ambrose at the ninth hour	Tuesday after St. Ambrose
Date of death	Not given	Immediately after the blow

Otherwise there is a fair amount of agreement between the two verdicts, which are presented in much the same order, although the roll alone gives the deceased's township and says that he was driving the cart, that there were four horses, that the blow was under the right ear, that the finder was the deceased's father, and that the hue and cry was raised.

Case 6

The parchment is quite different in shape from the rest of the file, being roughly 3½ inches (9 cm.) wide and 12½ inches (32 cm.) long. It appears to be dominated even more than Cases 2 and 4 by the list of jurors, which occupies the top half of the long, narrow membrane. The first two are bracketed together and described as tithingmen of Wolvey. They are separated from the remaining sixteen by a small space. The verdict, which is fairly succinct, begins in line with the last juror, introduced by the words: 'jurati qui dicunt super sacramentum suum quod . . .' It ends 'Et hoc presentant iiij villate [named]'. On the roll the usual final statement is omitted, while the verdict is said to be presented 'per sacramentum xij juratorum iiij^or villatarum . . .' The jurors are not named, but the four townships are given in the same order as in the file. Only one other case on Waver's roll is in this form, the penultimate one, which immediately follows Case 6 and which is not represented in the file.

Neither file nor roll gives the date of death, and only the roll has the date of the inquest. They agree on the date of the finding of the body, but the roll also gives the hour. Both, exceptionally, use days of the month and not feast days. In the file the year is interlined.

The verdicts are substantially the same, with the facts in the same order except that the finder is named at the beginning on the roll and at the end in the file. The roll has an unintended omission in the description of the place of death, but, unlike the file, records that the body was uninjured, death was sudden and nobody was suspected. According to the file the finder had one surety, John Hesonde, but the roll names two, John Isonde and Robert Bonde.

An attempt must now be made to see what conclusions can be drawn from this analysis of the cases. Physical appearance immediately suggests that each case might result in as many as four documents before enrolment. The first would be the list of all the potential jurors summoned. The half-erased list on the membrane containing Case 1 is an example of this. It contains many more names than the twelve on the roll, and its value must have ceased when the twelve had been empanelled and recorded elsewhere. It was obviously not needed by the enrolling clerk because it was overwritten with an inquest which had been heard earlier and which was enrolled first. Secondly, rough notes must have been made during the hearing of the inquests, although our file contains none now. The list of jurors summoned would seem the natural place for such notes, but the half-erased list has none and for that case, at least, they must have been written on a second membrane. Cases 2, 4, and 6 in the file appear to represent a third stage. They look very scrappy and they are dominated by jury lists, the verdicts having apparently been inserted as briefly as possible in any available space. Nevertheless, in each case the jurors and verdict appear to have been written by a single clerk at much the same time, and it may be assumed that the verdicts, which are too elaborate to have been rough jottings made during hearings, were added to the panels shortly after the inquests had ended. Finally, there are Cases 1, 3, and 5 in the file, which are handsomely and spaciously engrossed, and expressed in terms commonly found in formal coroners' inquests. It might reasonably be deduced that in every case earlier draft versions were recast, shortly before the visitation of King's Bench, in this more polished and also more stereotyped form, possibly with the help of a precedent book,[1] ready for enrolment.

There is no need to try to impose this pattern rigidly upon all six inquests. Items from the files of near-contemporary Shrewsbury and Northamptonshire coroners' files prove that coroners and their clerks cared little for complete consistency.[2] Thus the manner in which both the tithingmen and the twelve are marked as jurors in Case 2 in the file suggests that there may have been no earlier and more extensive jury list. The same may be true of Case 6 if only twelve of the eighteen listed really sat: the membrane certainly looks as though it began life simply as a jury panel. It is also true that the Hemlingford inquest from the file, which is sewn to the roll, is unlike either of the two Knightlow groups, falling somewhere between them. It is written on a long strip of parchment, about 2 inches (5 cm.) wide and 12½ inches (32 cm.) long, but very neatly. Moreover, although the jurors stand out, as in Cases 2, 4, and 6, they were not written first.[3] But this inquest derives from Waver's first period of office and is the product of an earlier clerk. Finally, the fact that Case 1 in the file was written by the clerk who wrote Waver's roll and Cases 3 and 5 by another is not necessarily significant. The surviving rolls show that more than one clerk was employed to deal with the files of the Warwickshire coroners who were no longer in office in 1387.

The hypothesis that our six inquests comprise three rough drafts and three fair copies must now be considered in the context of the variations between the file and the roll. Miscopying could account

---

[1] Only a few precedent books containing model entries of coroners' cases are known (*Am. Journ. Leg. Hist.*, iii. 117). Professor R. B. Pugh has kindly drawn my attention to one: B.M. Lansdowne MS. 560, ff. 34–5.

[2] Two jury panels from a Shrewsbury coroners' file consist of many names, some marked as jurors, with the verdicts endorsed. A third has just the twelve jurors listed at the top and the verdict written beneath them (J.I. 2/143, m. 1, schedules). Some pieces from a Northamptonshire coroner's file closely resemble our Cases 2 and 4 with the verdicts written on the same irregular and scrappy pieces of parchment as the jury panels, while others have the panels and verdicts on separate small membranes (J.I. 2/117A, m. 4, schedules).

[3] At the top there is a paragraph beginning 'Inquisicio capta apud . . . per . . . die . . .' There follows the heading *Franciplegii*, and under it in a column six names. Then comes the heading *Inquiciscio* (*sic*), followed by fourteen more names in column. A final paragraph begins 'Jurati dicunt per sacramentum suum quod ita contigit apud . . .'

for some of the differences, particularly in surnames such as Blont for Bont (Case 3), Bilneye for Bynley (Case 4), and Anneys for Dunes (Case 5), and for the different townships in Case 5, as explained earlier. Also, some of the additional information on the roll could be the result of a deliberate improvement of the file version by the enrolling clerk, aided by his precedent book and inspired by a desire to represent the coroner as efficient and to protect the neighbourhood and individuals from amercement. Thus the last four inquests, which are undated in the file, were held on the day after the deaths or the finding of the bodies according to the roll. The enrolling clerk could have added this on his own initiative to suggest that Waver executed his duties promptly.[1] Similarly the extra information that the hue and cry was raised (Cases 2, 3, 4, 5) may represent the enrolling clerk's desire to safeguard the first finder;[2] and that the felon fled and had no chattels (Case 2) and that nobody was suspected (Cases 4, 6) could have been safely inferred from the absence of contrary evidence in the file. Minor additions, such as the coroner's name or usual description, could have been made in the interests of consistency.

But when all such possibilities have been allowed for, there remains other information on the roll in every case, including Case 1, which is either completely absent from our file version or differs markedly from what is there; and Cases 3 and 5 show almost as many and as serious variations as the three which are represented by less polished verdicts. Sometimes the same facts are given in utterly different forms, as in the narrative section of Case 3 where both words and tenses are different. Also the discrepancies in descriptions of places may be more apparent than real. There is not necessarily any essential conflict, for example, between the statements that the same body was found at Princethorpe and at Stretton Wood in Stretton on Dunsmore (Case 1), because Princethorpe was a hamlet in the parish of Stretton; and the minor places in Case 4

---

[1] By contrast in Case 1, where the date of the inquest is in the file version, it was held five days after the finding of the body. It is true that the roll shows a lapse of four days between death and inquest in Case 2, for which the file gives no inquest date, but this could have been to allow for Christmas, the death having occurred on 23 Dec.

[2] For the first finder's obligation to raise the hue and cry see *The Medieval Coroner*, pp. 10, 25.

can be similarly reconciled. Nevertheless, even these examples prove that none of the enrolled cases was copied blindly from the surviving file version or from a fair copy of it. The new facts on the roll which could not have been guessed, and the completely conflicting sections of the two surviving versions, are more serious and feature in every case. The outstanding examples are the details of the wound and weapon in Case 1, the weapon in Case 2, the finding of money on the deceased in the file which became a statement about the deodand on the roll in Case 3, the very considerable extra information in Case 5, and the different information concerning dates in most of the cases. The only possible explanation is that for every inquest the enrolling clerk had additional material which no longer survives, and not just a rough draft and fair copy.

The source of this additional material must have been the second presentment. There were two separate juries for every inquest, which must originally have been represented in the file by two verdicts on separate membranes, one returned by the twelve freemen and the other by the tithingmen of the townships. Thus the verdicts of Cases 2, 3, and 5 which survive in the file are those of the townships, and so it can be assumed that most of the differences in the enrolled versions, which are said to be the verdicts of the twelve, represent differences in their original written presentments. The confusion over the townships in Case 5 strongly suggests that they were copied on to the roll from the surviving inquest, but this in no way affects the view that the other verdict was the roll's main source. Certainly the variations in the names of the twelve jurors prove that they were not enrolled from our file membrane. But even in these three cases a major problem remains. Our file version of Case 3 states that the twelve agreed with the tithingmen's verdict, and the naming of the twelve in the similar Case 5 may safely be taken to signify their agreement. Also, every case on the roll states, despite the clerk, that the townships made the same presentments as the twelve. Clearly this did not mean that their verdicts were identical.

The other three inquests are more complex. The file version of Case 1 seems genuinely to be a fair copy made by the enrolling clerk, probably as a 'trial run' as it was the first to be enrolled. The two original verdicts were presumably at his disposal, and the discrepancies between the fair copy and the enrolment must be his last-minute substitutions from the verdict, almost certainly that of the townships, which had not been his main source. The small differences in the order of the narrative must also be 'improvements', probably inspired by his precedent book, made as he copied the fair copy on to the roll.

The differences between the two versions of Case 4 are so great that the enrolment must be based largely on the verdict which does not survive. But both the enrolment and the surviving file inquest purport to be the verdict of twelve jurors, although only seven were apparently common to both panels. There are three possible explanations of this. One is that the five frankpledges were included among the twelve on the roll in error. Secondly, on the possible analogy of Case 6, all seventeen jurors listed in the file, the five frankpledges and the twelve, may have returned that verdict, being loosely described as twelve. But most probably the verdict is really that of the frankpledges and was erroneously attributed to the final twelve when written because it was necessary for reasons of space to write it beside them, the townships having already been written to the right of the frankpledges. On this theory the relationship between file and roll would be essentially the same for Case 4 as for Cases 2, 3, and 5 and, at one remove, for Case 1.

These five cases suggest that, whatever the form of the inquests in the file, the enrolling clerk had a standard form of words, described in the analysis of Case 1, for their beginning and end. Unfortunately Case 6 is completely out of pattern. The surviving file verdict, being that of the eighteen listed, or perhaps twelve of them, should in consistency have been the basis of the enrolment. No serious recasting was needed: it even ends with the roll's usual final sentence. Yet this is omitted from the enrolment, which gives the verdict as that of twelve unnamed jurors of (*recte* and) the four townships. This suggests that either the surviving file verdict was not consulted during enrolment or the enrolling clerk considered the eighteen, because they are headed by two tithingmen, to be the townships' representatives; and that, either way, the townships' presentment did not name the twelve.

In short, there is no consistent pattern to the development of Waver's inquests. Of our six it is unlikely that any but Case 1 went through the fair copy stage. The others were probably recast in the standard form straight from the original verdicts as they were enrolled, which would account for some of the erasures, substitutions, and interlineations on the roll. The enrolled cases are either a conflation of two very conflicting verdicts or, as is more likely, are based mainly (and Case 6 perhaps exclusively) upon one of them—always the one which has not survived and usually that of the twelve freemen.

Inevitably some questions remain unanswered. Why were Cases 3 and 5 written so neatly and formally for the file and the other verdicts of townships much more roughly? Why are the twelve freemen named on the townships' verdicts, even in Cases 3 and 5 which were never jury panels, when they were also on their own written presentments? Finally and most important, why had the two versions such marked differences when it was always emphasized that both juries returned the same verdict?

The last question is the most worrying. In every case there is agreement in broad outline between file and roll: on the circumstances in which death occurred and whether by felony or misadventure. But such facts are of little general value unless they exist in very large numbers, when they can be used for statistical and comparative purposes; and not enough coroners' inquests survive from the Middle Ages for valid statistical surveys to be possible. Inquests are therefore used in other ways: the weapons, deodands and valuations of goods and chattels for social and economic history, the field names for local topography, the jurors and other persons for genealogy, and so on. For these purposes it is the details that are important, and it is the details which cannot be taken at their face value.

Some have an inherent interest and importance whether or not they are completely true of the particular case. Also, in our six inquests some of the information on the roll is much more probable, or at least more relevant, than the conflicting statements in the file. For example, there is no reason to distrust the roll in the matter of the deodand in Case 3. The townships may well have been correct in returning that 2*s*. 1*d*. was found on the deceased, but the enrolling clerk must, rightly, have considered this irrelevant, and we may safely assume that he used the relevant information in the other verdict instead. But in the majority of instances where the roll and file disagree, as on dates and jurors' names, we cannot know which is correct, although we may be sure that the enrolling clerk normally based his version on the file verdict which does not survive. The inquests were held years before the compilation of the roll for the visit of King's Bench, and the enrolling clerk would rarely have been able to judge between conflicting facts in the two verdicts in the file. When allowance has also been made for the perils inherent in copying, there is probably a slightly less than even chance in each variation that the roll is right.

The conclusion is sadly obvious. Normally only an enrolment or, more often, a fair copy of an inquisition now survives. It is seldom possible to discover how much of it can be trusted: which jurors and sureties or even more essential people are ghosts, which dates and valuations are genuine, what exactly happened. It has long been realized that medieval chronicles must be approached with caution, but at least historians can usually recognize and allow for the chronicler's bias. The reliability of many official records seems to be no greater, and from their haphazard mixture of fact, fiction, and error the complete truth can rarely be distilled.

APPENDIX

The cases are printed in the same order as they appear in the enrolment in Coroners' Rolls (J.I. 2), no. 184, m. 3 and dorse. The last inquest entered on the face, which is not now represented in the file, is not printed, nor are the two final inquests on the dorse, of which only the last has left any trace on the file today—the half-erased jury panel on J.I. 2/255/8, m. 6. The order in which the cases from this file are printed below is membranes 6, 4, 1, 2, 5, and 3. The lay-out of the various pieces of information on the file membranes is described in the case-by-case analysis above.

The records printed here contain a number of errors of latinity, mainly wrong cases. The majority have not been noted individually as they are fairly obvious and do not confuse. Punctuation and capitals have been changed slightly in the interests of clarity and consistency. Headings and marginalia in the manuscripts are printed in capitals.

CASE I

File version (Plate 4)

KNYHT'. Inquisicio capta coram Roberto de Waure uno de coronatoribus domini regis in comitatu Warr' apud Stretton die Sabbati proximo post festum Apostolorum Simonis et Jude anno regni regis Edwardi tercii post conquestum xlvj^{to} per sacramentum Johannis de Grendon Johannis Colet Ricardi Taillour Thome Rondulf Henrici Wryhte Roberti Smyth Johannis Wryhte Thome Hosebond Willelmi de Grendon Ricardi Folk Willelmi Offechirch de Prensthorp et Roberti de Wodecote qui dicunt per sacramentum eorum quod contigit apud Prensthorp die lune proximo ante festum Sanctorum Simonis et Jude anno regni regis Edwardi tercii post conquestum xlvj^{to} quidam homo extraneus cuius nomen ignorant inventus fuit[1] interfectus cum quodam cultello percussus ad cor unde moriebatur. Per quos interfectus fuerat ignorant. Cuius inventor fuit[2] Johannes Irysh de Stretton qui levavit hutesium et invenit manucaptores Robertum Smyth et Johannem Wryhte etc.[3] Et dictus cultellus appreciatur ad j d. unde villata de Stretton oneratur. Et hoc presentant predicti xij juratores iiij villatarum Stretton Bobenhull Wolricheston et Ruyton.

Enrolment

STRETTON SUPER DONESMOR. INFORTUNIUM. Inquisicio capta coram Roberto de Waure uno coronatorum domini regis in comitatu Warr' apud Stretton super Donesmor die Sabbati proximo post festum Apostolorum Simonis et Jude anno regni regis Edwardi tercii post conquestum xlvj^{to} super visu corporis cuiusdam extranei ibidem interfecti per sacramentum Johannis de Grendon Johannis Colet Ricardi Taillour Thome Rondulf Henrici Wryhte Roberti Smyth Johannis Wryhte Thome Hosebond Willelmi de Grendon Ricardi Folk Willelmi Cochel et Roberti de Wodecote qui dicunt super

---

[1] *fuit* is interlined.　　　　[2] *Cuius inventor fuit* is written over an erasure.
[3] *etc.* is interlined.

PLATE 4

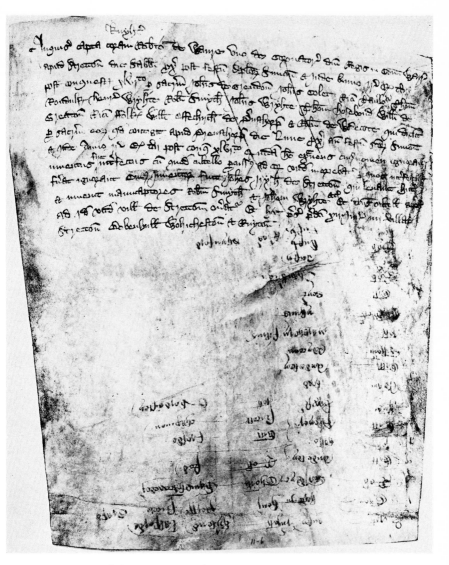

Coroner's inquest on an unknown stranger, 30 October 1372

sacramentum eorum quod contigit apud Stretton super Donesmor die lune proximo ante festum Apostolorum Simonis et Jude anno regni regis Edwardi tercii post conquestum xlvj^{to} quod cum quidam Johannes Irysh communis pastor animalium eiusdem ville pergens in campo eiusdem venisset in quodam bosco vocato Stretton Wode invenit ibidem quemdam extraneum occisum diversis plagis vulneratum cuius nomen ignorant. Levatum hutesium. De morte cuius neminem habent suspectum nisi per insultum latronum extraneorum qui statim post factum fugerunt. Plegii Johannis primi inventoris Johannes Wryhte et Robertus Smyth. Et hoc presentant predicti juratores iiij^{or} villatarum de Stretton Ruyton Bobenhull et Wolricheston.

CASE 2

File version

KNYHT'.[1] Willelmus Martyn Johannes Colvyle decennarii de Rokeby; Johannes Wedyntone decennarius de Mortone et Hulle; Johannes de Bordesle Nicholaus Sowstere Willelmus Forst decennarii de Beltone; Willelmus Herde Ricardus Wyshed decennarii de Clifton; jurati.

Idem decennarii dicunt quod Johannes Bocher percuttit Jiliam uxorem suam cum uno cultello qui vocatur broche precii de xviij d. Item juratores dicunt quod eodem Johannes percuttit predictam Jilianam in fronte semel quo obiit cum uno broche in vigilia Sancti Thome Apostoli circa horam nonam.

Johannes de Bylneye Robertus de Bretforde jurati; Rogerus Bayli Johannes Warde jurati; Henricus of ye Grene Johannes Blettesho jurati; Johannes Melewart Henricus Thorston jurati; Radulfus Westone Johannes Trot jurati; Johannes Ricardessone Willelmus Scharp jurati.

Enrolment

ROKEBY. JOHANNES BOCHER. CATALLA NULLA. Inquisicio capta coram Roberto de Waure uno coronatorum domini regis in comitatu Warr' die lune proximo post festum Sancti Thome Apostoli anno regni regis Edwardi tercii post conquestum xlvj^{to} apud Rokeby super visu corporis Juliane uxoris Johannis[2] Bocher de Rokeby ibidem interfecte per sacramentum Johannis de Bilneye Roberti de Bretforde Rogeri Bailly Johannis Warde Henrici atte Grene Johannis

---

[1] *Robertus Bretforde* is written on the dorse.   [2] *Johannis* is interlined.

Bletsho Johannis Muleward Henrici Thurstan Galfridi de Weston Johannis Trot Ricardi filii Ricardi et Willelmi Sharp qui dicunt super sacramentum eorum quod contigit apud Rokeby in vigilia Sancti Thome Apostoli anno regni regis Edwardi tercii post conquestum xlvj^to quod Johannes Bocher de Rokeby circa horam nonam percussit Julianam uxorem suam cum quodam baselardo in fronte capitis de quo vulnere obiit tercio die sequente; et sic felonice eam interfecit. Hoc facto hutesium levatum fuerat et dictus Johannes fugit; et nulla habet catalla. Et dicunt quod dicta Juliana habuit jura eccliastica.[1] Et hoc presentant predicti juratores iiij^or villatarum de Rokeby etc.

CASE 3

File version

KNYHT'. Accidit apud Stonleigh die veneris in crastino Epiphanie domini anno regni regis Edwardi tercii a conquestu xlvj^to quod quidam[2] Johannes Shoteswell Johannes Fishere et Johannes Saweyer inventi fuerunt mortui etc. Inquisicio inde capta coram Roberto Wouere coronatore domini regis super visu corporum eorundem hominum etc. Nicholaus Fisher Johannes of the Medewe Johannes Bedenhale et Willelmus Fox desennarii de Stonleigh; Thomas Herbert et Thomas Broun desennarii de Starton; Robertus Gibbes et Johannes Yerdeleye desennarii de Bobinhull; Johannes Pebbe et Matheus Irishman desennarii de Cobynton; qui dicunt super sacramentum quod predicti Johannes Johannes et Johannes in nocte Epiphanie domini venire voluissent de Asho a Stonleigh. Et eciam quando predicti homines veniebant apud Avene predicti Johannes Shoteswell et Johannes Fisscher ibant in una parva navicula et predictus Johannes Sawere saltat in predictam naviculam ita quod predicta navicula jusum vertit. Et sic predictus Sawer se ipsum demersit et Johannes Shoteswell et Johannes Fisscher similiter; et nuli alii inde male creditur. Inventor illorum Willelmus Fresel; plegii inventoris Johannes Westwale et Johannes Bont. Item presentant quod ij s. j d. cum eis fuerunt inventi.

XIJ JURATORES Johannes Jacokes Thomas Blakenhale Willelmus Braundon Adam Hebbe Willelmus Stoctun Johannes Eton Johannes Thenale Robertus Jelion Johannes Verdon Willelmus Philippes

---

[1] This is clearly a contraction of *ecclesiastica*, but there is no mark of contraction.
[2] *quidam* is interlined.

Willelmus Irishman et Thomas Dymmok qui dicunt super sacramentum suum quod predicti desennarii quo ad presentacionem[1] bene et fideliter presentant.

Enrolment

STONLEYE. INFORTUNIUM. DEODANDA XL D.[2] Inquisicio capta coram Roberto de Waure uno coronatorum domini regis in comitatu Warr' die Sabbati proximo post festum Epiphanie domini anno regni regis Edwardi tercii post conquestum xlvj^{to} apud Stonleye super visu corporum Johannes de Shoteswell Johannis Fyssher et Johannis Sawyer ibidem submersorum per sacramentum Johannis Jeuecokes Thome Blakenhale Willelmi de Braundon Ade Hebbe Willelmi de Stokton Johannis de Eton Johannis de Thornhale Roberti Julian Johannis Verdun Willelmi Phelippes Willelmi Irysh et Thome Dymmok qui dicunt super sacramentum eorum quod contigit apud Stonleye die veneris proximo post festum Epiphanie domini anno regni regis Edwardi tercii post conquestum xlvj^{to} quod Johannes de Shoteswelle Johannes Fissher[3] et Johannes Sawier venientes de villa de Assheso noctanter[4] voluerunt transmeare aquam de Avene. Dicti Johannes de Shoteswelle et Johannes Fyssher posuerunt se in quendam limbum essentem super eandem aquam et dictus Johannes Sawier saltavit ad eos et eundem limbum subvertebat ita quod iidem Johannes Johannes et Johannes ceciderunt in dictam aquam unde submersi sunt. Primus inventor eorum fuit Willelmus Fresel qui levavit hutesium; plegii eius Johannes Webbe et Robertus Blont. Et dictus limbus appreciatur ad iij s. iiij d. unde abbas de Stonleye oneratur pro deodanda regis. Et hoc presentant predicti juratores iiij^{or} villatarum de Stonleye Staverton Bobenhull et Cobynton.

CASE 4

File version

KNYHT'. Willelmus of Kuchene Ricardus Dawe francipleggii de Kyrk' Monachorum; Johannes Herbard Johannes Kyng Thomas Nichol francipleggii de Brokhurst Strotardeston et Wipetoft; Johannes Creste Johannes Hugge; Galfridus Pikard Johannes Bynley; Robertus Hert Willelmus Scheperd; Thomas Iblot Willelmus

---

[1] MS. has *ad pres'*, which could be extended as *ad presens*.

[2] Information concerning the deodand is recorded in K.B. 27/505, fines and forfeitures, m. 2d.

[3] *Fissher* is written over an erasure.   [4] *noctanter* is interlined.

Molend';[1] Johannes Harry Henricus Cartwryght; Johannes Wely Willelmus Andekyn.

Isti duodecim homines jurati presentant Ricardum de Walton pauperum submersum in quadam rivera[2] aque inter villam de Kyrkeby[3] et pratum prioris quod vocatur Stocwelmed die lune circa noctem proximo ante festum Purificacionis Beate Marie anno regni regis Edwardi tercii post conquestum quadragesimo septimo. Inventor istius adventus Johannes Potatden; plegii Davit of Braundone Walterus Argent.

Enrolment

KIRKEBY. INFORTUNIUM. Inquisicio capta coram Roberto de Waur' uno coronatorum domini regis in comitatu Warr' die martis proximo ante festum Purificacionis Beate Marie Virginis anno regni regis Edwardi tercii post conquestum xlvij° apud Kirkeby Monachorum super visu corporis Ricardi de Walton pauperi ibidem submersi[4] per sacramentum Willelmi Ofthe Cuchene Ricardi Dawe Johannis Herbard Johannis Kyng Thome Nichol Johannis Cosse Johannis Hugge Galfridi Picard Johannis de Bilneye Roberti Hert Thome Ibelot et Johannis Harrys qui dicunt super sacramentum eorum quod contigit apud Kirkeby Monachorum die lune proximo ante festum Purificacionis Beate Marie Virginis anno regni regis Edwardi tercii post conquestum xlvij° quod Johannes Porter transiens juxta[5] quamdam riveram aque juxta Brochurstmede invenit quemdam Ricardum de Walton pauperum[6] submersum in eadem rivera hora vesperarum; et neminem habent[7] suspectum de morte eiusdem Ricardi. Hutesium levatum. Dictus Johannes Porter invenit plegios David de Braundon et Walteri Forgo. Et hoc presentant predicti juratores iiij°ʳ villatarum de Kirkeby Brochurst Strotardeston et Wibetoft.

CASE 5

File version

KNYHT'. Contigit apud Streton super Dunnismor die martis proximo post festum Sancti Ambrosii anno regni regis Edwardi tercii post

---

[1] Probably *Molendinarius*, for Miller.
[2] *rivera* is interlined above *meatu*, which is struck through.
[3] *et Brokhurstmede die lune proximo* is written after *Kyrkeby* but is struck through.
[4] *ibidem submersi* is interlined.   [5] *juxta* is written over an erasure.
[6] *pauperum* is written over an erasure.
[7] *et neminem habent* is written over an erasure.

conquestum xlvij[to] quod quidam Willelmus Wattez inventus fuit mortuus etc. Inquisicio inde capta coram Roberto Wouere coronatore domini regis super visu eiusdem corporis Thomas Randolf de Stretton desennarius Prynsthorp; Thomas Starlyng desennarius Bobenhull; Robertus Gibbes desennarius Ruitoun; Willelmus Couherde Ricardus Tailour desennarii Fraunkton; Henricus Ansty desennarius; qui dicunt super sacramentum suum quod unus equs[1] in una caretta cum perde felonice[2] percussit predictum Willelmum Wattes die lune proximo post festum Sancti Ambrosii predictis die et anno ad horam nonam; et nulli alii inde male creditur. Primo invenit ipsum Rogerus Watte; plegii inventoris David Denes et Willelmus Horner. Et eciam dicunt quod predictus equs apreciatur xx s. unde villata respondeat domino rege.

JURATORES Thomas Berforde Willelmus Prynsthorp Willelmus Marchel Ricardus Oliver Henricus Hobben Ricardus Mathu Johannes Wright Ricardus Folke Willelmus Mathu Johannes Wlston Robertus Dunes Johannes Smyth.

Enrolment

STRETTON[3] SUPER DONESMOR. INFORTUNIUM. DEODANDA XX S.[4] Inquisicio capta coram Roberto de Waur' uno coronatorum domini regis in comitatu Warr' die mercurii proximo[5] post festum Sancti Ambrosii anno regni regis Edwardi tercii post conquestum xlvij° apud Stretton super Donesmor super visu corporis Willelmi Wattes de Franketon interfecti per sacramentum[6] Thome de Berford Willelmi Cochel Willelmi Smyth Ricardi Olyver Henrici Hobben Ricardi Matheu Johannis Wryhte Ricardi Folk Willelmi Matheu Johannis de Wolston Roberti Anneys et Johannis Smyth qui dicunt[7] super sacramentum eorum quod contigit apud Stretton super Donesmor die martis proximo post festum Sancti Ambrosii anno regni regis Edwardi tercii post conquestum xlvij° quod cum Willelmum[8] Wattes de Franketon fugabat iiij[or] equos tranctantes quamdam carettam

---

[1] *unus equs* is written over an erasure.
[2] *perde* is an error for *pede*; *felonice* is interlined.
[3] *Stretton* is written over an erasure.
[4] Information concerning the deodand is recorded in K.B. 27/505, fines and forfeitures, m. 2d.
[5] *die mercurii proximo* is written over an erasure.
[6] *Willelmi Wattes de Franketon interfecti per sacramentum* is written over an erasure.
[7] *qui dicunt* is repeated and struck through.
[8] *Sic.* The final 'm' of *Willelmum* is written over an erasure.

unus equs de dictis iiij^{or} equis cum uno pede suo percussit dictum Willelmum sub dextra auricula unde statim obiit. Primus eius inventor fuit Rogerus Wattes[1] pater dicti Willelmi. Hutesium levatum. Idem Rogerus invenit plegios Robertum Anneys et Willelmus Horner. Et dictus equs appreciatur ad xx s.; villa de Stretton oneratur. Et hoc presentant xij juratores iiij^{or} villatarum de Stretton Prensthorp Bobenhull et Franketon.

CASE 6

File version

KNYHT'. Ricardus Cartere Johannes Reve decennarii de Wolveye; Ricardus Kyng Willelmus Taundy Johannes Broun Reginaldus Warde Johannes Lincoln Willelmus Hyde Thomas Baily Galfridus Craft Willelmus ofthe Dyn Rogerus Cartewright Nicholaus Walsale Johannes Cokes Willelmus Jelion Johannes Hencokes Robertus atte Well Johannes Laurenc'; jurati qui dicunt super sacramentum suum quod quedam mulier xvj die mensis May anno xlvij° [2] inventa fuit mortua etc. Inquisicio inde capta coram Roberto Wauer coronatore domini regis etc. Et eciam dicunt super sacramentum quod predicta mulier predictis die et anno inveta[3] fuit mortua in Wegynpet de Haukislowe in campo de Wolvaye; et nichil aliud sciunt dicere. Primo invenit ipsam Willelmus[4] Fleshewer; plegius inventoris Johannes Hesonde. Et hoc presentant iiij villate Wolvaye Whithibrok Shulton Bulkynton.

Enrolment

WOLVEYE. INFORTUNIUM. Inquisicio capta coram Roberto de Waure uno coronatorum domini regis in comitatu Warr' xvij° die Maii anno regni regis Edwardi tercii post conquestum xlvij° apud Wolveye super visu cuiusdam mulieris extranee ibidem[5] invente mortue per sacramentum xij juratorum iiij^{or} villatarum de Wolveye Withibrok Shulton et Bulkynton qui dicunt super sacramentum eorum quod contigit apud Wolveye xvj die Maii anno supradicto quod cum[6]

---

[1] The 's' of *Wattes* is formed out of a previously written letter or letters.
[2] *anno xlvij°* is interlined.
[3] For *inventa*, but there is no mark of contraction.
[4] *Willelmus* is written over an erasure.
[5] *ibidem* is interlined.
[6] *cum* is interlined.

quidam Willelmus Flesshewer pergens in campo hora tercia venisset in quodam[1] vocato Haukesloue invenit ibidem quamdam mulierem extraneam corpore illesam mortuam; de morte cuius neminem habent suspectum nisi quod subito moriebatur. Plegii predicti Willelmi primi inventoris Johannes Isonde et Robertus Bonde.

R. F. HUNNISETT

---

[1] At least one word is missing here, possibly *loco* or, in view of the file version, *puteo in quodam loco.*

XI

Ecclesiastical Causes in Chancery

RECORD sources dominate the study of English history in the later Middle Ages. As the narrative accounts of chronicles became fewer in number and more localized in interest, administrative agencies were recording and preserving new categories of archives which reflect more sophisticated techniques in the organization of business. So great is the quantity of Public Records alone surviving from the fourteenth and fifteenth centuries that today, after many years of intensive exploitation, the historical potential of some groups has not yet been fully realized; a number have been little explored and certain classes of files from the courts of King's Bench, Common Pleas, and Chancery are still being sorted and listed. Faced with this abundance of material, searchers have tended to confine their inquiries to restricted ranges of record classes, often to the products of particular offices of state or courts of law. Specialization of this nature has yielded valuable studies of the operation and development of administrative and judicial institutions, explaining how the king's government worked and, to a more limited extent, allowing inferences about the pressures to which it was subjected at certain times. Sources of this kind have their limitations: they were created for particular purposes, to record transactions of immediate interest to those engaged upon certain administrative functions and not to answer the inquiries of remote generations of historians. This very functional limitation, however, gives records their unique value. If a certain fact of wider historical significance is alluded to, almost incidentally because it was in some respect relevant to a department's routine administrative work, that detail often commands greater credibility than the most solemn assertion of a deliberate narrative writer.[1] Records,

[1] Thus Henry IV's intention to remove Archbishop Scrope from York is revealed in signet and privy seal warrants dated a week before the day of Scrope's execution (8 June 1405), but the context in which this was shown was a commonplace transac-

indeed, can report history almost by accident. Consequently some classes of records can be of great value to historians whose subjects have little relation to the work of the departments which created them. Research at the Public Record Office is, of course, not monopolized by administrative historians; in fact, there is probably no topic of interest to any scholar concerned with late medieval England which cannot be supplemented by some detail of information enshrined in the archives of royal government, but his ability to find it may require luck as well as sufficient knowledge of the sources in general to know where to look.

In the field of ecclesiastical history it is also the case that the majority of scholars who pursue sustained inquiries concern themselves with institutions. Such is the impersonality of records that even the most documented group of medieval personages, the bishops, can rarely be revealed in other than their role as ruler of a diocese. In the present century our knowledge of the English Church in the later Middle Ages has been greatly extended by the study and publication of bishops' registers. It has been possible to modify conclusions once drawn only from the critical and often adversely biased accounts of ecclesiastical practice and clerical behaviour provided by contemporary works of literature and political manifestoes. Instead, copious details have been found of the ordering of church life in the memoranda of the day-to-day administration of dioceses recorded without any motive beyond having records of transactions available for future reference, again for administrative purposes. On the foundation of archival impartiality and sobriety provided by episcopal registers, therefore, modern scholars have shown how the late medieval church provided itself with an organization capable of discharging the responsibilities

---

tion of little moment, viz. Henry's grant to an under-clerk of his kitchen of the pension 'which he who is next created archbishop of York shall have to pay to one of our clerks'. Thus subsequent assertions in literary sources that the king was unwillingly stampeded into ordering Scrope's 'trial' and execution can be discounted. Since royal patronage was almost invariably prompted by petitions from hopeful beneficiaries, it would seem that reports of Henry's plans had reached the ears of his domestics no later than 1 June (P.R.O., Privy Seal Office, warrants for the privy seal, series 1 (P.S.O. 1) file 3, no. 138; Chancery, warrants for the great seal, series 1 (C. 81), file 626, no. 4359; R. L. Storey, *Thomas Langley and the Bishopric of Durham* (London, 1961), p. 18).

of the episcopal office, even in dioceses where the bishops' presence
was a rare occurrence. Whether this administrative machinery did
actually achieve its objectives is less certain. Even the wisest and
richest of rulers could only employ the most capable ministers
available at the time. The effectiveness of medieval government
cannot be assumed because its processes were painstakingly recorded. Only rarely can the information provided by bishops'
registers be supplemented by the court books of their officials and
of subordinate jurisdictions. The regular sequence of commissions
precisely recorded in the former and the judicial proceedings of the
latter give an impression of unruffled regularity. The records of
royal justice, although far more abundant in volume and no less
carefully made, provide, superficially, the same picture of judicial
competence. It is only too well known, however, that the legal
institutions of late medieval England were unable to restrain the
lawless propensities of its society. With disorder so rampant, it is
inconceivable that the records of ecclesiastical jurisdiction are less
deceptive and that in reality social conditions allowed the church
courts to function undisturbed by the pressures of maintenance and
intimidation. Reference to the contemporary archives of the royal
courts could correct estimates of the efficiency of ecclesiastical
administration at any particular time.[1] They can also provide
additional information about the operations of church courts and
details, sometimes of an unexpected kind, of the lives of some
ecclesiastics.[2] One class of Public Records, Early Chancery Proceedings, is particularly fruitful as a source for the ecclesiastical historian,
and although its value in this connection was demonstrated in 1907
it has been little exploited since then.[3] It is the purpose of this paper

---

[1] For instance, compare R. M. Haines, *The Administration of the Diocese of Worcester
in the First Half of the Fourteenth Century* (London, 1965), pp. 321–2, and *Select Cases in
the Court of King's Bench under Edward II*, ed. G. O. Sayles (Selden Society, vol. 74,
1957), pp. liii–v.

[2] e.g., in 1387 the juries of several hundreds in Gloucestershire each accused
sequestrators of the bishop of Worcester of making extortionate charges (cited) for
grants of probate; one jury indicted the bishop (Henry Wakefield) of the rape of one
woman on 4 Oct. 1383 (a Sunday) and of her mother on 12 Nov. following (P.R.O.,
King's Bench, Ancient Indictments (K.B. 9), file 32).

[3] C. T. Martin, 'Clerical Life in the Fifteenth Century, as illustrated by Proceedings
in the Court of Chancery', *Archaeologia*, vol. 60, part 2 (1907), pp. 353–78. *Monastic
Chancery Proceedings (Yorkshire)*, ed. J. S. Purvis (Yorkshire Archaeological Society,

to illustrate from the discussion of certain themes how this material, although originating in a secular court of law, can add a new dimension to the study of the English Church and simultaneously reveal failures in the vigilance of its own apparatus for disciplinary surveillance and so point to some deficiencies in bishops' registers.

From the last quarter of the fourteenth century, Chancery began regularly to exercise and record what has come to be known as its equitable jurisdiction. From the beginning, a good number of litigants appealing to this court were clerks; indeed in its early years, the proportion of clerical plaintiffs alleging wrongs of an ecclesiastical nature was higher than after 1417, when the volume of actions initiated by laymen began to swell. Chancery offered the opportunity to redress grievances which the common law either could not or would not remedy. In the early years, the pleas made to the chancellor concerned matters of a very miscellaneous nature.[1] That members of the clergy were quick to appreciate the facilities offered by Chancery is hardly remarkable. Chancery itself was staffed with men in clerical orders, and clearly word soon went through the profession that the court was ready to entertain pleas for redress of unusual injustices. To this time belong the bills alleging that their authors had been expelled from benefices by papal provisors.[2]

One early litigant in Chancery was an officer of the duchy of Lancaster. This was John Elvet who, as archdeacon of Leicester, complained that John Belgrave had attached a scurrilous libel to the door of St. Martin's, Leicester, the night before Walter Barnak, Elvet's official, was to hold an archidiaconal court there. In this Belgrave compared Barnak to the elders who condemned Susanna, stating that he did justice that was not rightful but oppressed the

Record Series, vol. lxxxviii, 1934) is an exception to this neglect. Its title is misleading: there is no Public Record Office class with this title, and the contents of the volume are a selection extracted from Early Chancery Proceedings.

[1] W. T. Barbour, 'The History of Contract in Early English Equity', *Oxford Studies in Social and Legal History*, iv, ed. P. Vinogradoff (Oxford, 1914), 68; M. A. Avery, 'The history of the equitable jurisdiction of Chancery before 1460', *BIHR*, xlii (1969), 132.

[2] P.R.O., Chancery, Early Chancery Proceedings (C. 1), bundles 3, no. 125; 4, no. 175; 7, no. 316; 68, nos. 68, 112, 237, 242, 252 (see below, p. 242 n. 1).

innocent and tolerated the wicked; he was 'un jugge de deable de iniquitee'. When the official sought to censure all concerned in this slander, Belgrave openly and 'pompousement' prevented him. Thus, Elvet concluded, his archidiaconal office could not be executed, and as more riots might ensue, he sought Belgrave's citation to Chancery.[1] Another bill from the first years of Chancery's new jurisdiction suggests that judicial processes in the diocese of Worcester could be manipulated by interested parties. According to John Todenham, Master John Middelton schemed to oust him from the rectory of Oddington, Gloucestershire. By making false allegations which would merit Todenham's deprivation, Middelton persuaded the bishop to appoint commissaries nominated by himself to hear the cause. This commission was revoked when the bishop was better informed, said Todenham, but it still proceeded, without citing him, 'by a process such as has never been seen before these days, to the great grief and scandal of the whole country'.[2]

The bills of plaintiffs form the majority of the records of Chancery jurisdiction before the sixteenth century. In most cases the only immediate guides to their dates are the addresses to certain chancellors, whose names only provide limits for dating, since some chancellors held office for several years, while different bishops of the same see, not otherwise named, held the great seal at various times in the fifteenth century. Many of the earliest bills, made before forms for drafting had been accepted, lack even this assistance. Such bills, however, are usually written in French or occasionally in Latin; from the 1430s bills applying for equitable relief were written in English, and thus this side of Chancery received the name which distinguishes it from its 'latin', or common law, side. There also exist many unsorted files of writs of *sub pena* and *corpus cum causa* relating to litigation in Chancery; these are dated and, when they can be made available for research, will doubtless enable many bills

---

[1] C. 1/68/83, addressed to the keeper of the great seal; thus 1394 or 1396, as Elvet was archdeacon of Leicester, 1392–1404. He was Gaunt's clerk of the wardrobe (J. Armitage-Smith, *John of Gaunt* (Westminster, 1904), p. 449).

[2] C. 1/68/20 (in French, not addressed). Middelton, who was Richard II's physician, was instituted by Bishop Wakefield to Oddington in 1388 and held the church for more than twenty years (A. B. Emden, *A Biographical Register of the University of Oxford to A.D. 1500* (Oxford, 1957–9), ii. 1276).

to be dated. Records of examinations of witnesses in Chancery and of judgements rarely exist before the middle of the fifteenth century. Consequently for most early suits the only evidence available is the initial complaints of plaintiffs. Petitions were always drawn up in the most abject terms, the innocence and honesty of the plaintiffs were fully stressed, and their wrongs and misery depicted in a heart-rending manner. They were designed, no doubt, to bring tears to the chancellor's eyes, and might have done so if he had not read hundreds of similar bills in the course of each year. The phraseology of petitions, in short, had many common-form elements which require that they should not be accepted at face-value. The subject matter must also be regarded with suspicion, for bills naturally give only the plaintiffs' versions of quarrels, and the answers produced by defendants may often have been found more convincing by the chancellor. Late medieval litigants and lawyers were highly skilled in the art of special pleading and in putting their cases suppressed all factors telling against themselves and made out that they had been wronged, whereas in fact they themselves may have been far from blameless. For instance, there are three bills from different clerks complaining, each one, that he was in peaceful and lawful possession of a church in the diocese of Lincoln until Master Stephen Tinwell, rector of West Deeping, came along with a gang of armed men, broke into the manse, smashing doors and windows in the process, and ejected the plaintiff and seized his goods. The particulars about the armed men and their military equipment are common form; so are the details of their violence. It is, moreover, hard to credit the collective evidence of these three bills that Stephen Tinwell, a graduate, notary, and beneficed clergyman, was a notorious despoiler of the rural clergy. It is more probable that he was a commissary of the bishop of Lincoln, or of a subordinate jurisdiction, and that he was sequestrating these livings in the course of his duties. Had he indeed been a kind of clerical brigand, the injured clerks could have appealed to their bishop. They chose Chancery instead, one suspects, for the very good reason that they knew that the bishop would show them no sympathy but would uphold Tinwell's actions. It would have been a remarkable coincidence if these three clerks had independently chosen this course of action against the same man; it is more credible that they acted in concert.[1] Here, then, are probable instances of bogus wrongs being brought into Chancery, and anyone who makes use of Chancery proceedings has to be cautious about such evidence.

All the same, many of these petitions provide circumstantial details which can be useful as evidence when detached from the gist of the actual grievances being reported. In the instances just mentioned, it may be accepted that the three clerks had been living at the rectories in question and that Stephen Tinwell had disturbed their possession. Chancery proceedings abound in informative details about clerical and monastic life, while parochial organization is reflected in numerous instances of litigation between incumbents and churchwardens or other parishioners. Those of Grayingham, Lincolnshire, sued their rector, Robert Conyng, who had erected an 'image' which prevented them from seeing the elevation of the Host. He excommunicated those who had protested, and when they procured an inhibition from the archdeacon, Conyng had them cited before the bishop.[2] The repair and construction of buildings are also illustrated. A London brazier told the chancellor that he had installed two bells in the church of Whitchurch Canonicorum,

---

[1] The plaintiffs were John Spalding, alleging expulsion from Standground (Isle of Ely), and John Osbern and William Sleford, both from Yaxley (Hunts.). The first two addressed their bills to the archbishop of York; Sleford's, which is in French, does not name the chancellor (C. 1/7/261, 281; 68/152). Tinwell was rector of West Deeping 1374–94 (L.A.O., Episcopal Registers, nos. 10, f. 64, and 11, f. 72. These references were kindly supplied by Mrs. J. Varley). The chancellor was thus Thomas Arundel and the bills of Spalding and Osbern belong to 1391–4. Osbern also petitioned an unknown chancellor, in French, that he had been instituted to Yaxley on the presentation of lay patrons and expelled by William Chesterton, a papal provisor (C. 1/68/252). This bill may be dated 1388: on 26 April Chancery ordered the arrest of a William Chesterton, who was to be brought before the king and council (*CPR*, 1385–9, p. 471; see also *CPL*, iv. 372). Chesterton's provision is not mentioned in the bill of Osbern against Tinwell, who might have been enforcing a judgement in Chesterton's favour; but as the plaintiff could have referred to this in order to expose Tinwell to charges of violating the statutes of provisors and *praemunire*, his failure to exploit this line of attack suggests that Tinwell's action was unconnected with Chesterton. More suspicious is the fact that both churches were in the patronage of Thorney Abbey, which was licensed to appropriate them in 1398 (ibid., v. 164). Tinwell may well have been employed by the abbey. He was a notary and witnessed a composition made by Thorney in 1390 (L.A.O., Episc. Reg. 12, f. 430, a reference kindly supplied by Miss Alison McHardy).

[2] C. 1/68/133 (in French, chancellor unknown). See the detailed lists of parties and summaries of complaints in *List of Early Chancery Proceedings*, vols. 1 and 2 (Public Record Office Lists and Indexes, nos. xii, 1901, and xvi, 1903).

Dorset. The arrangement, he said, was that the vicar should have them on trial for a year before he would be required to pay. When the year had passed, the brazier went to collect his money, but the vicar said that the bells had not met his specifications. It would appear that the vicar was trying to avoid his debt because a neighbouring rector, called in evidence, said that the bells sounded well enough to him.[1] Again, some bills give information about litigation at the papal curia, because English agents in Rome petitioned the chancellor when their clients failed to pay their fees and costs, and circumstantial details are given about how these expenses had been incurred.[2]

Among this material there is evidence of the way certain clergy did business with each other over the possession of church livings. They made agreements about benefices in the same way as laymen made contracts about land and other secular matters, and they were equally prepared to go to law when these arrangements were not carried out. This general conclusion is permissible despite the observations just made about the partial, one-sided nature of Chancery petitions, because the statements about this trafficking in benefices are made by the plaintiffs. They do not conceal the fact that they made these agreements, because the burden of their petitions is that the contracts were not carried out by the defendants. Actions for breach of contract in all kinds of business, secular as well as ecclesiastical, became a regular and important category of Chancery proceedings. The court offered a remedy in this matter which was not available by resort to common law. A civil court might award damages if a case for breach was proven, but Chancery could order that a contract should be performed in accordance with its terms. Moreover, common law offered no means for remedy where the parties had made their agreement only by word of mouth, exchanging no written record except, perhaps, bonds to pay certain sums of money; in such cases, Chancery provided the frustrated party his only opportunity for remedy.

Chancery proceedings illuminate three principal types of contracts concerning benefices. The largest category brought to the

---

[1] C. 1/68/144 (in French, chancellor unknown).
[2] C. 1/10/325 and 11/328 (both 1432–43); 43/112–16 (with examinations, 1469).

court is of disputes over the farms of rectories and some other livings, when the incumbents had made over their revenues and responsibilities in return for stipulated annual payments. These farms were made for periods of years and the incumbents did not surrender their titles to the farmers, who were generally laymen. In the other two groups, the contracts were between clerics and involved title. Here the larger number of cases in Chancery concerned exchanges of livings. The practice whereby clerks exchanged benefices between each other was a common one in the fourteenth and fifteenth centuries and bishops' registers record many transactions of this kind. Every exchange required a considerable amount of official documentation. A bishop's register would record the resignations of their livings by the two clerks concerned, the letters of the patrons presenting each clerk to the benefice vacated by the other's resignation, the bishop's examination of the reasons for the exchange and his issue of letters of institution and mandates for induction. If the benefices being exchanged happened to be in different dioceses, the bishop of one would empower the bishop of the other to carry out the exchange, and his commission would also be entered as part of the formal record. A bishop's register, however, records only the final stage in the arrangement of an exchange which had probably been preceded by lengthy and complex negotiations. The same formal language appears in the record of every exchange; even the bishop's reasons for approval are often given in a stereotyped formula. He is said to have found the reasons for the exchange true and lawful: had he not done, there would presumably have been no exchange and thus no reason for any of the record to be registered. A register reports only what had been done by a bishop, rarely giving his reasons or the preliminary stages necessary before any business could be performed.

It would therefore be unrewarding to search bishops' registers of the fifteenth century to discover the motives of clerks who exchanged livings. For one category of clerks it is permissible to draw inferences from these formal records. This is the class of ecclesiastical administrators, the graduates who pursued careers as canon lawyers and proceeded to offices like sequestrator general, official, and vicar general. Sometimes these men moved from the service of one bishop to another and then exchanged livings in the diocese of the first for others in the diocese where they would be working. A bishop translated to another see might bring some of his ministers and they would similarly arrange their own translation to new benefices.[1] Reasons for exchanges between other clergy can rarely be established. It may sometimes be assumed that some exchanges were arranged to enable clerks to escape the ill will of their diocesan. Thus Master William Pelleson, dean of Lanchester, was in 1417 threatened with proceedings for persistent absenteeism and prudently retired from the diocese of Durham by making an exchange with a rector in York.[2] There may have been cases when a bishop applied pressure to move a man from a parish[3] or even from the diocese, although when an incumbent had a thoroughly bad record his bishop had powers to deprive him of his benefice.

Petitions to the chancellor sometimes declare motives for exchanges. Philip Tregilla, presumably a Cornishman, had a rectory in Suffolk. In his old age, his heart turned towards his native land and he tried to obtain an exchange to a benefice closer to it.[4] A vicar of Thaxted, Essex, told the chancellor that he planned to move to a church in Leicestershire, because he had been born in that county.[5] Henry Newton, rector of Adwell, Oxfordshire, proposed to exchange with Thomas Rithe, who had a chantry in St. Paul's, London. This rector seemingly fits Chaucer's description of the parson who

> 'Leet his sheep encombred in the myre
> And ran to London, unto Seynt Poules,
> To seken him a chaunterie for soules'.

The priest Rithe was agreeable to the exchange because he 'had proposid to have goon to scole'. His desire for a university education, however, did not survive the shock of discovering how poor the rectory was. The rector had told him its annual value was £16

---

[1] R. L. Storey, *Diocesan Administration in the Fifteenth Century* (St. Anthony's Hall Publications, no. 16, York, 1959), pp. 19–20, 23–4.

[2] Storey, *Thomas Langley*, p. 186.

[3] An instance is given in M. Bowker, *The Secular Clergy in the Diocese of Lincoln 1495–1520* (Cambridge, 1968), p. 120.

[4] C. 1/68/27 (in French, chancellor unknown). The church was Willingham.

[5] C. 1/27/425 (see p. 252 below).

and produced witnesses who confirmed this valuation. Rithe later found that the church of Adwell was hardly worth 100*s.* p.a.,[1] a figure which is confirmed by surviving records of its taxation.[2] Philip Tregilla had been prepared to make some sacrifice to be nearer Cornwall. His church in Suffolk was worth £13 6*s.* 8*d.*, but he would have exchanged for one of £10 in another diocese.[3] These clerks, even when they had a respectable motive for an exchange, were practical enough to consider their stipends. Financial advantage may well have been the first consideration with some parties to exchanges. If some clerks were ready to sacrifice some of their income in moving to a more congenial area, those they exchanged with would clearly have profited. Moreover, it is notorious that many benefices were held by non-resident clergy, by men with full-time employment in the service of the king or pope, or of bishops and secular lords; while the more fortunate scholars at universities were also supported by the fruits of benefices. Non-resident clergy also exchanged livings. An absentee rector might well prefer to become the canon of a cathedral or collegiate church, where his non-residence would not incur official censure. When, for instance, a king's clerk exchanged one rectory for another and remained fully in royal service, it may be presumed that he made the exchange for a financial reason.[4] It is possible, too, that some exchanges between financially incompatible benefices were accompanied by a cash payment as compensation; such an arrangement had obvious attractions for an elderly or infirm parson, unable to cope with a large cure, or to one in urgent need of capital.[5]

There is little doubt that the practice of exchanging benefices permitted mercenary transactions. Financial considerations apparently inspired the great increase in numbers of exchanges in the fourteenth century. The gravity of this abuse prompted the

---

[1] Petition printed as an example in Appendix, pp. 258–9 below. Chancery presumably annulled the contract because Newton soon made other arrangements to leave Adwell. He had resigned by 27 Nov. 1440, when Henry Sharpe, bachelor of laws, was instituted (Lincoln Registers 18, f. 172).

[2] *VCH Oxford*, viii. 13.   [3] C. 1/68/27 (see p. 245, n. 4 above).

[4] Cf. A. L. Brown, pp. 278–9 below.

[5] John Wycliffe's expenses in litigation may thus explain why he exchanged Fillingham rectory for a much poorer benefice in 1368 (K. B. McFarlane, *John Wycliffe and the Beginnings of English Nonconformity* (E.U.P., 1952), p. 29).

convocation of Canterbury to legislate in 1392. It had been discovered that some clergy were being deceived into exchanging their livings for poorer ones; they were impoverished by exchanges, while mercenary clerks, heedless of their eternal damnation, were waxing fat. It was enjoined that in future bishops were to ensure that, when any two clerks requested an exchange, the benefices were to be of equal value. Convocation attributed the development of these corrupt practices to certain 'sons of iniquity, blasphemers of the clergy and Church, partners in the crime of Gehazi and Simon, commonly called choppechurches'. These were the agents who arranged fraudulent exchanges. Archbishop Courtenay believed that they plied their trade mainly in the city of London and he ordered its bishop to command them to abandon their nefarious business under pain of excommunication.[1] Commenting on this mandate, Professor Hamilton Thompson wrote that if it 'did not stop the abuse, at any rate it seems to have warned the traffickers in benefices to proceed with more caution'.[2]

It is quite clear, however, that this ecclesiastical outlawry of chopchurches did not extinguish their profession. In 1414 a statute required that the full legal name of a person should include his rank or trade,[3] and from the following years notices may be found in governmental records of men whose occupation is given as 'chop-church'. William Gannet of Crewkern, Somerset, gave 'chopchurch' as his occupation when he bought a general pardon in 1415.[4] William Wey and John Steregrave, both chopchurches of London, were accused of causing grievous bodily harm at Stepney in 1422. Thomas Meleman was another London chopchurch who, with a 'soudiour', was said to have robbed Finchley church in 1427. Edmund Raket of Waterford in Ireland, chopchurch, was said to be a member of a gang of miscellaneous origins who plundered a house in Harrow. A second Somerset man, Henry Down of Sevenhampton, was described as a chopchurch when charged with robbing a clerk's house in 1436. Another common law indictment of this time named

---

[1] *Concilia Magnae Britanniae et Hiberniae*, ed. D. Wilkins (London, 1737), iii. 215–17.

[2] A. H. Thompson, *The English Clergy and their Organization in the Later Middle Ages* (Oxford, 1947), p. 109.

[3] *Statutes of the Realm*, ed. A. Luders and others (R.C., 1810–28), ii. 171.

[4] P.R.O., Chancery, Supplementary Patent (Pardon) Rolls (C. 67), no. 37, m. 42.

Walter Geoffrey of Norwich as a chopchurch.[1] He appears to have
been a man of some consequence in his city. Chopchurching was not
his sole occupation, for he was also referred to as both scrivener and
poulterer. Geoffrey had been a member of the patrician gild of St.
George; he was expelled from it in 1436 because of his support for
the political aspirations of Norwich's lesser tradesmen.[2] Scriveners
in London also were involved in the benefice market and so was
at least one saddler.[3] A Devonshire husbandman petitioning in
Chancery alleged that he had been wrongfully prosecuted in church
courts 'bi subtill ymaginacion of one John Polyng, clerc, otherwise
called chopchirch, of Excestre'. Polyng is known to have been an
ecclesiastical lawyer practising in Exeter diocese between 1432 and
1455; he prospered sufficiently to be a benefactor to Exeter College,
Oxford, which observed his obit from 1461.[4]

Chopchurches therefore continued to flourish long after convocation's legislation against them in 1392, and not only in London but
in other parts of the country. Those who can be further identified
appear to have been men of some standing and were probably considered respectable members of their urban communities. The business of chopchurching was apparently not the sole occupation of
any of these men, but it was still regular enough for them to have
'chopchurch' cited in legal records as part of their correct description. Moreover, it seems that they were not regarded as outcasts
from society; there was no particular stigma attached to their
business. Convocation's statute had soon been forgotten.[5] The
obvious reason for chopchurches existing after 1392 was that the

---

[1] K.B. 9/218/1, no. 8; 221/1, nos. 15, 52; 230B, no. 78; 231/1, no. 51.

[2] *The Records of the City of Norwich*, ed. W. Hudson and J. C. Tingey (Norwich and
London, 1906), i. 346; ii, p. cxlii.   [3] C. 1/9/78; 17/348.

[4] C. 1/17/86; Emden, *Oxford Graduates*, iii. 1495.

[5] One petition does end with a prayer to avoid the scandals which could arise 'per
hujusmodi chopchirches'. The complaint was against John Boure 'vulgariter dictus
chopchirche'. He allegedly came to John Pudde and promised to obtain for him a
prebend worth £20 p.a. in Penkridge royal free chapel (Staffs.) if he was paid £18.
Misled by Boure's 'sermonibus blandis et blesis', Pudde agreed—and paid—but was
provided only with a chantry worth 100s. (C. 1/73/57, chancellor unknown; an
abstract appears in *Collections for a History of Staffordshire* (William Salt Archaeological
Society), N.S. vii (1904), 291–2). The date is probably 1417, when John Boure, 'chopchirch', undertook to appear in Chancery; this he did and was dismissed *sine die* (*CCR,
1413–19*, p. 525). Boure was himself the plaintiff in another suit in 1417–24; this
concerned an exchange of benefices (C. 1/4/70).

need for their services remained. Every rector wanting to exchange his benefice could hardly have travelled until he found another willing to exchange. Apart from the obvious hazards and inconveniences, he would run the risk of attracting the suspicions of his diocesan. It was simpler to go to a chopchurch, who probably kept memoranda of other clerks wanting to exchange, and was ready to find and persuade others to do so. Like estate agents today, chopchurches were useful as brokers; the derivation of the word 'chop' from the meaning 'to practice barter' makes their function clear.[1] It is unlikely, moreover, that all chopchurches were dishonest. Some were accused of malpractices in Chancery proceedings, but other bills refer to these middlemen without rancour when this is reserved for the other parties to proposed exchanges. No chopchurch is accused of corrupt dealings in more than one bill, and it seems improbable that a man's legal occupation could be given as 'chopchurch' if he negotiated only one exchange. Eight chopchurches have been traced in circumstances unconnected with exchanges of livings: presumably these men were known to have been fairly frequently engaged as brokers in church livings, but they are not known to have been accused of wrongful practices in this connection.

A certain proportion of exchanges were arranged without the help of chopchurches. Once two clerks wanting to exchange had made contact, with or without the services of a chopchurch, they had to arrange many details before they could ask their bishop or bishops to carry out the exchange. The parties gave each other valuations of their benefices. They discussed the timing of their exchange; this was important, because a large proportion of the revenues of a rectory came from tithes, and harvests were gathered at different times in different parts of the country. The parties also discussed how they would persuade their respective patrons to present the other to his living. When all the details had been arranged, the parties made bonds carrying financial penalties which they either exchanged or lodged with a third party. These bonds were the guarantees for each clerk that the other would perform his

---

[1] See *O.E.D.* From *c.* 1700 'chopchurch' was applied to a clergyman who himself moved from benefice to benefice.

part of the agreed arrangements, although the conditions themselves were not necessarily stated in writing. The next step was to
seek the consent of the patrons to the changes in the incumbency
of their livings, and this could be a lengthy operation. Only after
both patrons had sealed and delivered their letters of presentation
could the clerks go to their bishop or bishops to request the expedition of the exchange.

Such was the programme for an exchange of benefices, but there
remained some possibilities that the operation would not go through
because one party failed to perform his part in the initial agreement;
or an exchange might be completed and a party feel that he had
been defrauded. The aggrieved clerk might then sue in Chancery
for a remedy, either to secure the enforcement of the initial contract or its annulment. The case of Thomas Rithe, who said that
he had been misled about the value of Adwell rectory, has already
been noticed. In 1440, John Farly, vicar of Milton, made a
similar complaint against John Baker, vicar of Shenley. Baker had
sworn that Shenley was worth £20 p.a. to live in or could be leased
for sixteen marks. In fact, said Farly, it was not worth £6. The two
men had sealed bonds for £20 which they had left 'in the scryveners
handes' and Baker was now trying to obtain possession of Farly's
bond.[1] There are two cases of clerks alleging that they had been
similarly deceived by chopchurches and their clients; bonds had
been exchanged, but as the plaintiffs were refusing to carry out the
exchanges of benefices, the other parties were seeking by litigation
to enforce the payment of the bonds.[2] Robert Doncaster, who
described himself as 'un auncien chapelyn', appears to have been
the victim of an ingenious plot by his curate, John Olive. He alleged
that Olive promised to make him rector of Tendring, Essex;
Olive, indeed, brought with him a chaplain who claimed to be
rector of Tendring and to be ready to exchange with Doncaster.
The latter agreed; his vicarage of Mendlesham was less valuable
than Tendring. He sealed a deed resigning Mendlesham and entrusted it to Olive. Olive then contrived to have himself presented
and instituted to a second vicarage worth 40s. p.a. Next he went to

[1] C. 1/9/78 (pledges for prosecution dated 13 Oct. 1440).
[2] C. 1/16/368; 17/348.

the bishop to deliver Doncaster's deed of resignation and to resign his own vicarage for the expedition of an exchange between them. As the bishop complied, Olive became vicar of Mendlesham and expelled his former master who now found himself, not rector of Tendring, but vicar of a church 'que fuist de si peti[t] value'.[1]

The degree of detail required in the planning of an exchange is best shown in a bill by John Lelye, who attached a schedule listing the goods which were to be left at the rectories being exchanged. Lelye and John Hertilpole also agreed to leave the little tithes due at Easter to the other. Lelye said that he observed these conditions when leaving the rectory of Mells, Somerset, but when he arrived at Sandy, Bedfordshire, he found that Hertilpole had removed the tithes and stripped the rectory of its furnishings.[2] John Depull exchanged the rectory of Esher, Surrey, for that of Chagford, Devon, with the consent of both patrons and ordinaries, and was instituted and inducted. His complaint was not against William Mayowe, the new rector of Esher, but against his own patron at Chagford, John Wybury. According to Depull, Wybury seized all his corn and some other goods and guarded the parsonage to prevent Depull from entering.[3] This bill may reflect a situation sometimes caused by exchanges of benefices, for it is improbable that every patron found an incumbent wished upon him by exchange entirely congenial to himself.

These petitions were made by clerks who had made exchanges which they subsequently regretted. Others complained that they had arranged exchanges which were not carried out. Robert Bukyngton apparently took the initiative in planning an exchange with John Drake, another Devonshire incumbent, for he promised to pay the expenses incurred in obtaining the consent of the patrons

[1] C. 1/11/329 (addressed to the bishop of Bath and Wells; as it is in French, it must belong to 1432–43). Doncaster said Mendlesham was worth £26. 13s. 4d. Its value in 1536 was £14. 18s. 1d., when Tendring's value was £16 (*Valor Ecclesiasticus*, ed. J. Caley and J. Hunter (R.C., 1810–34), i. 442; iii. 480). For another case of a feigned rector see C. 1/12/179, and for a fraudulent proctor in another exchange see C. 1/68/59.

[2] Lelye said he was unable to obtain a remedy at common law because Hertilpole was a master in Chancery. He abandoned his suit there in 1432 (C. 1/11/329). The exchange had taken place in 1429 (*Register of Bishop Stafford*, ed. T. S. Holmes (Somerset Record Society, 1915–16), part i, p. 66).

[3] C. 1/7/308 (addressed to the archbishop of York).

of both livings. He alleged that he secured letters of presentation from both patrons at a cost of forty marks, but that Drake then refused to complete the exchange.[1] The vicar of Thaxted who wished to return to his native Leicestershire was likewise disappointed. He said that, by the mediation of friends, he made a full agreement for an exchange with William Shawe, rector of Ayleston. Each undertook, verbally, to go to his patron to obtain his consent and presentation of the other. After several journeys, the vicar eventually persuaded his patron, the dean of Stoke-by-Clare, to present Shawe to Thaxted. Shawe claimed to have failed in his attempts to win the consent of his patron, Sir William Vernon, and urged the vicar to approach Vernon. The vicar then, he said, 'often' went to London and Derbyshire to see Vernon, and as he did not know him, induced several friends, among them lords, to write to Vernon on his behalf. At length, after spending more than £40, he secured Vernon's consent, only to discover that Shawe was no longer willing to leave Ayleston.[2] The reason for his change of mind is suggested by the valuations of the two livings: Ayleston had double the income of the vicarage of Thaxted.[3] John Drake's belated decision to remain at Ermington was probably due to a similar reason, for he would have exchanged an income of £33 for a mere 44*s.* at Broad Nymet.[4]

The omission of these details about revenues emphasizes the danger of accepting the statements of plaintiffs in Chancery at face value. In the last two cases, it is apparent that the plaintiffs had attempted to deceive the defendants, who broke their agreements to exchange when they belatedly discovered how much to their disadvantage the exchanges would have been. It is possible that some of the plaintiffs in the other cases already described may not have been as disingenuous as their bills suggest. It is, at least, permissible to conclude that in all these cases either the plaintiff or the

[1] C. 1/44/197 (in English, addressed to the bishop of Bath and Wells). There is no reference in *The Register of Edmund Lacy*, ed. G. R. Dunstan (C.Y.S. lx–lxiii, 1963–71), to either Bukyngton as rector of Broad Nymet or Drake as vicar of Ermington. The date must therefore be later than 1455 and thus in 1465–73.

[2] C. 1/27/425 (addressed to George [Neville], bishop of Exeter, and thus 1460–5). Shawe was rector of Ayleston 1450–78 and William Vernon its patron 1451–67 (J. Nichols, *History and Antiquities of the County of Leicester* (London, 1795–1811), iv, part i, pp. 30, 27).   [3] *Valor Ecclesiasticus*, i. 438; iv. 186.   [4] Ibid., ii. 348, 378.

defendant had attempted to defraud the other. What is more generally evident, however, is the materialistic attitude of all parties to their ecclesiastical benefices. They regarded them as pieces of property to be traded in a secular manner, employing the forms of commercial practice in their transactions and going to law over their disagreements in the same spirit. The dividing line between such mercenary exchanges and simony pure and simple was a thin one. A clerk who exchanged his benefice for another did not offend canon law, even if his motive was his financial betterment. When clergy could look upon their benefices as negotiable properties, however, it is not remarkable that a number were tempted to exchange them for monetary payments. The extent of simony in the late medieval church cannot be measured. Only rare notices of its detection appear in episcopal registers. A single instance appears, for example, in the register for the thirty-one years of Thomas Langley's episcopate at Durham, and that came to light because the two chaplains concerned made a technical error in arranging the resignation of the church; this caused them to be cited before the bishop, who then extracted an admission of simony,[1] and he might not have exposed them had he not, as a former chancellor of England, become expert in the examination of witnesses and in acquaintance with the uncanonical dealings practised by clerical litigants appearing in Chancery. Clergy who engaged in the forbidden practice of simony appear to have concealed their operations from the ecclesiastical authorities by a variety of subterfuges, even though contemporary moralists proclaimed their prevalence.[2]

There are a number of petitions among Early Chancery Proceedings which give some evidence about the practice of simony in the fifteenth century. Sales of benefices were arranged in the same way as exchanges. The parties met, arranged details, and sometimes

---

[1] An inquiry into the presentation to the church of Kirkhaugh, Northumberland, in 1432, revealed that Thomas Stayndrop had, *ex impericia*, resigned into the hands of the lay patron. William Denton, who had been presented, then confessed that he had promised to pay Stayndrop ten marks for resigning. Stayndrop was then required to forfeit this money but Denton received the benefice (*The Register of Thomas Langley, Bishop of Durham 1406–1437*, ed. R. L. Storey (Surtees Society, 1956–70), vol. iv, nos. 1019, 1035; and vi, no. 1577).

[2] P. Heath, *The English Parish Clergy on the Eve of the Reformation* (London, 1969), pp. 36–8.

made bonds to each other as guarantees that each would perform his side of the transaction. As in the case of exchanges, these bonds could be the cause of litigation in Chancery. When Bishop Langley was chancellor, he received a petition from the executors of Robert Drax, who had been vicar of Rydon, Suffolk. This clerk had made a bond in £40 to a layman; its condition, which had been expressed only by word of mouth, was that Drax should resign his church for the benefit of the layman's cousin. This he had done, but the layman retained the bond and was demanding payment.[1] An intending incumbent might also make a bond with the clerk resigning in his favour. Master John Toly said that he had sealed a bond in £10 to John Brown, rector of Thornham Magna, Suffolk; the verbal condition was that he should pay all the charges which Brown would incur when resigning a 'poure vikeriage' for Toly's benefit. This condition had been fulfilled, Toly alleged, and he had received the vicarage, but Brown was retaining the bond.[2] Richard Tame claimed that he exchanged bonds in 100 marks with John Newers, rector of Didcot, in 1433. Newers then failed to keep to his undertaking to resign the church. As this condition had not been recorded on the bond, and as Newers had recently died, Tame had no remedy at common law.[3] In contrast, no bonds were made when, according to John Hynde, Walter Staple promised to resign the rectory of Monks Eleigh, Suffolk, 'to thentent' that Hynde should have it. The latter then 'laboured' with the ordinary and the patron and won their agreement, but then Staple 'trustyng in his conceyt that the seid suppliant shculde not thus have don, refuseth all utterly to resigne', nor would he refund Hynde his costs.[4]

As with exchanges, some clergy appear to have made arrangements for the disposal of their livings as if these were their private property. An agreement to resign a benefice so that a particular clerk should succeed to it was not a lawful contract. The right to nominate a future incumbent did not belong to the incumbent for the time being, but to the patron of the living. The parties to these

---

[1] C. 1/4/90 (1417–24).   [2] C. 1/74/20 (in English, chancellor unknown).

[3] C. 1/11/296 (addressed to the bishop of Bath, with references to the eleventh year of the then king and to Robert Wakefed as a bedel of Oxford). The latter is noticed as holding office in 1430 in Emden, *Oxford Graduates*, iii. 1955.

[4] C. 1/75/46 (chancellor unknown).

transactions always recognized that the patron's consent to a change was required, but they generally, and usually rightly, presumed that this would be given. The explanation why patrons were prepared to connive at these dealings may lie in the references by plaintiffs to their great costs in obtaining the consent of patrons. Many patrons did regard their advowsons as economic assets, to be exploited for the direct benefit of clerical kinsmen or dependents or for their own immediate gain by sale of nominations to vacancies.[1] There are some petitions to Chancery which show how some patrons sold their patronage. John Mey alleged that Thomas Lyghes, esquire, promised him a church worth twenty marks a year if he paid forty shillings.[2] John Beintbowe said that he was to have a vicarage resigned in his favour. The patrons, the prior and convent of Tickford, were 'welwylled and disposid godly'. When Beintbowe went to collect his letter of presentation from the prior, however, the latter refused to deliver the letter until Beintbowe gave him forty shillings. Beintbowe righteously asserted that he declined to make this payment, 'which to do is opyn symoney'. In his examination in Chancery, the prior denied the charge of simony but said that it was usual for the convent's presentees to give it twenty shillings 'by waye of almys', which Beintbowe had refused to do; he said, moreover, that his real reason for rejecting Beintbowe was that he would not exhibit the previous vicar's letter of resignation.[3]

Apart from the question of the patrons' co-operation, there remains the problem of why incumbents were willing to resign their benefices to other clerks. They were giving up sources of income and it is inconceivable that they did this without expecting some return. Its nature is disclosed in the petition of Richard Tame, who said that he agreed to pay Newers a pension of £12; if the bishop agreed, this would be charged on Didcot rectory, otherwise Tame would arrange for the annuity to be paid by a religious house.[4] Lawrence Aynderby obtained the rectory of Mablethorpe,

---

[1] Heath, op. cit., pp. 32, 38–9.

[2] C. 1/69/283 (in French, chancellor unknown).

[3] C. 1/43/169, 170 (addressed to the bishop of Bath and Wells). As the prior's name was William, the date must be 1468–73 (cf. *VCH Buckinghamshire*, i. 364–5).

[4] C. 1/11/296. For another abortive arrangement to pay a pension, with the ordinary's consent, see C. 1/16/220.

Lincolnshire, from Thomas Keleby upon undertaking to pay him an annuity of ten marks. Aynderby had then farmed the church to a layman who failed to pay the pension, and in consequence his bond to do this had been forfeited and Keleby was suing for its execution.[1] The assignment of pensions to clergy retiring from their livings was not a forbidden practice. Bishops sometimes arranged for pensions to be paid to an incumbent compelled to retire by age and infirmity. These arrangements for pensions reported in Chancery, however, were made privately and before the bishop knew of an impending resignation. They were also guaranteed by bonds, which suggests that a bishop would not be required to provide machinery to enforce payment. It is not certain that the parties to contracts for a resignation would necessarily seek the bishop's consent to a pension; such consent is not mentioned in every bill concerning resignations and Tame's bill shows that provision had been made for an alternative arrangement if the bishop's agreement was not obtained. The practice of retiring on pension by arrangement with the successor in a benefice did become increasingly common towards the end of the fifteenth century, and bishops began to issue licences to authorize the making of such arrangements in order to indemnify those concerned from charges of simony.[2] There was more than one explanation for a retiring incumbent seeking to secure a pension by private negotiation. Had he been an old or sick man, he may well have preferred to obtain the most generous provision available rather than rely on the bishop's assessment. On the other hand, these retiring parsons might not have been eligible for pensions in their bishops' estimation. John Newport, for instance, complained in Chancery that he had obtained Hockcliffe hospital, Buckinghamshire, by promising a pension to his predecessor. He did not then know that this predecessor had been deprived for misgovernment.[3] Alternatively, the retiring incumbent may have been a pluralist

---

[1] Aynderby was instituted in 1456 (Lincoln Registers, no. 20, f. 124ᵛ). He said that after 'the feld of Wakefeld' Thomas FitzWilliam compelled him to give him the farm for five years, by indenture. The bill (C. 1/27/180, addressed to the bishop of Exeter) therefore belongs to 1461–5.

[2] Heath, op. cit., pp. 183–4; K. Major, 'Resignation Deeds of the Diocese of Lincoln', *BIHR*, xix (1942–3), 63.

[3] C. 1/16/328 (addressed to the archbishop of Canterbury). A similar case is cited in Heath, op. cit., 37.

like John Brown, who kept his rectory while resigning a 'poure vikeriage' to John Toly, for what price the latter did not state in his bill.[1]

The number of cases of collusive resignations recorded in proceedings in Chancery is undoubtedly small, an average of only one in each decade of the period 1400–80. These were, however, cases of arrangements which had fallen through, where one party felt that he had a case for applying to Chancery for remedy. It cannot be certain that every aggrieved party in so delicate a matter saw fit to ventilate his grief in Chancery. It may be presumed that many more arrangements of this nature were completed to the satisfaction of both the parties concerned. Other categories of evidence confirm the prevalence of collusive resignations. In 1441, for instance, Thomas Hanwell petitioned the king 'to considir howe that your said oratour ys disposid to leve his chirch to thentent that Maister Robert Tatman, doctour of divinite, may have it and suceed hym in the same'. The king granted this request to present the petitioner's nominee to the church of Scrayingham, Yorkshire.[2] There are other examples of petitions like this among Privy Seal Office records when the king, as patron, issued letters of presentation subsequent to collusive resignations.[3] It occasionally appears in a bishop's register, moreover, that clerks seeking institution brought with them not only letters of presentation but also instruments recording the resignations of their predecessors.[4]

Critics of the clergy therefore had some justification for their allegations of simoniacal practices. Edmund Dudley had ample substance for making his charge against 'suche as will adventure the danger of symonie to have promotion', for he had negotiated the sales of royal presentations to aspirants to cathedral dignities.[5] Dean Colet in his convocation sermon in 1510 denounced the pride and greed of clergy who ran, 'ye[a], almost out of brethe, from one benefice to another, from the lesse to the more, from the lower to the hygher'.

[1] C. 1/74/20.

[2] P.R.O., Exchequer, Treasury of Receipt, Council and Privy Seal (E. 28), file 66 (endorsed 14 Feb. 19 Henry VI); cf. *CPR, 1436–41*, p. 542.

[3] E. 28/32, 60, 62.

[4] e.g. *Register of Thomas Langley*, iii, no. 838; iv, nos. 1009, 1108–9, 1208.

[5] E. Dudley, *The Tree of Commonwealth*, ed. D. M. Brodie (Cambridge, 1948), p. 5; F. C. Dietz, *English Government Finance, 1485–1558*, 2nd edn. (London, 1964), p. 41.

He deplored also the 'so great pensions assigned of many benefyces resygned', and he attributed to the covetousness of worldly clerks the pursuit of tithes and other profits which was rousing the ill will of the laity. Colet called for a revision of the laws against simony which 'so crepeth nowe abrode'.[1] This convocation had been called to discuss the hostile attitude of the laity towards the clergy, and Colet was blaming the 'evil life' of the clergy themselves for this lay malevolence.[2] The records in Early Chancery Proceedings bearing upon clergy's negotiations about the disposal of benefices thus have some relevance to a consideration of the background to the Reformation in England, particularly to the formation of its anticlerical element. There is a further connection. In the statute of 1534 'for the submission of the clergy to the king's majesty', clergy were forbidden to make judicial appeals to the pope. Instead, their applications for remedy were to be made to Chancery.[3] It may be said that for 150 years prior to this date clergy had themselves been making precedents for this manner of bringing their legal causes into the king's jurisdiction.

APPENDIX

Petition of Thomas Rithe (1440)

Unto right reverent Fader in god right worshipfull
and right gracious lord Chauncellor of Inglond.

Besechith full mekely youre simple pore servant and chapelein Thomas Rithe chauntrye preste in the chirche of Seint Paule in London, where that oon sir Henri Newton parson of the chirche of Adwell in the Countee of Oxenford in the diocese of Lincolln came to ȝoure seid besecher asking hym if that he wold permute his seid Chauntrye with the seid parsonage of Adwell, where upon youre seid besecher askid the forseid Parson of what value his seid chirche was yerely. To the whiche the seid Parson answered saying that he

---

[1] J. H. Lupton, *Life of John Colet* (London, 1909), pp. 295–6, 300.
[2] A. G. Dickens, *The English Reformation* (London, 1964), p. 90.
[3] *Statutes of the Realm*, iii. 461.

wold warrante the seid parsonage to be worth yerely xxiiij marcs
and that he wold make good and fynde good proves there of. And
there upon the seid parson brought with hym other iiij diverses
parsons and prestes whiche seyden and witnessid that the seid
chirche shold be worth yerely xxiiij marcs. Whereupon the seid
parties were bounden everich of hem to other in xl li. be two diverses
obligacions upon certein condicions indentid betuene hem, that
everich partie shold bringe yn to other his presentacion be the daye of
the Apostles Simon and Jude[1] next comyng. Now it is soo that ȝour
seid besecher hath pl[ain] k[no]wleche[2] that the seid parsonage is not
worth yerely c s. unto grete deceite of your seid besecher. Please it
unto your most reverent Faderhod and gracious lordship tenderly
to consider how that ȝoure seid besecher had proposid to have ȝoon
to scole with that the seid benifice had ben of that value whiche is
now provid the contrarie, and ȝoure seid besecher there of gretely
deceyvid, and there upon in as moche as youre seid besecher is with
oute remedie atte commone lawe graciousely to graunte a writte
sub pena for the seid parson, hym charging to appere before the king
in his chauncerye atte a certain day limitid and he there to be
examyned of this matier, and there upon to ordeigne a remedie, for
Goddes love and in wey of charite.

Memorandum[3] quod quintodecimo die Octobris anno regni nostri
decimo nono[4] Petrus Stucle clericus et Willelmus Rous coram dicto
domino rege in cancellaria sua personaliter constituti manuceperunt,
videlicet uterque eorum, pro prefato Thoma quod in casu quo ipse
materiam in hac supplicacione specificatam veram probare non
poterit, tunc prefato Henrico omnia dampna et expensas que ipse ea
occasione sustinebit satisfaciet juxta formam statuti inde editi et
provisi etc.

Source: Early Chancery Proceedings (C. 1), bundle 75, no. 3.
Description: Parchment, 15·5″ (39·6 cm.)×4″ (10·2 cm.).

R. L. STOREY

[1] 28 Oct.
[2] MS. torn.
[3] Added in a Chancery hand.
[4] 15 Oct. 19 (Henry VI, i.e. 1440). See also p. 246, n. 1, above.

XII

The Privy Seal Clerks in the Early Fifteenth Century

IT is not difficult to find material about the clerks who worked in the major royal offices in later medieval England. Their names are likely to appear occasionally in one connection or another on the Chancery rolls, in receipt of money in the Exchequer or clothes in the Great Wardrobe, or in some other record source; and in many cases a brief outline biography can be compiled from these references. It is normally difficult, however, to add flesh to these bones and see these men as personalities, and this is why this narrow subject is particularly worth discussing. By fortunate chance a good deal more information survives about three clerks who worked together in the Privy Seal Office in the early fifteenth century. Thomas Hoccleve, a man who never rose above an established clerkship in the Office, has left some 13,000 lines of verse containing an unusual amount of autobiographical material,[1] as well as the best Office formulary to have survived (B.M. Add. MS. 24,062). Robert Frye began at the bottom of the ladder like Hoccleve, but was promoted to the important and lucrative post of clerk of the Council, and later became the secondary, or second in command of the Privy Seal. Frye also has left a formulary (Edinburgh University Library MS. 183, formerly Laing 351a), and, more important, thirty of his private letters have survived in the Office files in the Public Record Office.[2] John Prophete was an Oxford

---

[1] There is a comprehensive bibliography of writing on Hoccleve in Jerome Mitchell, *Thomas Hoccleve* (Urbana, Ill., 1968). The verses have been edited in the Early English Text Society, Extra Series: *The Minor Poems*, ed. F. J. Furnivall and I. Gollancz (vols. lxi and lxxiii, 1892 and 1925) and *The Regement of Princes*, ed. F. J. Furnivall (vol. lxxii, 1897). Two manuscripts of *The Regement* contain an illumination of Hoccleve presenting the book to Prince Henry.

[2] Twenty-six letters are in a group in P.R.O., Exchequer, Treasury of Receipt, Council and Privy Seal (E. 28), file 29, three more scattered in the same file, and another (a petition to Frye) is in file 23.

graduate, a Privy Seal clerk in the early 1390s, secondary in the Office, the first clerk of the Council, and between 1406 and 1415 keeper and head of the Office. He was an important man, socially and politically superior to Hoccleve and Frye, with every expectation of a bishopric, and unfortunate not to receive one. There are many references to Prophete and a volume of letters in the British Museum (Harleian MS. 431) contains some of his correspondence.[1] Each of these men could be the subject of a paper, but what I intend to do here is to discuss the lives of the Privy Seal clerks in general terms, and then use the careers of Hoccleve, Frye, and Prophete to draw attention to some facets of clerks' lives which are never mentioned in the records.

The Privy Seal Office in the fourteenth century is well known from Tout's work,[2] and it did not change much in the early fifteenth, though it can be better documented then. It was primarily a writing-office where decisions by the king, the Council, and royal officials were translated into formal royal letters and authenticated with the privy seal. It was a 'clearing-house', sending out formal warrants to Chancery, Exchequer, and other offices, sending 'missive' letters to royal officials in England, Wales, Ireland, Gascony, and Calais, to individuals, towns, cathedral chapters, universities, and all manner of people, and sending diplomatic letters to foreign rulers. Hoccleve's formulary, containing almost 900 forms of letters arranged in sections, is the best guide to the range of business it transacted. Thousands of letters must have gone out in most years, letters that were not so formal that they required the authentication of the great seal, and yet were too important to go out under the signet. Little independent administrative work was done there, and the strength and purpose of the Office was to write clear, acceptable, polished letters in the king's name. The traditional establishment under the keeper was four clerks,[3] but in the fourteenth century there were often more, and in the early fifteenth century the staff was certainly larger. Tout listed 54 Privy Seal clerks known between

---

[1] I deliberately refrain from describing this as John Prophete's 'Letter-Book', because this title, though often used, is quite misleading. See below, p. 278, n. 2.

[2] T. F. Tout, *Chapters in the Administrative History of Medieval England* (Manchester, 1920–33), v.

[3] Ibid., v. 77.

1307 and 1399,[1] and 26 men are mentioned in connection with the Office between 1399 and 1425, the majority described at least once as 'clericus in officio privati sigilli'.[2] The number known in any one year, however, varies from six in 1400 to twelve in 1422. Part of the explanation is the chance survival of sources, and part probably a genuine fluctuation in the number of clerks employed. In 1422, for example, the Office had been divided into two sections for five years, one in France, the other in England, and the staff had no doubt expanded. Later in the century a distinction was drawn between clerks and under-clerks. In 1444, for example, five clerks and seven under-clerks in addition to the secondary received an allowance of clothes,[3] and though the word *subclericus* first appears, as far as I know, in this connection in 1421, some distinction like this probably existed in practice earlier. The evidence is far from clear and consistent, but it looks as though there were normally five or six senior established men, and as many or more young clerks. Frye is described as Prophete's clerk in 1394; Welde as Hoccleve's clerk between 1414 and 1417; Frank as Frye's clerk in 1423; and there are several more cases like these. It seems that the normal method of entry was to begin work under an established clerk, become accepted and entitled to an annual allowance of clothes, and progress to an established clerkship with a privileged position in the Office, say as regards fees, and the expectation of rewards from the king. In 1483 Richard III ordered the keeper to dismiss a clerk who had obtained the post by bribery and other means, 'contrary to the old

---

[1] Tout, *Chapters*, v. 110–12.

[2] The 26 men with the dates they are known to have served in the Office—which are probably almost all too conservative—are William Alberton (*c.* 1406–*post* 1447), William Alton (1422), John Auncel (1420), John Bagot (1423), John Baillay (*c.* 1390–?*c.* 1420), Henry Benet (*ante* 1422–*post* 1459), Thomas Burdet (*ante* 1401), John Claydon (*c.* 1415–*post* 1437), William Donne (*c.* 1388–*post* 1400), Thomas Felde (1406–*post* 1414), William Flete (*ante* 1398–?*post* 1422), Thomas Frank (*c.* 1418–*c.* 1454), Robert Frye (*c.* 1387–*post* 1425), Abel Hessil (*ante* 1401–*post* 1427), John Hethe (*ante* 1398–?*post* 1422), Thomas Hoccleve (?*c.* 1388–*c.* 1424), John Holme (1401), John Offorde (*c.* 1408–*c.* 1422), Richard Prior (*c.* 1404–*post* 1446), Robert Rolleston (1401), John Stone (1414), John Welde (*ante* 1408–*c.* 1418), William Weluaston (*ante* 1408–*post* 1409), John Wendelyngburgh (*ante* 1374–*post* 1399), and two men, Arondel and Prentys, known only from a reference in Hoccleve's *Minor Poems* (p. 35), to them as 'me countrefete' who liked to lie in bed.

[3] H. C. Maxwell-Lyte, *Historical Notes on the Use of the Great Seal of England* (H.M.S.O., 1926), pp. 33–4.

rule and due order in admitting of clerkes' and 'in grete discoraging of the underclerkes whiche have long contynued therin to have thexperince of the same' and 'have spended the flour of their ages in the same',[1] and no doubt this was the rule in the early part of the century. There is, however, normally little evidence about the early years of a clerk's career. Hoccleve, for example, is described as a king's clerk in 1392 when he acted as a mainpernor in a suit involving a Privy Seal clerk; he received several rewards later in the nineties; but he is described as a Privy Seal clerk only in 1399 when he was given an annuity for his good service there 'a longo tempore'. In *The Regement of Princes*, however, written about 1411–12, he says that next Easter he will have been twenty-four years in the Office.[2] Frye's early career is almost equally obscure. In 1399 he received an annuity for twelve years service in the signet and Privy Seal Offices, and in 1394 is described as clerk to John Prophete, then secondary in the Privy Seal and clerk of the Council.[3] Perhaps as a promising junior clerk in the signet he had been taken into the Privy Seal by Prophete. It is likely that the favour of the keeper and a senior clerk was the key to what was after all a comfortable but not a major post.

Most clerks were men of humble and obscure backgrounds. All we can say of Hoccleve is that his name suggests that he came from Hoccleve in Bedfordshire; Frye came from Wilton or Salisbury, and his letters suggest that his family were of very modest means. Neither was a university man, and Prophete with his 'good connections in Herefordshire and the adjacent Welsh March',[4] his Oxford M.A., and his experience as an administrator in the service of the archbishop of Canterbury, was a quite exceptional clerk whose clerkship in the Privy Seal was only incidental to his work as clerk of the Council. The Hoccleves and the Fryes were not, however, uneducated men. They must have come to the Office literate and with a grounding of secretarial skill, perhaps obtained in a 'business' college, and then learned the ways of the Privy Seal. English was, no doubt, their native language. Hoccleve's poems

---

[1] B.M. Harleian MS. 433, f. 123ᵛ.

[2] *CCR, 1389–92*, p. 564; *CPR, 1399–1401*, p. 61; *The Regement*, p. 30.

[3] *CPR, 1396–9*, p. 463; P.R.O., Exchequer of Receipt, Issue Roll (E. 403), no. 546 (20 Jan. 1394).   [4] Tout, *Chapters*, v. 97.

are in English and so too are some of the Frye letters, though contrary to what one might have expected, French is the commonest language among the Frye correspondence, even in the letters to and from his family in Wiltshire. In the Office it was French and to a much lesser extent Latin they used most in their day-to-day work and because many formal grants and letters were first drafted there, the clerks had to be able to compose and translate from one language to another. English became the common language for signet letters in the second decade of the century, and an increasing proportion of the petitions that came into the Privy Seal were in English, but in Hoccleve's formulary written in the early twenties not one of the letters is in English. It was only in the thirties that many privy seals came to be written in English, and by the forties it was common. Letter-writing itself was a professional skill. Both Hoccleve and Frye included in their formularies collections of proverbs, phrases, exordies, even forms of wills, as well as old diplomatic letters considered to be good examples of composition, and forms of the letters they wrote day by day. Diplomatic letters going out of the Office sometimes conformed to the rules of the *Cursus Curiae Romanae*, and Frye may have owned a copy of the popular dictamenal collection, the *Epistolarum* of Petrus de Vineis.[1] All the clerks to a lesser or greater extent must have had the same skills.

---

[1] The evidence is Edinburgh University Library MSS. 182–3, formerly Laing 351 and 351a, which were once bound up together. The former consists of some fragments of the *Epistolarum*, some pages of a year-book of Edward III's reign, and a page of proverbs in Frye's handwriting; the latter is a signet/privy seal formulary owned and in part written by Frye. This is the manuscript from which Professor E. Perroy printed many documents in his *Diplomatic Correspondence of Richard II* (Camden Society, 3rd ser. xlviii, 1933). The formulary consists of two parts. The first (ff. 81–120) is a signet formulary written after mid 1389, the date of the latest document in it. The second (ff. 27–80 and 121–54) is a privy seal formulary apparently begun in the 1390s and added to in the early fifteenth century. Frye wrote the additions and he may well have written all the privy seal formulary. The evidence is first the handwriting, and Frye's hand in the early fifteenth century is distinctive and well known, and second, the large ornamental 'F' which appears on ff. 39, 42, and 141 of the manuscript. The same 'F' is on two Frye letters in E. 28/29 (see reference below, p. 275, n. 3). Frye certainly owned the manuscript; he added some of the documents and many of the rubrics; and he may have written the entire privy seal section. He was originally a signet clerk and he may well have brought the signet formulary to the Privy Seal with him and added to it. His connection with Laing 351 and the *Epistolarum* is obviously more problematical, but not unlikely. Petrus de Vineis was a popular author in England and it was his service with Archbishop Pecham which no doubt explains why selections from Pecham's register formed the bulk of the Latin section

Both Hoccleve and Frye served for almost forty years, and, as the list of clerks shows, a working life of twenty, thirty, or forty years was common for established Privy Seal clerks. Normally it was a settled life in London and Westminster, working perhaps in a corner of Westminster Hall or in some of the rooms in the Palace.[1] Occasionally the seal and some at least of the clerks were obliged to accompany the king on a campaign in England or to a council or parliament outside London. There was no rule about this, administrative convenience determined when the seal should travel or remain at Westminster on any particular occasion; sometimes they journeyed to Windsor or Berkhampstead or another of the royal castles or manors near London where the king often lived; and between 1417 and 1422 some of the clerks went with a section of the Office to France. But most of the time the Privy Seal and its clerks were part of the administrative complex of Council and departments at Westminster. Every day several hundred clerks, officers, and councillors walked or rode or went by boat from London to their work at Westminster. The Privy Seal clerks were not paid salaries and most of them probably lived in the hostel provided by the keeper from his allowance of one pound a day. As late as 1409 the Exchequer was maintaining the fiction that this was paid only until arrangements were made for the keeper and the clerks to live in the king's household, but the separation had taken place long before. The hostel was normally a bishop's house hired for the purpose and the favourite area was outside Temple Bar. The bishop of Bath's house there was the hostel in 1382;[2] so too was Chester's Inn, the bishop of Chester's house, where Hoccleve lived when he wrote *The Regement of Princes* about 1411–12; it was to the bishop of Chester that a correspondent in Harleian MS. 431, perhaps Prophete, wrote to complain that the dividing wall between his *hospicium* and the bishop's was broken down;[3] and the bishop of Exeter's house, which the king asked the bishop to hire to the

---

of another early fifteenth-century collection of letters, All Souls MS. 182 (see *Anglo-Norman Letters and Petitions*, ed. M. D. Legge (Anglo-Norman Text Society, iii, 1941)).

[1] Tout, *Chapters*, v. 74, cites references to a table with a green cloth, benches, chests, and even a calculating table bought for the Office in the fourteenth century, and I can add nothing to this.

[2] Ibid., v. 71.   [3] B.M., Harleian MS. 431, f. 23.

keeper in 1417, excusing him accordingly from parliament, was in the same area.[1]

Only occasional references to the hostel survive to give an impression of what it was like. Four Middlesex villages, Great Stanmore, Little Stanmore, Edgware, and Kingsbury were assigned to the keeper to buy provisions for it;[2] coal was bought regularly from a collier in Croydon;[3] and Henry Ware bought sixty beasts for his hostel 'a Londres et y entour' at one point during his keepership between 1416 and 1418.[4] Henry IV ate there in 1400,[5] and the impression one gets is of a fairly large establishment. In addition to the keeper, the secondary, sometimes at least the clerk of the Council, and most of the clerks and sub-clerks, there would probably be servants from the Office, and the personal servants of the keeper. Some indication of the state a keeper might keep is given by the bequests in John Prophete's will. He died, not a bishop but dean of York, ten months after resigning the keepership, and his will mentions John Cheser, the steward of his household, Thomas Wycton, his chamberlain, Walter Ayleston, who received forty marks for unspecified long and faithful service, two chaplains, Edmund, who received ten pounds, and Robert, who received a breviary, Thomas Marshall, a valet, who received ten marks, as well as unnamed servants, valets, grooms, pages, and chaplains— apparently a number of each—who were given smaller sums.[6] Clearly Prophete, and surely the other keepers also, maintained a large household, and it is not surprising that Hoccleve worried about the 'poor cot' he would live in when he retired.

A clerk who left the hostel would indeed be in a precarious

---

[1] E. 28/33. Another bishop, probably in the 1390s, excused himself from parliament because his hostel was occupied by the keeper (Harleian MS. 431, f. 23 $^{r-v}$).

[2] In E. 28/9 (28 Mar. 1400) there is a privy seal letter patent ordering royal officers not to purvey corn, cattle, hay, oats, straw, carts, or poultry, nor other things against the wishes of the inhabitants or the keeper, and in 1415 the new keeper, John Wakering was given the assignment as other keepers had it (*CPR, 1413–16*, p. 329).

[3] B.M. Add. MS. 24,062, f. 107^v. This is a patent of protection for the collier.

[4] Ibid., f. 111^v. This is another patent of protection.

[5] Maxwell-Lyte, p. 151. A petition is endorsed that the king granted it 'in domo custodis privati sigilli quando rex comedit cum eo'.

[6] The will is printed in *Testamenta Eboracensia* (Surtees Soc., 1864), iii. 53–5, from Archbishop Bowet's register and in a fuller version in *North Country Wills* (Surtees Soc., 1908), pp. 10–11, from Archbishop Arundel's Canterbury register.

position because clerks were not paid wages by the king. In the mid fourteenth century daily wages had been paid, but this practice gradually died out and finally ceased in August 1399.¹ It was replaced for a time by grants of annuities. In 1399, for example, Frye and Hoccleve received annuities of £10 a year until they were promoted to a benefice without cure of souls worth £20 a year, and a few other clerks received annuities in similar terms.² Hoccleve often complained about the non-payment of his annuity, without much justification in fact, but he was fortunate because after Henry IV's reign few new annuities were granted, and the younger clerks had presumably to rely for an income on fees and favours and miscellaneous grants. The king might give a small cash payment for some special service, for going abroad or for particularly burdensome extra work. In 1401, for example, Hoccleve asked for and obtained a reward with seven other s[ervitors] in the Privy Seal because of the great amount of work they had done since the beginning of the reign.³ It was more common, however, for a clerk to petition for one of the desirable things such as a new-creation pension,⁴ a corrody, some forfeited goods, a benefice, or a secular office which came into the king's hands from time to time. The king was besieged by petitions for things like these, particularly from his own clerks, and he clearly tried to strike a balance. Hoccleve, for example, received a corrody in Hayling priory in 1394 and he shared a £40 forfeit with Frye and the other clerks in 1398, but after the grant of his annuity in 1399, increased in 1409, he is not known to have received anything further of this kind until 1424,

¹ Tout, *Chapters*, v. 84–92. Tout (p. 86) antedates the last payment of Wardrobe wages to Privy Seal clerks for on 12 June 1400 the treasurer and barons of the Exchequer were ordered to allow in the accounts of John Carp, Richard II's keeper of the Wardrobe, the 7½d. a day wages paid to John Wendelyngburgh from 1 Oct. 1395 to 31 Aug. 1399 and to Thomas Feriby from 18 Jan. 1398 to 24 Aug. 1399 as Privy Seal clerks (P.R.O., Exchequer K.R., Memoranda Roll (E. 159), no. 176, Brevia Directa Baronibus, Trinity, rot. 10).

² *CPR, 1396–9*, p. 463; *1399–1401*, p. 61. The annuities granted about this time were: 1396, Donne (£10), 1399, Frye (£10), Flete (£10), Hoccleve (£10), and Hethe (20 marks); 1402, Baillay (£10); 1409, Hoccleve (increased to 20 marks); and 1412, Offorde (20 marks). All save Donne, who died about 1414, had their annuities confirmed by Henry V.

³ E. 28/9 (23 July 1401). They were given £40 to be divided according to length of service, work done, and the income each already received.

⁴ For an example, see R. L. Storey, pp. 236–7, n. 1, above.

just before he retired, when he received a corrody in Southwick priory, near Southampton.[1] The same is true of the other clerks; they could expect grants, but not a continuous stream of grants. Some seem to have chosen to ask for grants of varying kinds; others preferred to concentrate on one type. John Baillay chose ecclesiastical preferment. Richard Prior in the twenties and thirties chose various minor offices such as stewardships and woodwardships in Wales; presumably he, like Hoccleve, was married, and thus not eligible to receive benefices. Whatever grants a clerk received, it is clear that they were primarily sources of income. Ecclesiastical or secular offices were intended to be performed by deputy; a corrody in most cases meant not free bed and board, but a patent under the conventual seal granting the clerk cash in lieu of maintenance or granting a specified maintenance, which could then be sold. Hoccleve's corrody in Southwick in 1424 may have meant a place of retirement, though I doubt it. More likely it was a source of profit like the Hayling corrody he received thirty years earlier. The latter is a revealing case; it was one of seven corrodies in various parts of the country left vacant by the death of William Gambon, an ex-official of the king's chamber, who had been given them twenty to twenty-five years before. Within a few days in January 1392, presumably on hearing of his death, four yeomen of the chamber, a serjeant of the Wardrobe, and three Privy Seal clerks asked for and obtained his corrodies.[2] William Flete apparently bought a corrody in 1404 for himself and his father and mother;[3] John Hethe bought an annuity for himself in 1408;[4] and transactions like this were probably common. There is nothing surprising in this impression

[1] CCR, *1392–6*, p. 249; CPR, *1396–9*, p. 408; CCR, *1422–9*, p. 151. In 1400 he gave up, which probably means he sold, his Hayling corrody to his colleague Hethe and another (CCR, *1399–1402*, pp. 126–7). One cannot be sure that we know all the grants a clerk received because minor grants of things like corrodies were not always enrolled, presumably because the recipient did not consider it worthwhile to pay to have this done.

[2] CCR, *1392–6*, pp. 248–9.

[3] CCR, *1402–5*, p. 293.

[4] Hethe had received a 20 marks annuity in 1399. In 1405 he surrendered this for a payment of £100; in 1408 he bought a 20 marks annuity from Thomas de Lancastre and the king confirmed the arrangement in 1409. Henry V confirmed this in 1413 but in 1415 Hethe surrendered this patent also for a cash payment of £50. Presumably he was desperate for ready cash (CPR, *1399–1401*, p. 180; *1405–8*, pp. 166–7; CCR, *1405–9*, p. 472; CPR, *1408–13*, p. 61; *1413–16*, p. 70; CCR, *1413–19*, p. 231).

of reward-seeking clerks; these men were not clerics who happened to be helping the king to govern the country; they were professional 'civil servants' who according to contemporary convention were mostly in minor orders, but were paid no wages and looked to the king for gifts and favours.

They had two further perquisites. They had an annual allowance of four ells of coloured cloth for robes each Christmas, and on special occasions such as the coronation of Queen Catherine in 1421 they might receive a special additional allowance.[1] The secondary received a double allowance of cloth and a piece of squirrel fur as well. They also could expect an income from fees and favours, but this is an obscure subject. The Privy Seal did not account to the king for fees, and though there is a good deal of sixteenth- and seventeenth-century evidence, there is little from the Middle Ages. Fees were certainly paid. Hoccleve complains that the clerks were often cheated of their fees; private accounts occasionally record sums paid in the Privy Seal; and it is difficult to believe that any private person who required a privy seal escaped without paying some fee in cash or kind. Probably routine warrants cost only a few shillings, but more important documents could bring in a few pounds.[2] On one occasion, in 1423, Hoccleve was paid two marks for writing a petition to the Council on behalf of the earl marshal and for the writing and sealing of the subsequent warrant to the treasurer and barons of the Exchequer.[3] And Frye's letters show that an experienced clerk at Westminster was much in demand to help suitors, who assuredly paid him in some way for it.

The general character of a Privy Seal clerk's life is, therefore, clear

[1] Tout, *Chapters*, v. 88–9, suggests that the clerks received a summer as well as a winter allowance of cloth, but this is certainly not true in this period.

[2] Maxwell-Lyte, pp. 34–5, 340–2, and 349, cites most of the evidence. In two cases in 1440 the clerk of the Council received over £7 and £8 respectively, and the Privy Seal clerks 46s. 8d. and 33s. 4d. respectively. In 1430 the York Merchant Adventurers spent more than £90 on an important charter including 20s. to the clerk of the Council House but only 6s. 8d. in the Privy Seal (*The York Mercers and Merchant Adventurers* (Surtees Soc., 1918), pp. 33–4). The statute 27 Hen. VIII, c. 11, lays down the fees payable in 1536.

[3] J. L. Kirby, 'An account of Robert Southwell, receiver-general of John Mowbray, Earl Marshal, 1422–3', *BIHR*, xxvii (1954), 196. This account records payments to other officials including 6s. 8d. to an usher of the Council House for his favour in letting Southwell into the Council House at an opportune moment to prosecute his case.

enough. Normally he came into the office as a young man, in time became an established clerk, and spent most of his working life at Westminster, living in a hostel in London, and enjoying a modest competence from fees and rewards of one kind or another. The records, however, tell almost nothing about, say, the interests, the conversation, of these men. This is where the stories of Hoccleve, Frye, and Prophete are particularly helpful.

Hoccleve is already well known. Tout, for example, quoted his poems a good deal, and there is no need to go over all his story. He was the author of some 13,000 lines of verse, wide-ranging, but fairly conventional in character. He was by no means a great poet, but he was well-read in European literature, well-known in court and magnate circles, and of some significance in the history of English literature. A remarkable feature of his poems, and the important thing in this context, is that they contain a quite unusual amount of autobiographical material. Hoccleve's own story is that he came into the Privy Seal as a young man in his late teens about 1387–8 and for a time enjoyed a fast life, spending his money freely, drinking in the Paul's Head tavern, chatting up the girls there, and so on. Always he was hoping for a benefice which would give him financial security; none came, and by 1410 he had married and become a chronic worrier; about 1415 he had a mental breakdown, recovered, and went back to work; and apparently spent the rest of his life there before his retirement about 1426 and his death in the spring of that year,[1] introspective, morbid, and anxious about the

---

[1] Contrary to all that has been written about this, the date of his death can be determined quite accurately, but the date of his retirement is problematical. It has been assumed that he had retired by Feb. 1423, because he was paid his annuity as 'nuper uni clericorum in officio privati sigilli domini Henrici nuper regis Anglie', but this means only 'late one of the clerks of Henry *IV*'. The word *nuper* is used in the same sense of several other clerks, and Hoccleve is described and describes himself as a Privy Seal clerk in 1424. He was buying parchment for the Office until 5 Dec. 1424, but the payment for this dated 4 Mar. 1426 described him as 'late one of the clerks in the office' (Issue Roll, no. 673). This is as close as I can define his retirement. He died soon after this last payment on 4 Mar. 1426 because on 8 May 1426 his corrody in Southwick Priory was granted to Alice Penforde to be held 'en manere et fourme come Thomas Ocle ja trespasse' (P.R.O., Chancery Warrants (C. 81), file 685, no. 1574). The grant, like many others, was not enrolled. 'Ocle' is an unusual spelling but it undoubtedly refers to Hoccleve and solves a question that has puzzled all who have written about Hoccleve.

future. Obviously Hoccleve was an unusual man, a competent writing-clerk, gifted, but to some extent unbalanced, and it is difficult to know how much of his story to believe. He was garrulous. In his formulary he corrects a mistake with the long explanation 'Heer made y leep yeer—ex negligencia etc; Witnesse on petebat etc. in the next syde folowynge which sholde have stonden on this syde. But how so it stonde, it is a membre of the matere precedent' (f. 194ᵛ); and earlier there is the surprising note 'Item, to bie me more beddyng for shame' (f. 35ᵛ). He wrote, and presumably talked, too much, but what he wrote was apparently in essence true. His service in the Privy Seal, his annuity, the hostel, even to some extent his breakdown, can be substantiated from the records.[1] He exaggerated his woes, particularly his financial worries, though to be fair he admitted as much. His real worry was that when he ceased to work and lost his day-to-day fees, his annuity might not be paid regularly, and his income would be reduced to six marks, presumably from sources like corrodies. In spite of his pious, strictly orthodox, religious beliefs and his attacks on wealth, money loomed large in his life. He often writes about the non-payment of his annuity though in fact the records show that here he had comparatively little of which to complain.[2] Money, he thought, could cure all ills:

> By coyn, I gete may swich medecyne
> As may myn hurtes alle, þat me greeue,
> Exyle cleene & voide me of pyne.[3]

Hoccleve was quite untypical of the Privy Seal clerks, but he probably reflects the common complaints of the men at the bottom

---

[1] In his 'Complaint' (*Minor Poems*, p. 95), written about 1420–1, perhaps during Lent 1421, Hoccleve states that he regained his sanity on 1 Nov., five years previously. This may be one reason why he did not come to the Exchequer personally between May 1414 and Mar. 1417 to collect payments due to him.

[2] The facts, with a few omissions, were collected by Furnivall in his introduction to the *Minor Poems* (pp. li–lxix). Hoccleve was paid 47 of 52 instalments of his annuity, perhaps 49 because two sets of rolls are completely missing. On average he was paid fourteen weeks after term-day, but this was distinctly sooner than most annuity holders, even his fellow Privy Seal clerks. It is fair to add, however, that though Hoccleve often complained about money, the begging poems about his annuity may all relate to terms when he was not paid.

[3] Ibid., p. 39.

of the administrative ladder. No doubt they all complained that their daily drudgery, stooping over the parchment at Westminster with pricking eyes and aching backs, was not appreciated and was certainly ill-rewarded. Most were probably as money-conscious as Hoccleve, but worried less, and indulged more freely in the pleasures of London. The cooks at Westminster gate, the taverns with their company and bawdy talk, hiring a boat on the Thames instead of walking, and the other things that Hoccleve mentions agree with the description of London in another contemporary poem, *London Lickpenny*, once attributed to Lydgate.[1] This is the society in which the clerks lived. Hoccleve with his literary interest, his dining club, and his scruples, was probably more cultured but more thin-skinned than the average clerk.

Robert Frye must have known London as well as Hoccleve, but his correspondence never mentions anything so frivolous. Frye represents in an extreme form something that was probably part of the life of any clerk: he was a man of business. His career began about 1387 as a signet clerk, but by 1394 he was John Prophete's clerk in the Privy Seal. Prophete was a quite important official, clerk of the Council and secondary in the Privy Seal, and perhaps took young Frye into the Office. Prophete gave up his posts about the end of 1395 but Frye remained, and by 1397 at the latest he himself was writing for the Council, and he continued to do so until 1421. In 1401 he began to be paid for doing so, and in 1406 his ten years work was rewarded when he was formally made 'clerk of the Council'.[2] He had a £10 annuity, a salary of £20, increased to 40 marks a year in 1406, a more than average number of gifts from the king, and a position of importance where people must often have sought and paid for his favour. He was a particularly efficient clerk who improved the filing system in the Privy Seal and made a considerable contribution to the development of the Council records. His employment at the Council ended in June 1421, but at the latest by December 1420, he had been appointed secondary in the Privy Seal, a position of dignity with furred livery and a salary of ten

---

[1] *Historical Poems of the XIVth and XVth Centuries*, ed. R. H. Robbins (New York 1959), pp. 130–4.

[2] This paragraph is based on my essay *The Early History of the Clerkship of the Council* (Glasgow University Publications, 1969).

pounds a year, but no very clear duties.[1] His writing is still found
in the files, and he was given charge of the office during the temporary absence of the keeper, but he appears to have been less active
and he was not paid as secondary after Easter 1425. He may have
retired to Wiltshire where his annuity was paid at least until Easter
1434, and he was certainly dead by December 1435.[2]

Frye's career was clearly a success. He had an important post and
by contemporary standards he was prosperous, though he never
enjoyed the range of employment and the rewards, such as prebends
and deaneries, that many graduates received.[3] He no doubt lived
well in the London that Hoccleve described, but there is no hint of
this in his letters. What they reveal are the business interests of a
successful clerk. Frye was agent and adviser to a number of people.
He collected the annuities and watched over the interests of John
Spertegrave and John Fairhood, two merchants trading overseas.
His relatives and neighbours in Wiltshire used his good offices. His
mother asked him to obtain a small piece of escheated land and its
stock for her husband and herself. Frye prudently obtained it for
himself.[4] He was asked to help delay an assize, obtain a general
pardon for two Wilton men, use his influence to obtain timber and
cuttings, and so on. Other people too appealed to him. Cecily
Tickell, a prisoner in Newgate, appealed for his help to be bailed;
the provost of St. Sever in Gascony wrote to him about some business concerning Jean de Béarn with which he was already engaged;
and there are various references to discussions, and assistance Frye

[1] The post of secondary had 'crystallised into a definite office' from 'a vague and
accidental supremacy' of one of the four clerks during Richard II's reign (Tout,
Chapters, v. 103–5). In 1382 William Dighton held it; Prophete held it at least between
1394 and 1395; but there was apparently no successor appointed until 1406 when
two days after Prophete became keeper, his nephew, Thomas Felde, who had no
Privy Seal experience, was appointed. Felde held it until 1414 or 1415, when he
entered the service of the archbishop of Canterbury, but he probably contributed
little to the office and was paid only £20 for all his service. There is no record of
another secondary until Frye in 1420, and none between 1425 and 1430, when
another distinguished lawyer, William Lyndwode, was appointed.

[2] Thomas Frank, a Privy Seal clerk, petitioned in Dec. 1435 for the corrody in
Halesowen which Robert Frye, chaplain, had when he was alive (E. 28/56).

[3] The major grants he received were five new-creation pensions or corrodies,
forfeited land worth 10 marks, a quarter share in a £40 forfeit, the office of subdeacon
in the conventual church of Wilton, and (in 1419) the church of Loughborough.

[4] Her humble letter in English (E. 28/29) led to Frye's petition to the king
(C. 81/1397, no. 55) and eventually to a patent (*CPR, 1399–1401*, p. 535).

has given. The purely family letters are disappointing, because they are almost entirely about business. Frye is given news about his mother's health; he is reminded about the curtains he promised; he orders his mother to be given twenty shillings; but mostly he is writing about his pension and his corrody, and his relatives are explaining what they have done about his business or begging his help. It must be confessed that most of the letters are pretty dreary and give no warm impression of Frye. The one letter to his mother, for example, is a stiff little Latin *de statu* letter as if from a formulary. Perhaps it was only an exercise. The letters are, however, incidentally revealing. They show for example how commonplace letter-writing was, even among ordinary people. Letters addressed to Robert Frye 'a le pryve seal' came from Wiltshire, Calais, St. Sever, even from cousin William Frye on pilgrimage to Rome to say that he was well and on his way home. They also show one way in which the formal, bureaucratic methods of government were tempered for ordinary people. You could turn to one of the civil servants and ask his help, though I am sure you had to pay him for doing so. Frye was in an unusually influential position as clerk of the Council, but no doubt all the clerks were prepared to write documents, give advice, and act as agents at Westminster.

Two letters stand out for me. The first is short and I give it in full. It is addressed 'A mon trescher compaignoun Robert Frye' and goes on:

> Trescher et tresfiable compaignoun. Je vous salve tressovent, vous enmerciant de voz honurables lettres. Et vous pri que touz autres novels nient specefiez en voz ditz lettres, 'si ascuns soient', en especial touchant levesche de Bathe, et auxi que serra gardeyn de prive seel, vous plese moi eartefier 'escript' en une 'petite' bille par le portour de cestes. Escrit a Salesbury le xiv jour Daugst.
>
> Vostre J. O(?).[1]

This must belong to 1400 or 1401 and refer to the wrangle over the bishopric of Bath when Henry IV refused to accept the papal

---

[1] The second initial has been galled and is problematical. The form of address suggests that the writer was a clerk like Frye; perhaps it was John Offorde, a signet clerk from at least 1403 and a Privy Seal clerk from at least 1408. But this is only a guess.

provision made in May 1400 of Richard Clifford, the keeper of the privy seal, which was settled only by his 'translation' to Worcester in August 1401. According to custom Clifford then resigned the keepership. The letter is of no consequence but it seems to me to reflect the gossipy, promotion-conscious world of the civil servants of the period. The second letter is a draft in French from Frye to the mayor and burgesses of Wilton, probably in 1406, thanking them for choosing him as one of their members of parliament, and promising to do all that he could for the borough. He served as one of their members in at least three parliaments, 1406, 1407, and 1413,[1] and was chosen no doubt because his services would be less costly and more effective than those of a townsman. The surprising thing is that he was a member at all because he had been in minor orders in 1395 and his annuity was granted in the usual form 'until promoted to a benefice'. In 1419, however, when he was presented to the parish church of Loughborough, the warrant specified 'so that he be preste or atte leste infra sacros withyn this yere',[2] and this suggests that he had given up his orders for a time.

Frye is much less of a personality to us than Hoccleve. He was clearly a skilled clerk,[3] a business-like, efficient man-of-affairs, successful, influential, caught up in the world of government. We never hear of him in any other connection, and this is probably no accident.[4]

The other clerks no doubt envied Frye's success, but he in turn probably envied the success of his graduate contemporaries for there was a widening gulf between the two groups. In the fourteenth century, for example, a Privy Seal clerk occasionally, though rarely, was promoted to be keeper, but in the fifteenth keepers were men of some mark outside the Office. The keeper was a great officer

---

[1] *Return of Members of Parliament* (1878), vol. i. There are no Wilton returns for the last three parliaments of Henry IV and Frye may well have served more often.

[2] C. 81/1365, no. 12.

[3] An unusual example of this skill is Frye's imitation of the usage of the French Chancery by adding *extra sigillum* notes to three privy seal letters patent of Richard II delivered to Charles VI (Pierre Chaplais, *English Royal Documents, King John–Henry VI* (Oxford, 1971), pl. 19).

[4] Three further Frye letters are printed in *Anglo-Norman Letters and Petitions*, pp. 80–2, and 88–9. They are to a Canterbury official seeking his help to obtain the archbishop's influence to have G.A. appointed gaoler of Newgate.

of state, normally a university graduate with administrative or legal experience, looking forward to a bishopric. John Prophete was both a clerk and a keeper, but he is not really an exception for his clerkship was only nominal. He was a Herefordshire man with respectable though not distinguished family connections. His will, that of his nephew, Thomas Felde, and other references enable us to identify quite a number of his relatives.[1] He was a graduate in arts, in all probability of Oxford, and a notary. His public career apparently began in 1382 as registrar to the court of Canterbury, and he then became 'secretary' to Archbishop Courtenay. The archbishop had been bishop of Hereford, and this may have begun the connection.[2] Prophete was already receiving grants from the king, and about 1386–7 became a royal clerk, probably attached to the Household. When Richard II resumed government into his own hands in 1389, Prophete was given the task of writing the records of the Council;[3] he became a Privy Seal clerk, at the latest by 1392, and in 1394 secondary in the Office, but his main work was at the Council. He was given the new title 'clerk of the Council' about 1392 and brought about a tremendous change in its records, but for some unexplained reason he gave up all these offices towards the end of 1395 and little is known about him until the revolution in 1399 when a more important phase of his career began. He was at once appointed a salaried councillor and the records show that he was one of the most active attenders at the Council; he was an intimate of Henry IV and in 1402 he became his secretary; and in October 1406, when Nicholas Bubwith became bishop of London and resigned the keepership of the privy seal, Prophete succeeded him. He retained this office through the political upheavals of the

---

[1] For Prophete's will, see above, p. 266; Felde's will is printed in *The Register of Henry Chichele, Archbishop of Canterbury*, ed. E. F. Jacob (C.Y.S., 1937–47), ii. 163–4. There are biographies of both in A. B. Emden, *A Biographical Dictionary of the University of Oxford to A.D. 1500* (Oxford, 1957–9). He had some family connection with Sir John Oldcastle or his wife Joan, more probably with Oldcastle who was also a Herefordshire man.

[2] In 1372 Courtenay ordained a John Prophete acolyte at Tiverton, but this may not be our Prophete (*Registrum Willelmi de Courtenay*, ed. W. W. Capes (C.Y.S., xv, 1914), p. 26). Some examples of Prophete's work for Courtenay and a bequest to him in Courtenay's will are cited in Joseph Dahmus, *William Courtenay, Archbishop of Canterbury* (University Park, 1966).

[3] This section is based on my *Clerkship of the Council*.

second half of the reign and resigned only in June 1415. Ten months later he was dead.

One cannot say that Prophete was typical of the keepers of the period because there was no typical keeper, but all had some things in common. They were educated men, most are known to have been university graduates, and they had served as administrators, lawyers, ambassadors, or had some comparable experience before they came to the Privy Seal. None save Prophete had served in the Office, but this did not matter, because the keeper's job was not to supervise the letter-writing, but to decide matters of difficulty and to be an assiduous councillor, one of the inner circle of administrators with the chancellor and the treasurer. To use a possibly misleading modern analogy the keeper was a cabinet minister rather than a civil servant. He was in orders and normally well endowed with churches, prebends, and other dignities when he came to the office. Nicholas Bubwith, Prophete's predecessor, estimated the value of his benefices at not more than 1200 marks a year in 1408,[1] and Prophete held the deanery of Hereford from 1393 until 1403–4, the deanery of York from 1406 until his death, and an impressive list of other benefices, valued at about the same figure.[2] It was men like these, not the ordinary Office clerks, who were the great pluralists. For example, Prophete held sixteen dignities or prebends in cathedrals at one time or another during his career; his nephew, Dr. Thomas Felde, held six; but none of the ordinary clerks ever held a single benefice in a cathedral. Indeed few of the Office clerks received benefices at all.

It is difficult to know what sort of man Prophete was, because though there are many, many references to him, none is so personal as Hoccleve's poems or even Frye's letters. There is a conventional representation of him on his brass at Ringwood in Hampshire, and in 1393 he was elected dean of Hereford because 'tanquam satis eis notum virum, sancta vita ac moribus approbatum, in spiritualibus providum et in temporalibus circumspectum', though obviously one cannot give much weight to so common-form a statement as

---

[1] *CPL*, v. 595–6.
[2] Ibid., vi. 141–2. This is a dispensation to hold his miscellaneous preferments 'value altogether not exceeding 1300 marks'.

this.[1] His career suggests that he was an able administrator and an agreeable man, and it is particularly significant that though he was very close to Henry IV in the first half of his reign, he continued in office through the upheavals of the second half, and even retained the keepership for a further two years in Henry V's reign. This suggests that though he was party to most of the great governmental decisions for a couple of decades, he had made few enemies and was recognized as a good, impartial administrator. His own correspondence and letters about him are almost entirely concerned with what to us is the least edifying aspect of an important clerk's life, his ecclesiastical career.[2] Prophete had a salary as a councillor, the normal expenses as keeper, and some secular gifts, but his rewards were almost entirely in the form of ecclesiastical preferment in churches and cathedrals. He can have rarely visited them, but his correspondence, and no doubt much of his conversation, was taken up with the administration of this ecclesiastical estate, seeking new gifts, negotiating exchanges of churches and prebends, asking for preferment for his friends and relatives, writing to his agent in Rome, begging for timber to repair his churches and rectories, and doing business at Westminster for his friends, most of them fellow ecclesiastics. The complicated story of his churches and prebends need not be told here, but it is striking how often he was involved in exchanges. Normally we do not know his motives. Sometimes they seem to have been convenience of administration, of collecting the revenues; for example, a single prebend in

---

[1] *Registrum Johannis Trefnant*, ed. W. W. Capes (C.Y.S., xx, 1916), p. 58.

[2] A few of his letters survive scattered in the Council and Privy Seal series, and there are references to him in many sources, but the most valuable single source is the letter collection, Harleian MS. 431, generally but misleadingly referred to as 'John Prophete's Letter-Book'. This is a complicated paper manuscript, basically a collection of documents from the first decade of the fifteenth century mainly relating to the Great Schism and the Council of Pisa, to which letters of private and formulary interest have been added. It is not Prophete's, nor even a collection of his letters; the number of his own letters is indeed greatly exaggerated in the catalogue of Harleian Manuscripts. The contents show a strong connection with Prophete and his nephew, Thomas Felde, though like other contemporary letter collections, the manuscript includes interesting letters from a number of people. Felde bequeathed a quire 'de litteris missivis in latinis' to Henry Penwortham, registrar to the archbishop of Canterbury, and it is tempting to link this with Harleian 431. But the whole subject requires fuller investigation along with other letter collections. Suffice it to say that the manuscript comes from the Prophete–Felde circle and reflects their interest in ecclesiastical affairs.

Chichester or Bath was better exchanged for a benefice near Hereford or London. Another motive, and not an uncommon one, was family arrangements. For example, within a few days in November 1407 Prophete held in succession three prebends in Hereford, exchanging them with his nephew, Dr. Thomas Felde, and another relative, Roger Hoore. These three often worked together, for example they had the grant of the custody of lands at Swindon in Gloucestershire from Archbishop Bowet during the minority of Roger Moryn.[1] Felde, an Oxford graduate and a modestly successful canon lawyer, diplomat, and commissioner, was clearly close to his uncle, and was being helped forward in his career. He became secondary in the privy seal two days after Prophete became keeper; he succeeded Prophete as dean of Hereford and in several preferments, and exchanged others with him; and he obtained Prophete's prebend of Leighton Buzzard within a few days of his death. He was given to reminding his correspondents of 'avunculus meus', the keeper of the privy seal, and he probably saw further promotion ahead if only Prophete could obtain a bishopric. He was clearly overshadowed by his uncle and, perhaps unjustly, it is difficult to be sympathetic to him.

An ecclesiastical career, however, had its worries and disappointments. Prophete's first major success was his election as dean of Hereford in 1393, but it seems likely that this turned sour. Among the Privy Seal archives there is a draft letter from the king to a cathedral chapter stating that because of strong complaints from them and the archbishop of Canterbury about the damage to the church caused by Prophete's long absence, he is giving him leave to exercise his deanery in person.[2] Prophete was dean of Hereford from 1393 until 1404, and of York from 1406 until his death, and the letter could refer to either. More probably it refers to Hereford, and it may explain his retirement from the Council after 1395, a time when the chapter was at odds with its bishop. It could be later, and it is certainly surprising to find Prophete resigning the deanery before 1404 even if he had a promise that his nephew would be elected to succeed him. It may be the action of a man who saw

[1] York, St. Anthony's Hall, Archiepiscopal Register 17, f. 24.
[2] E. 28/23.

he had no prospect of being much in Hereford and was under criticism for his absence. Two years later Innocent VII, no doubt at the instigation of Henry IV, provided Prophete to the richer deanery of York, but the pope died before the letters were drawn up and Henry IV wrote to his agent at the Curia particularly to ensure that the new pope, whoever he was, would renew Prophete's appointment.[1] Gregory XII did so and in June 1408 gave him leave to be non-resident for seven years. It may not be without significance that in June 1415 Prophete ceased to be keeper or that earlier that year he had a licence to exchange the deanery.[2] Prophete's major disappointment, however, was his failure to obtain a bishopric as almost every other keeper did. In Harleian MS. 431 there is a sad letter from his nephew, Thomas Felde, to an archbishop asking his assistance in obtaining the bishopric of Ely for his uncle.[3] It recounts that his friends had asked Prophete why he had not obtained a bishopric through the king's good offices with the pope 'prout alii custodes dicti sigilli se promoveri fecerunt temporibus retroactis'. Prophete's answer was that he would accept the dignity if it were voluntarily given to him by the pope, but that he would not ask either the king or the pope for it, and this meant it was impossible. Felde tried to guide the Holy Spirit by writing this letter on the assumption that John Fordham, bishop of Ely since 1388, was dead or dying. Fordham, however, though an old man and frequently unwell, outlived both Prophete and Felde, and in fact it was probably the longevity of the English bishops which deprived Prophete of his great reward. He did not obtain a bishopric in the first half of the reign, and few fell vacant between 1407 and 1415.

Prophete was an able administrator and a trusted councillor who was closely involved with great affairs for at least twenty-four years. Like most other leading professional administrators he was a cleric, and in the thick of ecclesiastical politics. No doubt, like Frye, he was much in demand as an adviser—in his case probably primarily to churchmen—though almost the only evidence of this

[1] F. C. Hingeston, *Royal and Historical Letters during the reign of Henry the Fourth* (R.S., 1860 and 1965), ii. 140; *CPL*, vi. 113–14.
[2] *CPL*, vi. 127 and 488–9.
[3] Harleian MS. 431, f. 94ᵛ.

is his service as a parliamentary proxy.[1] Inevitably he was an ecclesiastical careerist, but to say this probably does not do him justice. He was a pluralist and an absentee like all active senior civil servants, but there is some evidence for believing that he was a conscientious man. If we can accept it, there is the evidence of Felde's letter about his bishopric; there is his resignation of the deanery of Hereford; he took some care of the buildings of his livings; he furthered the interests of his cathedral chapters, particularly York; and the collection of documents in Harleian MS. 431 about the Council of Pisa suggests that he and his circle were interested in the problems of ending the Schism, though the story that Prophete himself was at Pisa is almost certainly untrue. The evidence is all rather problematical, but certainly my own impression of Prophete is a sympathetic one.

The stories of these three men obviously do not add up to a balanced impression of the Privy Seal. Nevertheless, they probably do represent some of the major emotions of the office, the fairly rough, only modestly rewarded, money-grubbing world of the average clerk; the scope that was open to an able clerk to become a man of business, helping clients in the administrative maze of Westminster and maintaining an extensive correspondence; and the rewarding world of the clerical careerist, rich in benefices and full of ecclesiastical gossip, but a world beyond the hope of all but a few highly qualified clerks.

A. L. BROWN

---

[1] In the collection of P.R.O. Parliamentary Proxies (S.C. 10), there are at least fourteen proxies to Prophete between 1391 and 1414, all but one from bishops and chapters.

XIII

Some Archdeacons' Court Books and the Commons' Supplication against the Ordinaries of 1532[1]

IT is now nearly twenty years since Brian Woodcock's thesis, prepared under the supervision of Professor Major, appeared in print. His untimely death cut short a tantalizing study into one of the most neglected areas of English church history: the ecclesiastical courts. Since that time a few attempts have been made to fill the gaps in our knowledge,[2] but as Woodcock noted after his study (which was based on the Canterbury documents alone), 'all modern scholars will be dead before a thousandth part of the *acta* of the English ecclesiastical courts can be printed so vast is their bulk.'[3] He might also have added that the difficulties which confront any serious student who wishes to use these records are immense. They were the product of a highly complex network of jurisdiction which differed from diocese to diocese[4] and which must be thoroughly

---

[1] An abridged version of this paper was submitted for the Alexander Prize Essay Competition of the Royal Historical Society in 1970 and it was awarded the prize.

[2] Notably for the Lincoln diocese by C. Morris, 'The Commissary of the Bishop in the Diocese of Lincoln', *JEH*, x (1959); id. 'A Consistory Court in the Middle Ages', ibid., xiv (1963); *An Episcopal Court Book for the diocese of Lincoln 1514–1520*, ed. M. Bowker (L.R.S. 61, 1967). Other dioceses had a very different jurisdictional structure: see especially R. A. Marchant, *The Church Under the Law: Justice, Administration and Discipline in the Diocese of York 1560–1640* (Cambridge, 1969); Dr. Marchant makes some useful comparisons with other dioceses, notably Norwich, and his book has a valuable bibliography, pp. 258–9, which will serve as an introduction to those seeking further information on the pre- and post-Reformation courts.

[3] B. L. Woodcock, *Medieval Ecclesiastical Courts in the Diocese of Canterbury* (Oxford, 1952), p. 140. Dr. Marchant has observed from his study of the post-Reformation ecclesiastical material that 'the sheer bulk of the records has deterred investigators, and I have become convinced that the statistical use of visitation and some other sources of information is preferable to printing a few random samples in full' (Marchant, op. cit., p. viii).

[4] See especially, 'Reports made to His Majesty by the Commissioners appointed to inquire into the Practice and Jurisdiction of the Ecclesiastical Courts in England

grasped before the relevance of the material can be assessed. But time has taken a heavy toll of many of the relevant documents, particularly those dealing with the lower ecclesiastical courts, those of the archdeacons and, in some dioceses, the commissaries. Ecclesiastical courts were, more often than not, itinerant, and registrars, whether diocesan or archidiaconal, were clearly sometimes in difficulties both with regard to finding paper on which to record processes and time in which to record them fully and clearly. As a result, some of the visitation and court proceedings which have survived are exceedingly torn and faded.[1] Many require 'heaven-sent moments' of inspiration to decipher at all.[2]

In addition to the problems created by the fifteenth-century scribes, the records have suffered at many hands ever since. Many books of archdeaconry *acta* have become so scattered that it is very difficult to find the relevant quires of the original book. Bedford Record Office, for instance, has in its keeping a book which contains for the most part wills and court process for the archdeaconry of Bedford, but it also includes some material for the diocese of London.[3] More daunting still is the problem of misclassification. Archdeaconry material has often not been recognized. The reason is not hard to find. In the Lincoln diocese, for instance, in the late fifteenth century, the archdeacon and commissary shared many duties including those of visitation, correction, and the granting of probate or letters of administration. Any book of archdeacon's *acta* might be expected, therefore, to show a wide diversity of material.[4] Any archivist unfamiliar with this material or used to the comparatively ordered ways of episcopal registrars is naturally torn between classifying this material as 'Visitation' or 'Probate' or 'Court Proceedings'. Since much of this material is not bound, and its foliation is frequently of a later date,[5] it has even happened that

and Wales', *Parliamentary Papers 1831–1832*, xxiv. The duties of officials principal were very different (see D. M. Owen, pp. 189–205, above).

[1] The most difficult I have tried to use so far are L.A.O., Viv. 2, 3, 4, 5.

[2] *Visitations in the Diocese of Lincoln 1517–1531*, ed. A. H. Thompson (L.R.S. 33, 35, 37, 1940–4), i. xx.   [3] Bedford Record Office, A.B.P./R. 1, ff. 1–4, 5ᵛ.

[4] B.R.O., D/A/We/1; this book contains all of these types of business.

[5] B.R.O., D/A/We/1 were given folio numbers by Marmaduke Claver, registrar for the archdeaconry of Buckingham from 1553. So confusing are his folio numberings that D/A/We/1 has been renumbered by the archivist. D/A/V/1 has two sets of

the archdeacon's *acta* for a single archdeaconry for a period of some twenty years have been separated. A very clear example of this has occurred in the case of the archdeaconry of Buckingham. Following the Probate Act of 1857, probate material for the archdeaconry was sent to Somerset House; other material which was more directly jurisdictional was sent to the Bodleian Library; while the fragments of a court book for the prebendal court of Buckingham were at Lincoln. Now that the material from the Bodleian Library and Somerset House has been deposited in the Buckinghamshire Record Office, a hitherto dismembered archdeacons' act book can be pieced together; on the backs of the so-called wills sent to Somerset House are the records of some 700 cases arising out of the archdeacon's duty of correction, and the fragments of some of his visitation proceedings. The Bodleian Library cases dovetail into this material, thereby providing at least part of an archdeacon's and commissary's act book for the period 1482 to 1522.[1] It is clear that the office of archdeacon's official and bishop's commissary was combined for much of the period, but while records of their activities were separated, not only the fact of the combination of offices, but also the records of their immense judicial activities, were 'lost'. Exactly the same phenomenon was noted by Woodcock in Canterbury; he recognized that the records of the old Canterbury probate registry contained 'much non-probate material . . . either as separate items or as entries in multi-purpose Act books'.[2]

How much more archdeaconry material remains hidden by what he charitably described as 'over-classification'[3] remains to be seen. But the sample of it for the Lincoln diocese indicates that there is a considerable amount of unused archidiaconal material which has a bearing, not only on the events leading up to the English

numbers on each folio (guaranteed to confuse), the Claver numbers (hereafter described as *old* foliation) and the recently given folio numbers (hereafter described as *new*). These books together with D/A/C/1 are in the course of being edited by Mrs. Elizabeth Elvey. I am grateful to her, not only for much help in unscrambling the otherwise baffling problems of foliation which the material presents, but also for the use of her invaluable transcript of D/A/We/1. All scholars of ecclesiastical courts will be in her debt when these records are published. It is hoped that they will appear under the auspices of the Buckinghamshire Record Society in the near future.

[1] B.R.O. D/A/We/1 and D/A/V/1 (formerly in Somerset House), and D/A/C/1 (formerly in the Bodleian Library).

[2] Woodcock, op. cit., p. 139.   [3] Ibid., p. 140.

Reformation, but on those that followed it. I can make no claim to
have discovered anything like all the fragmented *acta* for the archdeaconries which comprised the Lincoln diocese, but in the material
which is coming to light, particularly in that for Buckinghamshire
and Bedfordshire, I already see problems for any student of the
English Reformation. Still more clear is the fact that if the historian
is to answer these questions he must rely on the archivist: he must
be able to depend on the proper classification of documents, and
hope that those of a given area are in a single place. Professor Major
has consistently demonstrated how important the work of archivists
and editors is in its own right, and she has also shown how fundamental is their contribution to the work of historians. In paying
tribute to her outstanding work, both as an archivist and as an
historian, this study may perhaps show how essential it is that the
two professions should be seen as complementary, since an archivist's mistake may create an historical myth. Some demythologiz-
ing may be necessary in trying to understand the ecclesiastical
courts in the early sixteenth century.

In the first three decades of the sixteenth century the ecclesiastical
courts came in for some harsh criticism;[1] this criticism had a long
history but the case of Richard Hunne brought the unpopularity
of the courts, at least in London and among the merchants and
gentlemen of the metropolis, into sharp focus.[2] This unpopularity
was used by Henry VIII, with great skill, to bring Convocation
into subjection, and ultimately to force its acceptance of the royal
supremacy. Convocation was intimidated in 1531 by a charge of
praemunire for their exercise of ecclesiastical jurisdiction,[3] and in
1532 by the Commons' Supplication against the Ordinaries.[4] Why

---

[1] H. C. Porter, 'The Gloomy Dean and the Law: John Colet 1466–1519', *Essays in Modern Church History in memory of Norman Sykes*, ed. G. V. Bennett and J. D. Walsh (London, 1966), pp. 18 ff.

[2] See, for instance, A. Ogle, *The Tragedy of the Lollards Tower: the case of Richard Hunne with its Aftermath in the Reformation Parliament 1529–32* (Oxford, 1949).

[3] J. J. Scarisbrick, 'The Pardon of the Clergy, 1531', *Cambridge Historical Journal*, xii (1956), 22–39.

[4] *English Historical Documents*, v, *1485–1558*, ed. C. H. Williams (London, 1967), pp. 727 ff. For a discussion of the origin of the Supplication, see G. R. Elton, 'The Commons Supplication of 1532: Parliamentary Manœuvres in the Reign of Henry VIII', *EHR*, lxvi (1951), 507–34; and J. P. Cooper, 'The Supplication against the Ordinaries reconsidered', *EHR*, lxxii (1957), 616–41.

this Supplication was submitted is anything but clear; it was not apparently a diplomatic move to add leverage to Henry's papal negotiations; nor does it make sense if it is seen simply as a means devised by Cromwell to deprive the clergy of their legislative rights. As Dr. Kelly has cogently shown, most of the Supplication was not about these rights, and the fact that they subsequently proved crucial should not lead us into confusing intention and result.[1] The intention of the document is to attack the ecclesiastical courts quite as much as the legislative power of the Church. Clauses 2–7 deal directly with judicial problems.[2] What exactly lies behind this intention? Why were the courts so unpopular? Why was the case of Richard Hunne seen as symbolizing something of great importance? Was this just part of English folklore immortalized by Chaucer in his portrait of the Summoner? Or were the courts a real source of scandal, and was Hunne's case just one example of many?

The records of the court of audience of the bishop of Lincoln 1514–20 lend no weight to the Commons' criticisms.[3] And it would seem that if we are to understand the Supplication, we must turn to the courts of first instance, to the courts of the archdeacons and commissaries, for elucidation. If there is a clear case to be made against the Church courts it is in the records of the local courts that we should expect to find it. The elusive archdeaconry *acta* may provide a missing link in the story; they may reveal more clearly what lay behind the undoubted hostility to the Church courts, which marked the first three decades of the sixteenth century and proved so important in 1532.

Archdeacons' *acta* survive for the period *c.* 1480 to 1522 in some form (however fragmentary that may be) for three of the eight archdeaconries which comprised the pre-Reformation diocese of Lincoln. Those for Buckinghamshire[4] and Leicestershire[5] are most complete, but the fragmented Bedfordshire material is also useful;[6] in addition there are records of grants of probate,

---

[1] M. Kelly, 'The Submission of the Clergy', *TRHS* 5th ser., xv (1965), 104–5.
[2] *Documents*, v, ed. Williams, pp. 733–5.
[3] *Episcopal Court Book*, ed. Bowker, pp. xxi ff.
[4] B.R.O., D/A/We/1; D/A/V/1; D/A/C/1.
[5] L.A.O., Viv. 2, 3, 4, 5.   [6] Bedford R.O., A.B.P./R.1.

particularly for the archdeaconries of Lincoln and Stow. These appear to have been preserved separately and not to have been kept in a composite act book, but they help to illuminate certain problems especially those affecting the frequency with which the courts sat.[1] The *format* of the three main sets of *acta*, Leicestershire, Buckinghamshire, and Bedfordshire, is so different that we can safely rule out any possibility that the registrars 'cooked the books'; the Leicestershire material is primarily visitational, and where there is a report of a fault the court process which aimed at its correction has been subsequently added, with all the consequent palaeographic difficulties which this kind of method involves. The Buckinghamshire *acta* are arranged under date, as are the scant records for Bedfordshire. Yet in spite of these different approaches, each set of *acta* appears normally to point to the same conclusions.

The first and most obvious feature of the *acta* is the evidence provided of the immense activity of the archdeacon's official and the bishop's commissary.[2] In spite of the fact that the surviving records are certainly incomplete, and that consequently they represent only a fragment of the total activity of these ecclesiastical officers, it is apparent that some form of court or chapter (*capitulum*)[3] took place at the very least once a month; and where our records are most complete, they suggest that a session might be held as frequently as once every three days. This is most striking in the case of Leicestershire. In the year 1509 William Mason combined the duties of both archdeacon's official and bishop's commissary.[4] The archdeacon was William Spark.[5] The *acta* do not always distinguish as precisely as they might whether visitations and court proceedings were held before the archdeacon in person, or his official, or whether they were held under the auspices of William Mason acting not in his capacity as archdeacon's official but as bishop's commissary.[6] But whoever it was who was acting,

---

[1] *Lincoln Wills 1505–1530*, ed. C. W. Foster (L.R.S. 5, 10, 1914 and 1918).

[2] For the respective duties of the two, see my *Secular Clergy in the Diocese of Lincoln, 1495–1520* (Cambridge, 1968), pp. 31 ff.

[3] B.R.O., D/A/V/1 *passim*.　　　　　　　　　　　　[4] L.A.O., Viv. 5 *passim*.

[5] John Le Neve, *Fasti Ecclesiae Anglicanae 1300–1541*, i, *Lincoln Diocese*, compiled by H. P. F. King (London, 1962), p. 13.

[6] See, for example, L.A.O., Viv. 5, f. 3. The visitation of the churches of St. Leonard and St. Nicholas prompted court processes on 27 July, 4 Aug., 29 Sept.; and on

in whatever capacity, as far as the archdeaconry was concerned
the impression created was one of activity on the part of the
ecclesiastical authorities. In April 1509 the archdeacon or his official
visited most of the archdeaconry and they continued to do so until
10 May.[1] The result was to reveal a number of faults which required correction; notes of when the correction took place were
later inserted though they do not indicate before whom the case
was brought. But whether one or two people were involved in
hearing the cases, the fact remains that in June 1509 an ecclesiastical court sat on twelve out of twenty-three potential court
days.[2] This activity tailed off somewhat in July and August (though
this may simply be an optical illusion caused by gaps in the records).
In September of that year visitations were resumed, and resulting
cases of correction and probate were held not less than once a week
throughout October, November, and December of that year.[3]
Sometimes the court seems to have sat, for however short a time,
for three consecutive days. A similar impression is conveyed by the
archdeaconry *acta* for Buckinghamshire. These cover a longer period
but they are far less complete, and missing pages of *acta* may yet be
found. There are no *acta* for the year 1504, for example, and they
are sparse for the years 1482–8, 1495–1520. Most material survives
for the years 1492–3; this indicates that a court was always held
monthly but that it frequently sat for several days running. In
July 1492, for example, the official of the archdeacon held a meeting
on the 2nd, 4th, 5th, and 6th.[4] In 1493 the court sat every month
and for several days; in May, for example, it sat from 20th to 25th
inclusive;[5] in January 1493/4 it sat from 13 January to 17 January
inclusive.[6] No formal law terms appear to have been kept, and the

---

21 July, 28 July, 2 Nov. and 16 Dec. respectively. There is no indication whether the
archdeacon who appears to have held the visitation heard or delegated the correction
proceedings.

[1] L.A.O., Viv. 5, ff. 1, 7, 8, 13, 14, 17, 22, 23, 28, 29, 32^v, 34^v. The records of visitations do not always appear in chronological order.

[2] Of the 30 days of June, four were Sundays, one was Corpus Christi day, and two
were Ember days. If we may assume that courts were not held on these days we are
left with 23 potential court days. For the sessions, see ibid., ff. 1, 2^{v2}, 8, 9, 13, 15, 30^2,
33^v, 35^3.   [3] Ibid., ff. 3, 4^5, 11^2, 16^2, 18^v, 19^{v6}, 20^2, 24^{v5}, 25^2, 25^{v3}, 31^v, 32^2.

[4] B.R.O. D/A/V/1, ff. 267, 269, 269^v (old foliation); ff. 2, 4, 4^v (new foliation).

[5] Ibid., ff. 259–259^v (old foliation), ff. 10–10^v (new foliation).

[6] Ibid., ff. 263–263^v (old foliation), ff. 14–14^v (new foliation).

itinerant nature of the courts was apt to involve the judge in considerable travelling: on 13 January 1493/4, the archdeacon's official was at Chilton, a village some seven miles west of Aylesbury; on the 14th he went to Whitchurch, which lies north of Aylesbury and at least nine miles from Chilton; the following day he went to Stone, three miles west of Aylesbury and nearly six from Whitchurch; he then went to Beaconsfield, a journey of at least sixteen miles, and finally to High Wycombe, a mere four miles away. He had therefore travelled about thirty-six miles in five days; easy by modern standards but not quite so comfortable in bad weather on horseback.[1]

What was the purpose and the result of this activity and does it have a bearing on the criticisms of the courts subsequently expressed in 1529 and thereafter?

A breakdown of the cases heard indicates that the need for court sessions was not solely created by the pressure of correction business. But again there is a chance of the surviving material misleading us by creating an optical illusion. A casual reading of the Leicestershire material, for instance, might lead one to suppose that the most important judicial duties of an archdeacon or his official were those of correction subsequent on visitation; records of grants of probate and letters of administration are present in the *acta* but not in any great quantity.[2] The great bulk of the probate material for 1509 is in the probate registry at Leicester,[3] while the correction-visitation *acta* are at Lincoln;[4] the two may well marry up together, but it will require a very skilful editor and the presence of the records under a single roof for the complete *acta* to be reconstructed. Conversely, the Bedfordshire evidence would suggest that the prime duty of the court of the archdeacon's official was that of granting probate to wills, since only fragments of correction process survive;[5] yet hidden among this probate material are some

---

[1] B.R.O., D/A/V/1, *passim*. The distance estimated is minimal, it presupposes a very direct route; in reality the distance travelled was probably twice that of my estimate. See also Woodcock, op. cit., p. 35.

[2] See for example, L.A.O., Viv. 5, ff. 16, 18, 19ᵛ, 23ᵛ, 24ᵛ, 35, 35ᵛ.

[3] For an index of these, see *Calendars of Wills and Administrations relating to the County of Leicester proved in the Archdeaconry Court of Leicester 1495–1649 . . .*, ed. Henry Hartopp (Index Library, vol. 27, 1902).   [4] L.A.O., Viv. 2, 3, 4, 5.

[5] See especially Bedford R.O., A.B.P./R.1, ff. 135–9, 145 ff.

folios that point to a quite incredible amount of judicial activity, either instance or correction, the records of which are lost. On the back of folio 139 and on the subsequent five folios are lists of letters received, perhaps by the rural dean, mainly arranged under deaneries and certainly datable to the years 1499–1500.[1] These lists are extraordinary, as the transcript for one deanery, that of Shefford indicates:

Decanatus de Shefford

In Primis pro privatis qui non habuerunt	lxxii letteras[2]
Item pro privatis qui habuerunt	xii letteras
Item pro paroch'[3] que non habuerunt	xxxvi letteras
Item pro paroch' que habuerunt	vi letteras
Item pro coniugatis qui habuerunt	vi letteras
Item pro coniugatis qui non habuerunt	xlviii letteras
Item pro rebellibus	v^{xx}

The deanery of Shefford had twenty-six churches and some chapels;[4] there are no accurate estimates of its population at this date; the distinction between the 'haves' and 'have nots' defeats me; if it is meant to indicate that the individuals have received the letters in question then *recepere* would have been the most likely verb for the scribe to have used, even given the limited Latin which he knew; the letters could conceivably be letters of indulgence, but the mention of *rebellibus* makes this improbable. The word occurs in some fifteenth-century ecclesiastical documents to denote contumacious persons.[5] If in a single year in one deanery there were as many as five score contumacious persons to be cited once or even twice to the ecclesiastical courts, there had to be a number of

---

[1] Bedford R.O., A.B.P./R. 1, f. 140. The surrounding material is all of this date. Of the rectors mentioned John Underhill of Houghton Conquest had resigned by 1509 (L.A.O. Register 23, f. 405$^\text{v}$). The material cannot be later than that date.

[2] *Sic.*

[3] In view of the ambiguous *que*, it is not absolutely clear how *paroch'* should be construed.

[4] This figure is Hamilton Thompson's (*Visitations*, i. 113). It does not exactly tally with that suggested by H. Salter, *A Subsidy collected in the Diocese of Lincoln in 1526* (Oxford Historical Society, vol. lxiii, 1913), p. 197; the difference lies in the exact status of chapels. At most there were thirty churches or chapels in the deanery.

[5] For a similar use of the word, see, for example, *The Register of Thomas Langley, Bishop of Durham 1406–1437*, ed. R. L. Storey (Surtees Soc., 1956–70), v. 76.

sessions, and certainly scribes and summoners had plenty to do. But the problems of interpretation which this document presents are too great for us to be able to begin to reconstruct from the Bedfordshire material the distribution of correction, probate, and instance business which, in reality, came before the archdeacon's court. It is here that the Buckinghamshire evidence is most helpful, because all kinds of archidiaconal business appear; there are fragments of visitations, notes of elections of penitentiaries,[1] grants of probate and records of both instance and correction cases. So mixed is the material that it is clear that, though much is missing, the missing folios could scarcely have contained a single type of material;[2] our picture of the ecclesiastical courts is therefore unlikely to be distorted by the *lacunae*. If we take one of the Buckinghamshire books alone,[3] we have the record of some 700 court cases as well as some visitation material and innumerable wills. Of these 700 nearly 50 are best described as purely ecclesiastical; they concern the failure of incumbents or churchwardens to repair books, enclose cemeteries, mend chancels, light candles or, in the case of rectors, make distributions to the poor. The remainder of the cases break down as follows:

Testamentary cases	41%
Unspecified instance cases	19·5%
Cases arising out of the failure to pay ecclesiastical dues	12%
Morality cases	9%
Defamation cases	8·5%
Perjury cases	6·5%
Marriage cases	3·5%

It is not always absolutely clear from the accounts of these cases who the prosecuting party was; whether in fact the case was an *office* case which arose out of the archdeacon's duty to correct the erring, or whether it was brought solely at the instance of two

---

[1] See especially B.R.O., D/A/We/1, ff. 136ᵛ, 148ᵛ, 150, 154, 166ᵛ.

[2] See above, p. 287. The missing evidence is mainly for certain years.

[3] B.R.O., D/A/We/1. This book covers fitfully the period 1483–1520 and there is little chance of counting cases twice as there are few adjournments. (Cf. B.R.O., D/A/V/1, ff. 263–4 (old foliation); ff. 14–15 (new foliation), where it is unclear in a case from Crendon whether the same parties are concerned in the same case or another.)

laymen, as were the bulk of marriage cases.[1] Between these two clearly differentiated groups lay a variety of cases. It is possible, for example, that in a case where it is noted that one man was cited at the instance of another, one of the parties might have been a churchwarden or clerk and that this is a concealed (or 'promoted') office case;[2] the same may be true of some of the defamation cases. The reverse obtains in perjury cases; it often appears that the Church is prosecuting but in fact it is doing so on information laid by another, usually for a failure to implement the provisions of a will, which was often described as perjury; technically these cases were *ex officio promoto*.[3] It is often more useful in attempting to classify cases, to dispense with the technical distinction of office and instance, and simply to ask at whose initiative the case was brought. We shall not be distorting the picture too greatly if we assume that unspecified instance cases, and marriage and defamation cases arose largely as a result of lay initiative, and that morality cases, cases involving ecclesiastical dues, and perjury cases arose normally as a result of a visitation or a report laid to the court by some ecclesiastical official, be he the apparitor or summoner or the local incumbent or churchwarden. If this classification is accepted we have 31·5 per cent of cases arising out of lay initiative, 27·5 per cent from detection by ecclesiastical authorities, and 41 per cent testamentary cases which do not properly belong to either group. Instance and probate business took up most of the court's time, and very few sessions of the court of the archdeacon of Buckingham or his official can be shown to have been held solely to deal with office business.

The Commons, in their Supplication against the Ordinaries, were very careful to make no mention whatever of instance cases

---

[1] Almost all marriage cases were concerned with allegations of pre-contract. There is, however, evidence of bigamy, and Thomas Godying was said to have sold one wife and taken another (B.R.O., D/A/We/1, f. 123). Bigamy was not apparently uncommon (see especially, C. A. McClaren, 'An Early Sixteenth Century Act Book of the Diocese of London', *Journal of the Society of Archivists*, iii, no. 7 (1968), 340). Since the London act book records the activity of five vicars general, the type of case which is recorded would seem more closely to resemble that coming before the court of audience at Lincoln.

[2] This can certainly be shown to be the case on a number of occasions (see especially B.R.O., D/A/We/1, ff. 140, 140ᵛ, 161ᵛ, 166, 192ᵛ).

[3] Woodcock, op. cit., p. 69.

eo nomine. They reserved their criticism for office and testamentary cases, cases in fact where all parties had no choice but to appear before the court. If there were defects in the conduct of instance business, the remedy for it lay squarely with the litigants themselves. They could ignore their quarrels with their neighbours: there was no absolute necessity which demanded that Nicholas Barton and Thomas Couley bring to the notice of the court that Nicholas in an angry mood (*animo irato*) had called Thomas 'Rusticum et servum' by saying 'Avaunte chorle and I wolde prove the a chorle of condicione'.[1] They had but to come to blows and the matter could come before the king's courts.[2] Similarly there was nothing to prevent litigants settling out of court, which on occasions they did. So the Commons (or their masters) omitted instance procedure from their scrutiny, for this would often have turned a supplication against the Church, the ordinaries, into one against themselves. They devoted their attention, as far as the courts were concerned, to office and testamentary cases.

Their grievance over testamentary cases was that 'notwithstanding the last statute thereof made, there is invented new fashions to charge your subjects for probate of testaments, that is to say long delays and tracts or the proof thereon can be admitted'.[3] They also complained that they were cited out of the shire even when the will could have been dealt with within it. The problem over these complaints is that we have little contemporaneous evidence. Our evidence mainly pre-dates the legislation of 1529 affecting probate fees. But if any weight may be attached to 'notwithstanding', we may assume that the grievance was more acute before 1529 than after it, and that consequently what evidence we have should reveal probate procedure at its worst. But in the case of Lincolnshire a comparison is possible between the period before and after the 1529 legislation. What then is the evidence for

---

[1] B.R.O., D/A/V/1, f. 266 (old foliation); f. 1 (new foliation).

[2] By the fiction of a breach of the peace which was used to serve similar ends in the royal courts; a case which technically might be considered to be within the scope of Common Pleas, because it was on a civil matter between two parties, could come before King's Bench if trespass was alleged (M. Hastings, *The Court of Common Pleas in Fifteenth Century England* (Ithaca, N.Y., 1947), p. 24).

[3] *Documents*, v, ed. Williams, p. 734.

the complaints which gave rise to the legislation of 1529, and how did the legislation affect them?

Clearly the longer it took to get a will proved the greater the expenses incurred were likely to have been, so the criticisms of delay and expense are intimately related. To determine how long it took to prove a will presupposes we know the date of the testator's death, and in the case of those of sufficiently lowly status it is almost impossible to be certain of the date of death. We do, however, have the date given to the will, though we have no certain indication why some wills were registered *in toto* and others were not, nor do we know whether the date given to the will is the date at which it was made, the date at which it first came to the notice of the court, or the date of the testator's death. There is a distinct probability that the practice varied from archdeaconry to archdeaconry. The Lincoln wills look as though they were dated from when the executors appeared in court, because too many wills bear the same date for the coincidence of simultaneous death to be very likely.[1] Those for Buckinghamshire and Bedfordshire seem to be the dates at which the will was made. But what can be said certainly is that in comparing the date given to the will and the date of probate we are considering the maximum time in which the executors of the deceased were being inconvenienced by the court. If we take a sample of fifty Buckinghamshire wills mainly dating from 1520,[2] fifty Bedfordshire wills dating from 1500,[3] fifty Lincolnshire wills dating from 1504 to 1521,[4] and fifty

---

[1] Canon Foster did not think this was the case (*Lincoln Wills*, ii, p. x).

[2] This selection is based on the first fifty wills in the books concerned for a given year; it was felt that since the fullest Bedfordshire evidence dated from 1500, it was desirable to select the first fifty from that year. There was an abundant choice for Buckinghamshire, so fifty wills of the later date were chosen. For Buckinghamshire the wills used were B.R.O., D/A/We/1, ff. 2², 4–25, 27–30, 35, 37–48, 51–4, 56–7, 59, 60, 65.

[3] Bedford R.O., A.B.P./R.1, ff. 10², 10ᵛ², 11², 11ᵛ, 12, 12ᵛ, 13, 14, 15³, 16ᵛ³, 17², 17ᵛ², 18, 18ᵛ, 19², 21, 23, 23ᵛ², 24², 24ᵛ, 25², 25ᵛ, 26², 27², 29, 29ᵛ, 30, 31², 31ᵛ, 32, 34, 35², 35ᵛ² 36, 36ᵛ. These wills are in print, but unfortunately the Latin and English wills were edited separately thereby destroying the chronological sequence of probate grants which is maintained very closely in the early part of the book itself. For the printed wills, see *Bedfordshire Wills 1480–1519*, ed. P. Bell (Bedfordshire Historical Record Society, vol. xlv, 1966), and *English Wills 1498–1526*, ed. A. F. Cirket (Bedfordshire Record Society, vol. xxxvii, 1957), pp. 1–82.

[4] *Lincoln Wills*, i. 20–96. Many of the wills in this volume could not be used because there is no date of probate.

more for the same area dating from 1530 to 1532,[1] the results are
as follows:

	Beds.	Bucks.
Probate in under one month	22	11
„ „ over one month and up to two months	15	25
„ „ over two months and up to three months	4	7
„ „ over three months and up to four months	2	1
„ „ over four months and up to five months	1	2
„ „ over five months	6	4

	Lincs.	
	1504–21	1530
Probate in under one month	12	12
„ „ over one month and up to two months	8	8
„ „ over two months and up to three months	7	9
„ „ over three months and up to four months	5	5
„ „ over four months and up to five months	5	1
„ „ over five months and up to six months	1	8
„ „ over six months and up to one year	4	6
„ „ over one year and up to five years	4	1
„ „ over five years	4	0

Two striking factors emerge from these figures: the first is that for
both Bedfordshire and Buckinghamshire the majority of wills were
proved in under two months and it was rare for a will to take

---

[1] *Lincoln Wills*, ii. 155–85. Care should be taken with the dates in this volume; confusion arises for the period 1 Jan.–25 Mar. since the dating of the originals is for a year commencing on 25 Mar.; the editor did not show this by the convention Mar. 1529/30. As a result, it would appear that the will of Robert Raynton (pp. 154–5) was proved *before* he made it!

longer than five months. In Lincolnshire probate was not so rapid, but there are no grounds for thinking that the time taken to gain probate increased as a result of the 1529 act; probate took between a week and four months in 34 cases of the two samples; in 1530 there were a marginally higher number in the four to six months category, but this is compensated for by the correspondingly lower number which took over six months (a mere 7 as opposed to 12 before the 1529 act). Unless the long delays precede the date given to the will, it is hard to see what the Commons had in mind in this matter. It looks very much as though it is a very old complaint which still had emotional overtones but no factual basis.

The complaint that executors could be cited out of the shire receives no confirmation from Lincoln evidence. No weight can be attached to this since the court to which the citation would be made was likely to have been the consistory court, the records of which do not survive. But there is evidence to suggest that the bishops of Lincoln were very aware of the criticism levelled at Wolsey by Archbishop Warham, when he wrote 'I would your Grace knew what rumour and obloquy is in these parts and also in London that no testaments can take effect otherwise than your grace is content.'[1] In all probability the Commons were referring to Wolsey's notorious practice of taking any case he fancied for himself irrespective of its place of origin; the bishops of Lincoln knew their man, and had made an agreement with Wolsey, thereby effectually preventing him from doing anything of the kind.[2] Indeed, throughout the diocesan and archidiaconal evidence, there is very little to suggest that inhibitions were frequent or that litigants adjourned a case from one court to another with any regularity.[3] But at the heart of the complaint about the duration and location of probate cases lay the deeper grievance of fees.

Complaints against fees of all kinds had a very long history, and probate fees were often singled out for special mention. In 1416 there were criticisms of 'the high and excessive perception of fees for the registration of such wills, and the hearing of the account and

---

[1] A. F. Pollard, *Wolsey* (London, 1929), p. 194.
[2] Bowker, *Secular Clergy*, pp. 8–9.
[3] For one example see B.R.O., D/A/We/1, f. 79ᵛ.

final discharge of the executors deputed therein.[1] Ordinances were made, especially by Archbishop Stratford, stating the exact scale of fees which might be taken,[2] and very severe penalties were attached to its infringement; Woodcock found that this scale laid down by Stratford was in use in the archdeacon's court of Sandwich between 1520 and 1523, and it looks as though it also was used in the archdeaconry of Maidstone.[3] The scale was as follows:

Goods valued at nothing to					£1. 10s. 0d.		no fees
,,	,,	,,	£1. 10s. 0d. to	£5.	0s. 0d.		1s. 0d.
,,	,,	,,	£5. 0s. 0d. to	£20.	0s. 0d.		3s. 0d.
,,	,,	,,	£20. 0s. 0d. to	£40.	0s. 0d.		5s. 0d.
,,	,,	,,	£40. 0s. 0d. to £100.		0s. 0d.		10s. 0d.
,,	,,	,,	£100. 0s. 0d. to £150.		0s. 0d.	£1.	0s. 0d.[4]

There is no conclusive evidence to indicate whether the Stratford scale was in force in the Lincoln diocese, but since its authority was that of a provincial constitution, it is likely that it was regarded as binding. But there was a certain ambiguity in the ruling; Lynd-wood, in glossing it, recognised that a scribe must have an adequate fee and that this should normally be 6d., but he recognized that in cases where the duties of the scribe were unduly onerous then it was proper for a higher rate to be charged; it is also not absolutely clear whether gradations in the scale *pro rata* were permissible though it looks as though they were.[5] These possible loopholes in the law may help to explain the archdeaconry evidence.

All the evidence for probate fees indicates that round figures were exceptional; 1s. 8d., 2s. 4d., and figures of this kind were the norm. This may be because they were charged *pro rata* or because they include the scribe's fee. Very few wills were proved in the court of the archdeacon or the bishop's commissary in which the deceased had goods which would necessitate that he pay a fee of more than 5s. 0d. Men with goods above the value of £40 were likely to have them in a variety of places; if any of the goods of the deceased lay

[1] *Register of Henry Chichele*, ii, p. xxxiv.
[2] W. Lyndwood, *Provinciale Seu Constitutiones Angliae* (Oxford, 1679), p. 181.
[3] Woodcock, op. cit., p. 73.
[4] Lyndwood, *Provinciale*, pp. 181–2.
[5] Ibid., p. 181, *ad verb. Insinuationes*, and p. 182, *ad verb. Accipere*. I am grateful to Professor Ullmann for his help in trying to penetrate the meaning of this ordinance.

outside the archdeaconry but within the diocese, then the will would be heard by the bishop, or more usually by his official principal; if the goods lay in places outside the diocese as well as within it and were of more than £10 in value, then probate lay, in theory, with the archbishop of Canterbury.[1] The archdeaconry records, therefore, are normally of grants of probate or letters of administration for the relatively poor, and in any event with those whose goods were all located within the archdeaconry. If we look at the grants of probate in the years from 1519 to 1521 (which are the nearest in time to the legislation of 1529 which have survived to us) it becomes clear that most of those whose wills were proved in the archdeaconry, and for which a fee is given, were being charged at low rates, if not pardoned altogether. Between 1520 and 1521 the registrar to the bishop's commissary for Buckinghamshire noted the fees for 44 wills; of these exactly half were not charged a fee at all, 'in forma pauperis'; seventeen paid between one and two shillings; three paid 3s. 4d. and one paid 6s. 8d. and one 23s. 4d.[2] A year previously the registrar to the archdeacon's official had noted the fees of nineteen wills; of these only four were dismissed 'in forma pauperis'; eleven were charged at the first rate of one shilling; three were charged at the second rate of over three shillings. The remaining one was charged 8s. 0d.[3] The critical question with regard to these sums is how they relate to the goods of the deceased; were they in excess of the Stratford scale?

The problem of determining the value of goods of the deceased is great, but for Buckinghamshire we have what appears, at first sight, to be a useful means of assessing their value in the happy survival of part of a subsidy roll for the year 1524,[4] and a muster roll for 1522 which gives the value of the lands and goods of individuals, even if both are nil.[5] But this apparent gold-mine of information proves to be at once tantalizing and unhelpful. In the first place it

---

[1] Bowker, *Secular Clergy*, pp. 10–11.

[2] B.R.O., D/A/C/1, ff. 2, 2ᵛ, 3ᵛ, 5, 5ᵛ, 6ᵛ, 8ᵛ, 9ᵛ.

[3] B.R.O., D/A/We/1, ff. 60 f.

[4] *Subsidy for the County of Buckingham Anno 1524* (Buckinghamshire Record Society, vol. 8, 1950), ed. A. C. Chibnall and A. V. Woodman.

[5] Bodleian Library Certificates of Musters (Bucks.), MS. Eng. Hist., e. 187. This roll is being edited by Professor A. C. Chibnall. I am most grateful to him for the use of his transcript.

post-dates the last records we have for Buckinghamshire probate fees. We have, therefore, to search the muster or subsidy rolls for the heirs of the deceased; this means that to the already hazardous task of identification is added the further one of keeping apart families of the same name. The muster roll evidence is made more difficult by its arrangement under villages; a man with a holding in two places thereby appears twice, and to trace a single testator's heirs through all the villages in Buckinghamshire, even when the muster roll is indexed, will be a chancy affair. The subsidy roll is arranged in such a way that the total wealth of a family is entered only once, but the subsidy was only levied on those with goods or lands over the value of 40s. 0d., on the very people in fact who do not appear very frequently in the archidiaconal records. Not surprisingly, therefore, an attempt to correlate fees with the evidence of the muster or subsidy rolls yields bizarre and contradictory results. The executors of John Cok of Quainton obtained probate for his will without fee on account of his poverty.[1] Less than eighteen months later, the muster roll shows that there were two Cookes (*sic*) in Quainton, Elizabeth and William; each possessed 13s. 4d. in goods.[2] If both may be assumed to be the heirs of John, and if both may be assumed neither to have lost nor gained any goods since John's death, then we might be able happily to conclude that John's goods were worth 26s. 8d., and therefore were less than the 30s. 0d. which would have made him eligible for the lowest fee. But the chances of error are great and are admirably demonstrated by the case of James Werner of Chesham. His executors were also granted probate without fee on account of the poverty of the deceased;[3] yet the muster roll for Chesham reveals only one Werner, Katherine, perhaps James's widow, who held £3 in land and £3 in goods.[4] Katherine either belongs to a different branch of the family, or she had means acquired independently of James; alternatively his executors deceived the court about the value of his estate. Examples could be multiplied, but it is absolutely clear that the chances of error are so great that no very convincing

[1] B.R.O., D/A/C/1, f. 2.
[2] Bodleian Library Certificates of Musters (Bucks.), MS. Eng. Hist., e. 187, f. 106.
[3] B.R.O., D/A/C/1, f. 2ᵛ.
[4] Bodleian Library, MS. Eng. Hist., e. 187, f. 219.

conclusions about the scale of probate charges can be drawn from a comparison of probate fees and muster roll evidence. We are left, therefore, with the subsidy roll; this is incomplete, and three years later than the last record of a probate fee. Here again the problem of heirs vitiates the evidence. In 1520 probate was granted to the will of Thomas Awdley of North Marston.[1] His executors were Katherine Awdley, his wife, and John and Henry his sons. They paid a fine, *finem* (the word seems to be used interchangeably with a fee),[2] of 2*s*. 8*d*. If we allow that 8*d*. went to the scribe, it is clear that Thomas's will was charged on a *pro rata* basis, and that his goods were valued at between £5 and £20. Katherine was assessed for the subsidy in 1524 on £2.[3] Was this the full value of the goods of the estate? Or had some been concealed for taxation purposes? Alternatively were the goods of the deceased really in the order of £10 to £15 but had they been distributed between the widow *and* her sons who, in the meantime, had moved from the area? Any interpretation may be the right one, but to pronounce about the exorbitance or justice of probate charges on this evidence is to invite disaster. We are left, then, with only one source from which to resolve this problem: inventories.

These are scarce enough in any case, and the chances of finding both an inventory and a note of the fees charged are not great. Nevertheless, a few have come to light which may indicate, however slightly, something of what the Commons' Supplication was about in so far as it touched probate fees. The goods of Thomas Dallyn of Lincolnshire were valued in 1515 as being worth £11 3*s*. 0*d*.[4] There is a note that letters of administration cost 6*s*. 8*d*. and that 'costes and charges Abowt the same 4*s*. 8*d*.' (*sic*). Letters of administration appear always to have cost 6*s*. 8*d*. in Lincolnshire, since William Burgeys whose goods were valued at £38 8*s*. 0*d*. was charged just the same;[5] but whereas the richer man bore scribal costs which amounted to 2*s*. 0*d*., Thomas was charged 4*s*. 8*d*. Even allowing for the vagueness of the scribe, and even if we allow that the complexity of the poorer man's affairs resulted in far

---

[1] B.R.O., D/A/We/1, f. 73.

[2] It is an odd usage but it would not seem that a genuine fine for non-appearance is meant.   [3] *Subsidy for Buckingham*, p. 40.

[4] L.A.O., Inventories 2, no. 61.   [5] Ibid., no. 90.

greater work for the scribe, the difference is still substantial, and both sums are far in excess of the normal scribal fee of 6*d.* envisaged by Lyndwood and only to be exceeded in exceptional cases.[1] Ayn (*sic*) Harrison's goods were valued on her death in 1524 as being worth £10 8*s.* 9*d.*; there is a note that the commissary was paid 3*s.* 0*d.*;[2] this is exactly the sum allowed in the Stratford scale. Yet in the same year Alane Johnson's goods were valued at £11 16*s.* 0*d.*; her fee to the commissary was 5*s.* 0*d.* and letters of acquittance cost a further 2*s.* 0*d.*,[3] instead of the 6*d.* normally envisaged by Lynd- wood.[4] In 1527 Roland Tyndall's goods were valued at £9 12*s.* 5*d.*, and it was noted that his fine was 3*s.* 0*d.*,[5] again exactly that allowed in the Stratford scale. All these inventories were of the goods of Lincolnshire folk; yet even within a single shire there are some indications of variations of rate.

The rates appear to have been slightly different in Buckingham- shire and Bedfordshire. William Willesley died intestate and his goods were valued at £2 17*s.* 9*d.*; letters of administration cost the administrators 2*s.* 4*d.*: in addition a further 2*s.* 4*d.* was charged for the acquittance of the administration and for its fine ('pro acquie- tancia administracionis et fine eiusdem'): the scribe took another 2*s.* 0*d.* for writing the inventory and registering the accounts and 11*d.* for computing expenses at various times. It looks in this case as though the acquittance and fine costs are too high and the scribal costs much too high: the inventory lists 15 items and 19 charges or debts,[6] hardly enough to warrant fees very much in excess of the 6*d.* allowed, let alone sufficient to warrant the further scribal bonus for computing the expenses. Scribes in Bedfordshire were also putting up their rates in excess of the Lyndwood scale, and 7*d.* or 9*d.* was not unusual.[7] In the archdeaconry of Huntingdon by 1527, registrars were taking as much as 1*s.* 0*d.* and 1*s.* 4*d.*, though both admittedly in cases where the probate fee was high, 6*s.* 8*d.* and 5*s.* 0*d.* respectively.[8] In the case of William Smith there was 8*d.* to pay to the registrar and a probate fee of 1*s.* 0*d.* It is hard to

[1] Lyndwood, *Provinciale*, p. 181, *ad verb. Rationabile.*
[2] L.A.O., Inventories 2, no. 37.   [3] Ibid., no. 39.
[4] Lyndwood, *Provinciale*, p. 182, *ad verb. Acquietantiarum literis.*
[5] L.A.O., Inventories 2, no. 43.   [6] B.R.O., D/A/We/1, f. 13ᵛ, no. 34.
[7] Bedford R.O., A.B.P./R.1, ff. 152–9.   [8] L.A.O., Vj. 6, f. 65ᵛ.

believe that in all these cases the scribe had unduly onerous duties.[1] It is clear that a certain amount of hard bargaining might lie behind fees. It was noted in one Buckinghamshire probate grant that 3s. 4d. was charged for the proof of the will but that the executors 'computaverunt cum officio' and were dismissed from further charges 'in forma pauperis'.[2] The Commons, therefore, may have come to recognize that the official fees and their scale, which they had thought were the problem in 1529, were not the only problem. The problem lay in the latitude allowable within a given scale. Their legislation allowed the judge 2s. 6d. and the registrar 1s. 0d. for an estate valued at £5–£40. For those leaving £5 in goods, these fees were heavy; for those leaving £40 they were light.

But probate fees were themselves only a part of a far larger problem which was that of ecclesiastical dues and fees of all kinds. These too were particularly singled out for complaint in the Commons' Supplication against the Ordinaries. It was the courts of Audience and the Arches which were especially said to be guilty of asking unduly high fees, but the charge of 'great and excessive fees' was made in general against all spiritual courts. The Commons alleged that as much as 2s. 6d. might be asked for a citation and 3s. 4d. for a personal citation and that there was 'exacted for serving the process after the rate of miles for every mile 2d.'[3] Once again it is very difficult to assess the evidence which lay behind these complaints. Citations to the Leicestershire archdeaconry courts appear to have a fixed rate of 8d.; the one exception from this seems to have been a certain Johanna Pudsey who was cited to answer on a charge for which she had already been corrected; she appears to have paid 4d. for this unjustified citation.[4] Absolution from incurring the sanction of suspension *ab ingressu* cost 11d.[5] In instance cases one party might be made to pay the expenses of the other: Thomas Fraunces of Hambledon was brought to court at the instance of the churchwardens; he admitted that he owed the church 6s. 8d. and was given eight days in which to pay it, together with 1s. 1d.

---

[1] L.A.O., Vj. 6, f. 65ᵛ.

[2] B.R.O., D/A/We/1, f. 188ᵛ; the account is sufficiently garbled for it to be possible that *officio* should read *officiale*.

[3] *Documents*, v, ed. Williams, p. 734.

[4] L.A.O., Viv. 5, f. 94.   [5] L.A.O., Viv. 5, ff. 3, 35, 40, 45ᵛ.

in expenses.[1] Conversely a defendant who was cited to the court but whose accuser did not appear was dismissed without charge.[2] These fees were not light; eightpence was a significant sum; it was at least the equivalent in the building industry of a craftsman's daily wage at this date, and for the labourer it represented two days hard work.[3] But sizeable though a citation fee might be, it was not as great as that for a letter of pardon obtainable from that most unscrupulous of all ecclesiastical 'officers', the pardoner. Letters of pardon cost 2s. 0d.;[4] but these are not mentioned in the Commons complaints. The reason is not hard to seek; no one was *bound* to buy letters of pardon, just as no one was bound to pay the heavy sums involved in being buried in a church as opposed to outside it or in the porch. But once cited in the court, a man was bound to come or else he risked the higher bills involved in obtaining absolution for his contumacy. Ecclesiastical fees were, in this respect, in the same category as any form of compulsory taxation; always unpopular, even if in fact it represented a small percentage of the wealth of the taxed. But whereas taxation normally took some account of poverty (subsidies were rarely levied on those with lands or goods worth less than forty shillings), fees apparently did not, with the sole exception of probate fees. Court fees were only to be avoided by keeping clear of the courts, and so wide was their jurisdiction that that might be very difficult.

It was, therefore, with very sound logic that the Commons' attack on fees directly follows in their supplication the complaints about the conduct of office cases:

Also divers and many of your said most humble and obedient subjects, and specially those that be of the poorest sort within this your realm, be daily convented and called before the said spiritual Ordinaries, their commissaries and substitutes, *ex officio*, sometimes at the pleasures of the said Ordinaries, their commissaries and substitutes, for displeasure, without any provable cause: and sometimes at the only promotion and suggestion of their summoners and

---

[1] B.R.O., D/A/V/1, f. 267 (old foliation); 1 (new foliation).
[2] Ibid., f. 260ᵛ (old foliation); 11ᵛ (new foliation).
[3] E. H. Phelps Brown and S. V. Hopkins, 'Seven Centuries of Building Wages', *Essays in Economic History*, vol. ii, ed. E. M. Carus Wilson (London, 1962), p. 177.
[4] B.R.O., D/A/We/1, f. 13ᵛ, no. 34.

apparitors, being very light and indiscreet persons, without any other lawful accusation or credible fame first proved against them, and without any presentment in the visitation or other presentment according to your laws.

They went on to complain that such accusations might result in prison or in the tricking of an innocent man into self conviction, with the result that the accused might be put to the shame of open penance.[1]

Two types of case really came within the scope of this criticism; morality cases which were brought nearly always as the result of a visitation or a report laid by an ecclesiastical officer, and cases arising out of a failure to pay ecclesiastical dues. The latter were often in the 'no man's land' between office and instance cases; the procedure adopted was instance procedure, but they could be classified as *ex officio promoto* since a third party was involved.[2] But in the cases of morality and ecclesiastical dues there was one important common factor: the Church, or one of its official representatives (whether a rector or apparitor), was prosecuting. The case was not brought at the request of the laity. Ecclesiastical dues, particularly tithe and mortuary, were singled out in their own right in the Supplication, and the Commons alleged that tithe was being asked in excess of what was customary, and mortuary in excess of the rate laid down by statute in 1529; as a result, they claimed, citations were being issued to defaulters to appear in court, either vexatiously, or unnecessarily, when a simple request would have yielded the desired result without the business of going to court ('. . . indeed if he would have charitably first demanded it, he needed not to have sued for the same, and should have had it with good will').[3]

The Commons may have had a good point here; it is very noticeable in the Buckinghamshire *acta* that cases involving ecclesiastical dues are rarely denied. Sometimes there is an attempt to delay a substantial payment by bidding for time by the well-known procedures of constituting proctors, asking for a postponement in

---

[1] *Documents*, v, ed. Williams, p. 733.

[2] See above, p. 292. For a clear exposition of this type of case see Woodcock, op. cit., p. 68.　　　　　[3] *Documents*, v, ed. Williams, p. 735.

which to assemble evidence and finally an appearance in which
settlement is reached.[1] Usually, however, the debt is acknowledged
and the guilty party is simply given a time in which payment must
be made.[2] This speedy admission of debt may well indicate that the
censures of the court were unnecessary, but it also has the unfortunate consequence that we can rarely reconstruct what lay behind
the case. We are just left with the tantalizing entry:

Wyrardesbury.[3] Johannes New ad instanciam vicarii de Wyrares-
bury in quadam causa subtraccionis decimarum. Pax et dimissus.[4]

There is no evidence for the appropriate period about the effect of
the 1529 statute on mortuary. Full tithe cases, slight though they
are, indicate that difficulties of calculation lay behind most of the
tithe disputes: the dates at which sheep were shorn, the date of
birth of their young, the exact number of lambs produced and
whether they were born while their mothers were grazing within
the parish or outside it, lay behind the case of John Sutton of
Dunton.[5] The whole concept of compulsory tithe was clearly
becoming increasingly outdated when prices were changing and
enclosure might be made of grazing land in more than one parish.
Customary tithe was unrealistic when prices had ceased to be
customary, and pasture land which sprawled outside the parish
made it possible for an astute farmer to avoid tithe altogether. The
next century would show that compulsory tithe was easy to
ridicule and certainly unpopular; the problem was how to replace
it. The Commons could hardly expect tithe to remain the same over
a hundred year period when prices had not; and double tithe, which
they claimed was sometimes asked,[6] was a desperate rector's retort
to an enclosing farmer. The criticism was as naïve as the tithe
system was unrealistic.

This note of naïvety again appears if we examine the straight
office cases which came before the archdeacon or his official. But it
takes a more subtle form. The great majority of the office cases

---

[1] B.R.O., D/A/We/1, ff. 57ᵛ, 61ᵛ, 67.
[2] Ibid., ff. 79ᵛ, 81ᵛ, 120ᵛ, 128ᵛ, 129, 130ᵛ², 131ᵛ², 132, 132ᵛ, 134², 137ᵛ, 139, 141, 143ᵛ, 144.   [3] Wraysbury.
[4] B.R.O., D/A/V/1, f. 279 (old foliation), f. 19 (new foliation).
[5] B.R.O., D/A/We/1, f. 67.   [6] *Documents*, v, ed. Williams, p. 735.

arose out of charges of immorality or other irregularities such as magic and witchcraft. Typical of the morality cases was that of Alice Frawnces, who was accused of having lived incontinently with Robert Walton. Alice admitted her fault and was given penance. Robert denied it, and was ordered to purge himself; Robert next appeared some time later; Alice swore that he had had intercourse with her, but Robert still protested his innocence and suggested that William Adderbury was really the guilty party and that Thomas Daves was not above suspicion either, since he was said to have lain with her in the 'milmede'. Both appeared in due course and were given time to prove their innocence; finally both Robert Walton and William Adderbury failed to purge themselves and admitted their guilt.[1] Alice was clearly the village whore and had the honesty to admit it; it was anyone's guess who had slept with her last, and cases like hers involved the Church courts in the morass of gossip and intrigue as well as unsavoury detail which are the inevitable concomitants of village prostitution. To unravel this case, and the many like it, the Church had to pry into the most personal details of mens' lives, and it had often to rely for evidence on the village gossip. Many of the office cases reveal the ecclesiastical authorities trying to come to grips with village life at its most ribald and its most primitive. A startling example of the latter appears in the case of Henry Lillingston of Broughton who was brought before the court in 1520. He was accused of using magic to heal the sick; they used to go to him and he would give them medicine saying as he did so 'Jhesus that savid bothe you and me from all maner deseasses I aske for seynt cherite Our Lord iff be your wille' (to heal). He told the court that the mixture generally helped the sick and chiefly victims of stone and colic; it consisted of 'hoorehound, alisander, the red knoppes of marygoldes' all mixed together, pounded, and cooked with good ale and 'triaculo Janue' (*sic*: for Genoese treacle). He confessed to being illiterate and to having no knowledge of medicine at all, but that he had knowledge of healing through the grace of God alone. There is no suggestion that anyone died from his ministrations (which is more than could be said of the activities of most 'qualified' Tudor

[1] B.R.O., D/A/We/1, ff. 58ᵛ, 62ᵛ, 65ᵛ, 69ᵛ.

doctors), but the ecclesiastical authorities took a serious view of his case. He was given the unusually heavy penance not only of preceding the procession every Sunday throughout Lent carrying a candle in his hand to offer to the priest, but also of fasting on bread and water every Wednesday and Friday for a year. As though that were not enough, he had in addition to make a pilgrimage, bare-footed, to the shrine of Walsingham. Henry accepted all these penances and promised to perform them, and the sick of Broughton, no doubt, were forced to seek their help elsewhere.[1] The case of Henry Lillingston has a graphic quality about it which makes it unique, and his penance was certainly severe; he had not attempted to deny the charge, nor was it a fictitious one, but he did have to go more than ten miles to Aylesbury for his case to be heard. There was not always such 'provable cause' for a case being brought, and the *acta* show that the Commons had something of a case, since in about half the morality charges where proof was especially difficult, a convincing denial was made; but the Commons' charge of men being brought great distances receives little confirmation from the archdeaconry *acta*. One man travelled eleven miles to Beaconsfield from Colnbrook in February,[2] but this was in an instance case and was presumably of his own choosing; in south Buckinghamshire it was rare to have to travel more than between five and seven miles; in the less populated north it was sometimes a little further, but where a long journey was involved it was nearly always in an instance case involving two laymen. Typical were two parties in a marriage suit who came to Aylesbury from Newport Pagnall and Swanbourne respectively: the lady had a good eight miles to travel but the gentleman had at least twenty.[3] These distances compare favourably with those travelled before a case could be heard in the royal courts.

'The peril of open penance' and its shame, to which the Commons referred so eloquently, is hard to measure. The peril of open penance depended on whether it included the discipline; if it did, an uncharitable curate or neighbour might inflict a substantial injury on

---

[1] B.R.O., D/A/We/1, f. 66.
[2] B.R.O., D/A/V/1, f. 264 (old foliation); f. 15 (new foliation).
[3] B.R.O., D/A/We/1, f. 80.

the penitent. In Leicestershire the discipline does seem to have been ordered in a few cases; two men were ordered to receive five strokes apiece and six others were to receive the more customary discipline at the four corners of the churchyard;[1] in Buckinghamshire there is an occasional mention of the discipline[2] but easily the most heavy penance was that of Henry Lillingston. But the shame of the usual penance of carrying a candle before the procession on a Sunday, barefoot, and clad only in a shirt, was obviously a subjective matter; some felt it, others did not. Thomas Piggott of Dinton said openly in the court that he would rather kill himself than undergo the shame of penance ('maluit potius se ipsum interficere quam penitenciam agere'). Rather than allow this to happen and because Thomas was contemplating marriage with the offending lady the judge 'ob certas causas racionabiles' deferred penance altogether.[3] It was in such cases as this that the Ordinaries were clearly right in telling the Commons that 'when open penance may sometime work in certain persons more hurt than good, it is commendable and allowable in that case to punish by the purse and preserve the fame of the party.'[4] So the Commons were trying to have it all ways; they objected to the shame of open penance but they also objected to the only alternative, the redeeming of 'the same penance for money'. What exactly then were the Commons trying to do? Are they trying chivalrously to rescue women like Alice Frawnces from 'the shame of open penance' as well as Thomas Piggott from a money payment?

This is clearly not the case, and what precisely the Commons have in mind is shown by their reference to episcopal prisons, as the Ordinaries in their reply were quick to notice.[5] The men and women who were most usually before the courts for magic, or for a tumble in the hay, were not the gentry of England, sitting in and represented by Parliament. They were, as the Commons themselves admitted, 'of the poorest sort'.[6] The gentry were but rarely

---

[1] L.A.O., Viv. 5, ff. 25ᵛ, 31, 32, 34ᵛ, 43ᵛ, 53ᵛ.

[2] e.g. B.R.O., D/A/We/1, f. 135ᵛ; D/A/V/1, f. 272ᵛ (old foliation); f. 7ᵛ (new foliation).

[3] B.R.O., D/A/We/1, f. 63ᵛ.

[4] *Documents Illustrative of English Church History*, ed. H. Gee and W. J. Hardy (London, 1896), p. 163.

[5] Ibid., p. 162.   [6] *Documents*, v, ed. Williams, p. 733.

censured outside the confessional for their extra-marital relationships, their station made it unlikely that anyone would inform upon them, and the deference due to them made any procedure against them difficult if not impossible. If we try to examine the status of those who were before the archdeacon's court in Buckinghamshire in 1519–20, we find that they were, for the most part, the poor and the extremely poor.[1] Of twenty-five straight morality cases brought in that period, it is impossible to trace from the muster roll of 1522 eighteen of the persons involved. Hazardous though the whole process of identification is, it seems likely that some of them may owe their 'anonymity' to their lack of possessions, and, in all probability, to the fact that they were part of an ever-shifting labour force.[2] Only two of the remaining seven could be said to be men of any substance: one was Henry Ball; he had goods to the value of £13 6s. 8d.[3] and was accused of keeping a bawdy house, but on examination this was not the real charge against him; he was a party to a very long and complicated matrimonial suit and the court appears to have taken no notice of the morality charge against him but to have seen it as part of a bigger struggle which was adjourned 'sub spe concordie'. His case in fact turns out not to have been a morality case at all.[4] The only other man of substance who came before the court was Richard Pers of Haddenham, accused of having had intercourse with his servant. In all probability this was Richard Pers senior who appears in the muster roll as possessing £15 0s. 0d. in goods and 8s. 4d. in lands[5] in Haddenham itself, and perhaps more elsewhere. As though aware of the difficulties of the accused and the shame which would be attached to open penance in his case, 'ex certis consideracionibus habitis', the judge

[1] Morality cases for this date have been selected solely because their cases are the last we have before the Muster roll of 1522, and there is, in consequence, a better chance of tracing defendants appearing before the court in 1520, than (say) 1492.

[2] B.R.O., D/A/We/1, ff. 58ᵛ², 60, 65ᵛ, 61, 62, 63ᵛ, 69, 69ᵛ, 79, 80ᵛ, 81. In many of these cases more than one defendant was concerned; in the case of Alice Frawnces (ff. 58ᵛ f.) there were four defendants. An attempt has been made to trace all defendants in these cases both by searching the muster roll for them under their place of origin, as given to the court, and by looking at the surrounding villages. It may be significant that of the 'untraceables' four were said to be from Aylesbury, considered a likely centre for migrant labour.

[3] Bodleian Library, MS. Eng. Hist., e. 187, f. 40.

[4] B.R.O., D/A/We/1, f. 81.   [5] Bodleian Library, MS. Eng. Hist., e. 187, f. 92.

took the unusual step of ordering penance in the form of a pilgrimage to Northampton.[1] Of the other offenders none could be said to be wealthy: William Adderbury who had offended with Alice Frawnces was reported in 1522 to have no lands or goods,[2] and Henry Lillingston who was accused of witchcraft only had £1 0s. 0d. in goods.[3] Of the other defendants, the richest had £4 in goods,[4] and the other two had goods or property under the value of £2.[5] It hardly looks as though the archdeacons' courts were often brushing shoulders with the gentry, and in the two cases where men of substance were involved, care was taken to safeguard their position. The highly influential were cited, if necessary, to appear before the bishop in his court of audience, and they used their power either to bend the court to their purposes, or, better still, not to appear before it at all.[6] As Skelton noted in 1522

> The *poor* people they yoke
> With summons and citations.[7]

As far as the ecclesiastical courts were concerned, the gentry could rely on a certain 'diplomatic immunity'.

But this immunity did not apply in heresy cases, and these were the only cases in which an accused man might be detained in prison; otherwise, the unenviable fate of lingering in an episcopal gaol was reserved for priests who had ravished their penitents, or those who claimed benefit of clergy and who, without it, would

---

[1] B.R.O., D/A/We/1, f. 71.

[2] Bodleian Library, MS. Eng. Hist., e. 187, f. 63. [3] Ibid., f. 295.

[4] B.R.O., D/A/We/1, f. 70: Henry Paggenham; in the muster roll there is an Edmund Paggenham who had £4 0s. 0d. in goods (f. 324) but the two are not necessarily identical.

[5] B.R.O., D/A/We/1, f. 60: John Okenden; in the muster roll he is said to have land worth £1 13s. 4d. and goods worth 5s. 0d. (f. 79). He may have had other lands and goods elsewhere. The remaining defendant was Richard Corner (D/A/We/1, f. 80ᵛ). There were three Corners in Shenley Brook End: Henry, John, and Thomas; John and Thomas owned nothing; Henry had £1 0s. 0d. in goods (f. 183). It is anyone's guess whether Richard is identical with any of these gentlemen or of a different family altogether.

[6] See especially *An Episcopal Court Book*, ed. Bowker, pp. xiv, xvi; and my *Secular Clergy*, pp. 20, 99.

[7] *The Complete Poems of John Skelton, Laureate*, ed. Philip Henderson, 3rd edn. (London, 1959), 'Colin Clout', p. 259. Italics mine. I owe this reference to Dr. H. C. Porter.

have been hanged.[1] Hunne's case began to bring home to the gentle-men of England that in certain cases the ecclesiastical courts were no respecters of persons. The fate of Richard Hunne and indeed the fate of Alice Frawnces and Henry Lillingston could be the fate of anyone, if heresy moved from being mere Lollardy, which was for the most part the concern of the lower classes,[2] to Lutheranism, which could engage dons and merchants, gentlemen and courtiers.[3] And once Lutheranism could be seen to have an appeal, then even the most devout and orthodox might inadvertently become caught up in a witch-hunt. This is precisely what had happened between 1520 and 1530. The very act of translating the Lord's Prayer into English could be construed as heretical. Lutheran books were circulating in London and outside it, and by 1531 there is strong evidence to suggest that a concerted attempt was being made to root out heresy.[4]

In this atmosphere of fear, the very efficiency of the ecclesiastical courts became a threat. Dr. Kelly rightly suggested that it was fear of heresy proceedings which lay behind the attack on the ecclesiastical courts in the Commons' Supplication; he brilliantly showed that it was the legislative efficiency of convocation rather than its torpor which proved its undoing.[5] But he did not then know, and the *acta* now reveal, that this fear would have been unfounded if the courts had not been so efficient. It was precisely because men did not have to be cited to appear miles from their

---

[1] Bowker, *Secular Clergy*, pp. 122–3; *An Episcopal Court Book*, pp. 67, 124.

[2] J. A. F. Thomson, *The Later Lollards 1414–1520* (Oxford, 1965), indicates that Lollardy had no secure foothold in the universities (pp. 211–19); and all the evidence indicates that early sixteenth-century Lollardy found its support among the poorer classes (see especially A. G. Dickens, *Lollards and Protestants in the Diocese of York 1509–1559* (Oxford, 1959), p. 8).

[3] W. A. Clebsch, *England's Earliest Protestants 1520–35* (Yale, 1964), pp. 5 ff.; A. G. Dickens, *The English Reformation* (London, 1964), pp. 68–82. Colet was accused of heresy, partly probably because of the audience at his sermons (Thomson, op. cit., p. 252); and Margaret Roper, daughter of Sir Thomas More, was indirectly in trouble for her translation of the Lord's Prayer. If the devout and famous were not above suspicion, who was? See J. K. McConica, *English Humanists and Reformation Politics* (Oxford, 1965), pp. 72 ff. More menacing still were the attempts made by the Chancellor to apprehend suspects; see G. R. Elton, 'Sir Thomas More and the Opposition to Henry VIII', *BIHR*, xli (1968), 22–5.

[4] In addition to the control of the book trade (McConica, loc. cit.), even a dubiously worded will could be construed as heretical (see Dickens, *English Reformation*, p. 96).   [5] Kelly, op. cit., p. 101.

homes, it was precisely because the courts were so near, with a representative in the form of a parish priest in every village, that they were so threatening. The dispatch with which the ecclesiastical courts dealt with the large amount of probate business, and the popularity which they seem to have enjoyed in conducting instance business, suddenly became an immense source of alarm. If this efficiency was harnessed to the desire to stamp out heresy, no one was safe; if a charge of heresy was preferred, the defendant had no option but an episcopal prison. The shame of open penance might, over night, become the danger of death in the Lollards' tower.

Once the Supplication of the Commons is seen, not as an outburst against bad governance, but as a statement of a fear of too much governance, the first answer made by the Ordinaries makes more sense and so does the subsequent history of the ecclesiastical courts. At each point, the Ordinaries' Answer, far from being evasive, can be shown to have a real basis of fact behind it in the surviving archidiaconal *acta*. The Ordinaries make no claim to absolute probity; they know that human nature is too fallible for that.[1] They admit to a certain bewilderment; they cannot understand why this storm of abuse has broken upon their heads. They do not accept the Commons' assertion that the uncharitable behaviour of the Ordinaries has provoked it, but they recognize the divisive and subversive influence of heresy as underlying much of the animosity.[2] They attempt to allay the fears expressed in the Supplication about their power to make canons.[3] They then turn to the specific criticisms made of the ecclesiastical courts. They recognize that there may be *ex officio* citations wrongfully made on insufficient grounds. But they make the obvious defence that one swallow does not make a summer: 'for though *in multis offendimus omnes*, as St. James saith, yet not *in omnibus offendimus omnes*.'[4] They deny imprisonment except in cases of suspected heresy,[5] and they deny confiscating the goods of excommunicate persons except in cases of heresy.[6] They argue that there must be latitude over the

---

[1] *Documents*, ed. Gee and Hardy, p. 161.   [2] Ibid., p. 155.
[3] Ibid., pp. 156-9.   [4] Ibid., p. 161.
[5] Ibid., p. 162.   [6] Ibid., p. 159.

giving of penance, and they deny any attempt, of which they have knowledge, to trick defendants.[1] They deny that men travel long distances to prove wills, and point out that, except where the deceased had *bona notabilia*, recourse could normally be made by executors to local courts of probate.[2] They face squarely the double-faced nature of the attack on tithe: they see that tithe is a spiritual duty and that time may change the form that the duty takes, but not the duty itself. 'The manner of payment and person unto whom to pay may be, in time, altered, but the duty cannot, by any means be taken away.'[3] They ask that curates who demand mortuary in a court before having asked for it should be reported. They could have added that there existed, both in the machinery of visitation and in the device of an instance suit of vexatious litigation, a remedy for this complaint.[4] They simply state 'these curates thus offending, if they were known, ought to be punished; but who thus doeth, we know not.'[5] They recognize that the court of the arches and the jurisdiction of Canterbury pose particular problems over fees and distances but these are in the process of reform.[6] They make no mention of instance procedure, because the Commons have not mentioned it; nor does either side complain of delays in instance procedure.[7]

The archdeaconry *acta*, as well as the surviving material for the court of audience at Lincoln, appear to support the contentions of the Ordinaries.[8] There were some abuses but in general these were few. The Answer of the Ordinaries may have been undiplomatic, but it was not 'very slender' nor, in light of the evidence, does it seem unduly brusque.[9] The difference between the first reply of the Ordinaries and the second lies in the shift of emphasis from the specific complaints against the courts to the whole question of the power to make canons. This may be, as Dr. Kelly suggests, because

[1] *Documents,* ed. Gee and Hardy, pp. 162–3.   [2] Ibid., pp. 165–6.
[3] Ibid., p. 169.
[4] Cases of vexatious litigation were heard (e.g. B.R.O., D/A/V/1, f. 261ᵛ (old foliation); f. 12 (new foliation)).
[5] *Documents,* ed. Gee and Hardy, pp. 169–70.   [6] Ibid., p. 166.
[7] Delays in procedure were the most usual complaints in the secular courts, and account for the early popularity of Star Chamber (see G. R. Elton, *The Tudor Constitution* (Cambridge, 1960), p. 163).
[8] *Episcopal Court Book,* ed. Bowker, pp. xxi–xxii.   [9] Kelly, op. cit., p. 110.

'Henry was consistently more responsive to theological argument than to anti-clerical agitation';[1] it may also be because Henry saw an authority which did not extend to matters concerning 'the maintenance of the faith and good manner in Christ's Church' as well as 'the reformation and correction of sin'[2] was not worth having. But it may also be that Henry knew his Commons. Hall reports the incident in which the Commons offered the king the Supplication and in the same breath asked that parliament be dissolved. He reports Henry as rebuking them by saying 'you requyre to have the Parlyament dissolved and to departe into your countreys, and yet you would have a reformacion of your griefes wyth all diligence'.[3] Henry knew at least on that occasion that the Commons could ask for the impossible, and that they could complain without cause; he also knew that in so far as the Supplication touched the ecclesiastical courts, the attack had served its purpose of intimidating, and that feelings would cool when heresy procedure changed, as it did in 1534. This may explain why he allowed the case against the courts to drop, and that against the canon-making powers of Convocation to go forward, and why the ecclesiastical courts were allowed to survive in all their vigour the many and various changes in religion of the sixteenth century.[4]

If the archdeaconry *acta* may be taken as a guide, the fundamental case against the ecclesiastical courts in the early sixteenth century was not that made against them by the Commons. It was that made by Erasmus. In the colloquy between the Butcher and the Fishmonger, the Butcher remarks on the inordinate number of rules and regulations which appear to bind the Christian more rigorously than the Mosaic law had ever done. 'Nowadays, besides so many prescribed and proscribed styles and colors of clothing, are added various modes of shaving the head, to say nothing meanwhile of the burden of confession and the load of human regulations, complicated tithes, tighter restrictions governing marriage, new laws of kinship through marriage, and many others that make the Jewish law seem not a little easier in this respect than is our lot.'

---

[1] Kelly, op. cit., p. 111.
[2] Ibid, p. 112.
[3] *Henry VIII by Edward Hall*, vol. ii, ed. C. Whibley (London, 1904), p. 203.
[4] For the next stage in the story see Marchant, *The Church under the Law*.

To this the Fishmonger replies, 'A Christian is bound by many things, by more difficult ones, and finally by heavier penalty; yet the greater power of faith and love added to them renders easy what are by nature extremely oppressive.'[1] The obligations on the Christian in the early sixteenth century were indeed many: he was expected to participate fully in the services of the Church as well as fulfilling the ethical demands of the Gospels; he was also expected to give his faith a financial component by paying tithe and other fees. All these duties could only be easy, and indeed are only easy, in any age, if there is faith and love—if they are the response of the believer to the grace and love of God. This response to God is undertaken in baptism and thereafter nurtured in prayer and through the sacraments. But if the response becomes enfeebled, then the duties which are its concomitants become burdens, and will eventually be disregarded. The problem confronting the Church in the sixteenth century was that it dealt more adequately with symptoms than with causes. It corrected the failure of the so-called faithful to fulfil their Christian duties, be they tithe payment or continence, but it was nurturing their faith much less adequately. The absence of an authorized vernacular Scripture,[2] the prevalence in its stead of a large amount of material about the saints (much of which was scarcely more than a series of cautionary tales) was hardly likely to nurture the response of love.[3] At best it nurtured one of fear. Mass was seen as a way of avoiding evil and damnation, not as the union of the believer with his Lord.[4] In these

---

[1] *The Colloquies of Erasmus*, edited and translated by C. R. Thompson (Chicago, 1963), p. 323.

[2] This is not to deny that there were many unauthorized versions of the New Testament in English circulating (see Thomson, *Later Lollards*, p. 242).

[3] This is seen particularly clearly in the analysis of sermons for the period in J. W. Blench, *Preaching in England in the late fifteenth and sixteenth centuries* (Oxford, 1964), note especially pp. 115–49, and pp. 228 ff.

[4] This was the impression conveyed by much popular literature on the subject which emphasized both that the Mass gave practical benefits (see C. W. Dugmore, *The Mass and the English Reformers* (London, 1958), p. 70) and that it was the occasion on which concentration was centred on the Passion of Christ and the sin of man (ibid., p. 78), rather than on meditation on the Incarnation, Resurrection, and Ascension. These latter together provide the believer with grounds for hope in the mercy of God as well as penitence for man's sin. Perhaps the almost morbid emphasis on the Passion, in isolation, may account for the pessimism of much later medieval preaching (see Blench, op. cit., pp. 233 ff.). The Passion without the Resurrection is a creed of despair.

circumstances, every time the Church corrected someone like Alice Frawnces for her prostitution, or John Sutton for his failure to pay tithe, the question is raised, Who is in the dock? Was the faith being taught in early Tudor England of sufficient vigour to sustain so many regulations? Fisher had diagnosed the actions of the Commons as arising from lack of faith.[1] Ironically, it may have been the right diagnosis, but located in the wrong place. In the particular circumstances of 1532, he was mistaken about the Commons. Their criticisms of the ecclesiastical courts were for the most part, as I have attempted to show, the product, not of lack of faith, but of fear. Once Henry VIII had become Head of the Church the immediate cause of that fear was removed. The enforcement of the Reformation statutes was a matter for the common law courts, and the gentry were not to come up against the ecclesiastical courts again until the reign of Elizabeth. But while it had suited them and their king, the Commons had taken up cudgels on behalf of less privileged citizens. In their case, Fisher's diagnosis was accurate. Henry Lillingston and Alice Frawnces and folk like them, were taught by their parish priest. He would retell the cautionary tales, which figure so largely in the sermons of John Mirk, and account for a great number of the early publications of Caxton.[2] Fisher was wrong to accuse the House of Commons for its want of faith, and the Ordinaries noticed that the House was made up of 'well-disposed . . . well-conscienced men'.[3] But if he and his colleagues had been less concerned with the immediate crisis facing them, both in Parliament and with respect to the king, and less concerned to avert the loss of their jurisdiction, they might have reflected that faith and love were not as strongly represented in the parishes of England as fear and law. Cavalcades of preachers and teachers should have been as familiar a sight as the cavalcades of ecclesiastical lawyers.[4] 'Faith and love' did not render 'easy' that which is by nature 'extremely oppressive'.[5]

MARGARET BOWKER

[1] *Henry VIII by Edward Hall*, ii. 167.   [2] Blench, op. cit.
[3] *Documents*, ed. Gee and Hardy, p. 155.
[4] Woodcock, op. cit., p. 35.   [5] *The Colloquies of Erasmus*, p. 323.

LIST OF MANUSCRIPTS CITED

A BIBLIOGRAPHY OF THE
WRITINGS OF KATHLEEN MAJOR

Compiled by A. E. B. OWEN

The following additional abbreviations have been used in references:

Lincs.   Lincolnshire.

Mag.   Magazine.

A.A.S.R.   *Associated Architectural Societies' Reports and Papers.*

L.A.A.S.R.   *Lincolnshire Architectural and Archaeological Society's Reports and Papers.*

Miss Major has also been responsible, as General Editor, for the publications of the Lincoln Record Society since December 1935, and for the first series (nos. 1–8) of Lincoln Minster Pamphlets, 1948–56.

1932

Episcopal *acta* in medieval capitular archives.
BIHR ix, no. 27, 145–53.

1933

A SHORT ACCOUNT OF THE CHURCH OF ST. MARY MAGDALEN, GEDNEY.
The *Familia* of Archbishop Stephen Langton.
EHR xlviii. 529–53.

1934

Some Early Documents Relating to Holbeach.
A.A.S.R. xli, part 1, 39–45.

1935

An Unknown House of Crutched Friars at Whaplode.
A.A.S.R. xli, part 2, 149–54.

1936

Conan Son of Ellis, An Early Inhabitant of Holbeach.
A.A.S.R. xlii, part 1, 1–28.
Records of the charities of Gedney Hill (formerly Gedney Fen), contained in the church chest.
Local Historian, no. 7, 4.

1937

THE REGISTRUM ANTIQUISSIMUM OF THE CATHEDRAL CHURCH OF LINCOLN, vol. iv (L.R.S. xxxii). With C. W. Foster.
Survey of parochial documents in the diocese and county of Lincoln.
Local Historian, no. 16, 4.

1938

Survey of parochial documents in the diocese and county of Lincoln.
Local Historian, no. 17, 2.
Parish history from diocesan records. I: The clergy; II: The laity.
Lincs. Mag. iii. 331–4, 374–9.
The census of parochial documents: an account of some of the practical methods adopted in various localities.
British Records Association *Proceedings,* no. 3, 3–10. K.M. and others.

1939

Lincoln copy of the Magna Carta.
Lincs. Mag. iv. 109–11.

1940

THE REGISTRUM ANTIQUISSIMUM OF THE CATHEDRAL CHURCH OF LINCOLN, vol. v (L.R.S. xxxiv).
Diocesan Records and their makers.
Lincoln Diocesan Mag., May, 75–6.
The Lincoln Diocesan Records.
TRHS 4th ser., xxii. 39–66.

1941

Lincoln Diocesan Records as Sources for the Genealogist.
Genealogists' Mag. ix, no. 5, 158–71.

1942

Resignation Deeds of the Diocese of Lincoln.
BIHR xix, no. 56, 57–65.
Commonwealth ordinations, Lincoln diocese.
Theology xlv, no. 268, 210–11.
The Dedication of Churches.
Lincoln Diocesan Mag., Oct. and Nov., 126–7, 138.

1944

The Nature of Diocesan Records.

L.A.A.S.R., N.S. ii, part 2, 129–40.

Sales of next presentation.

Lincoln Diocesan Mag., June, 294–5.

1945

The Massingberd Deeds and Papers at Gunby Hall, Spilsby.

L.A.A.S.R., N.S. iii, part 1, 8–11.

The Lincoln Diocesan Record Office.

L.A.A.S.R., N.S. iii, part 1, 12–17.

REVIEW

Formularies which bear on the history of Oxford, c. 1204–1420, vols. i and ii, ed. H. E. Salter, W. A. Pantin, and H. G. Richardson.

Oxoniensia x. 108.

1946

The Thornton Abbey Chronicle (Bodleian Library, Tanner MS. 166) with extracts relating to the fabric of the Abbey.

Archaeological Journal ciii. 174–8.

1947

The Basis of Local History.

Lincs. Historian i, no. 1, 3–7.

1948

Fifteenth-Century Presentation Deeds in the Lincoln Diocesan Record Office.

In *Studies in Medieval History presented to Frederick Maurice Powicke*, 455–64.

REVIEWS

The History of Beelsby by A. C. Sinclair.

Lincs. Historian i, no. 2, 74–5.

Canonization and Authority in the Western Church by Eric W. Kemp.

Oxford Mag. lxviii, no. 3, 91–2. 'K.M.'

1949

Some notes on the Principal Printed Sources for the History of Churches and Incumbents in Lincolnshire.

In *Local History: Its Interest and Value*, 2nd edn. (Lincs. Local History Soc.), 28–37.

1950

THE REGISTRUM ANTIQUISSIMUM OF THE CATHEDRAL CHURCH OF LINCOLN, vol. vi (L.R.S. xli).

THE REGISTRUM ANTIQUISSIMUM OF THE CATHEDRAL CHURCH OF LINCOLN. Facsimiles of charters in vols. v and vi (L.R.S. xlii).

A SHORT ACCOUNT OF THE CHURCH OF ST. MARY MAGDALEN, GEDNEY. Revised edn.

A SHORT ACCOUNT OF ALL SAINTS' CHURCH, HOLBEACH. (Further edns. in 1959, 1965, 1967.)

ACTA STEPHANI LANGTON CANTUARIENSIS ARCHIEPISCOPI A.D. 1207–1228 Canterbury and York Society, part cxviii (vol. l).

The Office of Chapter Clerk at Lincoln in the Middle Ages.

In *Medieval Studies presented to Rose Graham*, ed. V. Ruffer and A. J. Taylor, 163–88.

1951

Original Papal Documents in the Bodleian Library.

Bodleian Library Record iii, no. 33, 242–56.

REVIEW

Notes on Recent Books.

Lincs. Historian i, no. 7, 291. 'K.M.'

1952

Notes on Some Terms in Ecclesiastical Records.

Lincs. Historian i, no. 10, 347–55.

REVIEW

The Episcopal Colleagues of Archbishop Thomas Becket by David Knowles. *Jnl. Theological Studies*, N.S. iii. 128–9.

1953

THE REGISTRUM ANTIQUISSIMUM OF THE CATHEDRAL CHURCH OF LINCOLN, vol. vii (L.R.S. xlvi).

A HANDLIST OF THE RECORDS OF THE BISHOP OF LINCOLN AND OF THE ARCHDEACONS OF LINCOLN AND STOW.

Record Publications and the Teaching of Diplomatic.

Archives ii, no. 9, 20–5.

1954

The Finances of the Dean and Chapter of Lincoln from the Twelfth to the Fourteenth Century: a Preliminary Survey.

JEH v, no. 2, 149–67.

1955

The *Familia* of Robert Grosseteste.

In *Robert Grosseteste: Scholar and Bishop*, ed. D. A. Callus, appendix 1, 216–41.

1956

REVIEW

Tudor and Stuart Lincoln by J. W. F. Hill.

Oxford Mag. lxxv, no. 3, 80. 'K.M.'

1957

REVIEW

The Register of Thomas Langley, bishop of Durham, 1406–1437, vol. i, ed. R. L. Storey.

JEH viii, no. 2, 247–8.

1958

THE REGISTRUM ANTIQUISSIMUM OF THE CATHEDRAL CHURCH OF LINCOLN, vol. viii (L.R.S. li).

REVIEWS

Facsimiles of Early Cheshire Charters, ed. Geoffrey Barraclough.

Archives iii, no. 20, 256–8.

The Register of Thomas Langley, bishop of Durham, 1406–1437, vol. ii, ed. R. L. Storey.

JEH ix, no. 2, 270–1.

1959

REVIEWS

Medieval Cartularies of Great Britain: a Short Catalogue by G. R. C. Davis.

JEH x, no. 1, 124–5.

Notarial Signs from the York archiepiscopal records by J. S. Purvis.

JEH x, no. 1, 126.

1961

St. Hilda's College.

American Oxonian xlviii. 57–60.

Obituary: Dr. Irene Churchill.

Archives v, no. 26, 108–9.

REVIEW

The Register of Thomas Langley, bishop of Durham, 1406–1437, vol. iii, ed. R. L. Storey.

JEH xii, no. 2, 264.

1962

Blyborough Charters.

In *A Medieval Miscellany for Doris Mary Stenton*, ed. P. M. Barnes and C. F. Slade. Pipe Roll Soc., N.S., vol. 36, 203–19.

REVIEWS

Thomas Langley and the Bishopric of Durham, 1406–1437, by R. L. Storey.
JEH xiii, no. 1, 101–2.

The Register of Thomas Langley, bishop of Durham, 1406–1437, vol. iv, ed. R. L.
Storey.
JEH xiii, no. 2, 264–5.

1963

REVIEW

Magna Vita Sancti Hugonis—The Life of St. Hugh of Lincoln, ed. Decima L.
Douie and Dom Hugh Farmer.
Medium Aevum xxxii, no. 3, 227–8.

1966

REVIEW

Medieval Lincoln by Sir Francis Hill (reissue).
The Municipal Review, April, 185.

1967

REVIEW

The Registers of Roger Martival, Bishop of Salisbury, 1315–1330: vol. i, ed.
Kathleen Edwards; vol. ii, ed. C. R. Elrington; vol. iii, ed. Susan Reynolds.
JEH xviii, no. 2, 260–1.

1968

THE REGISTRUM ANTIQUISSIMUM OF THE CATHEDRAL CHURCH OF
LINCOLN, vol. ix (L.R.S. lxii).
The Teaching and Study of Diplomatic in England.
Archives viii, no. 39, 114–18.

REVIEW

Thomas Arundel: a Study of Church Life in the Reign of Richard II by Margaret
Aston.
JEH xix, no. 2, 247–8.

1970

REVIEW

Hubert Walter, Lord of Canterbury and Lord of England by Charles R. Young.
EHR lxxxv. 154–5.

In the press

THE REGISTRUM ANTIQUISSIMUM OF THE CATHEDRAL CHURCH OF
LINCOLN, vol. x (last volume).